Gateway 2000 Inc.
http://www.gw2k.com

General Electric
http://www.ge.com

General Motors Corp.
http://www.gm.com

Golden Rule Insurance Company
http://www.goldenrule.com

W. L. Gore Associates
http://www.gore.com

Guidestar (The Donor's Guide to The Nonprofit Universe)
http://www.guidestar.org

Hasbro
http://www.hasbro.com

Honeywell Inc.
http://www.honeywell.com

Hot Coupons Savings Club
http://www.hotcoupons.com

InterActive Custom Clothes Company
http://www.ic3d.com

International Accounting Standards Committee
http://www.iasc.org.uk

International Brownie
http://www.internationalbrownie.com

International Commerce Exchange Systems
http://www.icesinc.com

International Organization for Standardization
http://www.iso.ch

The Internet Business Network (A Web Guide to the Job Search)
http://www.interbiznet.com/hunt/tools.html

Intuit Inc.
http://www.intuit.com

IRS
http://www.irs.ustreas.gov

JAMTV Music Network
http://www.jamtv.com

JCPenney
http://www.jcpenney.com

Jeep Home Page (Chyrsler Corp.)
http://www.jeepunpaved.com

JobSmart (Job Search Guide)
http://www.jobsmart.org

Joe Boxer
http://www.joeboxer.com

Johnson & Johnson
http://www.jnj.com

JumboSports
http://www.jumbosports.com

Junkbusters
http://www.junkbusters.com

Just For Feet
http://www.feet.com

Juno Online Services
http://www.juno.com

Kmart Corporation
http://www.kmart.com

Levi Strauss
http://www.levi.com

Lexus
http://www.lexus.com/clapton

LifeSavers
http://www.candystand.com

Lincoln Electric Co.
http://www.lincolnelectric.com

Liz Claiborne
http://www.lizclaiborne.com

M.Y.O.B. Accounting
http://www.myob.com

Madam C. J. Walker Enterprises Inc.
http://www.madamcjwalker.com

McDonald's
http://www.mcdonalds.com

Microsoft
http://www.microsoft.com

Microsoft Financial Forum
http://www.microsoft.com/msft

Monarch Marking Systems
http://www.monarch-marking.com

Money Hunter
http://www.moneyhunter.com

The Monster Board–DSC Communications
http://www.monster.com

MONY
http://www.mony.com

Motorola
http://www.motorola.com

MSBET & Microsoft joint venture
http://www.msbet.com

Multimedia 2000
http://www.m-2k.com

Music Boulevard
http://www.musicblvd.com

MySki Inc.
http://www.myski.com

Nantucket Nectars
http://www.juiceguys.com

NASCAR
http://www.nascar.com

National Association of Securities Dealers Automated Quotation System
http://www.nasdaq.com

National Center for Employee Ownership
http://www.nceo.org

National Fraud Information Center
http://www.fraud.org

National Highway Traffic Safety Administration
http://www.nhtsa.dot.gov

Netscape
http://www.netscape.com

Netstock Direct
http://www.netstockdirect.com

Network Associates
http://www.networkassociate.com

New York Stock Exchange
http://www.nyse.com

NordicTrack
http://www.nordictrack.com

Nortel Northern Telecom
http://www.nortel.com

OPEC (Organization of Petroleum-Exporting Countries)
http://www.opec.org

Oracle Education
http://www.oracle.com

Parent Time at Work
http://www.parenttime.com

Pink Jeep Tours
http://www.pinkjeep.com

PriceSCAN
http://www.pricescan.com

Procter & Gamble
http://www.pg.com

Prufrock Press
http://www.prufrock.com

Contemporary Business 2000

Louis E. Boone

Ernest G. Cleverdon Chair of Business and Management

University of South Alabama

David L. Kurtz

The R. A. and Vivian Young Chair of Business Administration

University of Arkansas

SOUTH-WESTERN

™

THOMSON LEARNING

Australia • Canada • Mexico • Singapore • Spain
United Kingdom • United States

SOUTH-WESTERN
™
THOMSON LEARNING

Contemporary Business 2000
Louis E. Boone, David L. Kurtz

Publisher:
Mike Roche

Acquisitions Editor:
John Weimeister

Developmental Editor:
Tracy L. Morse

Market Strategist:
Lisé Johnson

Project Editor:
Kathryn Stewart

Art Director:
Bill Brammer

Project Manager:
Darryl King

Project Management:
Elm Street Publishing Services, Inc.

Printer:
RR Donnelley & Sons
Willard, OH

For permission to use material from
this text or product, contact us by
Tel (800) 730-2214
Fax (800) 730-2215
http://www.thomsonrights.com

Library of Congress Catalog Card
Number: 99-74473

ISBN: 0-03-026256-9

To the 2.9 million students around the globe who began their business studies using *Contemporary Business* in their classes, making it the most widely used business text in history

and

to the Text and Academic Authors Association, which awarded *Contemporary Business* the first William Holmes McGuffey Award for Excellence and Longevity.

Dear Fellow Introduction to Business Instructor:

The first course I ever taught was introduction to business. As a neophyte instructor, I found it to be a fascinating, often frustrating, and constantly challenging assignment. Questions were posed from every business discipline, causing me to often respond with, "I don't know the answer to that question, but I'll find out and let you know." It was a memorable experience, one that played an important role in my decision to remain in academia.

In fact, I liked everything about teaching the class except the textbook. It was one of the market leaders at the time, filled with lists and definitions, and appeared to cover the subject of business adequately. What it lacked was the heartbeat of business—its vitality, its ability to solve societal and ethical problems, its importance in determining the standards of living we enjoy, and its choices of meaningful careers in which each student could achieve personal and professional goals and contribute to society. I hoped that one day I would have the opportunity to create a book that would convey this to college students.

Years later I was fortunate enough to form a writing partnership with my talented friend and colleague Dave Kurtz. The result was *Contemporary Business*—a book that vaulted to market leadership within months of its first release and has never wavered from its position as the unquestioned leader in the introduction to business market. At last count, 2.9 million students have begun their academic careers in business using *Contemporary Business* as their text. We are also especially proud that our U.S. and Canadian colleagues who write college textbooks recently honored our text with the McGuffey Award as one of the best business texts written in the second half of the twentieth century.

Dave and I understood and practiced the concept of continuous improvement years before it became a management buzzword. We are convinced that leadership of any industry is accompanied by a commitment to make each new edition better than its predecessor. Rather than resting on the laurels of the success of the current edition, we practice the philosophy embodied in the statement, "First, we will be best. Then we will be first."

I have taught sections of these courses on a regular basis, using the classes as real-life laboratories in which to experiment with new chapter materials, new teaching approaches, and new assignments. Although Dave and I visit dozens of classrooms on college campuses throughout the nation and use market research feedback, check-off questions on mail questionnaires can never replace the immediacy of conducting classroom sessions and receiving feedback firsthand from students and other instructors.

The result of this classroom experimentation, combined with feedback from students and introduction to business professors at numerous other colleges and universities, is *Contemporary Business 2000*. The new edition responds to these requests:

- "We want more applied, 'how-to' practical information in the text—information our students can use immediately."
- "We want more emphasis on entrepreneurship as a viable career alternative for students."
- "We want more coverage of technology—and especially the Internet—as a key ingredient in America's success in the twenty-first century."
- "We want more emphasis on business ethics and social responsibility in the new edition."
- "We want more experiential, hands-on assignments for our students."

As Dave and I will demonstrate in the following pages, we have worked hard to serve our instructor and student customers by addressing these requests. We are confident that you will be delighted with the results.

Sincerely,

Louis E. Boone

Preface

NEW 2000 UPDATE

Throughout the publication history of *Contemporary Business*, currency has been a goal and driving force. But never before has the pace of change in business been so rapid. Innovative use of technology and the Internet, a new spirit of entrepreneurship, the critical importance of relationships with customers, and emphasis on ethics and social responsibility have revolutionized the face of business today. These changes have made it all the more important to offer students and instructors a current business text—more current than the standard three-year revision cycle allowed. The result is *Contemporary Business 2000*. This new edition, containing all new vignettes, new Web sites, and many new boxed features, allows instructors to involve their students in the excitement of today's business world. Here's just a sample of late-breaking events covered in *Contemporary Business 2000*.

▼ The ongoing legal battles of Microsoft and the U.S. Department of Justice

▼ The comeback of the VW Beetle

▼ The cyberspace merger between America Online and Netscape

▼ The fallout from the NBA basketball strike

▼ The frenzy over the Furby animated toy

▼ The successes of Sun Microsystems and its unconventional CEO, Scott McNealy

Contemporary Business 2000 is also offered in a new paperback format, making it more affordable for students. The book's retail price is approximately 35 percent less than the previous edition and well below the price of competing hardcover texts. An instructor's addendum is available on the *Contemporary Business* Web site that describes the differences between the hardcover and paperback.

New for *Contemporary Business 2000* is more Web support. Southwestern is committed to assisting adopters with Web-based education materials. Framework includes reading assignments, goals, self-quizzes, Web-based activities, and more. Your local Southwestern sales representative can provide you with more details.

CONTENT FEATURES

Emphasizing Technology

Contemporary Business 2000 embraces technology, integrating it into every aspect of the text and package, resulting in the most innovative, exciting product on the market.

A high-tech student preface includes a glossary of helpful Internet terms and information on getting online, search engines, private data sources, and the text's personal World Wide Web directory.

In-depth, practical coverage of technology begins early in Chapter 1 and is thoroughly integrated throughout succeeding chapters and in the package components.

The Boone & Kurtz Home Page connects the new-technology theme to the real world. Completely integrated with the text, the Web site plugs students into additional sources of information and teaches them how to use the Internet as a business tool. The site links professors to valuable teaching resources and educational information. A new *Web Instructor's Manual* also helps professors navigate through the site and use it effectively within their courses.

Web addresses are included in each chapter to give students access to additional online information. Each chapter opens with a vignette detailing a success story involving technology. Online addresses are included for the company. "Nothing but Net" end-of-chapter application exercises plug students into the Internet, sharpening student surfing skills.

Part V, "Managing Technology and Information," features a stronger emphasis on high-tech issues. The part now contains two technology chapters—one on businesses' use of technology and the Internet to remain competitive and one on the use of technology to manage information.

Chapter 17, "Using Technology and the Internet to Succeed in Business," gives students practical insight into how to most effectively use the new and emerging technology to get ahead in the business world. It describes how applications of new technologies are important keys in maintaining a competitive edge and taking advantage of global opportunities. Applications of new technologies ranging from e-mail, smart cards, and product design to human resource education and training and continuous improvement are treated here. Likely breakthroughs in new technology are also explored.

The second half of the chapter is devoted to one of the most important current technologies: the Internet. The roles played by the Internet in electronic commerce, research, job searches, and online selling are examined. In addition, the chapter looks at costs and sources of revenue from Web sites, describes the typical Internet user, and examines the problems facing business executives who rely heavily on the Internet in their organizations. Finally, the chapter discusses organizational communications through intranets and their advantages and disadvantages.

Practical applications featured in the chapter include:

▼ "Tips for Creating a Successful Web Site"

▼ "Navigating the Net"

▼ "Choosing the Right Internet Service Provider"

Appendix A, "Your Career in Business," is tied directly to the *Discovering Your Business Career* CD-ROM, as well as to relevant material on the Boone & Kurtz Web site.

Emphasizing Entrepreneurship as a Career Alternative

Contemporary Business 2000 has an underlying entrepreneurial theme, encouraging students to look at issues from the perspective of business owners. It also corrects the unbalanced emphasis on giant business found in most business texts by analyzing entrepreneurship as an alternative for business students. The text offers practical information to future entrepreneurs, equipping them with facts needed to succeed in business.

Entrepreneurship is introduced within the first pages of the text and then completely integrated throughout. Each chapter contains checklists, questionnaires, and self-scoring exercises, re-emphasizing key chapter concepts and helping students learn about their personal business style and their aptitude for entrepreneurial success. These practical, interactive features help students create a toolbox of information about themselves as future business executives. Most of the opening vignettes focus on entrepreneurs who have successfully applied emerging technologies to business challenges.

Part II, "Starting and Growing Your Business," gives students practical insight into two of the most critical stages of business ownership: starting and growing a new venture. The section explores strategies for avoiding the high failure rate associated with many new businesses.

Chapter 6, "Starting Your Own Business: The Entrepreneurship Alternative," is written from a "you" approach, placing students in the role of new entrepreneurs. It is completely integrated with the *Discovering Your Business Career* CD-ROM.

Emphasizing Business Success in the Relationship Era

Chapter 7, "Strategies for Business Success in the Relationship Era," combines material on business strategy and planning with a major new emphasis on relationships. Features include strategic alliances (in production, finance, human resources, communications/information systems,

marketing, international business), the relationship era in marketing, and roles played by databases.

Emphasizing Ethics and Social Responsibility

Continuing to lead the market in its emphasis on ethics and social responsibility, the new edition introduces the topics even earlier—within the first few pages of Chapter 1 and in Chapter 2, "Achieving Business Success by Demonstrating Ethical Behavior and Social Responsibility."

Ethical and societal issues are often best understood when various positions are examined through class discussions and assignments. A feature of each chapter is "Solving an Ethical Controversy," in which students are presented with an experiential activity related to an ethical dilemma. Some of the topics included are:

▼ Should Intel Be Baking Your Cookies Online?

▼ Should the Public Tolerate Child Labor?

▼ Should Whistle-Blowers Get a Share of the Money They Help Recover?

▼ Are Big Oil Companies Merging into Dangerous Giants?

▼ Should Company Auditors Act as Bean Counters or Gumshoes?

▼ Should Hedge Funds Expect to Be Rescued from Their Greed?

Greater Emphasis on the Applied, "How-To" Approach

The most common student suggestion for improving all business textbooks can be summed up as, "Give more real-life information that I can apply." In *Contemporary Business 2000,* we do just that.

▼ The new edition integrates a "how-to" approach in text chapters from chapter titles to new boxes and exercises.

▼ End-of-chapter Experiential Exercises and "Nothing but Net" Internet assignments move the student beyond memorization and focus on applications.

▼ "Business Tool Kits" placed throughout the text give students "how to" information they can apply immediately.

PEDAGOGY AND TEXT FEATURES

Focus on Essential Concepts

Each chapter includes 10 essential business terms, further emphasizing the most important concepts. Additional business terms are also highlighted in each chapter.

Skill Development Emphasis

SCANS (Secretary's Committee on Acquiring Necessary Skills) features continue to be integrated throughout the text, such as critical-thinking questions that are included at the end of boxed features in every chapter, career development exercises, video cases, Internet-based exercises, and practical tips. These features give students real-world feedback on specific topics.

Business Hall of Fame and Shame Boxes

"Business Hall of Fame" and "Business Hall of Shame" boxes in each chapter detail actual business strategies that scored big as well as those that flopped. Presented in a punchy, eye-grabbing format, these stories give students an inside view of the results of actual business decisions.

Solving an Ethical Controversy

"Solving an Ethical Controversy" boxes in each chapter highlight real-world ethics and diversity issues. These topics are excellent springboards for classroom discussions and debates.

Business Tool Kits

"Business Tool Kits," included in each chapter, equip students with hands-on business insight and information they can apply to their lives immediately. Topics include tips for creating a Web page, choosing software, and creating an electronic resumé.

Business Directory

The student-friendly "Business Directory" defines key terms in a highlighted box on the two-page spread in which they appear.

End-of-Chapter Activities

New end-of-chapter material includes Ten Business Terms You Need to Know, Questions for Critical Thinking, an Experiential Exercise, and Nothing but Net Web exercises.

Continuing Video Case

Hard Candy, the novel nail-polish company that shook up established industry giants, is the subject of the new Continuing Video Case that appears at the end of the text. Separate sections of the case focus on issues related to each section of *Contemporary Business 2000,* implementing new topics as students learn them. The accompanying video is also divided into parts corresponding to the text and the written case.

Custom-Made Modules

Three new four-color, 32-page modules are available separately or packaged with the text at **No Additional Charge.**

Hispanic Americans in Contemporary Business

Reflecting the increasing number of U.S. Hispanic-owned companies as well as burgeoning opportunities with Mexico-based operations, this new module highlights contributions from Hispanic American business owners and executives, features leadership success stories, discusses the impact of NAFTA, and explores demographic, employment trends and career opportunities for Hispanic Americans.

African Americans in Contemporary Business

Mirroring a more diverse marketplace and the increasingly powerful African American segment, this module explores opportunities for African Americans in today's business environment, analyzes employment trends and demographics, features African American business role models and leaders, details entrepreneurial success stories, and spotlights contributions by African Americans as they relate to U.S. business. This module was extensively reviewed by leading African American academic and business leaders.

In-Class Exercises and Technology Module

Tied directly to our increased technology emphasis, this innovative resource features detailed and practical tips for effectively navigating the Internet, includes interactive Web exercises, and focuses on the fast-paced advances in technology and their impact on business in the 21st century. In addition, this interactive supplement features tips and ideas for cross-functional teaching, as well as additional exercises and cases focusing on issues affecting actual companies, enabling students to apply chapter concepts to hands-on, real-world exercises and experiences.

THE MOST COMPLETE AND INNOVATIVE SUPPORT PACKAGE ON THE MARKET

Boone & Kurtz's *Contemporary Business 2000* continues to lead the market with the most innovative, technologically advanced package and packaging available. Completely integrated with the text, this high-tech resource illustrates key chapter concepts with hands-on, real-world applications for students. For instructors and students, it provides support unrivaled by any package on the market. Along with cutting-edge, new features, the package also includes some of Boone & Kurtz's precedent-setting originals, revised and updated for this new edition.

NEW! Web Instructor's Manual

Created to help instructors integrate the Boone and Kurtz Web site into the course with ease, the *Web Instructor's Manual* includes detailed outlines of the Web site, instructor's teaching notes for company profiles and exercises, and detailed notes on how the instructor can integrate the Web site into the course.

Video Package

The innovative video package for the new edition integrates the book's technology, entrepreneurship, and societal themes. The videos take a problem-resolution approach, with problems and solutions featuring concepts directly from the text chapters. Custom produced for *Contemporary Business,* the videos were created in partnership with successful, well-known companies, giving students a real-world perspective of how business professionals meet the challenges of the new century. Here are some examples of the 21 end-of-chapter videos included in the new edition:

▼ Chapter 3, "Economic Challenges Facing Global and Domestic Business"
Video Case: Fossil—Watching the World
This designer and manufacturer of popular fashion watches has offices in both the United States and Hong Kong. The video examines new business challenges facing the firm now that Hong Kong has returned to Chinese authority.

▼ Chapter 6, "Starting Your Own Business: The Entrepreneurship Alternative"
Video Case: Two Artists or Two Executives? The Story of Two Women Boxing
Linda Finell and Julie Cohn launched this successful venture 14 years ago. Two Women Boxing creates one-of-a-kind handmade boxes, picture frames, and hand-decorated photo albums. In addition to their product lines, the two entrepreneurs are now licensing their designs to such outlets as Neiman Marcus, Silvestry, and Chronicle Books.

▼ Chapter 7, "Strategies for Business Success in the Relationship Era"
Video Case: Paradigm Simulation—Reality Bites in the Virtual World
Paradigm has enjoyed a mutually beneficial relationship with Nintendo, creating innovative 3-D software games such as *Pilot Wings*. In addition, Paradigm is now creating games for the Sega Channel and will soon launch its first game on the Internet.

▼ Chapter 17, "Using Technology and the Internet to Succeed in Business"
Video Case: A Search Engine Named Yahoo!
This inspiring video details how two young college students turned their hobby—collecting fun sites on the World Wide Web for their friends—into a tremendously successful business. That was April 1994. Today the two founders are multimillionaires, and their business is now a global Internet service.

▼ Chapter 18, "Using Technology to Manage Information"
Video Case: Human Genome Sciences
Founded by Harvard genetics guru William Hazeltine and a group of private investors, HGS is engaged in the competitive race to match components of DNA in the scientific quest to identify all of the genes in the human body. The team is striving to identify human genes and their functions. Collected database information will eventually be sold to pharmaceutical companies to help them develop treatments and cures for life-threatening diseases and illnesses.

Continuing Case Supported by Video

The new edition of *Contemporary Business* includes a special continuing video case featuring Hard Candy. Hard Candy, a cosmetics company for Generation Xers, was born when pre-med student Dineh Mohajer began mixing unusual nail polish colors in the bathtub of her apartment and selling them to trendy boutiques on Melrose Avenue. The firm's transition from a sole proprietorship to a full-blown (and highly profitable) global corporation is traced in the memorable video segments. This exciting video can be packaged with each copy of *Contemporary Business 2000*.

The continuing case feature is a new component of this new edition that students won't quickly forget.

Boone & Kurtz Web Site

The Internet Business Connection is located at www.contemporarybusiness.com. This online resource connects professors and students alike with countless business resources. From this site, users can select the home page for any chapter or appendix in the textbook. The individual home pages contain company profiles, exercises, numerous resources associated with chapter topics, links to other sites related to chapter material, interactive simulations for applicable chapters, and much more. For example, the "Reading Room" allows users to access online business magazines such as *Fortune, Forbes, Money,* and *BusinessWeek,* as well as the business sections of many regional and national newspapers such as *USA Today,* the *New York Times*, and the *Washington Post*. Additional online exercises help students review chapter materials. In addition, instructors are linked to teaching resources, bibliographies of articles related to text material, and ideas on how to use the Internet in class. The *Internet Business Connection* also includes a comprehensive Web page for Appendix A, "Your Career in Business." Students see links to over 30 sites where current business jobs are posted or sites for researching and locating employers. They also receive helpful tips to maximize their job searches, including specific search words or phrases they can use for each of the seven business careers explored in the *Discovering Your Business Career* CD-ROM. For faster browsing and convenience, users can download the *Internet Business Connection* and install it on their computers. It runs in a special Web browser inside the *Discovering Your Business Career* program.

Internet Guide

An *Internet Guide* can be packaged with each copy of *Contemporary Business 2000*. All students can be Internet savvy with this invaluable guide to the Internet. The handbook's Internet terms and popular Web site addresses—over 160 ranging from the American Stock Exchange to the White House—get students where they want to go on the Internet.

Discovering Your Business Career CD-ROM

This interactive, multimedia program guides students as they explore business career options such as accounting, corporate financial management, information systems, risk management/insurance, retail bank management, sales, and store operations. Offering practical insight, the CD-ROM walks students through the entire career-search process, from assessing their compatibility with different careers and determining the depth of their interest to effectively implementing a job search strategy. The program helps students pinpoint careers of interest based on their answers to questions about their preferences for specific job activities, as well as personal priorities about work environment, compensation, and advancement. For each potential business career, students can view a custom video summarizing what their responses reveal about how well the career suits them and also receive a three- to six-page report detailing how each of their responses on relevant items may or may not indicate a good career match. Students can access comprehensive profiles on a variety of careers, including videos, audios, and extensive text detailing skill requirements, compensation trends, and actual job responsibilities. A list of associations, directories, and other relevant information is also included. This CD-ROM can be packaged with each copy of *Contemporary Business 2000*.

PowerPoint/CD-ROM Media Active Presentation Software

Classroom lectures and discussions come to life with this innovative presentation tool. Extremely instructor friendly and organized by chapter, this program enables instructors to custom design their own multimedia classroom presentations, using overhead transparencies, figures, tables, and graphs from the text, as well as completely new material from outside sources.

Transparency Acetates, Masters, and Teaching Notes

Over 200 full-color overhead transparency acetates are available. The acetates—many of which are new to this edition—illustrate key concepts discussed in the text. Most are original, but some are copies of key text figures and graphs. Transparency masters highlight actual figures and graphics found in the text. A complete set of teaching notes is included for both the acetates and masters.

Distance-Learning Instructor's Resource System

In a continuing effort to provide the most innovative package system available and to meet the changing needs of this growing marketplace, Boone & Kurtz have provided Web-based materials for instructor's use in distance-learning courses. In addition, a *Distance-Learning Study Guide* is available for students.

Media Instructor's Manual

This separate media manual features easy-to-use guidelines to help instructors incorporate the videos and Power-Point presentation software into lectures and classroom presentations. It also includes important information for each of the videos, including teaching objectives, a list of chapter concepts illustrated in the video, outlines of the videos, answers to in-text video case questions, and experiential exercises.

Instructor's Resource Manual

Instructors have asked for a more user-friendly resource, and we have delivered the most innovative *IRM* on the market. The *IRM* includes the following helpful sections for each chapter:

▼ Changes in this new edition

▼ New coverage

▼ New terms

▼ New features

▼ Internet addresses included in each chapter

▼ Annotated learning goals

▼ Lecture outline

▼ Ten business terms you need to know

▼ Other important business terms

▼ Answers to Business Hall of Fame/Shame critical-thinking questions

▼ Answers to review questions

▼ Answers to end-of-chapter critical-thinking questions

▼ Experiential exercises

▼ Teaching notes for Nothing but Net

▼ Answers to video case questions

▼ Additional teaching resources for chapter
   experiential exercises
   supplemental cases
   guest speaker suggestions

Supplemental Modules

Three separate supplemental modules—Quality, Diversity, and Business Math—provide additional coverage for instructors who want to further emphasize any of these areas.

Assessment Module

This unique module enables instructors to assess student mastery of text concepts. Organized by chapter, it includes chapter learning goals, review questions, essay questions, and unique assessment exercises.

Electronic Instructor's Manual and Study Guide

This innovative instructor resource system includes electronic versions of the *Instructor's Resource Manual* and *Study Guide* on disk.

Test Bank

Double- and triple-checked for accuracy, the revised and updated *Test Bank* includes 3,500-plus questions, more than half of which are new. Questions are keyed to chapter learning goals, text page number, and type of question (knowledge or application). Questions include multiple choice, true/false, and a short essay for each learning goal. Mini-cases with multiple-choice questions and critical-thinking questions emphasize the importance of the concepts presented in each chapter.

Computerized Test Bank

Available in IBM-, Windows-, and Macintosh-compatible formats, the computerized version of the printed *Test Bank* enables instructors to preview and edit test questions, as well as add their own. The tests and answer keys can also be printed in scrambled formats.

RequesTest and Online Testing Service

Dryden Press makes test planning quicker and easier than ever with this program. Instructors can order test masters by question number and criteria over a toll-free telephone number. Test masters will be mailed or faxed within 48 hours. Dryden can provide instructors with software to install their own online testing program, allowing tests to be administered over a network or on individual terminals. This program offers instructors greater flexibility and convenience in grading and storing test results.

Web-Based Stock Market Game

The fastest path to learning is through hands-on application, which is exactly what students gain when they use this interactive new program. Through this Web-based supplement, students create a stock portfolio they manage and manipulate throughout the course.

Computer Simulation

The computerized game *Chopsticks*—created by Professors Eugene J. Calvasina, James Leon Barton, Jr., Ava Honan, Richard Calvasina, and Gerald Calvasina of Auburn University—challenges students to develop and experience the business concepts presented in the text and to utilize frequently used business decision-making tools. The game is accompanied by an *Instructor's Manual* that provides instructions and student worksheets. The simulation game is available on disk for use with IBM and IBM-compatible PCs.

Web-Based Computer Cases Supplement and the B&K Business Disk

These innovative Web-based components are designed to assist instructors who want to include analytical problems as homework assignments or to use such tools as personal computers in the basic business course. The computer cases supplement includes three to five business problems and solutions per chapter, focusing on key concepts. The business disk includes complete programs for the computer cases and the solutions to each case.

Web-Based Portfolio of Business Papers

Available on the Boone & Kurtz Web site, this comprehensive collection of actual business documents helps students understand the variety of official papers required in a modern business organization. Teaching notes are included.

Study Guide

An invaluable tool for helping students master business concepts, the *Study Guide* includes a brief outline, experiential exercises, a self-quiz, cases, short-answer questions, and crossword puzzles for each chapter. Solutions appear at the end of the guide.

Alternate Study Guide

Answers and solutions are not included with this alternate guide. When required as a part of the course materials, instructors can assign homework from the guide, using it to evaluate how well students are retaining concepts covered in the text.

Computerized Self-Study

A computerized Windows-based study aid for students. Modified Test Questions are organized by chapter and give students the opportunity to test their knowledge of key chapter concepts. Available on a 3½-inch disk or as a downloadable file on the *Contemporary Business* Web site.

ACKNOWLEDGMENTS

The authors gratefully acknowledge the following colleagues who reviewed all or part of the new edition and its ancillaries. We are extremely grateful for the insightful comments of the following people:

Alison Adderly-Pitman
Brevard Community College

David Alexander
Angelo State University

Charles Armstrong
Kansas City Kansas Community College

Charles Beem
Bucks County Community College

Carol Bibly
Triton College

Steven E. Bradley
Austin Community College

Willie Caldwell
Houston Community College

Edward Friese
Okaloosa–Walton Community College

Stephen W. Griffin
Tarrant County Community College South

Annette L. Halpin
Beaver College

Nathan Himelstein
Essex County College

Eva M. Hyatt
Appalachian State University

Gloria M. Jackson
San Antonio College

Steven R. Jennings
Highland Community College

Bill Kindsfather
Tarrant County Community College

Charles C. Kitzmiller
Indian River Community College

Fay D. Lamphear
San Antonio College

Paul Londrigan
Mott Community College

James McKee
Champlain College

Linda S. Munilla
Georgia Southern University

George Otto
Truman College

Alton Parish
Tarrant County Community College

William E. Rice
California State University, Fresno

Catherine A. Sanders
San Antonio College

Gene Schneider
Austin Community College

Nora Jo Sherman
Houston Community College

James B. Stull
San Jose State University

The authors also would like to recognize the professors and individuals who participated in keeping the *Contemporary Business 2000* supplements an outstanding and innovative package:

Hal Babson
Columbia College

Jeanne Bartimus
University of South Alabama

Kathy Daruty
Los Angeles Pierce College

Douglas Hearth
University of Arkansas

Eric Sandburg
President of Career Design Software

Amit Shah
Frostburg State University

Raymond Shea
Monroe Community College

Bill Syvertsen
California State University, Fresno

Gary Thomas
Anne Arundel Community College

Roland D. Tollefson
Anne Arundel Community College

David Wiley
Anne Arundel Community College

The authors also would like to respectfully acknowledge and thank the professors and ancillary authors whose comments and efforts helped create a successful revision of the eighth edition of *Contemporary Business:*

James Leon Barton, Jr.
Auburn University

Robb Bay
Community College of Southern Nevada

Eugene J. Calvasina
Auburn University

Gerald Calvasina
Auburn University

Richard Calvasina
Auburn University

Rowland Chidomere
Winston–Salem State University

Robert Cox
Salt Lake Community College

Norman B. Cregger
Central Michigan University

Kathy Daruty
Los Angeles Pierce College

Jodson Faurer
Metropolitan State College at Denver

Blane Franckowiak
Tarrant County Community College

Milton Glisson
North Carolina AT&T State University

Don Gordon
Illinois Central College

Stephen Griffin
Tarrant County Community College, South

Douglas Heeter
Ferris State University

Paul Hegele
Elgin Community College

Tom Heslin
Indiana University, Bloomington

Ava Honan
Auburn University

Vince Howe
University of North Carolina, Wilmington

Geraldine Jolly
Barton College

Dave Jones
La Salle University

Kenneth Lacho
University of New Orleans

Thomas Lloyd
Westmoreland County Community College

Martin St. John
Westmoreland County Community College

Eric Sandburg
President of Career Design Software

Joan Sepic-Mizis
St. Louis Community College at Florissant Valley

Raymond Shea
Monroe Community College

E. George Stook
Anne Arundel Community College

Roland Tollefson
Anne Arundel Community College

Sheb True
Loyola Marymount University

Robert Ulbrich
Parkland College

W. J. Walters
Central Piedmont Community College

Tom Wiener
Iowa Central Community College

David Wiley
Anne Arundel Community College

Joyce Wood
Northern Virginia Community College

Gregory Worosz
Schoolcraft College

Last, but not least, we want to thank our good friends at our publisher and Elm Street Publishing Services. Our acquisitions editor, John Weimeister, our developmental editors Tracy Morse and Karen Hill, our project editors, Kathryn Stewart and Phyllis Crittenden, our designers, Bill Brammer and Melissa Morgan, our production managers, Darryl King and Barb Lange, our market strategist, Lisé Johnson, and our photo and permissions editors, Jan Huskisson and Abby Westapher, have been most supportive and helpful. We are especially appreciative of the numerous contributions of our research associates Jeanne Bartimus, Marlene Bellamy, Douglas Hearth, Carolyn Lawrence, and Nancy Moudry.

Business has gone high tech. And never has there been a more exciting time to study this dynamic field. New technological advances have created an industry of endless opportunities—limited only by business's creativity.

Contemporary Business 2000 is wired for the new high-tech advances, integrating a technology emphasis throughout the text and package. Internet, CD-ROM, multimedia—these are some of the new tools you'll use to learn about traditional and emerging business concepts and issues.

For example, *Contemporary Business* has an especially strong connection to the Internet, including its own student-friendly site on the World Wide Web. The Internet offers countless exciting opportunities for businesses. With Boone & Kurtz, you'll learn firsthand what an effective business tool this—and other high-tech applications—can be, as well as experience the intricacies of effectively navigating the Information Superhighway.

The Internet is literally the application of all business principles:

1. The Internet is all about advertising—from advertising goods and services to creating an image through the home page.

2. Many companies gather data over the Net—practical information about competitors, suppliers, and customers. Many firms include questionnaires on the Web for data gathering.

3. Companies can test-market new ideas or product and service enhancements over the Net.

4. Home pages often include e-mail addresses or links, offering another avenue for helpful information.

5. Legal issues are reviewed on the Web. Issues such as product liability or the Communications Decency Act may be investigated. Instructions are also offered for reporting consumer complaints to various agencies.

6. The Web opens the door to international companies or governments. It is especially insightful to investigate legal issues regarding business in other countries.

7. Many special-interest groups have home pages. Ethical and environmental issues, for example, are frequently reviewed.

8. The Web is a unique channel for distributing goods, services, and information.

9. Direct access to producers by consumers may significantly change the nature of selling.

10. The Internet may be used for job searches. Many companies post job openings on their home pages. Several online job search services are also available.

As you can see, the applications are endless. And *Contemporary Business* is your direct link to business innovation. Visit the Boone & Kurtz *Contemporary Business* Web site at www.contemporarybusiness.com

STUDENT GLOSSARY OF HELPFUL INTERNET TERMS

Bookmark. A browser feature that places selected URLs in a file for quick access.

FTP (file transfer protocol). A tool for transferring files between computers on the Internet, often used to transfer large files of statistics, scientific experiments, and full-text articles.

Gopher. A text-based Internet search engine developed by the University of Minnesota that provides subject access to files on the Internet through menus.

Home page. The first hypertext document displayed on a Web server. A home page is often a menu page with information about the developer and links to other sites.

HTML (hypertext markup language). Code in which World Wide Web documents are written and presented.

HTTP (hypertext transfer protocol). The protocol used by the Web to transfer hypertext documents.

Hypertext. Documents that contain links to other documents, allowing the user to jump from one document to another.

URL (uniform resource locator). Web address that gives the exact location of an Internet resource.

Usenet. A group of systems that enable users to exchange discussion on specific topics through news groups.

World Wide Web (WWW). A hypertext-based system for finding and accessing Internet resources.

HOW TO GET ONLINE

Learning to use the basic tools will make surfing the Net more profitable and enjoyable for you. Each site has an address, which is referred to as a URL, or uniform resource locator. Using a URL is a fast way to get to a site. Setting a bookmark makes getting to a useful site at a later time even faster. If you do not know a specific URL, you can use any of the various search engines (for example, Yahoo!, Infoseek) to conduct a search.

YOUR PERSONAL WORLD WIDE WEB DIRECTORY

Contemporary Business provides students with an in-text World Wide Web directory. Online addresses are included in the textbook for companies and organizations highlighted in extended-text examples, boxed features, opening vignettes, and photo illustrations. Company Web addresses are also listed alphabetically inside the front and back cover pages of the text.

For additional resources, you can reach the Boone & Kurtz *Contemporary Business 2000* home page at www.contemporarybusiness.com

Because the Internet is a constantly changing network of networks, no subject list is ever complete. Each day addresses change, new sites are added, and old sites disappear without warning. Following is a list of search engines and private data sources that provide links to numerous other sites relating to business and businesses themselves.

SEARCH ENGINES

If you don't know the URL for a site, you can use various search engines to perform a keyword search by developer or subject name. As with everything on the Internet, these search tools change daily, and new features are constantly added. The following search engines can help track down online information on a variety of topics:

Search.com (http://search.cnet.com/). This site gives access to more than 300 specialized indexes and search engines.

Metacrawler (http://www.go2net.com/). This tool submits your query to nine of the top search engines at once.

Altavista (http://www.altavista.com/). This service provides one of the largest search indexes on the Web.

Infoseek Guide (http://infoseek.go.com/). This search index includes millions of listings.

Yahoo! (http://www.yahoo.com/). This useful search index divides reference sites into logical groups.

GOVERNMENT DATA SOURCES

U.S. Census Bureau (http://www.census.gov/). This site provides free access to many census data reports and tables, including international census data from many countries.

U.S. Bureau of Economic Analysis (http://www. bea.doc.gov/). This site provides national and regional economic information, including gross domestic product by industry.

U.S. Bureau of Labor Statistics (http://stats.bls.gov/). This site gives access to the BLS survey of consumer expenditures, a report on how U.S. consumers spend their money.

Department of Commerce/STAT-USA (http://www. stat-usa.gov/). This subscription-based site provides access to hundreds of government-sponsored business research studies and other statistical information.

FedWorld (http://www.fedworld.gov/). This site provides a central access point for locating government information. If you need data from the government but don't know where to find it, start here.

PRIVATE DATA SOURCES

Knight-Ridder Information (http://www.dialog.com/). This extensive database provides access to thousands of business research reports, industry and competitor information, and trade publications. Although it proves itself an excellent source for secondary data of all types, a typical search can be expensive. Knowledge Index, available on CompuServe, provides access to many of the Dialog databases for an hourly fee.

Lexis-Nexis (http://www.lexis-nexis.com/). This is another extensive—and expensive—database of directories, trade publications, and legal information.

HOW TO CITE INTERNET SITES

If you plan to use the information you have retrieved from the Internet in a research paper or in homework assignments, you need to know how to cite the information correctly. Although formats are still being developed for the various types of electronic documents, new editions of most of the accepted style manuals have a section on citing electronic resources, including the Internet.

The University of Michigan's Internet Public Library has a list with links to recommend electronic information citation guides such as
http://www.uvm.edu/~ncrane/estyles,
which offers citation formats based on the forthcoming book by Li & Crane, *Electronic Styles: An Expanded Guide to Citing Information,* according to the Modern Language Association styles.

DISCOVERING YOUR BUSINESS CAREER CD-ROM

Included free with each new copy of *Contemporary Business 2000* by The Dryden Press is a CD-ROM titled *Discovering Your Business Career.* It contains three programs, each of which may be used in conjunction with your course: *Discovering Your Business Career, Career Design,* and *The Internet Business Connection.* Detailed instructions for these programs are included at the end of each part in the text.

Discovering Your Business Career

Discovering Your Business Career helps you learn about and assess your compatibility with seven major business career areas. They were selected not only to represent the diversity of business opportunities available but also for the number of jobs in these fields.

- ▼ Accounting
- ▼ Corporate financial management
- ▼ Information systems
- ▼ Risk management/insurance
- ▼ Retail bank management
- ▼ Sales
- ▼ Retailing

For each career, you receive broad guidance and practical advice on everything from clarifying the depth of your interest in that career to preparing and implementing an effective job search strategy.

The first step in your business career exploration is to complete a questionnaire. You rate a broad range of business-related job activities from "very appealing" to "very unappealing." For example, you rate the statement "Making financial forecasts about your company's profits based on the assumptions you have made about how many units will sell, the selling price, and the expenses." You also rate yourself according to ten broad career factors that measure your priorities about your work environment, compensation, and progression in your career. The program then matches your responses to specific business careers and indicates which may be of greatest interest to you. For each business career, you can view a personal video summarizing what your responses reveal about how well the career suits you. You can also read a detailed three- to six-page report explaining how each of your responses from the questionnaire may or may not indicate a good career match.

In addition to learning about your compatibility with different business careers, you can access complete career profiles about each of them. Through videos, multimedia slide shows, and extensive textual content, the profiles present a detailed, up-to-date picture of actual job responsibilities, career paths, and skills required to be successful. You also learn about current compensation levels and associations, directories, books, and other information about the business career of interest. To ensure that the profiles realistically reflect current job opportunities in the business field, researchers conducted extensive interviews with top professionals and executives from prominent companies, including AT&T, IBM, General Mills, Procter & Gamble, Ford, General Electric, Hewlett-Packard, McDonald's, Reebok, Bank of America, NationsBank, Chase Manhat-

tan, Bankers Trust, Citicorp, PricewaterhouseCoopers, Arthur Andersen, KPMG Peat Marwick, JC Penney, Kimberly-Clark, USX Corp., John Hancock Mutual Life Insurance, Allstate Insurance, Neiman Marcus, Wal-Mart, Sears, and Kmart.

Career Design

Also included on the *Discovering Your Business Career* CD-ROM is a free copy of *Career Design,* the landmark career planning software program that is based on the work of John Crystal, the major contributor to the most widely read career book of all time, *What Color Is Your Parachute?,* by Richard N. Bolles. *Career Design* has received worldwide coverage and praise from both the business and computer press, including *BusinessWeek, Fortune, The Wall Street Journal, The Financial Times, The London Times, PC Magazine,* and *PC Computing.* The student version provides general career exercises and resources in the following sections:

- ▼ Interests—Uncovering your business interests.

- ▼ Skills—Identifying the strengths you offer a prospective employer, including technical skills achieved through formal training and education and nontechnical skills, such as leadership and communications.

- ▼ Entrepreneurship Quotient—Completing a questionnaire to determine your level of entrepreneurial orientation.

- ▼ Personal Finance—Finding out how much earning power you need. In a spreadsheet, you enter anticipated expenses upon graduation under such categories as "Insurance," "Loan Payments," and "Rent/Mortgage." The program then applies current federal and state income taxes to calculate the gross income before taxes that you must earn to maintain your chosen lifestyle.

- ▼ People Preferences—Identifying the types of people with whom you want to spend your time, including at work.

- ▼ Work Preferences—Identifying your preferred working conditions.

- ▼ Business Adventure—Writing about how you want to spend two weeks in a business-related activity, such as "Learning about the step-by-step process a bank or other lender follows in approving a multimillion-dollar loan for a large real estate project."

- ▼ *BusinessWeek* Article—Writing an imaginary article about what you or your future company has accomplished in the business world.

▼ Setting Goals—Clarifying your personal and professional direction by setting specific goals.

▼ Resumés—Preparing a resumé after comparing and choosing from one of three available formats: chronological, functional, or results oriented.

Internet Business Connection

The *Internet Business Connection* is the name of the Web site for *Contemporary Business*. From this site, you can select any chapter or appendix in the textbook. Each chapter and appendix has its own home page from which you can access company profiles, exercises, and resources associated with chapter topics. On the home page for the *Contemporary Business* Web site, you can select the "Reading Room" to access online business magazines such as *Fortune, Forbes, Money,* and *BusinessWeek,* as well as the business sections of many regional and national newspapers such as *USA Today,* the *New York Times,* the *Washington Post,* the *San Francisco Chronicle,* and more.

For faster browsing and convenience, you can download the *Internet Business Connection* and install it on your computer. It runs in a special Web browser inside the *Discovering Your Business Career* program.

The *Internet Business Connection* also includes a comprehensive Web page for Appendix A, "Your Career in Business." You have links to over 30 sites where current business jobs are posted or sites for researching and locating employers. You also receive helpful tips to maximize your job search, including specific search words or phrases you can use for each of the seven business careers in *Discovering Your Business Career.*

Together, *Discovering Your Business Career, Career Design,* and the *Internet Business Connection* offer an invaluable enhancement to your business course by enabling you to connect what you learn with exciting career opportunities in the field. Through the *Internet Business Connection,* you can seamlessly integrate the vast resources of the Web with what is covered in your course to bring the world of business closer to you.

Louis E. Boone, Ph.D., holds the Ernest G. Cleverdon Chair of Business and Management and serves as coordinator of the introductory business course at the University of South Alabama. He formerly chaired the Division of Management and Marketing at the University of Tulsa and has taught courses in management and marketing in Australia, Greece, and the United Kingdom.

Following recent major heart surgery, Dr. Boone has returned to active teaching, writing, and research. In addition to authoring numerous marketing and business texts and computer simulation games, he recently published *Quotable Business*, Second Edition (Random House, 1999). His current research focuses on event and sports management and marketing. Dr. Boone's research has been published in such journals as the *Journal of Business Strategy, International Journal of Management, Journal of Business Research, Sports Marketing Quarterly, Journal of Psychology, Business Horizons, Journal of Marketing,* and the *Journal of Business of the University of Chicago.* He is the 1999 recipient of the Outstanding Scholar Award from the University of South Alabama and is listed in *Who's Who in America.*

David L. Kurtz, Ph.D., is the R. A. and Vivian Young Chair of Business Administration at the University of Arkansas. He was formerly the head of the Department of Marketing and Transportation at Arkansas.

Prior to returning to his graduate alma mater, Dr. Kurtz held the Thomas F. Gleed Chair in Business and Finance at Seattle University. Earlier, he was department head at Eastern Michigan University. Dr. Kurtz has also taught at Davis & Elkins College and Australia's Monash University.

Dr. Kurtz has authored or co-authored 36 books and more than 120 articles, cases, and papers. His work has appeared in such publications as the *Journal of Business Research, Journal of Marketing, Journal of Retailing,* and numerous other well-known journals.

Dr. Kurtz has been active in many professional organizations including president of the Western Marketing Educator's Association, and vice-presidentships in the Academy of Marketing Science and the Southwestern Marketing Association. He is also the recipient of an honorary doctorate in pedagogy from Davis & Elkins College.

Contents in Brief

Contents

PART I
BUSINESS IN A GLOBAL
ENVIRONMENT 2

Opening Vignette
Prospecting Online with
Levi Strauss
Business Hall of Fame
(Under) Feeding the Furby
Frenzy
Business Hall of Shame
Cinemex: Struggling to
Revamp Mexico's Movie
Industry
Solving an Ethical
Controversy
Should Intel Be Baking Your
Cookies Online?
Business Tool Kits
• Avoiding the Fine-Print
  Trap
• How to Line Up a Great
  Summer Job
• How to Develop Critical
  Thinking and Creative
  Skills

Opening Vignette
Microsoft: Predator or
Gentle Giant?
Business Hall of Fame
Bill Strickland: Modeling the
Future with Education,
Training, and Hope
Business Hall of Shame
Trouble Keeping an Eye on
the Ball at adidas
Solving an Ethical
Controversy
Should Whistle-Blowers Get
a Share of the Money They
Help Recover?
Business Tool Kits
• Before You Accept a Job,
  Review Your New
  Employer's Code of Ethics
• Protect Your Privacy
• How to Be Charitable
  without Being a Chump

Opening Vignette
**Workers of America Can
Even Unite Online**
Business Hall of Fame
**Working toward a Leaner
Labor Organization**
Business Hall of Shame
Losing Points at the NBA
Solving an Ethical
Controversy
**Should the Public Tolerate
Child Labor?**
Business Tool Kit
• **To Buy or Not to Buy**

Opening Vignette
**Fine-"Tooning" Production
at DreamWorks SKG**
Business Hall of Fame
Chrysler's Cyber Cars
Business Hall of Shame
McDonald's Quality Problem
Solving an Ethical
Controversy
**Are Celebrities Responsible
for the Products They
Endorse?**
Business Tool Kit
• **Affordable CAD**

Opening Vignette
**Streamline Offers a Lifestyle
Solution**
Business Hall of Fame
**Bath & Body Works
Cleans Up**
Business Hall of Shame
**Good-Bye to Good Buys at
Woolworth**
**Solving an Ethical
Controversy**
**Should Large Retail Chains
Try to Censor the Music
They Sell?**
Business Tool Kit
- **How to Find the Right
  Independent Sales Rep for
  Your Product**
- **Attracting Customers on a
  Shoestring Promotion
  Budget**

Opening Vignette
**Joe Boxer Sells Skivvies
with "Guerrilla" Marketing**
Business Hall of Fame
**NASCAR Drives Home Sales
for Sponsors**
Business Hall of Shame
Swept Away
**Solving an Ethical
Controversy**
**Can Internet Marketers
Ethically Solicit Business
from Children?**

Business Tool Kits
• **Choosing Software**
• **Are You Ready for 2000?**

Opening Vignette
Finding Financial Figures for Johnson & Johnson Online
Business Hall of Fame
Need an Accountant?
Consider a Virtual One
Business Hall of Shame
The Perils of Taking on Too Much Debt
Solving an Ethical Controversy
Should Company Auditors Act as Bean Counters or Gumshoes?
Business Tool Kit
• **Remedies for the Cash-Flow Blues**

PART VI
MANAGING FINANCIAL RESOURCES   654

Opening Vignette
Uncle Sam Levels the Playing Field with EDGAR
Business Hall of Fame
Small Firms Can Bank on New Services
Business Hall of Shame
ATM Fees—Making People Pay to Use Their Own Money
Solving an Ethical Controversy
Are Credit Card Issuers Responsible for Rising Consumer Debt?
Business Tool Kit
• **Tips from Two Venture Capitalists**

Opening Vignette
Online Trading—Just a
Keystroke Away with
Ameritrade
Business Hall of Fame
Turning Customers into
Investors
Business Hall of Shame
A Web of Deception
Solving an Ethical
Controversy
Should Hedge Funds Expect
to Be Rescued from Their
Greed?
Business Tool Kit
• Selecting a Stockbroker

junkbusters.com

wethe

LOCKHEED
MARTIN

http://www.lmco.com

PART I | Business in a Global Environment

Labor

http://www.bls.gov/

cnewsusa.com
Commercial News USA

LEVISTRAU

mercedes
-benz.

wat

Refresh   Home   Search   Mail

www.odci.gov/cia/publications/

Today's Links   Web Galler

wto.org
WORLD TRADE
ORGANIZATION

mys

chapter 1

Business: Blending People, Technology, and Ethical Behavior

LEARNING GOALS

1. Describe the private enterprise system and the roles played by individual businesses, competitors, and entrepreneurs within the system.

2. Explain how the historical development of the U.S. economy continues to influence contemporary business.

3. Outline the challenges and opportunities that businesses face in the relationship era.

4. Describe how technology is changing the way businesses operate and compete.

5. Relate the importance of quality and customer satisfaction in efforts to create value for customers.

6. Explain how individual businesses and entire nations compete in the global marketplace.

7. Describe how changes in the workforce are leading to a new employer-employee partnership.

8. Identify the skills that managers need to lead businesses in the new century.

9. Explain how ethics and social responsibility affect business decision making.

10. List four reasons for studying business.

Prospecting Online with Levi Strauss

Who would have believed it? A company with a brand name as well recognized as Coca-Cola, McDonald's, and Nike is scrambling to retain its customer base. The firm, born in 1873 in the aftermath of the California gold rush, enjoyed decades of sales and profit growth until the 1990s. By 2000, its share of the men's jeans market had dropped to 25 percent, down from 48 percent just ten years earlier.

A big factor in Levi's current problems is the vastly increased competition in the apparel industry. In addition to competing directly with brands like Lee and Wrangler, and trendier names like Old Navy, The Gap, Tommy Hilfiger, and Calvin Klein, many of the retail stores that carry Levi's have begun offering their own branded merchandise. JCPenney, a leading Levi's outlet, also offers its Arizona brand, and Sears sells its Canyon River jeans.

Another problem resulted from a brand image that many teenagers and young adults considered stodgy. Teens don't want to wear the same brands their parents wear. And Levi's has been criticized for being slow to spot the fashion changes, illustrated by its failure to lead the recent trends for super wide-bottom slacks and cargo pants, which have large pockets on the thighs.

Although Levi's management hasn't pushed the panic button, changes are already under way. To hold down production costs, company-owned manufacturing plants in the United States and Canada are being replaced by lower-cost contract manufacturing companies in Mexico, Central America, and South America. Levi's has also offset some of its sales slippage in jeans by focusing on its successful line of casual and dress pants, Dockers and Slates. These brands have matched up well with the growing popularity of casual attire work policies where khakis—not jeans—can pull double duty at work and play.

To compensate for slippage on the product focus on successful products

One major move by this longtime king of the denim empire is into the world of electronic commerce. How do you sell jeans on the Net, you ask? When you visit www.levi.com or www.dockers.com, you can get fashion tips from virtual salespeople, mix and match clothes in your own virtual dressing room, and even order your jeans in custom-tailored styles.

.WWW.

www.levi.com
www.dockers.com

Once Levi's decided to focus more strongly on consumer needs, the jump to the Web was a logical move. Web sites offer more items than department stores can stock. They also make possible the much ballyhooed notion of mass customization—a production method that allows goods and services to be produced in lot sizes of just one or a few at a time. Want a new pair of jeans guaranteed to fit? Levi's Personal Pair jeans are sewn to your body measurements. These data are entered into a computer, which selects from 500 design choices to find your best match. The order travels via modem to the nearest Levi's factory where the jeans are made by altering standard Levi's patterns. For about $65, a customer can get a pair of personalized jeans in just three weeks.

This new focus on matching products to individual needs is reflected in the firm's advertising. In one recent print ad, a young dreadlock-sporting youth wears dark, baggy Levi's while standing on a sidewalk with a sign that reads, "Conformity Breeds Mediocrity."

To develop lasting relationships with its legions of customers in 76 markets worldwide, Levi's employs powerful tools like computer databases to provide continuing links in the form of direct-mail advertising and other promotions. For example, a recent mailing contained activity books and contest information to young customers to promote brand awareness and increase store traffic.[1]

CHAPTER OVERVIEW

The U.S. economy is riding high on a tremendous wave of prosperity that is likely to continue well into the 21st century. A quick glance at a few statistics illustrates the many benefits that these good times bring in people's lives:

▼ Over 95 percent of U.S. workers are employed, the highest level in almost a quarter-century.

▼ Total output of goods and services is growing at approximately 4 percent a year.

▼ Despite lost sales in markets affected by the Asian economic recession, U.S. corporate profits are up, and the millions of people who own shares of stock—either directly or through their retirement accounts—are beaming as the stock market continues to hit new all-time highs.

▼ In addition to balancing the federal budget, Congress has promised tax cuts of more than $135 billion over the next 5 years.

▼ High employment, low inflation, and growth in wages have combined to boost consumer confidence to record levels. As a result, sales of homes and durable goods are marching upward at a steady pace.

▼ Businesses are investing in new technology and improvements in order to take advantage of new consumer markets.

▼ In surveys, 90 percent of executives express confidence about the continued growth of the U.S. economy and nearly one-third plan to add workers to their labor pools.[2]

How does all this optimism affect you? Simply put, the economic growth opens doors of opportunity for those who are prepared to put ideas into action. Dineh Mohajer has provided another example of today's entrepreneurial spirit. A 23-year-old college student, Mohajer invested $200 to make and sell wildly colored nail polishes with funky names. Today, just 3 years later, her company, Hard Candy, is confronting cosmetics industry giants like Revlon and L'Oreal. And trusted names like Levi's are seeking new ways to compete through online sales and global manufacturing.

In the new century, everyone is facing new challenges posed by the technological revolution that is changing the

rules of business. The combined power of telecommunications and computer technology is creating inexpensive, global networks that transfer voice messages, text, graphics, and data within seconds. These sophisticated technologies create new types of products, and they also demand new approaches to marketing existing products. Technology is also speeding the rate of change in the business world, where new discoveries rapidly outdate inventions created just months before.

Promotional messages, like the one from Merrill Lynch shown in Figure 1.1, illustrate the impact of technology on people's daily lives. Merrill Lynch, America's leading stock brokerage firm, is increasingly a global company. The ad shows how technology permits it to quickly locate information from experts in different countries and use it to advise its clients.

Innovative technologies are also globalizing today's business world. Businesses can now easily manufacture, buy, and sell across national borders. You can order a Big Mac or a Coke almost anywhere in the world, while Japanese and Korean companies manufacture most of the consumer electronics products sold in the United States. Mercedes Benz manufactures sport utility vehicles in Alabama, while many General Motors automobiles are assembled in Canada.

Figure 1.1 **Technology: Responding to Market Needs, Creating Global Markets, and Making Existing Products Obsolete**

This rapidly changing business landscape compels businesspeople to react quickly to shifts in consumer tastes and other market dynamics. Success requires creativity, split-second decision making, and innovative vision. Whether you decide to start your own business, as David Marcheschi did, work for a small, family-run business, or sign on with a large international corporation, your achievements will depend on your ability to maintain the constant pace of change in today's world.

Contemporary Business explores the strategies that allow companies to compete in today's interactive marketplace and the skills that you will need to turn ideas into action for your own career success. This chapter sets the stage for the entire text by defining *business* and revealing its role in society. The chapter's discussion illustrates how the private enterprise system encourages competition and innovation while preserving important individual freedoms. Later sections highlight the most important challenges and opportunities businesspeople will face in the 21st century.

WHAT IS BUSINESS?

What image comes to your mind when you hear the word *business?* Some people think of their jobs, others think of the merchants they patronize as consumers, and still others think of the millions of firms that make up the world's economy. This broad, all-inclusive term can be applied to many kinds of enterprises. Businesses provide the bulk of employment opportunities as well as the products that people enjoy.

Business consists of all profit-seeking activities and enterprises that provide goods and services necessary to an economic system. Some businesses produce tangible goods, such as automobiles, breakfast cereals, and computer chips; others provide services, such as insurance, music concerts, car rentals, and lodging.

Business drives the economic pulse of a nation. It provides the means through which standards of living improve. The United States leads the world in national, per-capita output of goods and services.

At the heart of every business endeavor is an exchange between a buyer and seller. A buyer recognizes a need for a good or service and trades money with a seller in order to obtain that product. The seller participates in the process in hopes of gaining profits—a critical ingredient in accomplishing the goals necessary to maintain constant improvement in standards of living.

Profits represent rewards for businesspeople who take the risks involved in blending people, technology, and information to create and market want-satisfying goods and services. In contrast, accountants think of profits as the difference between a firm's revenues and the expenses it incurs in generating these revenues. More generally, however, profits serve as *incentives* for people to start companies, expand them, and provide consistently high-quality, competitive goods and services.

Consider, for example, the role of profits in the U.S. newspaper industry over the past few years. In the early 1990s, newspapers saw their income from advertising drop as advertisers cut back because of the recession. At the same time, newspaper operating costs, especially the cost of paper, rose. The combination of dropping income and rising costs squeezed profits, and many newspapers were forced to make some tough decisions. The *Los Angeles Times,* for example, laid off 3,000 workers. Other newspapers simply closed up shop. By the mid-1990s, however, operating costs, including newsprint prices, had dropped again; as the economy improved, advertising revenues also increased. Once again, newspapers began to enjoy rising profits, allowing many of them to implement expansion plans. The *Los Angeles Times* is hiring again, and it has expanded its news coverage. Other papers have resumed marketing and community-relations programs they axed to cut costs in the early 1990s.[3]

Although the quest for profits is a central focus of business, businesspeople also recognize social and ethical responsibilities. To succeed in the long run, companies must deal responsibly with employees, customers, suppliers, competitors, government, and the general public.

Not-for-Profit Organizations

What characteristics link the National Football League, the U.S. Postal Service, the American Heart Association, and C-SPAN? For one, they are all classified as **not-for-profit organizations,** business-like establishments that have primary objectives other than returning profits to their owners. These organizations play important roles in society by placing public service above profits. Not-for-profit organizations operate in both the private and public sectors. Private-sector not-for-profits include museums, libraries, business associations, charitable and religious organiza-

Business Directory

business the profit-seeking activities of those engaged in purchasing or selling goods and services to satisfy society's needs and wants.

profits the financial rewards received by a businessperson for taking the risks involved in creating and marketing want-satisfying goods and services.

tions, and most colleges and universities. Additionally, government agencies, political parties, and labor unions are classified as not-for-profit organizations.

A good example of a not-for-profit organization is New York's Metropolitan Museum of Art. Like profit-seeking businesses, the Met must generate funds to cover its operating costs. Revenues come from a number of sources, including individual donations, memberships, government grants, gift-shop sales, and special fund-raising drives. The organization also uses such business techniques as advertising. The ad in Figure 1.2 describes a special exhibition of Florentine paintings. Such events provide added value to museum members and attract thousands of occasional and first-time visitors, who may become members.

Since 1970, the number of not-for-profit organizations in the United States has grown four times faster than the national economy as a whole. Excluding U.S. government agencies, 1.2 million not-for-profit organizations control more than $1 trillion in assets. These operations employ more people than the entire federal government and all 50 state governments combined.[4] Additionally, millions of volunteers work for them in unpaid positions. Not-for-profits find funding both from private sources, including donations, and from government sources. They are commonly exempt from federal, state, and local taxes.

Although they focus on goals other than generating profits, staff members of not-for-profit organizations face many of the same challenges as those of profit-seeking businesses. For example, Andrea Rich, president of the Los Angeles County Museum of Art, runs her organization like a business. She must find ways to serve and satisfy the museum's customer groups, including visitors, taxpayers, and donors. Rich must also manage a large and diverse staff of employees, ensuring that everyone from the custodians to the art curators efficiently performs her or his job. In addition, Rich manages a $30 million annual operating budget.[5]

As in the world of profit-seeking businesses, the new century will bring changes to the not-for-profit sector. An aging and increasingly diverse population may require not-for-profits to find new ways of delivering services. Government funding is also declining, a trend that will force not-for-profit executives to develop new cost-cutting methods. Faced with increased competition for limited funding, not-for-profits will also have to boost their effectiveness at marketing and

| Figure 1.2 | The Metropolitan Museum of Art: A Private-Sector, Not-for-Profit Organization |

fund-raising. These changes and others will require leaders with strong business skills and experience.[6] Therefore, many concepts discussed in this book will apply to not-for-profit organizations as much as to profit-oriented firms.

Factors of Production

Capitalism, like other economic systems, requires certain inputs for effective operation. Economists use the term **factors of production** to refer to the four basic inputs: natural resources, capital, human resources, and entrepreneurship. Table 1.1 identifies each of these inputs and the type of payment received by firms and individuals who supply them.

Natural resources include all productive inputs that are useful in their natural states, including agricultural land, building sites, forests, and mineral deposits. For example, Hershey uses 700,000 quarts of milk a day in producing almost 33 million chocolate Kisses. The milk used in Hershey's Kisses alone keeps 50,000 dairy cows "employed" full-time.[7] Natural resources are the basic inputs required in any economic system.

Human resources are also critical inputs in all economic systems. Human resources include anyone who works, from the chief executive officer of a huge corporation to a self-employed auto mechanic. This category encompasses both the physical labor and the intellectual inputs contributed by workers. Figure 1.3 emphasizes the importance of human resources to organizational goals by depicting a concert hall in which different musical instruments indicate the various skills of the members of the orchestra.

Capital, another key resource, includes technology, tools, information, and physical facilities. These elements frequently determine whether a fledgling computer firm, like Compaq or Microsoft, becomes an industry leader or remains a small operation. *Technology* is a broad term that refers to such machinery and equipment as production lines, telecommunications, and basic inventions. Information, frequently improved by techno-

logical innovations, is another critical success factor, since both managers and operating employees require accurate, timely information for effective performance of their assigned tasks.

Money is necessary to acquire, maintain, and upgrade a firm's capital. These funds may come from investments by company owners, profits, or loans extended by others. Money then goes to work building factories; purchasing raw materials and component parts; and hiring, training, and compensating workers. People and firms that supply capital receive factor payments in the form of interest.

Entrepreneurship is the willingness to take risks to create and operate a business. An entrepreneur is someone who sees a potentially profitable opportunity and then devises a plan to earn those profits. One such entrepreneur created the wildly popular Furby discussed in the Business Hall of Fame box. Some entrepreneurs set up new companies and ventures; others, such as the executives at Levi Strauss, revitalize established firms by keeping the organizations open to market changes and expansion possibilities.

To see how one firm utilizes the factors of production, consider Arnold Lund's new business, Windflower Corp. Lund sees opportunity in wind. He's spent 20 years developing the technology for a turbine-powered windmill that can produce 10,000 kilowatt hours of energy a year, about the same amount used in an average home. Lund's employees and technicians (human resources) are already working on the first unit, priced at $10,000, for a home in Palm Springs, California. In addition to wind, Lund's firm will require steel and other natural resources to build the units. Lund sold another firm he owned in the early 1990s to raise the $2 million in capital he needed to develop and market the windmills. Although Lund is confident that his windmills will serve a market need, he admits that he is taking an enormous risk, just as other entrepreneurs before him have done.[8]

The next section looks at how the factors of production are allocated and used within the private enterprise system, the economic system in which U.S. businesses currently operate.

Table 1.1	Factors of Production and Their Factor Payments	
Factor of Production		**Corresponding Factor Payment**
Natural resources		Rent
Human resources		Wages
Capital		Interest
Entrepreneurship		Profits

THE PRIVATE ENTERPRISE SYSTEM

No business operates in a vacuum. All operate within a larger economic system that determines how goods and services are produced, distributed, and consumed in a society. The type of economic system employed in a society also determines patterns of resource use. Some economic systems, such as communism, feature strict controls on business ownership, profits, and resource allocations, in order to accomplish government goals.

In the United States, businesses function within the **private enterprise system,** an economic system that rewards businesses for their ability to perceive and serve the needs and demands of consumers. A private enterprise system minimizes government interference in economic activity. Businesses that are adept at satisfying customers gain access to necessary factors of production and earn profits.

Another name for the private enterprise system is *capitalism.* Adam Smith, often identified as the father of capitalism, first described the concept in his book *The Wealth of Nations,* published in 1776. Smith believed that an economy is best regulated by the invisible hand of **competition,** the battle among businesses for consumer acceptance. Smith felt that competition among companies would assure consumers of receiving the best possible products and prices, because less efficient producers would gradually be driven from the marketplace.

This invisible hand concept is a basic premise of the private enterprise system. In the United States, competition regulates economic life. To compete successfully, each firm must find a basis for **competitive differentiation,** the unique combination of organizational abilities and approaches that sets a company apart from competitors in the minds of consumers. Eyeglasses retailer Lenscrafters has differentiated itself from competitors through service. Customers get their new lenses in about an hour. Wal-Mart uses discount pricing on brand name products to attract customers.

Businesses operating in a private enterprise system face a critical task of keeping up with changing marketplace conditions. Firms that fail to adjust to shifts in consumer preferences or ignore the actions of competitors leave themselves open to failure. Consider, for example, Dydee Diaper. For 60 years, the Boston-based company laundered and delivered cloth baby diapers to parents. As women entered the workforce in increasing numbers, however, busy working mothers began to prefer the convenience of disposable diapers. Dydee started losing customers to giant manufacturers like Kimberly-Clark and Procter & Gamble. Dydee, one of the last diaper services left in the country, recently filed for bankruptcy.[9]

Throughout this book, the discussion will focus on the tools and methods that 21st-century businesses will apply to compete and differentiate their goods and services. Each Business Hall of Fame feature explains how an individual businessperson or company has developed successful strategies for competitive differentiation. The book will also discuss many of the ways in which market changes will affect business and the free enterprise system in the years ahead. Chapter 3 focuses specifically on how businesses function within other economic systems.

| **Figure 1.3** | **Human Resources: A Critical Factor of Production** |

Business Directory

factors of production basic inputs into the private enterprise system, including natural resources, human resources, capital, and entrepreneurship.

private enterprise system an economic system that rewards firms based on how well they match and counter the offerings of competitors to serve the needs and demands of customers.

competition the battle among businesses vying for consumer acceptance.

BUSINESS HALL OF FAME

(Under)feeding the Furby Frenzy

From Barbie dolls to teddy bears. From yo-yos to Cabbage Patch kids to Tickle Me Elmo. The steady stream of toys, gadgets, and gizmos keeps the toy industry on its toes—ready for innovation and growth. A recent toy fad is Furby, an interactive bundle of fuzz that speaks its own language (Fur-

bish); learns English phrases; and responds to touch, sound, and light. Creator Dave Hampton got his inspiration from the Tamagotchi virtual pet (the LED companion that dies without constant and intense nurturing). "That's not a pet," said Hampton. "I want to make something that kids can hold . . . something that would seem alive." He has delivered on that vision. Furbies sing, dance, laugh, snore, make rude noises, and talk to other Furbies. They even teach kids to talk Furbish.

Along with the demanding little furballs came *Furby frenzy*—whipped up by the media, which began hyping Furbies right after February's Toy Fair '98. Even though the toy wouldn't be ready until fall, shoppers were interested. In fact, parents were clamoring for Furbies before the toys were even shipped from the factory.

Some accuse Hasbro, Furby's manufacturer, of using fad marketing to create the intense demand. If true, Hasbro wouldn't be the first to use such tactics. Look at De Beers and others in the diamond cartel who deliberately produce fewer diamonds than they can just to drive prices up and make diamonds more desirable. Even the Ty toy company removes various models

of Beanie Babies from the market before demand is satisfied—supporting the belief among consumers that the inexpensively made stuffed animals have some kind of collector's value. Of course, retailers are perfectly happy with manufacturers who undersupply because they won't be stuck with unsold inventory.

However, Hasbro's Tiger Electronics unit (which makes Furbies) claims that it did not conspire to tighten supply. Tiger's publicist says that before September, retailers had ordered 1 million Furbies. Confident that the toy would sell well, Tiger manufactured 1.3 million. But, in fact, after all the media coverage had stirred up so much interest, closer to 5 million Furbies could have been sold. So people got caught up in Furby frenzy.

Whether the scarcity was intentional or unplanned, Hasbro wasn't making Furbies fast enough, and stores were running out of them before parents could say "kah a-tay" (Furbish for "I'm hungry"). That's when millions of shoppers attempted to find Furbies on the Internet. Some Web sites didn't even try to sell the few Furbies that were still available. eToys (www.etoys.com) gave away one Furby a day until Christmas. You just

Basic Rights within the Private Enterprise System

Certain rights critical to the operation of capitalism are available to citizens living in a private enterprise economy. These include the rights to private property, profits, freedom of choice, and competition, as shown in Figure 1.4.

The right to **private property** is the most basic freedom under the private enterprise system. Every participant enjoys the right to own, use, buy, sell, and bequeath most forms of property, including land, buildings, machinery, equipment, inventions, and various intangible kinds of property.

The private enterprise system also guarantees business owners the right to all profits (after taxes) earned by their

activities. Although a business is not assured of earning a profit, its owner is legally and ethically entitled to any income it generates in excess of costs.

Freedom of choice means that a private enterprise system relies on the potential for citizens to choose their own employment, purchases, and investments. They can change jobs, negotiate wages, join labor unions, and choose among many different brands of goods and services. People living in the capitalist nations of North America, Europe, and other parts of the world are so accustomed to this freedom of choice that they sometimes forget its importance. A private enterprise economy maximizes individual human welfare and happiness by providing alternatives. Other economic systems sometimes limit freedom of choice in order to accomplish government goals, such as increasing industrial production.

had to visit the site every day and sign up. Of course eToys was glad to have you pick up one or two other gift items while you were visiting. Some Web sites sold Furbies for as long as they had the toys in stock. For FAO Schwarz (www.faoschwarz.com), the stock of Furbies lasted until the day after Thanksgiving. Still other sites were inundated. At the Toys R Us site (www.toysrus.com), shoppers got only "network error" messages when they tried to search for Furbies.

Several sites did have Furbies a few days after Thanksgiving. At eGift (www.egift.com), for example, you could order a Furby for $147.95—some five times the suggested retail price. And before Christmas was over, some sites were charging as much as ten times the suggested $29.99. Even so, people were more than willing to pay for a guaranteed delivery and especially for a chance to avoid the malls and their Furby-frantic crowds.

The question is, does Furby mania "have legs"? Can the cuddly toy retain its popularity? Some owners are finding out that Furbies can be demanding and loud. On the *Today* show, Katie Couric asked Tiger publicist Marc Rosenberg, "Can you get them to shut up now?" Whether Furby joins the ranks of teddy bears, yo-yos, and Barbies depends on the toy's ability to turn fad appeal into the sticking power of a toy classic. Will Furby keep its hot-toy

status, or is Hasbro's hit already a has-been? The competition is stiff.

Challenging Furby are Anakin Sky-walker and Darth Maul, along with other *Star Wars* prequel characters. Also in the running are the Furby-inspired interactive toys that not only say a few words but can even hold a conversation. Mattel's entry is the CD-ROM that lets kids drive and crash Hot Wheel cars on a Hollywood sound set. The World Wrestling Federation modeled the Stone Cold Steve Austin figure after its famous wrestler to protect a kid's room as a talking security system, with light sensor and motion detector. Not the least of Furby's challengers are PBS's Teletubbies (Tinky Winky, Dipsy, Laa-Laa, and Po), which are interactive and which sport an LED "tummy screen" in three colors.

So how will Furby fare? Can Furby fend off the *Star Wars* prequel characters and the Teletubbies? True, Furbies have flashier coats. Hasbro has spruced them up, giving them patterned fur in giraffe, tiger, Dalmatian, and snow leopard prints. But will new fur be enough?

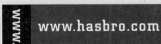
www.hasbro.com

QUESTIONS FOR CRITICAL THINKING

1. Do Furbies and other fad toys revitalize Hasbro by keeping it open to new possibilities? Give an example of how Furbies could inspire innovation at Hasbro.

2. Did Web sites solve the problem for shoppers when the demand for Furbies far exceeded supply? How did the Internet help allocate scarce resources? Could online sources do anything to hurt the toy's appeal or popularity?

3. If you were a toy entrepreneur, what is the biggest risk you would face trying to bring your toy to market?

Sources: Isabel Forgang, Kevin Penton, and Bill Hutchinson, "Furby Rules High-Tech Toys," *New York Daily News Online*, accessed at www.mostnewyork.com, February 9, 1999; Jason Ocampo, "Furby, PC Games Fuel Hasbro Profits," *Gamenews*, accessed at www.gamecenter, February 9, 1999; Benjamin Fulford, "Don't Flood the Market," *Forbes*, December 28, 1998, p. 56; "Flyin' Furbies," *People*, December 14, 1998, p. 88; Elizabeth Weise, "Stalking Rare Furbies in Web Wilderness," *USA Today*, Section D, December 2, 1998, p. 1; John Cloud, "How the Furby Flies," *Time*, November 30, 1998, pp. 84–85.

The private enterprise system also permits fair competition by allowing the public to set rules for competitive activity. For this reason, the U.S. government has passed laws to prohibit "cutthroat" competition—excessively aggressive competitive practices designed to eliminate competition. It also has established ground rules that outlaw price discrimination, fraud in financial markets, and deceptive advertising and packaging.

The Entrepreneurship Alternative

One of the options offered by capitalism is entrepreneurship. Indeed, entrepreneurial spirit beats at the heart of private enterprise. Individuals who recognize marketplace opportunities are free to use their capital, time, and talents to

pursue those opportunities for profit. The willingness of individuals to start new ventures drives economic growth and keeps pressure on existing companies to continue to satisfy customers. If no one were willing to take economic risks, the private enterprise system wouldn't exist.

The Small Business Administration reveals the extent to which entrepreneurial spirit fuels growth in the U.S. economy. Approximately 1,200 new businesses are launched every day, most of them small. The 20 million U.S. small businesses, defined by the SBA as companies with less than $6 million in net worth, create most of the new jobs in the country and are expected to grow at twice the rate of larger companies over the next 15 years. If U.S. small business constituted a separate economy, it would rank as the world's third-largest economic entity, behind the United States as a whole and Japan.[10]

Entrepreneurs often find novel ways to use natural resources, technology, and other factors of production. Englishman Simon Pratt, for example, saw an opportunity in a new invention, a tough, polyurethane bag that could be filled with liquids and still float. Since many countries suffer from severe fresh water shortages, he saw an opportunity to use tug boats to pull the bags full of fresh water to thirsty people around the world. Pratt figures that his firm, Aquarius Water Trading & Transportation Co., will accept nearly $40 million worth of contracts to deliver water over the next few years.[11]

Entrepreneurship is also important to existing companies in a private enterprise system. Large firms often encourage entrepreneurial thinking, hoping to benefit from enhanced flexibility, improved innovation, and new market opportunities. Take Bix Norman, a top-notch salesperson for office furniture manufacturer Herman Miller. He felt that his company was missing an opportunity by building only high-priced, premium-quality office furniture, ignoring the grow-ing number of small, home-based businesses. Norman convinced top management to let him start a new subsidiary that would manufacture a line of well-made but low-priced furniture. Last year, thanks to Norman's entrepreneurial insight and drive, the new division sold $200 million worth of desks, chairs, and bookcases.[12]

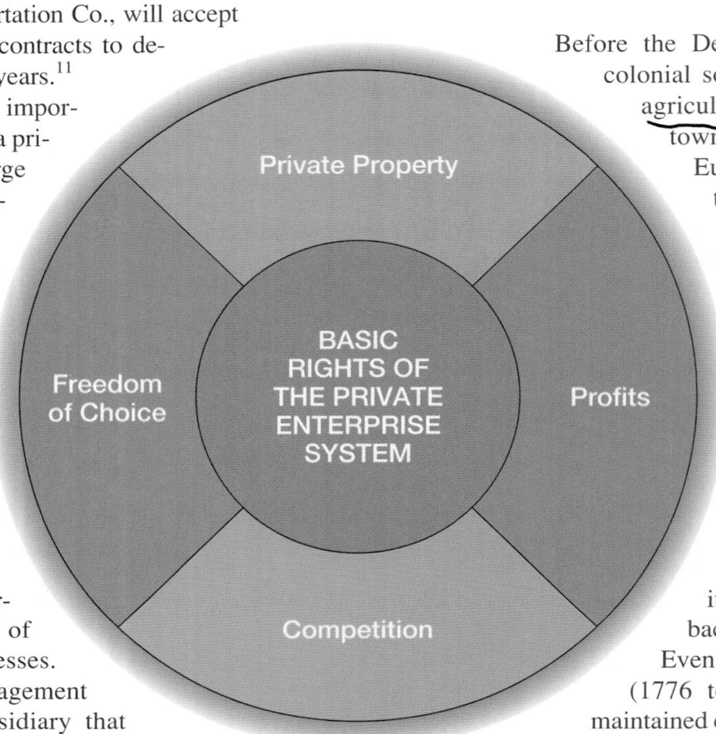

Figure 1.4 **Basic Rights within a Private Enterprise System**

As the next section will explain, entrepreneurs have played a vital role in the history of American business. They have helped to create new industries, developed successful new methods for conducting business, and improved the U.S. standing in global competition. Chapter 6 returns to the subject of entrepreneurship and Chapter 5 looks more closely at how individuals start their own businesses.

SIX ERAS IN THE HISTORY OF BUSINESS

In nearly four centuries since the first European settlements appeared on the North American continent, amazing changes have occurred in the size, focus, goals, and use of technology by U.S. businesses. As Table 1.2 indicates, U.S. business history is divided into six distinct time periods:

(1) the colonial period, (2) the industrial revolution, (3) the age of industrial entrepreneurs, (4) the production era, (5) the marketing era, and (6) today's relationship era. The next sections describe how events in each of these time periods have influenced U.S. business practices.

The Colonial Period

Before the Declaration of Independence, colonial society emphasized rural and agricultural production. Colonial towns were small compared to European cities, and they functioned as marketplaces for farmers, craftsmen, doctors, bankers, and lawyers. The economic focus of the nation centered on rural areas, since prosperity depended on the output of farms and plantations. The success or failure of crops influenced every aspect of the economy.

Colonists depended on England for manufactured items as well as financial backing for infant industries. Even after the Revolutionary War (1776 to 1783), the United States maintained close economic ties with England. British investors continued to provide much of the financing for developing the U.S. business system, and this financial influence continued well into the 19th century.

The Industrial Revolution

The industrial revolution began in England around 1750, moving business operations from an emphasis on independent, skilled workers who specialized in building products one by one to a factory system that mass-produced items by bringing together large numbers of semiskilled workers. The factories profited from the savings created by large-scale production, bolstered by increasing support from machines over time. As businesses grew, they could often purchase raw materials more cheaply in larger lots than before. Specialization of labor, limiting each worker to perform only one specific task in the production process, also improved production efficiency.

Influenced by these events in England, business in the United States began a time of rapid industrialization. Agriculture became mechanized, and factories sprang up in cities. During the mid-1800s, the pace of the revolution was increased as newly built railroad systems provided fast, economical transportation.

The Age of the Industrial Entrepreneur

Building on the opportunities opened by the industrial revolution, entrepreneurship increased in the United States during the late 19th century. Inventors created a virtually endless array of commercially useful products and new production methods.

Will fresh water soon become an internationally traded commodity? Entrepreneur Simon Pratt is betting on this possibility. Here, the water transporter stands on Aquarius's 200,000-gallon water bag off the Greek island of Aegina.

▼ Eli Whitney introduced the concept of interchangeable parts, an idea that would later facilitate mass production on a previously impossible scale.

▼ Robert McCormick designed a horse-drawn reaper that reduced the labor involved in harvesting wheat. His son, Cyrus McCormick, saw the commercial potential of the reaper and launched a business to build and sell the machine. By 1902, the company was producing 35 percent of the country's farm machinery.

▼ Cornelius Vanderbilt, J. P. Morgan, and Andrew Carnegie among others saw enormous opportunities waiting for anyone willing to take the risk of starting a new business.

▼ Cleveland bookkeeper John D. Rockefeller saved and borrowed to finance his own dry goods trading business. The business thrived and Rockefeller decided to go into oil refining. By age 31, he was well on his way to becoming one

of the richest men in the world. The company he founded, the Standard Oil Company, is now a multibillion-dollar global business.[13]

The entrepreneurial spirit of this golden age in business did much to advance the U.S. business system and raise the overall standard of living. That market transformation, in turn, created new demand for manufactured goods.

The Production Era

As demand for manufactured goods continued to increase during the early years of the 20th century, businesses focused even greater attention on the activities involved in producing those goods. Work became increasingly special-

Table 1.2	Six Eras in Business History	
Era	**Main Characteristics**	**Time Period**
Colonial	Primarily agricultural	Prior to 1776
Industrial revolution	Mass production by semiskilled workers, aided by machines	1760-1830
Industrial entrepreneurs	Advances in technology and increased demand for manufactured goods, leading to enormous entrepreneurial opportunities	Late 1800s
Production	Emphasis on producing more goods faster, leading to production innovations like assembly lines	Prior to 1920s
Marketing	Consumer orientation, seeking to understand and satisfy needs and preferences of customer groups	Since 1950s
Relationship	Benefits derived from deep, ongoing links with individual customers, employees, suppliers, and other businesses	Began in 1990s

ized, and huge, labor-intensive factories dominated U.S. business. Assembly lines, introduced by Henry Ford, became common business equipment. Business owners turned over their responsibilities to a new class of managers trained in operating established companies. Their activities emphasized efforts to produce ever more goods in quicker processes.

In 1917, U.S. Steel Co. was the largest company in America, with 286,000 workers producing 23 million tons of metal a year to meet the growing demand for industrial materials. The company operated blast furnaces, rolling mills, hopper cars, barges, coal mines, ships, and shipyards around the clock. In today's dollars, U.S. Steel's assets at the time would be worth $31 billion.[14]

During the production era, business focused attention on internal processes rather than external influences. Marketing was almost an afterthought, designed solely to distribute products generated by central company activities. Little attention was paid to consumer wants or needs. Instead, businesses tended to make decisions about what the market would get. For example, if you wanted to buy a Ford Model T automobile, you had no choice in color. Henry Ford's factories produced cars in only one color— black—because that decision simplified the manufacturing process.

The Great Depression of the early 1930s changed the shape of U.S. business yet again. As incomes nose-dived, businesses could no longer automatically count on selling everything they produced. Managers began to pay more attention to the markets for their goods and services, and sales and advertising took on new importance. During this period, *selling* was often synonymous with *marketing*.

Demand for all kinds of consumer goods exploded after World War II. Suddenly, consumers were buying again. At the same time, however, competition also heated up. Soon businesses began to think of marketing as more than just selling; they envisioned a process of determining what consumers wanted and needed and then designing products to satisfy those needs. In short, they developed a **consumer orientation.**

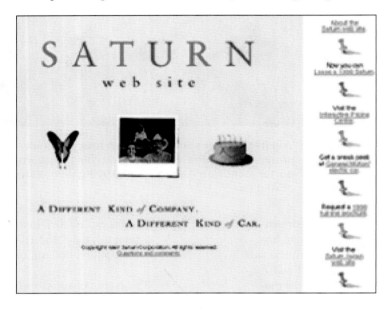

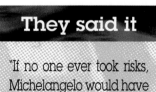

Businesses throughout the United States formed marketing research departments to analyze consumers' desires before beginning actual production. Consumer choice skyrocketed. Today's automobiles no longer come just in black; instead, car buyers can choose from a wide range of colors.

Businesses also have discovered that they need to distinguish their goods and services from those of competitors. **Branding,** the process of creating an identity in consumers' minds for a good, service, or company, is one tool used by marketing oriented companies. A **brand** can be a name, term, sign, symbol, design, or some combination that identifies the products of one firm and differentiates them from competitors' offerings.

One of the early masters of branding was Ray Kroc, the founder of the McDonald's restaurant chain. Kroc insisted that every one of his restaurants follow the same operating procedures and offer similar menu items, reinforcing the nationwide image of the growing restaurant franchise in consumer minds across the country. Today, the golden arches are among the best-known company symbols in the world.

A more recent example of a successful consumer orientation and application of branding is General Motors' Saturn Corp. In the 1980s, most U.S. car manufacturers were struggling to compete with imports from foreign auto makers. GM created Saturn as a separate company to offer high-quality automobiles, but the new firm's real success derived not from its quality but from its ability to develop and implement a consumer orientation. For example, recognizing that many consumers hated buying a new car, Saturn took pains to improve the experience. Prospective car buyers entering a Saturn showroom don't face the high-pressure sales tactics normally associated with car salespeople. Instead, they are served by "sales consultants" who are trained to treat customers with respect. No one haggles over price. Saturn sets prices to satisfy customer expectations, while still allowing the firm to make a profit. As a result, nearly 87 percent of Saturn buyers say they would recommend Saturn to their friends.[15]

The marketing era has had a tremendous effect on the way business is conducted today. Even the smallest business owners recognize the importance of understanding what customers want and the reasons why they buy.

The Relationship Era

Contemporary business is poised on the cusp of a new age. Unlike the industrial revolution, which was powered by manufacturing advances, this new era is driven by advances in information technology. Powerful computers, online connections, and other technologies are helping businesses to form deep, direct links with their customers, employees, suppliers, and other organizations. During this new era, the relationship era, business will focus on developing and leveraging relationships for mutually beneficial returns.

Traditionally, business activities have focused on increasing the number of exchanges, or transactions, between buyers and sellers with only limited attention to communications and little or no ongoing relationships between the parties. The goal has simply been to get as many customers as possible to buy at least once. Techniques like price discounts, coupons, and prizes in cereal boxes influence short-term purchase decisions. However, firms are realizing the limitations of this approach for long-term operations. Not only is it an expensive and inefficient way to do business, but it builds little protection against competitors' efforts to attract customers to their goods and services.

Businesses gain several advantages by developing ongoing connections with customers. Since they can serve existing customers less expensively than they can find new ones, businesses that develop long-term customer relationships successfully reduce their overall costs. Long-term relationships with customers enable businesses to improve their understanding of what customers want and prefer from the company. As a result, businesses enhance their chances of sustaining real advantages through competitive differentiation.

USAA is already firmly entrenched in the relationship age. The San Antonio company began selling auto insurance in the 1930s to U.S. military officers stationed around the world. The company builds relationships with customers by paying careful attention to quality and service. A sophisticated computer database keeps track of USAA's interactions with its nearly 3 million customers. All customer information and correspondence is consolidated into each customer's electronic file. With one phone call to a customer service representative, a policyholder can make changes in or ask questions about any of his or her insurance policies without frustrating transfers from department

to department. The USAA representative immediately commands all of the information necessary to provide personal service to that customer.[16]

USAA also seeks to forge lifelong links with customers by finding products to fill their changing needs. In addition to auto, life, and homeowner's insurance, USAA customers can turn to the company for home mortgages, credit cards, and even purchases of jewelry and home furnishings. USAA has accomplished this impressive level of service by setting up a network of alliances with other businesses, which actually provide the goods and services. When a customer calls USAA to apply for a credit card or home mortgage, for instance, the call connects him or her to a USAA ally firm. USAA's partners must agree to meet the company's strict criteria for providing quality service at reasonable cost.[17]

USAA and other businesses have discovered that the relationship era is an age of connections. Connections, not just between businesses and customers, but also between employers and employees, technology and manufacturing, and separate companies, are fueling economic growth. The economies of countries around the world are also becoming increasingly interconnected, as businesses expand beyond their national boundaries. In this new global economy, techniques for managing networks of people, businesses, information, and technology are of paramount importance to business success.

Each new era in U.S. business history has forced managers to reexamine the tools and techniques they formerly used to compete. The relationship era is no different from the others. Tomorrow's managers will need creativity and vision to stay on top of rapidly changing technology and to manage complex relationships in the global business world. The rest of this chapter and other elements throughout the book explain some of the ways in which businesses are preparing for the fast-paced 21st century.

> ## They said it
>
> "You must learn from the mistakes of others. You can't possibly live long enough to make them all yourself."
>
> **Sam Levenson (1911-1980)**
> **American humorist**

MANAGING THE TECHNOLOGY REVOLUTION

As the last section discussed, the relationship era is driven by new technologies that are changing nearly every aspect of people's lives. To succeed in the 21st century, business leaders must understand how technology is changing the shape, not just of business, but of the world as a whole.

This insight can begin with a definition of **technology** as a business application of knowledge based on scientific discoveries, inventions, and innovations. In business, technology can streamline production, creating new opportunities for organizational efficiency. A factory may rely on automated machinery to produce finished products. In an office, computers may simplify the process of managing the information involved in running a business.

Technological breakthroughs such as supercomputers, laser surgery, and electric cars result in new goods and services for consumers, improved customer service, reduced prices, and more comfortable working conditions. Technology can make products obsolete, just as cassette tapes and CDs wiped out the market for vinyl records. It can also open up new business opportunities.

Changes in technology can also create whole new industries and new ways of doing business. Technological innovations ranging from voice recognition and scanners to advanced fiber optics and online services are playing critical roles in advancing nations' standards of living as they approach the next century.

The Internet

Perhaps the most talked about technological innovation of the past few years is the **Internet,** a worldwide network of interconnected computers that, within limits, lets anyone with access to a personal computer send and receive images and data anywhere. The roots of the Internet began when the U.S. Department of Defense created a secure military communications system in the late 1960s.

Over time, other government and business computer networks were also created and interlinked. In 1986, the National Science Foundation facilitated comprehensive connections among many of these computer networks by dedicating five supercomputers that allowed all of the various networks to communicate with each other.

In 1993, Internet usage began to spread to individual users with the development of the **World Wide Web (Web or WWW),** an interlinked collection of graphically rich information sources within the larger Internet. The Web has opened new opportunities for organizations and individuals to communicate their messages to the world on **Web sites,** the data pages of the WWW. Most Web sites offer some interactive elements. A user simply clicks on a highlighted word or picture to receive information—text, photographs, charts, or even a song or movie clip. The number of Web sites has increased at an astounding rate in recent years, from about 18,000 Web sites in 1995 to 740,000 today.[18]

Another Internet communications tool is electronic mail, commonly called **e-mail,** the electronic delivery of messages via Internet links. Using e-mail, individuals and businesses can instantly send messages and information around the globe. E-mail also allows for documents, pictures, and spreadsheets to be sent almost anywhere in the world. By the turn of the century, analysts expect more than 6.9 trillion e-mail messages to be sent annually.[19]

What does the Internet mean to industry? For one thing, it represents a huge community of prospective customers. Some 200 million users are now connected to the Internet, and 45 percent of them are expected to buy almost $100 billion in goods and services directly through Internet connections this year.[20] As Figure 1.5 shows, residents of most of the world's nations now have Internet access.

The Internet is also facilitating new interactive relationships between businesses and their customers. Instead of relying on intermediaries such as retailers, agents, and brokers to reach customers, businesses can now connect directly with customers. This tool may dramatically change traditional business practices in some industries. For example, what role will travel agents play when most customers learn to book their own reservations with hotels and airlines directly over the Internet? Also, automobile-related transactions on the Internet are now nearing $1 billion a year. In the future, car buyers may be able to order units directly from the factories, completely bypassing dealers.[21]

The Internet is also opening up new ways of interacting with customers, suppliers, and employees. Many firms have invested in **intranets,** closed network systems using Internet standards that allow for information sharing among employees, divisions, and geographically diverse locations. Other firms have created **extranets,** secure networks accessible from outside, but only by trusted third parties such as familiar customers or suppliers.

The Internet's interactive capability also allows businesses to customize their goods and services for individual customers around the world. Need a new pair of skis? MySki Inc. lets you design your own via the Internet. Skiers indicate their level of expertise, the conditions they encounter when skiing, the colors they prefer, and even personalized messages they want imprinted on their skis.

DID YOU KNOW?

A recent poll identified the automobile as the invention most Americans said they couldn't live without. The light bulb came in second, followed by the telephone. One respondent in five listed television, good enough to rank it as the fourth most essential invention. Aspirin ranked fifth, followed by the microwave oven, blow-dryers, and the personal computer. Moral: Americans most highly value mobility, light, communication, freedom from pain, and, of course, great hair.

Business Directory

Internet a worldwide network of interconnected computers that, within limits, lets anyone with access to a personal computer send and receive images and data anywhere.

Figure 1.5 **How Nations Compare in Internet Access and Freedom of Content**

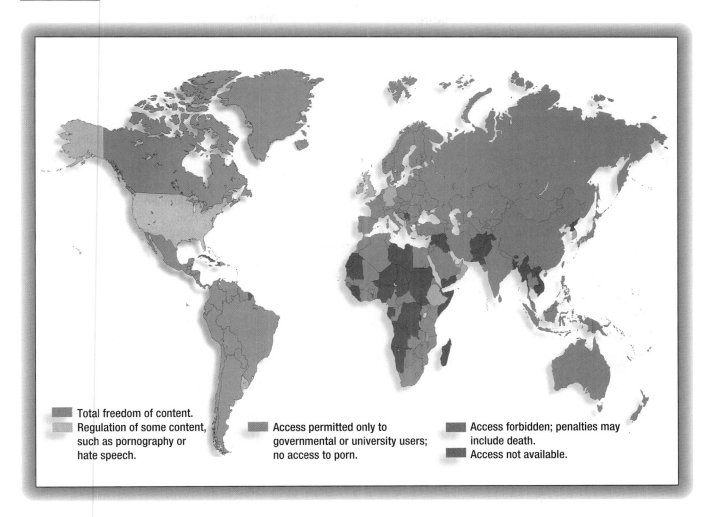

- Total freedom of content.
- Regulation of some content, such as pornography or hate speech.
- Access permitted only to governmental or university users; no access to porn.
- Access forbidden; penalties may include death.
- Access not available.

www.evoski.com

MySki's Web site automatically creates an animated 3D preview. After a buyer places an order, the company makes a pair of skis according to the stated preferences. After 3 weeks, the new skis are delivered to the buyer's doorstep. Chris Jorgensen, president of MySki, says that skis are just the beginning. He has plans to open MySnowboard, My-Furniture, and MyCar Internet sites in the future.[22]

Chapter 17 will explain more about how businesses are managing technology, including Internet resources. Technology's role in various business functions is also a recurring theme throughout this book. Many of our Business Hall of Fame and Business Hall of Shame inserts report on firms' efforts to leverage technology for competitive advantage.

FROM TRANSACTION MANAGEMENT TO RELATIONSHIP MANAGEMENT

As the world enters the 21st century, a significant change is taking place in the ways companies interact with customers. Since the industrial revolution, most businesses have concentrated on building and promoting products in hopes that enough customers would buy them to cover costs and earn acceptable profits, an approach called **transaction management.**

In the relationship era, however, many businesses are taking a different, longer-term approach in their interactions with customers. These firms are seeking ways to actively nurture customer loyalty by carefully managing every interaction. They earn enormous paybacks for their efforts. A company that retains customers over the long haul reduces its advertising, sales, and account initiation costs. Since customer spending tends to accelerate over time, revenues also grow. Companies with long-term customers often can charge premium prices, and they find that many new customers come from loyal customer referrals.[23]

Increasingly, therefore, business focuses on **relationship management,** the collection of activities that build and maintain ongoing, mutually beneficial ties with customers and other parties. At its core, relationship management involves gathering knowledge of customer needs and preferences and applying that understanding to get as close to the customer as possible.

Hickory Farms, for example, fosters close ties with customers by building on its knowledge of individuals' preferences and needs. A central computer information system stores data about these preferences as a way to create ongoing ties with customers. If you sent gift baskets to friends and relatives last year, this year Hickory Farms will remind you who received your gifts, what you sent them, and even the wording of the accompanying greeting cards. All you need to do is let Hickory Farms know what gifts you want sent for this year and your gift-giving work is done. Hickory Farms customers who order regularly also work with personal sales representatives who are rewarded for satisfying individual customers.[24]

Hitachi Data Systems (HDS), a $2 billion computer equipment and service firm, has developed an even more comprehensive system of relationship management. The company invites an advisory panel of customers to regular, 3-day meetings with HDS executives and engineers. During the meetings, HDS gains first-hand feedback on service issues, product performance, and technological developments that help the company to stay ahead in a highly competitive, rapidly changing industry.[25] In a very real sense, HDS has moved its relationships with customers beyond buyer-seller interactions to a partnership in which customers have an important say in the company's future plans and direction.

Strategic Alliances and Partnerships

Businesses are also finding that they must form partnerships with other organizations in order to take full advantage of available opportunities. A **partnership** is an affiliation of two or more companies with the shared goal of assisting each other in the achievement of common goals. One such form of partnership between organizations is a **strategic alliance,** a partnership formed to create competitive advantage for the businesses involved.

For example, Bill Hanley knew that the only way to keep his business growing was to team up with his competitors. Hanley's company, Galileo Corp., manufactures fiber optic elements for military defense systems. In the early 1990s, when government defense spending fell to new lows, so did the demand for fiber optics. Hanley approached his top five local competitors and suggested they pool their resources and marketing efforts to capture a larger overall slice of the remaining defense fiber optics market. The companies joined together to form the Center for Advanced Fiber Optic Applications (CAFA). CAFA coordinates research and new product development among all member companies to win defense and international business for all of the partners in the alliance.[26]

Chapter 7 will take a closer look at other strategies that businesses are using to strengthen relationships with customers and other firms.

CREATING VALUE THROUGH QUALITY AND CUSTOMER SATISFACTION

Today's savvy consumers want the satisfaction of acquiring more than ordinary goods and services. Their demands extend beyond just low prices. Firms seeking to tighten bonds with customers must provide value to customers in order to earn their long-term loyalty.

Value is the customer's perception of the balance between the positive traits of a good or service and its price. Customers who feel that they have received value—that is, positive benefits for a fair price—are likely to remain satisfied and continue their relationships with a firm. However, when customers perceive an inequitable balance between benefits and price, they become dissatisfied and start to look for opportunities outside their relationship with the business. Value is also an important way to differentiate goods and services from competing offerings. A firm that provides real value to customers often enjoys superior advantages and wider opportunities in the marketplace.

Consider Mercedes Benz. You may not recognize the newest Mercedes Benz model offered for sale in Europe. The A140 is just 141 inches long with a tiny 82-horse-power engine. In fact, the car's only recognizable trait is the familiar three-pronged logo on the hood. Mercedes believes that customers will choose the A140 over similar, lower-priced offerings by Toyota, Chevrolet, and Volkswagen because they value the Mercedes reputation for qual-

Business Directory

customer satisfaction the ability of a good or service to meet or exceed buyer needs and expectations.

ity, service, and performance over competitors' price advantages—even for a Lilliputian Mercedes.[27]

Mercedes, like other companies, has discovered that customer value perceptions are often tied to **quality,** the degree of excellence or superiority of a firm's goods and services. Technically, quality refers to physical product traits, such as durability and performance reliability. However, quality also includes **customer satisfaction,** the ability of a good or service to meet or exceed buyer needs and expectations.

Technology wields a double-edged sword for customer satisfaction. On one hand, the use of technology can give a business the ability to improve interactions with customers. General Electric Medical Systems (GEMS), for example, is a $4 billion global manufacturer of high-tech medical equipment. GEMS customers, primarily large hospitals and clinics, were dissatisfied with the amount of training and support they were receiving. In response, GEMS set up its own television network to carry live training broadcasts via satellite directly to customer workplaces, which led to dramatic improvements in customer satisfaction.[28]

On the other hand, technologies like online communications, computerized engineering, and satellite communications have led customers to expect more from firms with which they do business. Customers are no longer content to wait for replies to their questions or complaints. They expect instant responses and personalized attention to their needs. They now insist on products that can perform expanded functions with improved reliability. Firms that do not keep up with customer expectations lose customers to rivals that do.

Businesses in all industries, therefore, face a common challenge of finding new ways to add value to customer interactions through increased customer satisfaction and quality. This statement introduces a recurring theme in this book—how businesses will compete in the relationship era. Chapter 7 focuses specifically on relationship management, and Chapter 12 discusses the specific methods by which businesses create value for their customers through quality and customer satisfaction.

COMPETING IN A GLOBAL MARKET

Businesses can no longer limit their sights to events and opportunities within their own national borders. The world's nations and their economies are developing increasing interdependence. To remain competitive, compa-

nies must continually search for both the most efficient manufacturing sites and the most lucrative markets for their products.

The global economy is currently expanding at an annual rate of about 4 percent. U.S. exports account for one-seventh of the world's exports, up from one-ninth in 1993. Major trading partners—led by Canada, Japan, Mexico, and China—are shown in Figure 1.6. The ten nations listed there purchase 64 percent of all U.S. exports. In addition,

Both shoppers and the retail outlets benefit from relationship management at Hickory Farms.

they account for two-thirds of all goods imported to the United States.[29] Recently, however, emerging economies in Latin America, eastern Europe, and Asia are presenting tremendous opportunities for trade. Rising standards of living in these countries have created increasing customer demand for the latest goods and services.

The prospects of succeeding in the global marketplace appeal to U.S. businesses, which can find huge markets outside North America. Of the world's 6 billion residents, less than 5 percent reside in the United States. U.S. giants such as Coca-Cola Co. and McDonald's have proved that they can duplicate their domestic success abroad, since 80 percent of both firms' sales come from non-U.S. customers. Similar sales patterns characterize Gillette, which generates two-thirds of annual sales from international markets, and Boeing, whose foreign sales account for 54 percent of its aircraft business. The largest U.S. exporters are shown in Table 1.3.

The United States is the world's leading exporter of cotton, wheat, fish, airplanes, fresh fruits, medical instruments, nuts, corn, soybeans, musical instruments, manufactured fertilizers, and movies. The United States even exceeds France in its exports of perfume.[30]

| Figure 1.6 | Top Ten U.S. Trading Partners |

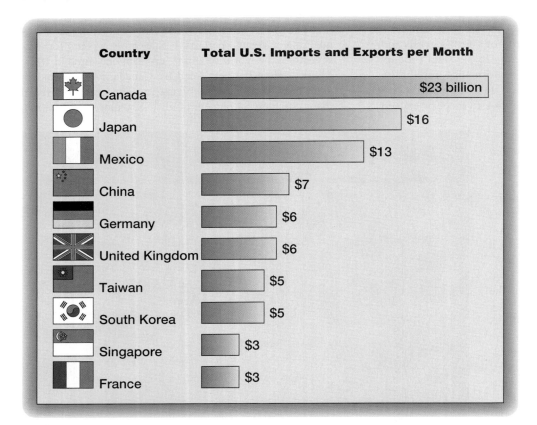

Country	Total U.S. Imports and Exports per Month
Canada	$23 billion
Japan	$16
Mexico	$13
China	$7
Germany	$6
United Kingdom	$6
Taiwan	$5
South Korea	$5
Singapore	$3
France	$3

Large corporations aren't the only businesses that export to the global market. Small and medium-sized businesses are increasingly active in foreign trade. An estimated 28 percent of these businesses are involved in some form of exporting activity. They enjoy faster growth in their revenues, profits, and employment than comparable, nonexporting firms.[31]

Going global helped to save Zippo Manufacturing. The maker of cigarette lighters faced stalled domestic sales tied to reductions in U.S. tobacco consumption. In response, Zippo's management targeted overseas markets, where smoking is still a socially acceptable practice and U.S. brand names are often valued. As a result, nearly 60 percent of Zippo's current sales are from overseas customers.

Many U.S. businesses are also finding that imported goods made by foreign manufacturers can create new oppor-

Mercedes Benz plans to parlay its reputation for luxury into a broader product line, ranging from this A140 subcompact to a U.S.-built sport utility vehicle. In seeking a broader market, the firm must avoid tarnishing its reputation among buyers of superluxury models.

tunities to satisfy the needs of domestic consumers. When an optometrist mentioned that he had difficulty finding eyeglass frames that fit the unique face shapes of African-Americans and members of other ethnic groups, Cynthia Bower saw an opportunity. Her company, Atlantic Optical Framewear, imports eyeglass frames from South America, Asia, and Africa and sells them through a network of domestic distributors.[32]

The United States also offers an attractive market for foreign competitors because of its size and high standard of living. Foreign companies like Matsushita, Mercedes Benz, Benetton, and Sun Life of Canada operate production, distribution, service, and retail facilities here. Foreign ownership of U.S. companies has increased as well. Pillsbury, MCA, and Firestone Tires are some well-known firms with foreign parents. Foreign investment in the United States means additional competitive pressures for domestic firms. One survey of U.S. firms found that 28 percent reported facing direct competition from non-U.S. companies.[33]

Productivity: Key to Global Competitiveness

Global competitiveness requires nations, industries, and companies to work efficiently at producing goods and services. As discussed earlier, firms need a number of inputs, or factors of production, in order to produce goods and services.

Productivity describes the relationship between the number of units produced and the number of human and other production inputs necessary to produce them. Pro-

Table 1.3	Top Ten U.S. Exporters		
Rank	**Company**	**Exported Products**	**Exports**
1	General Motors	Motor vehicles and parts, railroad locomotives	$16.1 billion
2	Ford	Motor vehicles and parts	11.9
3	Boeing	Commercial aircraft	11.8
4	Chrysler	Motor vehicles and parts	9.4
5	General Electric	Jet engines, turbines, plastics, medical systems	8.1
6	Motorola	Communications equipment	7.4
7	IBM	Computers	6.3
8	Philip Morris	Tobacco, beer, and food products	4.9
9	Archer Daniels Midland	Meats, vegetable oils	4.7
10	Hewlett-Packard	Measurement and computation products	4.7

ductivity is, therefore, a ratio of output to input. When a constant amount of inputs generates increased outputs, an increase in productivity occurs.

Total productivity considers all inputs necessary to produce a specific amount of outputs. Stated in equation form, it can be written as follows:

$$\text{Total productivity} = \frac{\text{Output (goods or services produced)}}{\text{Input (human/natural resources, capital)}}$$

Many productivity ratios focus on only one of the inputs of the equation: labor productivity or output per labor-hour. An increase in labor productivity means that the same amount of work produces more goods and services than before.

Productivity is a widely recognized measure of a company's efficiency. In turn, the total productivity of a nation's businesses has become a measure of its economic strength and standard of living. Economists refer to this measure as a country's **gross domestic product (GDP)**—the sum of all goods and services produced within its boundaries. GDP is based on the per-capita output of a country; in other words, total national output divided by the number of citizens. U.S. GDP is currently growing at an average rate of 2.7 percent a year. As Figure 1.7 shows, it remains the highest in the world.

However, some economists argue that this measure doesn't necessarily prove that the United States is the most productive or competitive nation in the world. They point out that Americans actually work longer hours and take fewer vacations than do workers in other countries. If national output is calculated on the basis of production divided by the total number of hours worked in a nation, France and Germany would show higher productivity levels and several other European countries would be close to the United States. In short, if Europeans simply worked longer hours, Americans would lag behind in productivity.[34]

Even though the United States leads the world in GDP, continued economic growth in countries such as Germany, China, and Japan has aroused fears about the global competitiveness of the United States. Some suggest that U.S. managers focus too much on short-term goals and devote insufficient attention to developing long-range plans for worldwide competition. Plant closings, business failures, and employee layoffs are seen as signs of the

Figure 1.7	**Nations with the Highest Gross Domestic Product**

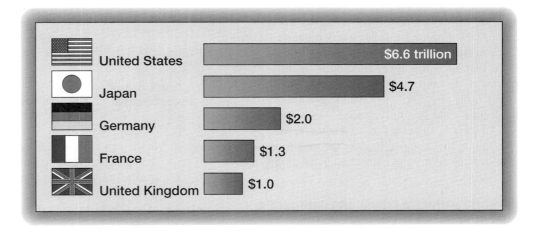

United States	$6.6 trillion
Japan	$4.7
Germany	$2.0
France	$1.3
United Kingdom	$1.0

need to invest more in long-term research, development, and innovation in order to remain competitive in the global market.

BUSINESS HALL OF SHAME

Cinemex: Struggling to Revamp Mexico's Movie Industry

Mexico's moviegoers had gotten used to visiting dumpy, aging theaters and receiving poor service. The theater owners had grown accustomed to struggling under heavy government regulation, and the movie moguls had acquired a taste for controlling the industry. But all that changed when the government decided to privatize its state-owned movie company and deregulate the industry as a whole.

Young Mexican entrepreneur Miguel Angel Davila couldn't wait to take advantage of the decision. Along with two of his classmates from Harvard Business School, Davila saw a chance to introduce Mexican moviegoers to American-style cinema: multiplex theaters offering modern decor, comfortable seats, and state-of-the-art sound systems. So the three partners launched Cadena Mexicana de Exhibición—Cinemex.

Even as risky and difficult as it can be to start a new company in the United States, launching a startup in Mexico proved even tougher. For one thing, the old movie moguls were elitist and clubby, so financing was difficult to come by. One potential investor stated, "We don't need some Harvard MBAs with their Rolls Royce dreams telling us where to invest our money." In fact, Davila was turned down by every financial institution he asked. Luckily, foreign business vendors and a few wealthy Mexican investors saw more potential in the project, so Davila and his partners were able to raise $21.5 million.

When Cinemex opened its first two theaters in Mexico City's most elegant shopping districts, every night brought sell-out crowds. When Cinemex expanded into some of the poorer neighborhoods, people were at first intimidated by the theaters. But after Davila sent employees out on the sidewalk to invite folks in for a look, business soared in the new locations as well. Unfortunately, patrons weren't the

---

Education is another factor in judging a country's productivity and overall competitiveness. High school graduation rates in Japan, Germany, Canada, and the United Kingdom are now at or near U.S. levels. Meanwhile, the number of U.S. college graduates has risen only slightly over the past 20 years, while the number of graduates in Japan has skyrocketed. Finally, although the overall literacy rate of U.S. adults is comparable to that of other industrialized nations, the percentage of American adults falling into the lowest literacy level is higher than comparable figures for nearly every other developed nation. "There is good reason to believe that such low-level literacy is an impairment to our economic growth and competitive position," says Paul E. Barton of the Educational Testing Service.[35]

Chapter 4 examines these and other factors affecting global competitiveness, as well as the strategies employed by companies competing in the global market.

DEVELOPING AND SUSTAINING A WORLD-CLASS WORKFORCE

A skilled and knowledgeable workforce is an essential resource for keeping pace with the accelerating rate of change in today's business world. Employers need reliable workers to foster strong ties with customers and partners. They must build workforces capable of the productivity needed to compete in global markets. Business leaders are also beginning to realize that the brainpower of employees plays a vital role in a firm's ability to stay on top of new technologies and innovations.

A world-class workforce can be the foundation of a firm's competitive differentiation, providing important advantages over competing businesses. Building a world-class workforce is a difficult task, however, made all the more complex by the changing characteristics of workers as well as the effects of recent business history.

They said it

"Here's a good way to tell you have a bad professor. You ask the guy about *haiku* and he says, 'Oh, that's a guy pitching for the Yankees.'"

David Letterman
American comedian

Preparing for Changes in the Workforce

In the new millennium, companies will face several trends that challenge their skills for managing and developing human resources. These trends include aging of the population, shrinkage in the pool of workers, increased mobility of workers, growing diversity, and the changing nature of work.

Aging of the Population Members of the baby boom generation, people born between 1946 and 1965, are nearing the peaks of their careers, and the oldest of them will begin

only people that Davila and Cinemex had to deal with.

A powerful theater union sent gangs of roughnecks to block Cinemex employees from entering theaters. Davila was even shoved around by some of these thugs. The theaters received regular bomb threats, and during sold-out shows, mice were released in the theaters to panic the audiences.

Still unsatisfied, union bosses called on government friends to cause other trouble. For example, labor authorities scheduled detailed inspections of Cinemex's operations—not common practice, even in Mexico. The officials expected bribes, but Davila said no. "These mobsters had enjoyed political power for many years," he said of the union bosses. "They weren't going to roll over and play dead." But Cinemex prevailed when the Mexican labor department eventually ruled that the

company could work with any union it wanted.

In addition to bureaucrats and unions, Davila and his partners must face competition from imitators. Dallas-based Cinemark has recently built multiscreen theaters in smaller Mexican towns, and Organización Ramírez operates movie screens throughout the country. To maintain its edge, Cinemex focuses on making the movie-going experience as pleasant as it can be, even providing valet parking. Also, Cinemex offers online reservations for movies and other cultural events.

Davila still faces an occasional mouse panic. And he still has to deal with bureaucrats in the guise of tax auditors and fire inspectors. But Cinemex is helping Mexico change not only the way it sees movies but also the way it does business.

www.cinemex.com.mx

QUESTIONS FOR CRITICAL THINKING

1. Why do you think a businessperson today needs an understanding of a foreign country's culture, economy, and politics before entering into a venture there?

2. In what ways do you think the Internet can help a businessperson prepare for doing business in a foreign country?

Sources: José Aguayo, "Thugs, Bureaucrats, and Mice," *Forbes*, May 4, 1998, pp. 74–76; Cinemex Web site accessed at www.cinemex.com.mx, February 9, 1999.

---

retiring shortly after the new century begins. Employers will have to deal with issues arising from reliance on older workers, such as retirement, disability programs, retraining, and insurance benefits. By 2025, 62.2 million Americans will be senior citizens—nearly double today's number. As these elderly Americans leave the workforce, they will attract attention by businesspeople eager to earn profits by serving their needs. Figure 1.8 illustrates how airlines such as USAir cater to this age group by offering a variety of discount fares.

Retirement also creates human resource problems for thousands of businesses, because Generation Xers, those people born between 1966 and 1976, represent only 21 percent of the population compared to nearly 42 percent for baby boomers. Experts predict a decline in the number of available adult workers as the new century begins.

Management of retailer Mervyn's recognizes that Generation Xers will be tomorrow's managers and that

Figure 1.8 **USAir: Serving the Needs of Older Travelers**

their attitudes about work differ from those of their predecessors. They value flexibility, training, and creative expression, so Mervyn's has developed a management training program to attract and keep Generation Xers. Trainees are allowed to choose their own pace as they work through the program, and development efforts pair them with experienced managers. After they graduate, they take responsibility for two or three departments in a store, supported by encouragement to apply new ideas and methods.[36]

Shrinking Labor Pool Throughout the 1980s and early 1990s, cost cutters at many large companies eliminated jobs as a way to boost profits. Now, managers face the opposite problem as the lowest unemployment rate in a quarter-century has led to a limited supply of skilled employees looking for jobs. In one study, nearly half of human resource executives at large and medium-sized companies reported difficulty finding workers. Most polled executives in mining, manufacturing, construction, and business and professional services expect the situation to worsen by 2000.[37]

The task of recruiting employees can be an even bigger challenge for small-business owners. Charles Whiteside owns Ana-Lab Corp., an environmental testing company in Kilgore, Texas, that employs 60 workers. Additional workers were needed, but those positions remained unfilled for several months. To attract more employees, Whiteside increased the firm's health insurance, sick leave, retirement, and education benefits. "There's not enough good employees for the demand," says Whiteside. "We pay a lot of overtime here because we don't have enough people."[38]

Increased Mobility of Workers Even after a firm's recruiters find the right employee for a job, the effort to keep that employee confronts them with increasing difficulties. Employees are no longer likely to remain with single companies for their entire careers. Men, in particular, are switching jobs faster than they did a decade ago.[39]

Fast-growing Cisco Systems, a manufacturer of computer network equipment, hires as many as 1,200 new employees a month. Cisco's trainers then concentrate on acclimating these workers to the firm in the hope that they will stay for the long term. Company systems track each new employee's orientation and ensure that each one starts with a fully functional workspace. Each new hire is assigned a "buddy," another employee who answers questions about working at Cisco and helps the newcomer to feel welcome.[40]

Increased Diversity Like the general population, the workforce is growing more diverse, a trend that will continue well into the next century. In 1980, ethnic minorities comprised just 18 percent of the U.S. population. By 2005,

members of these groups will represent 28 percent of the population, and by 2050, nearly 50 percent of Americans will belong to nonwhite ethnic groups. Hispanics and Asians represent the fastest-growing segments of the population.[41] Managers must be able to work effectively with diverse ethnic groups, cultures, and lifestyles in order to develop and retain a superior workforce for their company.

To benefit from diversity, executives of many companies develop explicit strategies to encourage and manage multiculturalism. As figure 1.9 explains, General Motors has an active program for recruiting minority employees. Inside the company, training programs help managers and workers to understand differences and similarities between various groups. Every GM division must spell out goals for encouraging diversity in its annual business plan.[42]

The Changing Nature of Work The United States is moving away from manufacturing as a basis for its economy and toward an economy based on service industries. This change will lead U.S. employers to rely increasingly heavily on service workers with sharp knowledge skills as well as manufacturing and technological skills. New work lifestyles are also becoming common elements of business life. The number of telecommuters who do their work at home for businesses located elsewhere has grown nearly 30 percent in the past 2 years.[43] Other employees are expecting employers to allow job flexibility so they can meet family and personal needs along with job-related needs.[44] Employers are also hiring growing numbers of temporary and part-time employees.[45]

Another business tool for staffing flexibility is **outsourcing,** contracting with another business to perform tasks or functions previously handled by internal staff members. In addition to reducing the continuing costs of hiring and training new employees, outsourcing can help a firm to compete by concentrating on the functions that pro-

| **Figure 1.9** | **Reaping the Benefits of Diversity at General Motors** |

"Going the extra mile... that's what makes the GM team approach so rewarding."

Forget what you've heard about gigantic departments with big-time anonymity. Teamwork is the keystone of GM's global success today. We've knocked down the walls. Opened up a free exchange of ideas and information. Where you have the chance to make a real difference. And the better your ideas and information, the faster your rise up the corporate ladder (that's one thing we haven't changed).

To join the team with the driving difference, send your resume to: GM Education Relations, Fax: (313) 556-9165. For additional information, visit our website at: http://www.gm.com/edu_rel Teamwork that touches the world.

General Motors
An Equal Opportunity Employer

Southwest Airlines employees are recognized as one of the company's greatest assets. The company gives employees the power to satisfy customers on the spot—and to have fun while they do it.

vide competitive differentiation and delegating others that do not add to customer value. The Sabre Group, for example, handles all of US Airways' computer functions. Sabre operates the US Airways data processing center, maintains all company computers, and even manages the airline's internal computer network. This arrangement frees US Airways staff to turn their attention to the strategic issues of running an airline.[46] Outsourcing is a popular choice among companies in many other businesses, such as telemarketing, accounting, and even human resource management.

The New Employer-Employee Partnership
To handle the challenges of a changing workforce and to gain competitive advantage by fully utilizing employee talents, many employers are trying to form new types of relationships with employees. They emphasize creating an employer-employee partnership that recognizes and encourages workers' important contributions to providing value and satisfying customers.

Southwest Airlines CEO Herb Kelleher identifies the key to his company's success as its ability to build an intelligent and motivated workforce. Southwest achieves this goal by hiring service-oriented employees, treating them with respect, and creating a fun and challenging work environment. While rules

and regulations are the basis for making decisions, Southwest employees are given latitude to make decisions that satisfy customers on the spot. Employees are encouraged to take active roles in suggesting and implementing new work methods and innovations. As a result, Southwest posts the best on-time performance record and receives the fewest customer complaints in the U.S. airline industry. "Competitors have tried and failed to copy us because they cannot copy our people," says Kelleher.[47]

Starbucks Coffee also treats employees as partners in the firm's success. The company offers stock options, dubbed "bean stock," to all employees at every level. If employees, through their efforts, make Starbucks more successful every year, their stock options increase in value. Starbucks CEO Howard Schultz credits the program with fostering a sense of ownership among employees that has encouraged them to submit innovative ideas about cutting costs, increasing sales, and creating value for customers.[48]

Reaping the Benefits of Diversity

As already discussed, today's workers come from many different ethnic, lifestyle, and age groups. Enlightened business leaders recognize the gain they receive from encouraging all of their employees to contribute their unique perspectives, skills, and experiences.

Diversity, blending individuals of different genders, ethnic backgrounds, cultures, religions, ages, and physical and mental abilities, can enrich a firm's chances of success.

Several studies have shown that diverse employee teams and workforces tend to perform tasks more effectively and develop better solutions to business problems than homogenous employee groups. This difference is due in part to the varied perspectives and experiences that foster innovation and creativity in multicultural teams.

Since nearly every business serves a diverse group of customers, diversity in its workforce can improve management understanding of customer needs and relationships with customer groups. Maybelline, for example, hoped to gain a share of the $55 million market for ethnic cosmetics by recruiting African-American, Hispanic, and Asian employees to develop product and marketing strategies for the new line. With their insights and input, Maybelline captured 41 percent of the ethnic cosmetics market.[49]

Also, practical managers know that attention to diversity issues can help them to avoid costly and damaging legal battles. Employee lawsuits alleging discrimination are now among the most common legal

> ## They said it
>
> "America is not like a blanket—one piece of unbroken cloth, the same color, the same texture, the same size. America is more like a quilt—many pieces, many colors, many sizes, all woven and held together by a common thread."
>
> **Jesse Jackson (1941-)**
> **American civil rights leader**

BUSINESS TOOL KIT

How to Line Up a Great Summer Job

Summer may seem like part of the distant future, but it's never too soon to start looking for a summer job that can give you a boost up the career ladder. Here are three tips for lining up a great summer job:

1. **Find an internship.** Prospective employers are impressed by students who have completed internships. Most colleges and universities maintain internship or career service offices. Professors might also provide leads. Not all internships are paid positions, but you can gain skills and experience worth the effort.

2. **Volunteer.** If you are an active volunteer, let prospective summer employers know about your experiences. If not, look for volunteer opportunities that fit your personality, skills, and career goals.

3. **Network.** Relationships with others may help you to land a great summer job. Let relatives, family, and friends know several months in advance what type of job you want. Find and join professional organizations in your area of interest. List 20 or 30 companies where you would like to work and write letters of introduction explaining your skills.

Source: Amy Lindgren, "Plan Now," *San Diego Union Tribune*, September 22, 1997, p. C2.

issues faced by employers. The median amount of compensation awarded in successful employee discrimination suits is now over $200,000.

Diversity and other issues related to human resource management will be discussed further in Part 3.

WANTED: A NEW TYPE OF MANAGER

Once, managers were encouraged to be "organization men," wearing identical gray flannel suits and working in a world of strict rules and rigid hierarchies. Companies no longer recruit only stereotyped, male managers; they look for someone with the ability to create and sustain a vision of how an organization can succeed. The 21st-century manager will need to apply critical thinking skills and creativity to business challenges, steer change, and manage an increasingly diverse workforce.

Importance of Vision

An important managerial quality needed in the 21st century is **vision,** the ability to perceive marketplace needs and what an organization must do to satisfy them. Business Hall of Fame illustrated, Dave Hampton created Furbies after seeing the Tamagotchi virtual pet and wanted to give kids something more. Another visionary entrepreneur is William Penzey, Jr. He started his spice-importing firm, Penzeys, Ltd., when he saw that consumers wanted exotic spices like Costa Rican cardamom pods and cinnamon sticks from Indonesia

and Vietnam—products that large spice companies refused to carry. Penzeys is now a $4-million-a-year mail-order business.[50]

The need for vision isn't limited to entrepreneurs. When Gary Mead took over as chief executive officer of La Quinta Inns in 1992, he didn't like what he saw. The hotel chain's units were in poor condition, and they offered even poorer service to customers. He knew that in order to compete, the firm's 248 hotels would need costly upgrades and repairs. Unfortunately, individual owner/managers of the properties didn't want to spend the money. Mead bought out all of La Quinta's independent franchisees in

Bill Penzey has built a $4 million business by selling exotic seasonings that big companies don't carry.

order to get the control he needed to fulfill his vision of a hotel chain offering consistent quality that would meet customers' demands. He then spent $270 million remodeling the properties, an investment that paid handsome dividends. Occupancy rates are up and profits have jumped 25 percent since 1996.[51]

Chapter 7 will explain how vision and the ability to turn ideas into action affect a firm's chances of success as part of the discussion of strategic planning.

Importance of Critical Thinking and Creativity

Critical thinking and creativity are essential characteristics of the 21st-century workforce. Businesspeople will need to look at a wide variety of situations, draw connections between disparate information, and develop future-oriented solutions.

Critical thinking is the ability to analyze and assess information in order to pinpoint problems or opportunities. The critical thinking process includes activities like determining the authenticity, accuracy, and worth of information, knowledge, and arguments. It involves looking beneath the surface for deeper meaning and connections that can help to identify critical issues and solutions. "In the past 20 years, the role of leadership has changed from being the person with the right answers to being the person with the right questions," explains Quinn Spitzer, CEO of consulting firm Kepner-Tregoe. To help you develop your critical thinking skills, critical thinking questions intended to stimulate discussion follow every Business Hall of Fame and Business Hall of Shame story and each chapter.

Creativity is the capacity to develop novel solutions to perceived organizational problems. While most people think of it in relation to artists, musicians, and inventors, they reveal a very limited definition. In business, *creativity* refers to the ability to see better and different ways of doing business. A computer en-

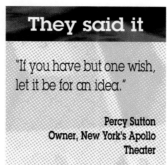

gineer who solves a glitch in a software program is executing a creative act; so is a mail-room clerk who finds a way to speed delivery of the company's overnight packages.[52]

In the highly competitive market for computer printers, even the most innovative manufacturers rely on creativity to devise novel ways to communicate with potential customers. Industry giant Hewlett-Packard used the amusing ad shown in Figure 1.10 to demonstrate the realism of its photo-quality images.

Communications systems manufacturer Lucent Technologies has developed an innovative way of fostering employee creativity through its IdeaVerse center. The center's purple walls, paintings on the ceiling, and beanbag chairs provide an environment where employees can nourish their creativity through seminars, books, videos, and speakers. The center also holds "ideation" sessions where groups of employees come together to brainstorm answers to particularly tough organizational problems.[53]

Creativity and critical thinking must go beyond generating new ideas, however; they must lead to action. In addition to creating an environment where employees can nurture ideas, managers must give them opportunities to take risks and try new solutions. The Business Tool Kit box contains tips on developing critical thinking and creative skills.

| Figure 1.10 | **Using Creativity to Communicate Product Superiority** |

Now you can print photo-quality images, on any paper. The HP DeskJet 722C uses special printing technology called PhotoREt II. Sharp detail and natural colors make for surprisingly lifelike realism. No matter what paper you use. Just $349. Visit www.hp.com/go/DJ722mouse or a store near you. And see what extraordinary things you can do with ordinary paper.

How to Develop Critical Thinking and Creative Skills

Open Your Mind

▼ Become aware of the need to improve your creativity.

▼ Recognize your routine patterns of thought and behavior.

Put Yourself in Someone Else's Shoes

▼ Pretend that you are a customer of a particular company and think of five things you would do to improve it.

▼ Repeat the exercise from the viewpoints of a sales representative for that company, an employee, and a dissatisfied customer.

Restate Issues in Reverse

▼ Name good ways for a company to *lose* customers.

▼ Name good reasons for *not* buying a product.

▼ List ways a company could destroy a good relationship with a customer or supplier.

Force Connections

▼ Select six photos of dissimilar items. Number the photos, roll a pair of dice, and match the two pictures with those numbers. Then create a statement that explains how these two items could be connected to create a new good or service.

▼ Select 50 nouns at random from a dictionary. Write each word on a card, shuffle the cards, draw two, and make a connection between the resulting pair of words.

Look for Inspiration in New Places

▼ Take a different route to school or work. What do you notice?

▼ Look for new ideas for goods or services in unusual places: an airport, doctor's office, theater, sporting event. What other sources can you identify?

Seek Multiple Solutions

▼ Choose a routine task that you frequently perform. Ask yourself, How else could I do this? What might happen if I were to do it another way?

Ability to Steer Change

Today's managers must guide their employees and organizations through the changes wrought by technology, marketplace demands, and global competition. Managers must be skilled at recognizing employee strengths and motivating people to move toward common goals as members of a team. Throughout this book, real-world examples demonstrate how companies have initiated sweeping change initiatives. Most, if not all, have been led by managers comfortable with the tough decisions that today's fluctuating conditions require.

Factors that require organizational change can come from both external and internal sources; successful managers must be aware of both. External forces might include feedback from customers, developments in the international marketplace, economic trends, and new technologies. Inter-

nal factors might arise from new company goals, emerging employee needs, labor-union demands, or production problems.

Apparel manufacturer Levi Strauss has compiled a long history of growth. Recently, however, the company found that consumers were becoming less loyal, retailers more demanding, and suppliers more numerous than before. As a result, Levi's management embarked on a companywide change program to prepare their firm for the 21st century. Top management set the goals, but the design and implementation of the transition was pushed down to middle managers and employees. Members of 20 teams composed of employees from different departments were asked to find new ways of moving products to stores, satisfying customers, and pleasing retailers. The 200 people on the 20 teams were designated as *change agents* responsible for explaining the new programs to their peers and following through to ensure achievement of goals. As the new programs were implemented, thousands of jobs were redesigned and many workers were asked to reapply for employment.

Thomas J. Kasten, a Levi's vice president, says that the changes weren't easy, but they've paid off in important gains. "There's no handbook for this stuff and I don't have a lot of personal experience to fall back on. I've had to dial up my personal learning quotient. But we're unearthing skills and talents that might not have surfaced otherwise."[54]

The role played by change agents is examined in more detail in Chapter 6. Teamwork is a major topic in Chapter 11.

MANAGING ETHICS AND SOCIAL RESPONSIBILITY

In recent years, headlines have been full of stories about misconduct by businesses and their employees. Texaco executives were caught on tape using derogatory terms to refer to African-Americans. A California firm illegally imported Mexican strawberries, resulting in thousands of elementary school students being exposed to hepatitis. Kathie Lee Gifford was compelled to apologize when news stories revealed that a line of clothing carrying her name was manufactured using child labor. These and other cases demonstrate the importance of ethics and social responsibility in business.

Business ethics refers to the standards of conduct and moral values involving right and wrong actions arising in the work environment. Poor ethical standards can lead to public image problems, costly lawsuits, high levels of employee theft, and a host of other expensive problems. Ethical decision making can also foster trust, a vital element of strong relationships with customers, employees, and other organizations.[55] It is particularly important for top executives to demonstrate ethical behavior, since studies have shown that employees emulate their behavior.[56]

Strong company and individual ethics are often the cornerstone of visionary companies. Drug manufacturer Johnson & Johnson has maintained a strong code of ethics for over 50 years. These ethical standards form a framework for decision making throughout the company. When bottles of Tylenol were found to have been laced with poison in the 1980s, for example, executives did not hesitate to recall the product or deal openly with the media, because their actions were guided by deeply ingrained principles.[57]

Working hand-in-hand with business ethics is **social responsibility,** a management philosophy that highlights the social and economic effects of managerial decisions. This chapter's ethical controversy box reports Internet companies' struggle to weigh their social responsibility against profit considerations as they decide what information to collect on Web surfers.

Businesses demonstrate their social responsibility in a variety of ways. Sounds True is a Boulder, Colorado, maker and distributor of audio tapes dealing with health, psychology, and spiritual topics. Through sponsorship of the Prison Audio Project, management encourages Sounds True customers to donate their used audio tapes to some 1.5 million U.S. prison inmates.[58] Phil J. Quigley, CEO of telecommunications giant Pacific Telesis Group, personally campaigned to get the company to donate $100 million to start Education First, a program with the goal of connecting all California public schools and libraries to the Internet.[59]

For managers and employees at Fujifilm, protecting the environment is both a social responsibility and an important company objective. The photo in Figure 1.11 shows Lita Lowder, Fuji's regulatory compliance coordinator, in front of South Carolina's Ace Basin, 350,000 acres of one of the most pristine and viable ecosystems in North America. Lowder and her 8,000 Fuji associates in the United States work to preserve and protect valuable natural resources.

Chapter 2 explores business ethics, social responsibility, and the influence of business on society as a whole in detail. Each chapter also presents a feature highlighting a current ethical controversy in business.

WHY STUDY BUSINESS?

As business moves into the 21st century, new technologies, population shifts, and shrinking global barriers are altering the world at a frantic pace. Businesspeople are catalysts for many of these changes, creating new opportunities for individuals who are prepared to take action. Studying contemporary business will help you to prepare for the future.

Throughout this book, you'll be exposed to the real-life stories of many businesspeople. You'll learn about the

Business Directory

business ethics standards of conduct and moral values involving right and wrong actions arising in the work environment.

social responsibility a management philosophy that highlights the social and economic effects of managerial decisions.

SOLVING AN ETHICAL CONTROVERSY

Should Intel Be Baking Your Cookies Online?

As a businessperson, you need to know as much about your audience as you can so your ads will grab attention and let you show off your product. But as a consumer, you need to know whether marketers can be trusted to collect and use the personal information they need without abusing your right to privacy. The Internet and its technology only intensify this dilemma.

Some Web sites leave *cookies* on your computer when you visit them. These user ID files are stored on your hard drive so that businesses can access data on you or your system and track your Web movements. Software-based security depends, in part, on how you enter information. And you can delete cookie files or even refuse to let them be deposited.

But Intel's new Pentium III chip contains an encoded serial number that can be read (like caller-ID) to trace any online communication to a single computer. Such hardware-based security reduces the chance of fraud, but critics are outraged over the power that such measures give marketers and over the loss of anonymity on the Internet. Intel was forced to disable the ID number as a consumer boycott brewed.

Privacy advocates see businesses stopping at nothing to get the data they want. In a *CIO* magazine poll, high-tech and business executives said it's more important to track customer information (64%) than to protect customer privacy (36%). A Federal Trade

Commission survey, however, found that four out of five respondents were worried about how online information would be used.

 Should Internet businesses be allowed to regulate themselves?

PRO

1. More access to such consumer information as purchases and Web visits means more effective goods and services for consumers.

2. The Direct Marketing Association already puts privacy restrictions on its members and helps consumers take their names off members' lists, so no additional protection is needed.

3. Online businesses need to have the freedom to grow. Government regulation will only slow growth and increase the cost of doing online business.

4. Online businesses need a more secure ID system to enhance privacy by reducing the risk of credit-card fraud and identity theft.

CON

1. Companies may collect data for one reason but find other, more profitable ways of using it, such as selling to marketers.

2. To get free loot or play games, many kids think nothing of giving out personal data, which is used by some companies to market to the very young.

3. Web site marketers and software vendors could coerce people into releasing hardware serial numbers before allowing them access to popular programs and Web sites.

4. Invasion of privacy on the Internet is one more way people are losing control of personal information.

SUMMARY

Shoppers in cyberspace need to feel as comfortable doing business on the Web as they do on Main Street. Other than the Children's Online Privacy Protection Act, which will eventually provide some protection, we currently have no set of laws protecting privacy on the Internet. Some experts say that the government already collects data and consumers have no privacy now anyway, so they should "just get over it." But privacy advocates want to make sure that businesses won't be tempted to use personal data in public ways.

Sources: Robert Lemos, "The Dark Side of the Digital Home," *MSNBC*, accessed at www.msnbc.com, February 8, 1999; Laura Gibbons Paul, "Careful What You Click For," *Family PC*, accessed at www1.zdnet.com, January 11, 1999; Lauren Gibbons Paul, "Hook 'Em Early and Often," *Family PC*, accessed at www1.zdnet.com, February 9, 1999; Ted Bridis, "Intel Yields to Privacy Concerns," the Associated Press, February 9, 1999; Ted Bridis, "CIO Magazine Survey Shows Chief Information Officers Side with Intel, Picking Customer Data Over Privacy," PR Newswire, February 3, 1999; James Lardner, "Intel Even More Inside," *U.S. News & World Report*, February 8, 1999, p. 43.

range of business careers available and the daily decisions, tasks, and challenges that they face. By the end of the course, you'll understand how marketing, accounting, and human resource management work together to provide competitive advantage for firms. This knowledge will help you to become a more capable employee and enhance your career potential.

Perhaps working for someone else isn't your dream. Like Dave Hampton, Furby creator, you may see yourself as an **entrepreneur,** building your own business and controlling your own future. Entrepreneurs are willing to take risks to create and operate a business. As earlier sections have explained, entrepreneurship can bring tremendous rewards—and enormous risk. As you read each chapter, you

Figure 1.11 **Fujifilm: Doing Well by Doing Good**

One Fujifilm employee thinks it's no coincidence that our boxes are green.

Lita Lowder, Fuji Photo Film, Inc., Regulatory Compliance Coordinator, photographed in South Carolina's ACE Basin

When your products are used to capture the earth's beauty, you obviously don't want that beauty to disappear. That's why Fujifilm employs experts like Lita Lowder. She's just one of 8,000 associates, at 43 facilities across the country, helping us to meet safety and environmental requirements. Her work is part of the Fujifilm GreenCare Program, our multi-faceted effort to preserve and protect valuable natural resources. Our support of South Carolina's Ace Basin, 350,000 acres of the largest, most pristine and viable ecosystems in North America is one part of this effort. So the next time you see one of our green boxes, remember Lita Lowder and Fujifilm's other associates because, in addition to putting the film inside, we're making sure there will always be a place to use it. **FUJIFILM**

Reading about the mistakes of other entrepreneurs in the Business Hall of Shame features will help you to avoid repeating these costly errors. Additionally, Chapter 6 concentrates specifically on how to start your own business. The information in this book will lay the foundation for the practical skills you need to launch a successful venture.

Even if you do not plan on becoming a businessperson, your daily life will still be affected by business. Every time you shop at a grocery store, buy a car, or visit your bank, you interact with the business world. Each chapter examines the tools and tactics used by firms to gain your business. Understanding these concepts will help you to make well-informed consumer choices, whether you are buying a new CD player or stock in IBM.

Finally, the business world has the resources and capabilities to solve—or create—many of the world's problems. This book discusses many examples of how organizations have shaped the world. The questions for ethical discussion in each chapter will help you to understand the important influences of industry on society, government, and economics. Armed with this knowledge, you'll be prepared to help cure society's problems as they emerge during this new century.

As you can see, business affects nearly every facet of life. In Part 1 of this book we take a detailed look at the ethical and social responsibility issues facing contemporary business. Other chapters discuss how economics influences business and people's everyday lives. Later chapters focus on the challenges and opportunities faced by businesses competing in global markets.

will learn about successful entrepreneurs in the Business Hall of Fame features. These entrepreneurs can serve as valuable role models for you.

Business Directory

entrepreneur a risk taker in the private enterprise system.

SUMMARY OF LEARNING GOALS

1. Describe the private enterprise system and the roles played by individual businesses, competitors, and entrepreneurs within the system.

The private enterprise system is an economic system that rewards firms based on how well they match and counter competitors' goods and services. Competition in the private enterprise system ensures success for firms that satisfy consumer demands. Entre-

preneurs are the risk takers in the private enterprise system. If no one takes risks, no successful businesses emerge, and the private enterprise system will not function.

2. Explain how the historical development of the U.S. economy continues to influence contemporary business.

Contemporary business has benefited from the experiences and strengths of each era of business history. The production methods developed during the industrial revolution and the production era have helped U.S. businesses improve efficiency at producing goods. The emphasis on understanding and meeting consumer needs during the marketing era has given U.S. businesspeople insight into how to differentiate their goods and services in the global marketplace.

3. Outline the challenges and opportunities that businesses face in the relationship era.

Business in the 21st century will be driven by relationships. Managers will have to find the best way to connect people, technology, and ethics in order to form strong partnerships with customers, employees, and other organizations. Opportunities will include advances in technology and growth of global markets.

4. Describe how technology is changing the way businesses operate and compete.

Technology is the application of science and engineering to do practical work. New technologies are allowing businesses to provide new goods and services for consumers, improve customer service, lower prices, and enhance working conditions. However, technology is also changing the shape of some industries, while it creates entirely new industries. Technology also opens new questions about business ethics and social responsibility.

5. Relate the importance of quality and customer satisfaction in efforts to create value for customers.

Today's savvy consumers expect more than they received in the past. They are looking for goods and services with positive traits offered at fair prices, the essence of value. A customer's perception of value is tied to quality, the degree of excellence or superiority of a firm's goods and services. Quality also includes customer satisfaction, the ability of a good or service to meet or exceed buyer needs and expectations. If customers feel they have received value—that is, quality for a fair price— they are likely to remain satisfied and continue their relationships with a firm.

6. Explain how individual businesses and entire nations compete in the global marketplace.

Global competitiveness requires nations, industries, and companies to work efficiently at producing goods and services. *Productivity* is the term that describes the relationship between the number of units produced and the human and other production inputs needed to produce them. Productivity is a widely used measure of a company's efficiency. In turn, the total productivity of a nation's businesses has become a measure of its economic strength, standard of living, and ability to compete.

7. Describe how changes in the workforce are leading to a new employer-employee partnership.

Employers today face increasing diversity, an aging population, and the changing nature of work itself. These factors and others have led to shrinkage in the workforce, making it more difficult to find and keep the quality employees needed for successful competition. As a result, many businesses are striving to develop partnerships with their employees by recognizing and rewarding their contributions.

8. Identify the skills that managers need to lead businesses in the new century.

Because the workforce is changing, managers need to improve their abilities to coach, mentor, and nurture employees in order to avoid labor shortages and benefit from diversity. Managers in the new century will need vision, the ability to perceive marketplace needs and how their firm can satisfy them. Critical thinking skills and creativity will allow managers to pinpoint problems and opportunities and plan novel solutions. Finally, managers will be dealing with rapid change, and they will need skills to help steer their organizations through shifts in external and internal conditions.

9. Explain how ethics and social responsibility affect business decision making.

Business ethics are the standards of conduct and moral values involving right and wrong actions in the workplace. Businesses that set high ethical standards avoid public image problems, costly lawsuits, customer mistrust, and other expensive problems. They can also offer guidelines for executives and employees to apply in making decisions. Social responsibility is a management philosophy that highlights the social and economic effects of business decisions and actions. Socially responsible firms seek to give back to their communities, customers, and employees.

10. List four reasons for studying business.

Business influences nearly every aspect of society. An understanding of contemporary business provides an excellent foundation for building the skills and knowledge needed to handle the challenges and opportunities of the new millennium. Studying business will help you in at least four ways: (1) to learn about different business careers, (2) to assess the advantages and disadvantages of starting your own business, (3) to become a better-informed consumer and investor, and (4) to learn how business can contribute to solving many of the problems of society.

TEN BUSINESS TERMS YOU NEED TO KNOW

business	Internet
profits	customer satisfaction
factors of production	business ethics
private enterprise system	social responsibility
	entrepreneur
competition	

Other Important Business Terms

not-for-profit organization	extranet
natural resources	transaction management
human resources	relationship management
capital	partnership
entrepreneurship	strategic alliance
competitive differentiation	value
private property	quality
consumer orientation	productivity
branding	gross domestic product (GDP)
brand	outsourcing
technology	diversity
World Wide Web	vision
e-mail	critical thinking
intranet	creativity

REVIEW QUESTIONS

1. Why are profits important in a private enterprise system? Would entrepreneurs start organizations if they saw no opportunity for profit? Why or why not?
2. What is competitive differentiation? Pick three products that you use regularly and explain how the businesses that provide them have distinguished their products from competitors.
3. What is meant by the term *relationship era?* Give an example of a business or organization whose managers have found new ways to make connections with customers.
4. How is the relationship era different from the way business was conducted in each of the historical periods listed below? How is it the same?
   a. colonial era
   b. industrial revolution
   c. age of industrial entrepreneurs
   d. production era
   e. marketing era
5. What is meant by the term *productivity?* How is the concept of GDP related to productivity?
6. What is value, and what role does it play in consumer preferences and buying decisions? Can a poor-quality product have value to consumers?
7. What are the main challenges that businesspeople will face in building world-class workforces in the 21st century?
8. Explain the difference between critical thinking and creativity. Which do you think is more important in school? In business? In your personal life?
9. In newspapers and magazines, find at least three examples of how business ethics and social responsibility have affected specific business organizations' performances.
10. Does a country's education level affect its ability to compete in the global marketplace? Why or why not?

QUESTIONS FOR CRITICAL THINKING

1. To face the challenges and opportunities of the 21st century, businesses will need managers with vision, creativity, and critical thinking skills. How can a business determine whether a prospective employee has these characteristics before making the hiring decision? Write a list of interview questions through which an employer could evaluate a prospective employee's creativity. Do you think these skills are something that can be learned? Suggest ways in which businesses can encourage vision, creativity, and critical thinking in employees and managers. Do you think these characteristics are more important for managers in large companies or for entrepreneurs?
2. Discuss the ethical considerations of the following situations. What would you do if faced with these situations? Explain your reasoning in detail.
   a. You are a manager who has caught an employee stealing a box of pencils.
   b. You are placed in charge of your company's payroll department. You know it would be easy to write an extra company check to yourself.
   c. Your department is 3 days late in meeting a deadline for an important client, and you worry that you will be unable to fill the order. Should you make up an excuse so the client will give you more time or should you tell the truth and face the consequences? What should you tell your boss?
   d. You uncover information that shows your boss is illegally meeting with a competitor to set prices.
3. To encourage creativity among employees, Wal-Mart's head of store operations picks one product in which he sees untapped potential and then challenges employees to find ways to promote it and sell more of it. This month's pick is duct tape. Suggest a plan for promoting and selling duct tape. What new uses might you suggest to encourage customers to buy more duct tape? How would you display duct tape in the store to catch their attention?
4. Hispanic consumer groups recently threatened to boycott American Airlines after revelations that an airline training manual warned that Hispanic customers tended to drink heavily and cause disruptions during flights. Using the concepts in this chapter, devise a plan to help American Airlines deal with this situation. Be as specific as possible.

5. For years, Volvo had an image as a maker of boxy cars with a devotion to reliable performance and vehicle safety. Volvo customers were highly loyal, many of them middle-class families with children. After several years of poor sales, Volvo now plans to introduce a sporty new coupe and a racy convertible, with prices starting at $40,000, more than $20,000 higher than last year's models. Volvo believes that it can capture a share of the luxury car market now dominated by Mercedes Benz, BMW, and Lexus. Examine how Volvo will need to change its relationships with customers, employees, car dealers, and suppliers in light of this new strategy. How might customer perceptions of value, quality, and satisfaction change? Do you believe that Volvo's strategy will work? Why or why not?

Experiential Exercise

DIRECTIONS: Following is a list of workforce trends discussed in the chapter. Column 1 identifies the trends. Columns 2 and 3 ask you to anticipate how the trends might affect you and your career. Columns 4 and 5 are based on the answers you get when interviewing an employee who has been out of college and working full-time five or more years.

1. Trends	2. Potential Impact on My Career	3. My Strategies to Capitalize on These Trends	4. Impact on Person Interviewed	5. Company's Strategies to Manage Trends
a. Aging of the population				
b. Shrinking labor pool				
c. Increased mobility of workers				
d. Increased diversity				
e. Changing nature of work				

Nothing but Net

1. **The Internet.** To help you get the most out of the "Nothing but Net"exercises that appear at the end of every chapter, visit one of the Web sites listed here. If you're new to the Internet, list three things you learned that will help you develop your "surfing" skills. If you're a proficient Net surfer, list three items of information you learned that will help you improve your "surfing" skills.

www.pbs.org/uti/begin.html

www.msn.com/tutorial/default.html

2. **Code of Ethics.** Use your search engine to find the code of ethics for three organizations. One site that contains several codes of ethics is

www.arq.co.uk/ethicalbusiness/frsrc/susa.htm

At that site, choose "Business Ethics Resources on WWW."
Compare the three codes to determine their similarities and differences in focus, approach, language, and emphasis. Provide possible reasons for the similarities and differences you noticed. How might you benefit as an employee working for an organization with a code of ethics compared with one without a code of ethics?

3. **The New Employer-Employee Partnership.** Visit the Web site of a corporation you're interested in learning more about as a prospective employee. What assumptions can you draw about the company from its Web pages on job opportunities, employee benefits, and the like? Some possible Web sites follow:

Levi Strauss: www.levistrauss.com

Southwest Airlines: iflyswa.com/

Marriott Hotels Resorts and Suites: www.marriott.com/marriott/

Starbucks Coffee: www1.occ.com/starbucks/index.html

Hewlett-Packard: www.hp.com

Note: Internet Web addresses change frequently. If you do not find the exact sites listed, you may need to access the organization's or company's home page and search from there.

FAST TRACK TO SUCCESS

Every business is rooted in an entrepreneurial idea. Today, a growing number of entrepreneurs are finding themselves on the fast track to success by skillfully blending people, technology, and ethical behavior. Following are descriptions of five such companies.

YAHOO!

In 1994, as Ph.D. students at Stanford, Jerry Yang and David Filo began compiling lists of their favorite Web pages, which eventually led them to create a search engine called Yahoo! Today, nearly 2 million users access the Yahoo! site every day. Over the past few years Yahoo! has formed several important strategic alliances with Netscape, Softbank, the Village Voice, Fodor's, and MTV.

Yang and Filo are also giving back to the community. Not only does Yahoo! help promote the development of Internet education and programming, the company is connecting classrooms to the Internet, provides free educational seminars, and offers exposure for not-for-profit organizations on its Web sites.

PARADIGM ENTERTAINMENT

In 1990, three out-of-work engineers took their expertise in 3-D military computer simulations and found success offering it to a much broader user group. Forming a strategic alliance with Silicon Graphics, Paradigm has won accounts with organizations such as BMW, NASA, Chrysler, and Boeing. Paradigm is currently creating products for Nintendo, Disney, and Sega and will soon release its first game on the Internet.

Paradigm gives back to the community through a scholarship fund it has created for engineering students. The company also offers scholarship recipients a job with the company upon their graduation.

DREW PEARSON COMPANIES

Drew Pearson, former Dallas Cowboys Super Bowl Champ, is CEO of Drew Pearson Companies (DPC) one of the nation's top designers and manufacturers of sports caps. DPC is one of only six companies to have scored licenses with the NFL, NBA, MLB, and NHL. "We were the first to use computers in our design process," says President Ken Shead. "We could generate art that showed variation in designs—three-dimensional front and back views—something our competition had no clues as to how we were generating those looks." DPC also set itself apart by negotiating exclusive licensing agreements with non-sports companies such as Disney.

TWO WOMEN BOXING

Artists Julie Cohn and Linda Finnell's decidedly low-tech approach to design garnered their handmade line of journals, photo albums, baby books, and picture frames an account list including Neiman Marcus, Bergdorf's, and Barneys. But the company faced growth and competitive problems. According to Cohn, "As we got computerized, we were really able to analyze the cost of our business in more scrutinizing fashion."

Cohn and Finnell decided to focus their attention on their greatest strength—designing. In an effort to combat their limited manufacturing capabilities, they began licensing their designs to other mass market companies. Licensing has allowed the business to grow and the women to remain true to their management style without stressing their in-house staff.

HUMAN GENOME SCIENCES

Human Genome Sciences (HGS) was founded in 1992 by Harvard Medical School professor Dr. William Haseltine and a group of New Jersey venture capitalists. HGS's objective is to be the first to discover most human genes and use this knowledge to create new gene-based medicines to predict, detect, treat, and cure disease.

HGS shares its proprietary information with partners including SmithKline Beechman and Schering-Plough Corporation. HGS is entitled to licensing and research fees and receives royalty payments on products created by its partners. HGS also plans on developing its own therapeutic products. Dr. Haseltine asserts HGS's mission is to use the new gene technology to improve human health, not to alter genetic destiny.

Questions

1. Would you describe these businesses as entrepreneurial? Why or why not?

2. What role has technology played in the success of these businesses?

3. How do these businesses demonstrate their social responsibility?

chapter 2

Achieving Business Success by Demonstrating Ethical Behavior and Social Responsibility

LEARNING GOALS

1. Explain the concepts of business ethics and social responsibility.

2. Describe the factors that influence individual ethics and common ethical dilemmas in the workplace.

3. Explain how organizations shape ethical behavior.

4. Relate the ways in which government regulation affects business ethics and social responsibility.

5. Describe the responsibilities of business to the general public, customers, and employees.

6. Explain why investors and the financial community are concerned with business ethics.

7. Describe the ethical and social responsibility issues facing businesses in the global marketplace.

Microsoft: Predator or Gentle Giant?

A recent joke reveals much of the background surrounding the legal battles between the federal government and Microsoft Corp.: "In the U.S. government's fight with Bill Gates, I'm for the federal government. I always like to root for the little guy." Who hasn't heard of Bill Gates, the founder and CEO of software powerhouse Microsoft, whose company stock holdings have made him the world's richest man? To many, Gates is a folk hero of today's cyberspace economy, whose brains and business savvy enabled him to build a software monopoly and who is now being falsely accused by jealous rivals. To others, Gates and his company represent a fierce predator that wields its power to crush the competition.

Which group is right? If Microsoft has become a monopoly, its potentially uncompetitive clout can be countered by federal laws like the Sherman Antitrust Act and the Clayton Act, both described on page 50. The answer can be found by examining how Microsoft has been operating in the industry.

Microsoft makes Windows, the operating system that runs 90 percent of the world's personal computers. This advantage makes it difficult for other

companies to challenge the software giant because Windows is currently the door to the computer world. But rivals accuse Microsoft of throwing its weight around to monopolize the entire industry—forcing PC purchasers to buy products they don't want, dictating which business relationships other companies can enter into, and even offering questionable incentives. Although Microsoft executives express their right to compete forcefully in the marketplace, they deny any strong-arm tactics. And so the company finds itself in the federal courts, accused by the U.S. Justice Department of anticompetitive behavior.

While the government's responsibility is to protect consumer choice and preserve competition, Microsoft argues that the government is attempting to kill its ability to satisfy customers and compete successfully. Microsoft's position is that in bundling its own Internet Explorer browser with Windows 95, it was simply adding value to the software.

Product bundling isn't the only area of dispute. The Justice Department also questions some of Microsoft's contracts with Web site operators and Internet service providers. Web companies seeking top billing in the *Channels* section of Windows 98 were required to create Web pages whose appearance would deteriorate if viewed with a browser other than Explorer. Microsoft also

WWW.
www.microsoft.com
www.usdoj.com

asked these companies to avoid business with rival Netscape; Intuit is one such firm. The government claims that these contracts cut off key distribution channels for Netscape, but Microsoft says that PC users can easily find Netscape's product by downloading it from the Internet.

The government points to other examples of unfair practices with respect to Netscape. Apple Computer execs claim that Microsoft threatened to withhold Microsoft Office for Macintosh unless Apple joined its war against Netscape. And the Justice Department claims that Microsoft offered Intuit $1 million to switch from Navigator to Internet Explorer. Microsoft labeled this an incentive. In fact, it argues that even though Netscape has lost market share, it still retains 40 percent of the total market. So Netscape is alive and offering consumers a competitive product.

Microsoft insists that it isn't a monopoly—and that the government simply doesn't understand the competition in today's global marketplace. After all, its industry dominance could be destroyed quickly by any programmer with a better idea. The rise of the personal computer 30 years ago cost IBM its overwhelming dominance. Will some high-tech giant slayer come looking for Microsoft?[1]

CHAPTER OVERVIEW

As discussed in Chapter 1, the underlying aim of most businesses is to serve customers at a profit. But the situation at Microsoft demonstrates that sole focus on profitability and beating the competition at any cost can have a dramatic downside. When does a company's self-interest conflict with society's and consumers well-being? And are seeking profits and upholding high principles of right and wrong mutually exclusive goals?

Today, a growing number of businesses of all sizes are answering "no." An organization that wants to prosper over the long term cannot do so without considering **business ethics,** the standards of conduct and moral values governing actions and decisions in the work environment. Business also must take a wide range of social issues into account, including how a decision will affect the environment, employees, and customers. A related term, *social responsibility,* refers to the philosophies, policies, procedures, and actions directed toward the enhancement of society's welfare as a primary objective. In short, businesses must find the delicate balance between doing what is right and doing what is profitable.

When that balance is skewed, they can experience serious consequences. Fruit

Business Directory

business ethics standards of business conduct and moral values.

and vegetable distributor Andrew & Williamson Sales found this out when an oversupply of Mexican-grown frozen strawberries filled its San Diego warehouse. When monthly storage fees for the fruit began cutting into the company's bottom line, the sales manager devised a plan to turn expense into profit. The frozen strawberries could be sold at discounted prices to school cafeterias across the country, except for one problem. Federal regulations require all fruit sold to schools to be domestically grown. Andrew & Williamson executives decided to disguise the Mexican-grown strawberries as domestically grown produce and sell them to schools through three independent food brokers.

The plan seemed to work well, until hundreds of Michigan school children became sick with hepatitis A. Government investigators quickly identified the source of the outbreak: All of the students had eaten frozen strawberries in their school cafeterias that had originated in the Andrew & Williamson warehouse. The company was forced to reveal that it had illegally sold Mexican strawberries to the schools. Most likely, an infected field worker in Mexico had inadvertently passed the disease to freshly picked strawberries. Several Andrew & Williamson executives were later indicted on criminal charges, and the company was left in financial ruin as a result of its unethical behavior.[2]

In business, as in life, deciding what is right or wrong in a given situation is not always a clear-cut choice. Businesses have many responsibilities—to customers, to employees, to investors, and to society as a whole. Sometimes conflicts arise in trying to serve the divergent needs of separate constituencies. Andrew & Williamson executives, for example, faced a conflict between the firm's desire for profits and its responsibility to customers and the law. In other cases, conflicts arise between ideal decisions and those that are practical in given situations.

As Figure 2.1 indicates, four main forces shape business ethics and social responsibility: individual, organizational, legal, and societal forces. Rather than oper-

ating in a vacuum, each of the forces interacts with the other three, and the interactions powerfully impact both the strength and direction of each influence.

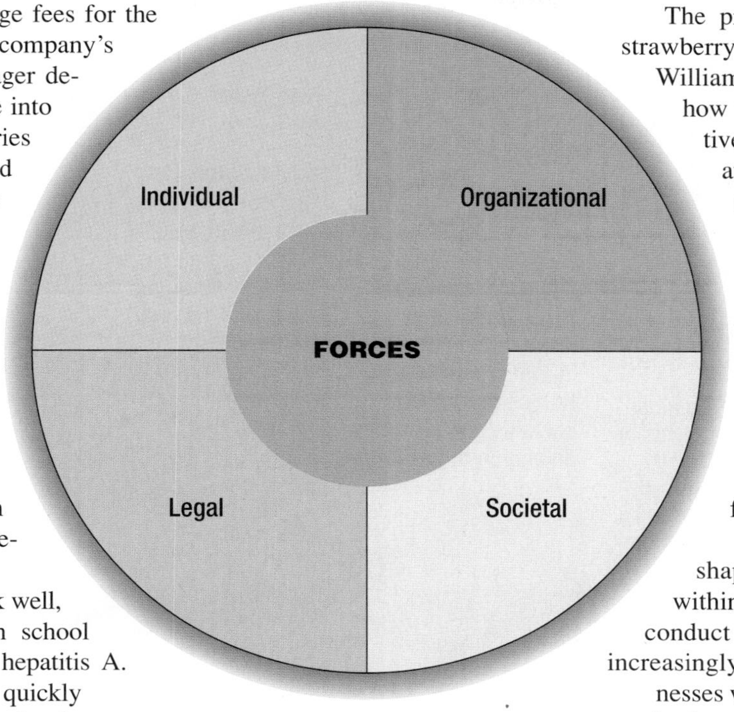

The problems resulting from the strawberry cover-up by Andrew & Williamson officials demonstrate how the ethical values of executives and individual employees at all levels can influence the decisions and actions a business takes. Throughout your business career, you will encounter numerous situations where you will need to weigh right and wrong before making a decision or taking action. Therefore, the discussion of business ethics begins by focusing on individual ethics.

Business ethics are also shaped by the ethical climate within an organization. Codes of conduct and ethical standards play increasingly significant roles in businesses where doing the right thing is both supported and applauded. This chapter will demonstrate how a firm can create a framework to encourage—and even demand—high standards of ethical behavior and social responsibility from its employees.

It is clear, however, that not all companies successfully set and meet the ethical standards of leading firms such as Nordstrom. As a protectionist move, federal, state, and local governments have enacted laws to regulate business practices. Many of these laws are examined in this chapter. It also considers the complex question of just what business owes to society and how societal forces mold the actions of businesses. Finally, it examines the influence of business ethics and social responsibility on global business.

INDIVIDUAL BUSINESS ETHICS

In today's business environment, individuals can make the difference in ethical expectations and behavior. As executives, managers, and employees demonstrate their personal ethical principles—or lack of ethical principles—the expectations and actions of those who work for them, as well as those who work with them, can change.

Figure 2.1 **Forces Shaping Business Ethics and Social Responsibility**

> **They said it**
>
> "The central business issue should be how to meet the needs of a group of people in a way that is fulfilling for employees, satisfying for customers, profitable for shareholders, and responsible in the community."
>
> **Mark S. Albion**
> **American business writer**

| Figure 2.2 | Stages of Moral and Ethical Development |

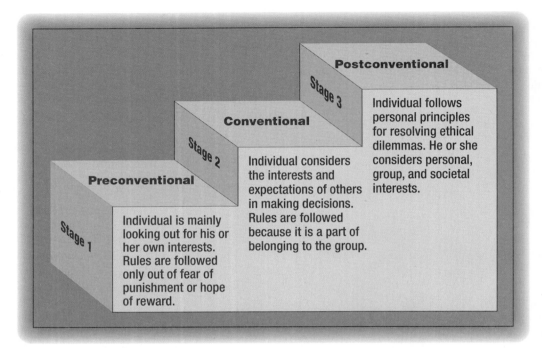

ical choices, the next section focuses on how personal ethics and morals are developed.

The Development of Individual Ethics

Individuals typically develop ethical standards in the three stages shown in Figure 2.2: the preconventional, conventional, and postconventional stages. In the preconventional stage, individuals primarily consider their own needs and desires in making decisions. They obey external rules only because they are afraid of punishment or hope to receive rewards if they comply.

In the second stage, the conventional stage, individuals are aware of and act in response to their duty to others, including their obligations to their family members, co-workers, and organizations. The expectations of these groups influence how they choose between what is acceptable and unacceptable in certain situations. Self-interest, however, continues to play a role in decisions.

The final, postconventional stage represents the highest level of ethical and moral behavior. The individual is able to move beyond mere self-interest and duty and take the larger needs of society into account, as well. He or she has developed personal ethical principles for determining what is right and can apply those principles in a wide variety of situations.

An individual's stage in moral and ethical development is determined by a huge number of factors. Past experiences help to shape responses to different situations. A person's family, educational, cultural, and religious backgrounds can also play a role. People can also have different styles of deciding ethical dilemmas, no matter what their stage of moral development. As Table 2.1 shows, one study suggests that men and women tend to use different techniques for resolving ethical situations.

To help you understand and prepare for the ethical dilemmas you may confront in your career, let's take a closer look at some of the factors involved in solving ethical questions on the job.

What is the current status of individual business ethics in the United States? Although ethical behavior can be difficult to track or even define in all circumstances, evidence suggests that many individuals act unethically or illegally on the job. Take employee theft as an example. It is estimated that U.S. businesses currently lose over $120 billion a year from employee theft of everything from cash to paper clips. Nearly 60 percent of workers in one survey also admitted to "time theft" in such forms as coming in late to work, leaving early, or lying about sick days.[3]

Employee theft is not the only questionable behavior on the job. In one survey of American workers, nearly half admitted to committing one or more unethical or illegal acts on the job during the past year. The most common acts included cutting corners on quality (16 percent), covering up incidents (14 percent), and lying to or deceiving customers (9 percent).[4] Another study found that 30 percent of managers admitted to filing deceptive internal reports.[5]

Given these findings, it is apparent that nearly every employee, at every level, wrestles with ethical questions at some point or another. Some rationalize questionable behavior by saying "everybody's doing it." Others act unethically because they feel pressured to hold their jobs or meet performance quotas. Some, however, avoid unethical acts that don't mesh with their personal values and morals. In order to understand the differences in the ways individuals arrive at eth-

They said it

"First, there is the law. It must be obeyed. But the law is the minimum. You must act ethically."

IBM employee guidelines

Table 2.1   Ethical Gender Gap

Typical Ways Men Resolve Ethical Dilemmas:	Typical Ways Women Resolve Ethical Dilemmas:
– Primarily Respect Rights	– Primarily Respect Feelings
– Ask "Who Is Right?"	– Ask "Who Will Be Hurt?"
– Value Decisiveness	– Avoid Being Judgmental
– Make Unambiguous Decisions	– Search for Compromise
– Seek Solutions That Are Objectively Fair	– Seek Solutions That Minimize Hurt
– Rely on Rules	– Rely on Communication
– Are Guided by Logic	– Are Guided by Emotion
– Accept Authority	– Challenge Authority

On-the-Job Ethical Dilemmas

In the fast-paced world of business, you will sometimes be called to weigh the ethics of decisions that can affect not just your own future, but possibly the futures of your fellow workers, your company, and its customers. As already noted, it's not always easy to distinguish between what is right and wrong in many business situations, especially when the needs and concerns of various parties conflict.

Consider the situation that William Haggett, CEO of Bath Iron Works (BIW), found himself in after a quarterly meeting with his shipbuilding firm's top client, the U.S. Navy. After the meeting, Haggett discovered that one of the Navy consultants had accidentally left behind a 67-page document marked, "Business Sensitive." Scanning the document, Haggett realized it detailed a competitor's proposal for a project on which BIW also was bidding. Haggett not only read the competitor's proposal, he discussed the contents with subordinates and had the document copied. When a subordinate told BIW's president about Haggett's actions, the president went to Haggett and convinced him to return the proposal to the Navy's consultant. Although a Navy investigation cleared Haggett of any serious wrongdoing, his BIW colleagues pushed him to resign. "With the benefit of hindsight, I see it was a bad decision on my part," he later explained at a news conference.

Lockheed Martin CEO Norman Augustine found himself in a similar situation. The day before his firm's proposal for a large government contract was due to be turned in, a mysterious package arrived in the mail. It contained a copy of a competing proposal for the same contract. With the information in hand, he still had time to change Lockheed Martin's proposal in order to gain the upper hand at winning the contract. Augustine immediately turned the data over to the government and informed Lockheed Martin's competitor about what he had received. Lockheed Martin didn't win the contract, which meant that some employees lost their jobs and shareholders lost money. But Augustine didn't regret his decision. He recalls, "We helped establish a reputation that, in the long run, will draw us business."[6]

What would you do in a situation like this? Would you do whatever seemed necessary to make sure your company made the big sale? According to one recent survey, 98 percent of salespeople said they would do "anything" to close a sale.[7]

As these two stories illustrate, several avenues can be taken to solve ethical dilemmas. In many cases, each possible decision will have unpleasant consequences as well as positive benefits that must be evaluated. The ethical dilemma that confronted Haggett and Augustine is just one example of many different types of ethical questions encountered in the workplace. Figure 2.3 identifies some of the more common ethical dilemmas that business-people face.

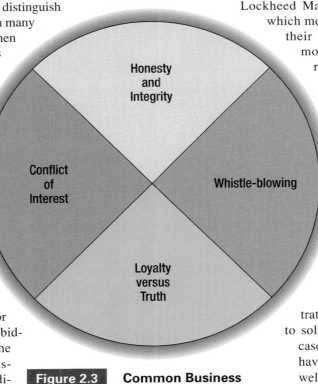

Figure 2.3   Common Business Ethical Dilemmas

Honesty and Integrity

Conflict of Interest

Whistle-blowing

Loyalty versus Truth

Conflict of Interest A **conflict of interest** exists when a businessperson is faced with a situation where his or her decision may be influenced by the potential for personal gain. Bribes are one type of conflict of interest. Joseph Escalon, for example, worked for the Federal Aviation Administration (FAA) processing applications for commercial airline pilot licenses. A pilot for Asiana Airlines, who hadn't completed required flight checks or met FAA training and experience requirements, offered Escalon money and a free trip if he would rush the application through the certification process. Escalon accepted the bribe, but his actions were later revealed. He was sentenced to four months in prison and a $2,000 fine.[8]

Questions regarding conflicts of interest extend beyond bribery. Consider the debate at Wake Forest University's Bowman Gray School of Medicine. Several of the faculty members at the medical school also conducted research for R. J. Reynolds Tobacco Co. Their research was intended to determine whether the effects of nicotine from cigarette smoking were as dangerous as anti-tobacco activists claimed. Critics say the faculty members had a conflict of interest. On the one hand, they were working to train future doctors; on the other, they were accepting funding from a company which manufactures a product viewed as a major health threat.[9]

Honesty and Integrity Honesty and integrity are traits highly valued by employers. In a survey conducted by

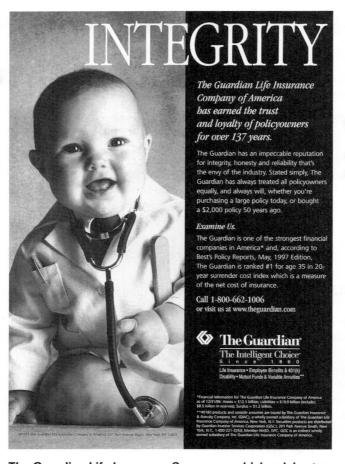

The Guardian Life Insurance Company, which celebrates its 140th birthday in 2000, highlights its strong reputation for integrity, honesty, and reliability in its promotional messages.

staffing firm Robert Half International, employers said the number one qualities they sought in job applicants were honesty and integrity.[10]

Integrity involves adhering to deeply felt ethical principles in business situations. It goes beyond being truthful—it means doing what you say you will do and accepting responsibility for mistakes.

Honesty is an ethical principle that permeates many work situations. Some people, for example, misrepresent their academic credentials and previous work experience on their resumes or job applications. Recent news stories have reported instances where individuals have misrepresented their military experience in order to qualify for burial in Arlington National Cemetery. One candidate withdrew from a political race after news reports surfaced that refuted his claims about a brother's racially motivated death during the civil rights struggles of the 1960s.

As already discussed, employee theft is an enormous expense for U.S. businesses. Research has shown that many employees also have few qualms about lying in order to protect themselves from punishment. Honesty is also a factor in developing strong customer relationships.

Loyalty versus Truth Businesspeople expect their employees to be loyal and to act in the best interests of the company. An ethical conflict can arise, however, when individuals must decide between loyalty to the company and truthfulness in business relationships. William Haggett and Norman Augustine both faced this issue in deciding how to handle situations where they had access to information about competitors' plans.

Whistle-Blowing When an individual does encounter unethical or illegal actions at

Business Directory

conflict of interest a situation where a business decision may be influenced by the potential for personal gain.

whistle-blowing an employee's disclosure to the media or government authorities of illegal, immoral, or unethical practices of the organization.

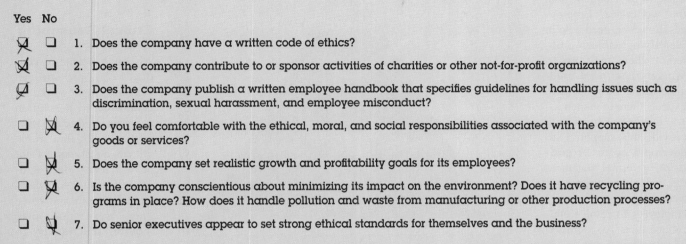

B U S I N E S S   T O O L   K I T

Before You Accept a Job, Review Your New Employer's Code of Ethics

How far would you go to satisfy your employer? If working for an ethical and socially responsible firm is important to you, look before you leap. Here are seven questions to help you evaluate how well a potential employer's ethical values mesh with your own.

Yes No

☑ ☐ 1. Does the company have a written code of ethics?

☑ ☐ 2. Does the company contribute to or sponsor activities of charities or other not-for-profit organizations?

☑ ☐ 3. Does the company publish a written employee handbook that specifies guidelines for handling issues such as discrimination, sexual harassment, and employee misconduct?

☐ ☑ 4. Do you feel comfortable with the ethical, moral, and social responsibilities associated with the company's goods or services?

☐ ☑ 5. Does the company set realistic growth and profitability goals for its employees?

☐ ☑ 6. Is the company conscientious about minimizing its impact on the environment? Does it have recycling programs in place? How does it handle pollution and waste from manufacturing or other production processes?

☐ ☑ 7. Do senior executives appear to set strong ethical standards for themselves and the business?

If you can answer "yes" to five or more of these questions, chances are you will find yourself working for an ethical and socially responsible firm.

---

work, he or she must decide what action to take. **Whistle-blowing** is the term for an employee's disclosure to the media or government authorities of illegal, immoral, or unethical practices of the organization. Nationwide Insurance agent John Askin faced an ethical dilemma in the early 1990s, and he decided that whistle-blowing was the only avenue available to him. Askin alleges that his boss gave him a map of Louisville, Kentucky, with a large *X* marked over several neighborhoods. Askin was told to avoid sales from these largely low-income, African American neighborhoods, but he refused and decided to alert government agencies. Although Nationwide has denied Askin's allegations, the Justice Department is investigating the company for illegally discriminating against minority groups.[11]

A whistle-blower must weigh a number of issues in the decision to come forward or not. Some may decide to try to work through internal channels within their organizations in order to correct the wrongdoing. If that fails, they must weigh the potential damages to the greater public good if they do not come forward. Although in many instances whistle-blowers are protected by state and federal laws, they may still experience dramatic retribution for their actions. For example, Mark Whitacre was an executive at Archer Daniels Midland (ADM) when he blew the whistle on his employer for illegally fixing grain prices. He cooperated with the FBI's investigation by se-

cretly taping meetings over a 3-year period in which the alleged misdeeds occurred. ADM later fired Whitacre and accused him of embezzlement, effectively destroying his career.[12]

Obviously, whistle-blowing and other ethical issues arise relatively infrequently in firms with strong organizational climates of ethical behavior. The Business Tool Kit gives guidelines that will help you to evaluate a potential employer's ethics. The next section examines how a business can develop an environment that discourages unethical behavior among individuals.

HOW ORGANIZATIONS SHAPE ETHICAL CONDUCT

No individual makes decisions in a vacuum. Choices are strongly influenced by the standards of conduct established within the organizations where people work. Most ethical lapses in business reflect the values of the firms' corporate cultures.

As shown in Figure 2.4, development of a corporate culture to support business ethics happens on four levels: ethical awareness, ethical reasoning, ethical action, and ethical leadership. If any of these four factors is missing, the ethical climate in an organization will weaken.[13]

Ethical Awareness

The foundation of an ethical climate is ethical awareness. As we've already seen, ethical dilemmas occur frequently in the workplace. Employees, however, need help in identifying ethical problems when they occur. Workers also need guidance about how the firm expects them to respond.

One way for a firm to provide this support is to develop a **code of conduct,** a formal statement that defines how the organization expects and requires employees to resolve ethical questions. An estimated 73 percent of companies have such codes of conduct in place.[14]

Figure 2.4 **Structure of an Ethical Environment**

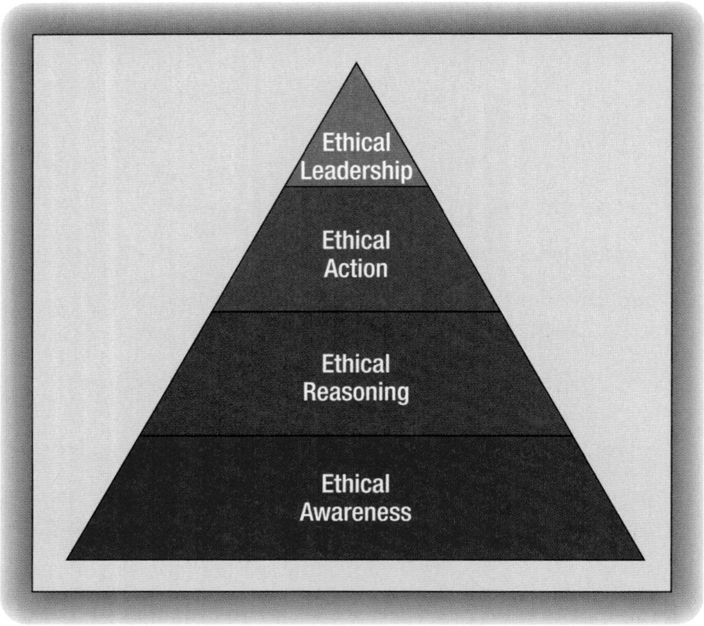

At the most basic level, a code of conduct may simply specify ground rules for acceptable behavior, such as identifying the laws and regulations that employees must obey. Other companies, however, use their codes of conduct to identify key corporate values and provide frameworks that guide employees as they resolve moral and ethical dilemmas.

Telecommunications giant Nortel views its corporate code of conduct as a way to put the firm's core values into practice. The company's code identifies the commitments the firm has made to five groups of stakeholders: employees, customers, suppliers, shareholders, and the global community in which the company operates. Nortel executives sought input and feedback from employees in developing the code. Over 36 discussions were held with groups of employees to pinpoint ethical areas where employees wanted and needed guidance. The company placed a draft of the code on its employee intranet, allowing all 63,000 Nortel employees to comment. After the code was finalized, Nortel posted it at the company's Web site.[15]

WWW. www.nortel.com/cool/ethics/home.html

Ethical Reasoning

Although a code of conduct can provide an overall framework, it cannot detail a solution for every ethical situation. Recall that some ethical questions do not have clear black-and-white answers. Many ethical dilemmas involve gray areas that may require individuals to sort through several options and potential consequences. Businesses must provide the tools employees need to evaluate these options and arrive at suitable decisions.

Many firms have instituted ethics training programs. Although some observers debate whether ethics can actually be taught, this training can give employees an opportunity to practice applying ethical values to hypothetical situations as a prelude to applying the same standards to real-world situations. At MONY insurance, everyone in the company, including senior management, must attend an ethics training course that focuses on specific situations employees might encounter in their jobs.[16]

WWW. www.mony.com

Lockheed Martin hired a consulting firm to develop an ethics training game called "The Ethics Challenge" based on the popular comic-strip characters Dilbert and Dogbert. Teams move game pieces around a board that resembles different parts of an office. As they move toward the finish line, teams must solve ethical problems from sample cases. The company believes that the board game encourages employees not only to discuss ethical situations but also to arrive at ethical choices working as a group.[17]

Business Directory

code of conduct a formal statement that defines how the organization expects and requires employees to resolve ethical questions.

Ethical Action

Codes of conduct and ethics training help employees to recognize and reason through ethical problems. However, firms must also provide structures and approaches that allow decisions to be turned into ethical actions.

Goals set for the business as a whole and for individual departments and employees can affect ethical behavior. A firm whose managers set unrealistic goals for employee performance may find an increase in cheating, lying, and other misdeeds, as employees attempt to protect themselves. One study of unethical behavior on the job found that 56 percent of workers who did mis-

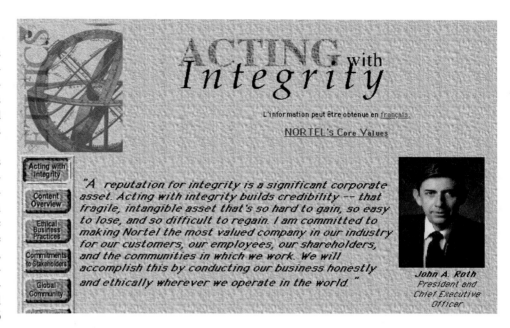

behave felt pressured to do so because of stress in the workplace.[18] Wetherill Associates, a Pennsylvania auto-parts distributor, tries to avoid this problem by not setting sales goals for its salespeople.

Other companies encourage ethical action by providing support for employees faced with dilemmas. One common tool is an employee hotline, a telephone number that employees can call, often anonymously, for advice or to report unethical behavior they have witnessed. Some companies also create ethics officers, individuals responsible for guiding employees through potential ethical minefields.

Nortel employees can call AdviceLine to discuss any questions they have regarding the company's code of conduct. In each region around the globe where Nortel operates, a local employee conducts classes on ethical behavior. Nortel believes that this helps to personalize each employee's relationship with the company by providing one-on-one access to a corporate business ethics representative.[19]

Ethical Leadership

Executives must not only talk about ethical behavior but also demonstrate it in their actions. This principle requires that they be personally committed to the company's core values and be willing to base their actions on them.

However, ethical leadership should also go one step further and charge each employee at every level with the responsibility for being an ethical leader. As such, each individual should be aware of transgressions and be willing to defend the organization's standards.

Unfortunately, not all organizations are able to build this solid framework of business ethics. The Business Hall of Shame discusses what can happen when companies as-

sume that others share their ethical concerns. Because the damage from ethical misconduct can powerfully affect a firm's stakeholders—customers, investors, employees, and the public—pressure is exerted on businesses to act in acceptable ways. The next section examines the legal and governmental forces that are designed to safeguard society's interests when businesses fail at self-regulation.

CONTROLLING BUSINESS BEHAVIOR THROUGH GOVERNMENT REGULATION

Although few would disagree that businesses should act ethically and responsibly, it is clear that not all companies behave this way. When businesses fail to regulate their own actions, consumers and other businesses can suffer serious consequences. Because of this threat, federal, state, and local governments sometimes step in to regulate business activity. Many of the major federal laws affecting business are listed in Table 2.2. Legal protections for employee safety and equal employment opportunities are covered later in this chapter. Many of the laws that affect specific industries or individuals are described in other chapters. For example, legislation affecting international business operations is discussed in Chapter 4. Laws designed to assist small businesses are examined in Chapter 5. Laws related to formation and operation of labor unions are described in Chapter 11. Finally, legislation related to banking and the securities markets is discussed in Chapters 20 and 21.

The history of government regulation in the United States can be divided into three phases: regulation of competition, consumer protection, and deregulation. Because an understanding of the political and legal environment in

Table 2.2 Major Federal Laws Affecting Business

Date	Law	Description
A. LAWS TO MAINTAIN A COMPETITIVE ENVIRONMENT		
1890	Sherman Antitrust Act	Prohibits restraint of trade and monopolization; delineates a competitive marketing system as national policy.
1914	Clayton Act	Strengthens the Sherman Act by restricting such practices as rice discrimination, exclusive dealing, tying contracts, and interlocking boards of directors where the effect {may be to substantially lessen competition or tend to create a monopoly."
1914	Federal Trade Commission Act	Prohibits unfair methods of competition; established the Federal Trade Commission, an administrative agency that investigates business practices and enforces the FTC Act.
1938	Wheeler-Lea Act	Amended the FTC Act to further outlaw unfair practices and give the FTC jurisdiction over false and misleading advertising.
1950	Celler-Kefauver Antimerger Act	Amended the Clayton Act to include major asset purchases that decrease competition in an industry.
1992	American Automobile Labeling Act	Requires a vehicle's manufacturer to provide a label informing consumers of where the vehicle was assembled and where its components originated.
B. LAWS TO REGULATE COMPETITION		
1936	Robinson-Patman Act	Prohibits price discrimination in sales to wholesalers, retailers, or other producers; prohibits selling at unreasonably low prices to eliminate competition.
1937	Miller-Tydings Resale Price Maintenance Act	Exempts interstate fair trade contracts from compliance with antitrust requirements. Repealed by passage of the Consumer Goods Pricing Act in 1975.
1993	North American Free Trade Agreement (NAFTA)	International trade agreement between Canada, Mexico, and the United States designed to facilitate trade by removing tariffs and other trade barriers among the three nations.
C. LAWS TO PROTECT CONSUMERS		
1906	Federal Food and Drug Act	Prohibits adulteration and misbranding of foods and drugs involved in interstate commerce; strengthened by the Food, Drug, and Cosmetic Act (1938) and the Kefauver-Harris Drug Amendment (1962).
1958	National Traffic and Safety Act	Provides for the creation of safety standards for automobiles and tires.
1966	Fair Packaging and Labeling Act	Requires disclosure of product identification, name and address of manufacturer or distributor, and information on the quality of contents.
1967	Federal Cigarette Labeling and Advertising Act	Requires written health warnings on cigarette packages.
1968	Consumer Credit Protection Act	Truth-in-lending law requiring disclosure of annual interest rates on loans and credit purchases
1970	Fair Credit Reporting Act	Gives individuals access to their credit records and allows them to change incorrect information.
1970	National Environmental Policy Act	Established the Environmental Protection Agency to deal with various types of pollution and organizations that create pollution.
1971	Public Health Cigarette Smoking Act	Prohibits tobacco advertising on radio and television.
1972	Consumer Product Safety Act	Created the Consumer Product Safety Commission with authority to specify safety standards for most products.
1975 1977	Equal Credit Opportunity Act	Bans discrimination in lending practices based on sex and marital status (as of 1975) and race, national origin, religion, age, or receipt of payments from public-assistance programs (as of 1977).
1990	Nutrition Labeling and Education Act	Requires food manufacturers and processors to provide detailed nutritional information on the labels of most foods.
1990	Children's Television Act	Limits the amount of advertising to be shown during children's television programs to not more than 10.5 minutes per hour on weekends and not more than 12.0 minutes per hour on weekdays.
1990	Americans with Disabilities Act (ADA)	Protects the rights of people with disabilities; makes discrimination against the disabled illegal in public accommodations, transportation, and telecommunications.
1993	Brady Law	Imposes a 5-day waiting period and a background check before a gun purchaser can take possession of the gun.
D. LAWS TO DEREGULATE SPECIFIC INDUSTRIES		
1978	Airline Deregulation Act	Grants considerable freedom to commercial airlines in setting fares and choosing new routes.
1980	Motor Carrier Act and Staggers Rail Act	Significantly deregulates the trucking and railroad industries by permitting them to negotiate rates and services.
1996	Telecommunications Act	Significantly deregulates the telecommunications industry by removing barriers to competition in local and long-distance phone and cable television markets.

which business decisions are made is closely linked to ethics and social responsibility, the following sections examine how each of these regulatory phases has shaped, and still influences, the business landscape.

Regulation of Competition

As Chapter 1 showed, competition is the cornerstone of a private enterprise economy. During the late 19th and early 20th centuries, however, government became concerned that power in many industries was too concentrated in the hands of small numbers of companies. These large, industry-controlling companies not only stifled competition, but they also had little incentive to act ethically. In response, the federal government began to intervene to regulate competition and commercial activities.

Some industries, such as electric utilities, became regulated. Throughout most of this century, government regulations allowed only one power company in a given market. Regulators reasoned that the large capital investment required to construct electric transmission lines made this type of regulation appropriate. In a **regulated industry,** competition is either limited or eliminated, and close government control is substituted for free competition. In most cases, regulated industries are those closely tied to the public interest where competition would be wasteful or excessive.

The second form of government regulation, enactment of statutes, has led to both state and federal laws that affect competition and various commercial practices. Over a century ago, the federal government began to regulate competition with the Sherman Antitrust Act of 1890. This act prohibits any contract or conspiracy that tends toward restraint of trade. It also declares illegal any action that monopolizes or attempts to monopolize any part of commerce.

Another major federal law, the Clayton Act of 1914, forbids such trade restraints as tying contracts, interlocking directorates, and certain anticompetitive stock acquisitions. A tying contract requires the exclusive dealer for a manufacturer's products to carry other, perhaps unwanted products in inventory. In interlocking directorates, competing companies have identical or overlapping boards of directors. The Clayton Act also forbids any purchase of another company's stock that reduces competition.

> ## They said it
>
> Anyone who sells butter containing stones or other things to add to the weight will be put into our pillory, then said butter will be placed on his head until entirely melted by the sun. Dogs may lick him and people offend him with whatever defamatory epithets they please without offense to God or King. If the sun is not warm enough, the accused will be exposed to the hall of the jail in front of a roaring fire, where everyone will see him."
>
> Edict of Louis XI (1421–1483)
> King of France

Both the Sherman Act and the Clayton Act are enforced by the Antitrust Division of the U.S. Department of Justice. Violators are subject not only to criminal fines or imprisonment but also to civil damage suits by competitors or other parties. In some cases, the government allows the accused firm to enter into a consent order, under which it agrees voluntarily to cease the conduct that the government alleges is inappropriate. The Celler-Kefauver Antimerger Act (1950) amended the Clayton Act to prohibit major asset purchases that decrease competition in an industry.

This chapter began by describing the antitrust suit recently filed by the Department of Justice against Microsoft for alleged tying contract violations. Microsoft imposed a requirement on personal computer makers that wanted to include its Windows software with their machines to also include Microsoft's Internet Explorer software. Among the companies testifying against Microsoft were Compaq and Netscape. Microsoft, however, argued that because its Internet Explorer was not a separate product but a new feature of Windows, it was not subject to the tying contract prohibition.[20]

The Federal Trade Commission Act of 1914 banned unfair competitive practices and set up the Federal Trade Commission (FTC) to administer various statutes that apply to business. The powers and investigative capacities of the FTC have grown rapidly over the years; today, it is the major federal regulatory and enforcement agency to oversee competitive practices. The FTC can sue violators or enter into consent orders with those that agree to cease questionable practices.

During the Great Depression of the 1930s, other laws aimed at protecting competitors were enacted when independent merchants felt the need for legal protection against competition from larger chain stores. Federal legislation enacted during this period included the Robinson-Patman Act and the Miller-Tydings Resale Price Maintenance Act.

www. **www.ftc.gov**

Business Directory

regulated industry an industry in which competition is either limited or eliminated, and government monitoring substitutes for market controls.

BUSINESS HALL OF SHAME

Trouble Keeping an Eye on the Ball at adidas

Everyone knows that to succeed in sports, you have to keep your eye on the ball. The same is true for succeeding in business, especially when the business is making sports equipment. Just ask adidas. The German sports manufacturer learned firsthand about what happens when you don't watch the ball—adidas was sued by laborer Bao Ge for the pain and suffering he endured while being forced to manufacture adidas soccer balls in a Chinese prison under the worst conditions of exploitation and torture.

The sports-equipment manufacturer has always taken great pride in how closely it monitors its production process. For example, when rival Nike lost sales due to media reports that its products were made in Asian factories with poor labor conditions, adidas reemphasized it code of conduct. The company joined 58 global sports-equipment makers in an agreement to curtail the use of children to produce soccer balls. And when CEO Robert Louis-Dreyfus first heard about adidas soccer balls being sewn in Chinese prisons, he promised, "If it turns out that even one item was made by slave labor or in a prison camp, heads will roll—maybe even my own."

How could this happen to such a diligent company? Maybe adidas wasn't watching the ball closely enough. Several Chinese manufacturers produce balls for adidas. Shanghai Union, one of China's oldest and largest sports-ball makers, says it makes adidas-brand balls for Japan's Molten Corp., which is licensed to manufacture and market adidas balls in Japan. However, adidas says that its contract with Molten "demands that they don't use child or prison labor." Likewise, Molten says subcontractor Shanghai Union assures that no prison labor is used on adidas soccer balls. But, Molten adds, it can't be certain those assurances are true. "We

---

This text covers many other specific business practices regulated by government in other sections and in Appendix C, Business Law.

Consumer Protection

Although the objective of consumer protection underlies most business-oriented laws—including the Sherman Act and the Clayton Act—many of the major consumer-oriented laws have been enacted during the past 40 years.

Federal and state legislation plays a major role in regulating product safety. The Consumer Product Safety Act of 1972 created a powerful regulatory agency called the Consumer Product Safety Commission (CPSC). The agency has the authority to ban products without court hearings, order recalls or redesigns of products, and inspect production facilities, and it can charge managers of negligent companies with criminal offenses. Other federal laws, such as the Poison Prevention Packaging Act of 1970, set guidelines for product labels of manufacturers in various

industries. Additionally, the dramatic rise in product liability lawsuits over the past two decades has pushed businesses in all industries to pay greater attention to customer safety issues.

A later section takes a closer look at consumer protection issues as part of a discussion of businesses' social responsibilities to customers.

Deregulation

Deregulation, the movement toward eliminating legal restraints on competition in various industries, has significantly reshaped the legal environment for many industries in the last two decades. Considerable controversy continues to surround the government's role in regulating the actions of businesses and the benefits of allowing industries to compete without intense government control.

During this phase, the federal government has worked to increase competition in a number of industries, including telecommunications, utilities, transportation, and banking, by discontinuing many regulations and permitting firms to expand their service offerings to new markets. The trend toward deregulation started in 1978 with the Airline Deregulation Act, which encouraged competi-

Business Directory

deregulation   a regulatory trend toward elimination of legal restraints on competition.

have a subcontracting agreement with Shanghai Union . . . nothing more. We can't be too inquisitive about them," says Molten's Hidesuke Kuriki.

Because stitching together 32 panels for one soccer ball is highly labor intensive, it is common practice in China to send the handwork out to rural areas where labor costs are low. However, when a company contracts hand labor with a Chinese factory, it is difficult to be sure that none of the work is being done by prisoners. Once raw materials are delivered to workshops in China, you can't be sure where the actual work is being done, says Frank Change, whose Shanghai-based Mortex Ltd. makes adidas soccer balls for export to Europe. As Chang points out, "Unless you have somebody there who watches when they sew, there's no way anyone can control that."

To its credit, adidas has canceled all orders for Chinese-made soccer balls. But the embarrassment the company has endured over this incident is a lesson for any company that contracts work in a country as poorly regulated as China. It's also a lesson to any businessperson: When ethics are involved, you really do have to keep your eye on the ball.

QUESTIONS FOR CRITICAL THINKING

1. **Discuss the ethical and social values involved in manufacturing products under poor labor conditions. How could adidas have made sure that its soccer balls would not be produced in prisons? Would any of these actions cut into adidas's profits?**

2. **When adidas canceled its orders for Chinese soccer balls, the decision was applauded by the Brussels-based International Textile, Garment and Leather Workers' Federation, whose member unions represent people employed in the production of soccer balls. Do you think the approval was based on the federation's concern for the human rights of all workers? Or was the move a chance for its members to get more work? Defend your answer.**

Sources: Bao Ge, "I Miss My Cellmates in the Prison," Digital Freedom Network, accessed at www.dfn.org, February 9, 1999; "adidas Cancels All Football Orders from China," Hong Kong Voice of Democracy, July 29, 1998, accessed at www.democracy.org.hk; and "Questions about Prison Labor Hits adidas," *The Wall Street Journal*, June 26, 1998, p. A13.

tion among airlines by allowing them to set their own rates and to add or abandon routes based on profitability.

Critics of deregulation often point out negative effects of the trend. Some say that deregulation may lead to increasing prices as competitors are eliminated. Others suggest that firms may sacrifice safety in the name of competition. All of these issues are legitimate concerns.

The latest industry undergoing deregulation is the electric utility industry. With 198 investor-owned utilities in the United States, it is also the largest industry to be deregulated so far. California became the first state to totally open electricity sales to free competition. Consumers and businesses can now choose to buy from several different electricity suppliers, either locally or from other states. Several months before deregulation, industry giant Enova began an intensive television advertising campaign in order to convince consumers to use its services. Other state regulatory agencies are poised to follow California's lead. Supporters claim that deregulation will slash consumer and business electricity costs by 20 to 30 percent over the next 5 to 10 years. Critics, however, say that savings are likely to be much smaller, especially for residential users.[21]

Government Regulation of Cyberspace

The newest regulatory frontier is the Internet. Regulation of business on the Internet is a major issue facing govern-

ments and businesses around the world. The Internet is a borderless market; for it to function as a global marketplace, governments must work together to develop a stable economic and legal environment in which firms can operate freely, regardless of jurisdiction. Policies such as encryption (coding) of sensitive information, regulation, and electronic payments can't be decided separately by each country.

To that end, the Clinton administration recently released its *Framework for Global Electronic Commerce*. The framework acknowledges that cyberspace is very different from traditional communications media, and many current laws may no longer be appropriate for it. The European Union and the United States support a market-driven approach to electronic commerce. The framework emphasizes self-regulation by the private sector rather than government restrictions. Among the recommendations are:

▼ Declaring the Internet a tariff-free environment for cross-border transactions

▼ Developing and implementing a consistent global commercial and legal framework for electronic commerce. Contracts, rather than laws, should govern e-commerce

▼ Protecting copyrights, patents, and trademarks

▼ Protecting privacy of personal data, especially with regard to children, through self-regulation rather than censorship.[22]

Protect Your Privacy

A recent investigation by *Money* magazine found that today's consumers face a very real threat to their privacy. Many companies resell data about their customers to other businesses. Criminals also can illegally obtain facts about you by hacking into computer databases. As a result, details such as your address, bank account numbers, buying patterns, and other personal information may be in the hands of more people than you think. Here are five tips to protect your privacy:

1. When buying over the Internet, be sure your order is encrypted, so the information you provide cannot be read by computer hackers.

2. Put your name on the Direct Marketing Association's free Mail Preference List. This step will cut down unsolicited mailings from marketers who've obtained your name and address from other companies. The DMA's address is P.O. Box 9008, Farmingdale, NY 11735. To cut down on unwanted e-mail solicitations, try registering with Junkbusters: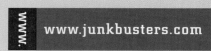

3. On the job, avoid sending personal e-mail or accessing nonwork-related Internet sites. Employers have the right to monitor any communications sent over office computers, and many do so.

4. Many Web sites place "cookies" into visitors' computers. A cookie keeps track of every site you visit and reports the information back to the original site. If you don't want a Web operator to keep tabs on your surfing, go to your computer's Find or Search feature, type in *COOKIES*, and then delete the text file.

5. At least once a year, order your credit report from a major credit bureau such as Trans Union (610–690–4909), or Equifax (770–612–2500). Check for any inaccuracies or false charges that may indicate someone has illegally gained access to your account.

Source: Ann Reilly Dowd, "Protect Your Privacy," *Money*, August 1997, p. 104.

Reaching an internationally agreed upon system for Internet communication and transactions will take years. Many international alliances, trade blocs, and treaties may affect Internet business, as well. Chapter 17 looks more closely at the issues surrounding Internet commerce. The Business Tool Kit discusses measures by which individual Internet users can protect their sensitive information.

ACTING RESPONSIBLY TO SATISFY SOCIETY

A second major issue affecting business is the question of social responsibility. In a general sense, **social responsibility** is management's acceptance of the obligation to consider profit, consumer satisfaction, and societal well-being of equal value in evaluating the firm's performance. It is the recognition that business must be concerned with the qualitative dimensions of consumer, employee, and societal benefits as well as the quantitative measures of sales, revenue, and profit, by which business performance is traditionally measured.

As Professors James F. Engel and Roger D. Blackwell point out, social responsibility is a concept easier to measure than business ethics:

Actions alone determine social responsibility and a firm can be socially responsible even when doing so under coercion. For example, the government may enact rules that force firms to be socially responsible in matters of the environment, deception, and so forth. Also, consumers, through their power to repeat or withhold purchasing, may force businesses to provide honest and relevant information, fair prices, and so forth. To be ethically responsible, on the other hand, it is not sufficient to act correctly; ethical intent is also necessary.[23]

Historically, a company's social performance has been measured by its contribution to the overall economy and the employment opportunities it provides. Variables such as wage payments often serve to indicate social per-

Business Directory

social responsibility management's acceptance of the obligation to consider profit, consumer satisfaction, and societal well-being of equal value in evaluating the firm's performance.

formance. While profits and employment remain important, today many factors contribute to an assessment of a firm's social performance. These include providing equal employment opportunities; respecting the cultural diversity of employees; responding to environmental concerns; providing a safe, healthy workplace; and producing safe, high-quality products.

A business is also judged by its interactions with the community. Many corporations highlight charitable contributions and community service in their annual reports to demonstrate their social responsibility. Among them:

▼ Ford recently paid about $1 million to sponsor an episode of the television show *Murphy Brown* dealing with breast cancer. Public service ads focused on the disease, its detection, and cure.

▼ AT&T is active in the Partnership for a Drug-Free America. An example of drug education and awareness programs sponsored in part by AT&T is shown in Figure 2.5.

▼ Johnson & Johnson gives the World Wildlife Fund a cut from sales of a special line of children's toiletries.

▼ American Express credit card users generated $22 million for Share Our Strength, a poverty-relief charity aimed at providing food for low-income households.[24]

Some firms measure social performance by conducting **social audits,** formal procedures that identify and evaluate all company activities that relate to social issues such as conservation, employment practices, environmental protection, and philanthropy. The social audit informs management about how well the company is performing in these areas. Based on this information, management may take steps to revise current programs or develop new ones.

Outside groups may conduct their own evaluations of businesses. Various environmental, religious, and public-interest groups have created standards of corporate performance. Reports on many of these evaluations are available

| Figure 2.5 | AT&T Contributions to the Partnership for a Drug-Free America |

Her dreams don't have to be limited by her reality.

The reality is that she witnesses a lot of drug abuse. She finds it in her neighborhood, at her school, and in the park. But thanks to the Partnership for a Drug-Free America, this reality doesn't have to define her future. Through drug education and awareness programs, sponsored in part by AT&T, children are learning how drugs can weaken ambition and take away dreams. They are about to discover the power of their own determination and how to use it in the fight against drugs. AT&T and the Partnership for a Drug-Free America are helping them realize their potential. The reality is that every child has the right to dream.

AT&T and the Partnership for a Drug-Free America are giving children back their childhood.

© 1996 AT&T

to the general public. The Council on Economic Priorities produces publications such as *The Better World Investment Guide,* which recommends basing investment decisions on companies' track records on various social issues, including environmental impact, nuclear weapons contracts, community outreach, and advancement of women and minorities. Other groups have used the Internet to publicize their evaluations and criticisms of the social responsibility of firms.

Many firms find that consumers evaluate their social track records in financial decisions, that is, by either buying or not buying the firms' goods and services. One study, for example, reported that 75 percent of consumers surveyed said they wouldn't buy, no matter what the price, from firms they considered socially irresponsible.[25] Other consumer groups organize boycotts of companies they find to be socially irresponsible. In a boycott, consumers refuse to buy a company's goods or services.

The *Boycott Quarterly,* a Seattle-based publication, reports that some 800 products currently are being boycotted by consumer activists. The AFL-CIO recently asked its members to boycott 20 companies it believes to have unfriendly policies against unions.[26]

As Figure 2.6 shows, the social responsibilities of business can be classified according to its relationships to the general public, customers, employees, and investors and the rest of the financial community. Many of these relationships extend beyond national borders.

Responsibilities to the General Public

The responsibilities of business to the general public include dealing with public-health issues, protecting the environment, and developing the quality of the work force. Additionally, many would argue that businesses have responsibilities to support charitable and social causes and organizations that work toward the greater public good. In other words, they should give back to the communities in which they earn profits. This is called **corporate philanthropy.**

Figure 2.7 summarizes these four responsibilities, which are discussed in the sections that follow. The Business Tool Kit on how to be charitable suggests some criteria for choosing these actions.

Public-Health Issues One of the more complex issues regarding business ethics and social responsibility to the general public revolves around public health. Central to this debate is the question of what businesses should do about products that are inherently dangerous.

For example, tobacco products represent a major health risk, contributing to the incidence of heart disease, stroke, and cancer among smokers. Furthermore, families and co-workers of smokers share this danger, as well, since their exposure to secondhand smoke increases their risks for cancer, asthma, and respiratory infections. Substance abuse, including alcohol abuse, is another serious public-health problem worldwide.

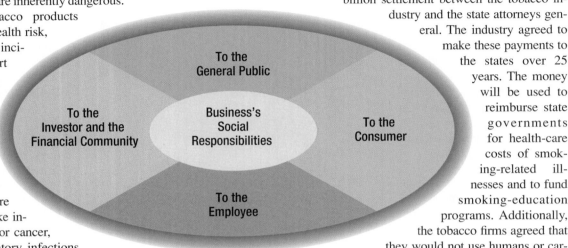

Figure 2.6   **Responsibilities of Business**

Motor vehicle accidents are a major killer, and drunk drivers cause many serious crashes. Alcohol abuse has also been linked to serious diseases such as cirrhosis of the liver. Other public-health dangers are posed by fatty foods, TV violence, handguns, and even motorcycles.

A second health-related question that businesses must answer involves the protection of vulnerable groups. Consider, for example, that 80 to 90 percent of smokers begin the habit before age 18. Over the last 5 years, the number of high school students who smoke has increased each year.[27] These young people will become tomorrow's work force, and their smoking habits will predispose them to a multitude of health problems. The tobacco industry has been repeatedly criticized for using advertisements aimed at children and teens. Until 1999, Joe Camel, for example, a cartoon figure used to promote Camel cigarettes, was one of the most widely recognized advertising symbols among young children. Absolut vodka ads have even become collector's items for many teens, raising concerns that the company is encouraging underage drinking. Both alcohol and tobacco companies have been criticized for targeting ethnic and racial minorities in their advertising.

Many consumers view both alcohol and tobacco advertising, whether aimed at adults or young people, as socially irresponsible. Some brewers have tried to counter these views by sponsoring advertising campaigns that promote moderation. Even firms who are not in these industries have faced controversy over this issue. For instance, the *San Francisco Bay Guardian* was recently picketed by antitobacco activists for accepting advertising from tobacco companies, even though the newspaper's editorial coverage had strongly criticized the tobacco industry in the past.[28]

Many of these concerns were highlighted in a huge $246 billion settlement between the tobacco industry and the state attorneys general. The industry agreed to make these payments to the states over 25 years. The money will be used to reimburse state governments for health-care costs of smoking-related illnesses and to fund smoking-education programs. Additionally, the tobacco firms agreed that they would not use humans or cartoons in ads, effectively killing off Joe Camel and the Marlboro Man. Tobacco ads, already banned on radio and television, may be placed only in newspapers, direct-mail pieces, and adult magazines. Transit and billboard advertising—which as recently as 1998 had totaled $150 million in the United States—are now prohibited. The tobacco settlement is likely to have repercussions for all products deemed dangerous to public health.[29]

Businesses also face challenges when dealing with the consequences of diseases like AIDS, a devastating virus that breaks down the body's ability to defend itself against illness and infection. AIDS is especially dangerous because, on average, 5 years pass between a person's first exposure to the virus and actual development of the disease. During this period, people may not show any symptoms, and they probably don't even know they have the infection, but they are still carriers who can transmit the disease to others. This large pool of unknown carriers accounts for the rapid spread of the disease.

AIDS has forced companies to educate their workers about how to deal with employees and customers who have the deadly disease. Health care for AIDS patients can be incredibly expensive, straining the ability of small companies to pay for health-care coverage. Do companies have the right to test potential employees for the AIDS

They said it

"Joe Camel is dead. He had it coming."

Bruce Reed
Assistant to President Clinton for domestic policy

virus and avoid this expense? Some people believe that this screening would violate the rights of job applicants; others feel that a firm has a responsibility not to place AIDS patients in jobs where they could infect members of the general public. These are difficult questions. In resolving them, a business must balance the rights of individuals against the rights of society in general.

Protecting the Environment Businesses affect the world's fragile environment in a variety of ways. They consume huge amounts of energy, which increases the burning of

Figure 2.7   **Business Responsibilities to the General Public**

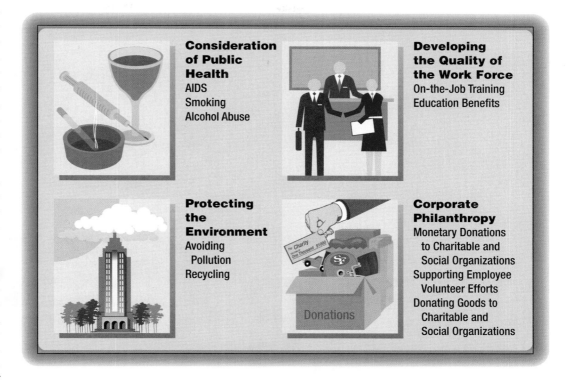

fossil fuels such as coal and oil for energy production. This activity introduces carbon dioxide and sulfur into the earth's atmosphere, substances that many scientists believe will result in dramatic climate changes over the next century. Meanwhile, the sulfur from fossil fuels combines with water vapor in the air to form sulfuric acid. The acid rain that results kills fish and trees and pollutes ground water. Wind can carry the sulfur around the entire globe. Sulfur from factories in the United States is damaging Canadian forests, and pollution from London smokestacks has been found in the forests and lakes of Scandinavia. Other production and manufacturing methods leave behind large quantities of waste materials that can further pollute the environment and fill already bulging landfills.

Pressures from government and the public have caused many businesses to reevaluate their impact on the environment. For many managers, finding ways to minimize the **pollution** and other environmental damage caused by their products or operating processes has become an important economic, legal, and social issue.

Perhaps no industry better demonstrates the changing relationship between business and the environment than the oil industry. When Royal Dutch/Shell Oil first explored the Amazon in search of oil in the mid-1980s, the company paid little attention to environmental issues. Workers cut

> ## They said it
>
> "Air pollution is turning Mother Nature prematurely gray."
>
> **Irv Kupcinet (1912 –)**
> **American newspaper columnist**

more than 1,250 miles of trails and roads through the rain forest, and mud and garbage from well drilling were dumped into rivers. After being strongly criticized by environmentalists for these and other actions, Royal Dutch/Shell promised Peru it would be more responsible in future natural gas projects. The firm has hired an anthropologist and a team of biologists from the Smithsonian Institute to survey the native plant and animal populations. This information will be used to return the project site to its natural state when the gas fields have been exhausted. To avoid road cutting, workers and equipment are shuttled into the site by air at a cost of $10,000 an hour. Special equipment is used to recycle potentially toxic waste, and whatever can't be treated or reused is hauled off the site.[30]

As Figure 2.8 points out, the world's rain forests are disappearing at the rate of an acre per second. Both socially conscious, profit-seeking firms like Mobil and not-for-profit organizations like the World Wildlife Fund are working to reverse this trend and to inform the world's citizens of the value of the rain forests to every individual.

Many consumers have more favorable impressions of environmentally conscious businesses; in fact, they often prefer to buy from such firms. To target these customers, companies use *green marketing*, a marketing strategy that promotes an environmentally safe product. For example,

Figure 2.8   **Protecting the Rain Forest and the World's Oceans**

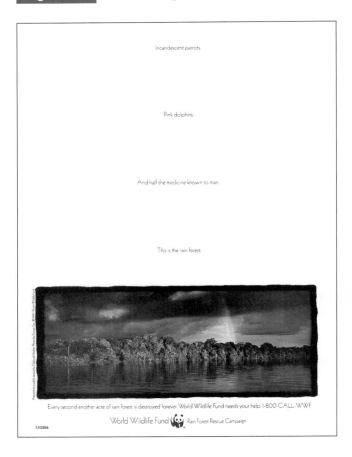

Incandescent parrots.

Pink dolphins.

And half the medicine known to man.

This is the rain forest.

Every second another acre of rain forest is destroyed forever. World Wildlife Fund needs your help. 1-800-CALL-WWF

World Wildlife Fund Rain Forest Rescue Campaign

It's two of the safest ships ever built.

It's Mobil's *Raven*, and inside the hull that keeps water out is another hull keeping the oil in. Between them is a safety zone 13 feet wide, enough distance between oil and ocean to have prevented most of history's collision-caused spills. The *Raven* is our second double-hull supertanker (our *Eagle* was the first ever built and operated by an oil company), and two more are in the works.

Even without double hulls, they're amazing vessels. Their navigation systems are so precise that a 50-yard course deviation (less than the ship's width) causes alarms to go off. And Mobil crew training never stops. With 2.2 million barrels of oil on board, no one is more aware of the risks than we are. No one is more watchful or invests more in safety either. To learn more, visit www.mobil.com.

Mobil The energy to make a difference.

one office manager chose Northeast Utilities for her company's electric supplier because it draws most of its power from hydroelectric dams rather than coal and nuclear plants. Choosing Northeast costs about $10 more a month but it "fits our environmental concerns."[31]

However, a business cannot simply claim that its goods or services are environmentally friendly. In 1992, the Federal Trade Commission issued guidelines for businesses to follow in making environmental claims. A firm must be able to prove that any environmental claim made about a good or service has been substantiated with reliable scientific evidence. Additionally, as shown in Figure 2.9, the FTC has given specific directions about how various environmental terms may be used in advertising and marketing.

Environmental concerns can lead to new technologies. General Motors, Honda, Toyota, and Ford, for instance, have developed electric cars that they hope will eventually

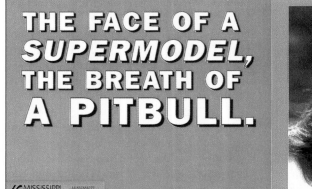

The need to be cool: The Mississippi State Department of Health uses part of the state's $3.4 billion settlement with the tobacco industry in an attempt to sway nonsmoking teens from ever picking up the habits of smoking or dipping (chewing) tobacco. The billboards appeal to a tried-and-true staple of high school worries—image.

BUSINESS TOOL KIT

How to Be Charitable without Being a Chump

Although your firm may be staffed with Good Samaritans, plenty of unscrupulous people are willing to take advantage of your good intentions. If you are unfamiliar with a charity, but think it's something you might like to support, first find out what the group does in your area. Then look for the following warning signs that can expose scams. If you encounter any of these practices, take a much closer look before shelling out a donation.

▼ *Solicitations designed to make you cry, not think.* Charities should provide specific information about their programs. If you're not sure what they intend to do with your money, call the group and ask.

▼ *Vague claims of charity donations from sales of a service or good.* Typically, less than 10 percent of the purchase price goes to the charity.

▼ *Requests for donations in cash.* Almost always a bad idea. Cash donations can be pilfered or lost, and there's no record of your contribution for tax purposes.

▼ *Phone solicitors who want personal financial information, such as your credit card or checking account numbers.* Ask the caller to mail you information, and hang up on anyone who tries to pressure you into making a donation right away. Honest charities willingly wait.

A valuable source of information to help givers find charities that suit their needs is Guidestar. Using IRS data, this service provides online reports detailing the finances and programs of more than 600,000 charities.

WWW. **www.guidestar.org**

Source: Warning signs reported in Sandra Block, "Warning Signs Can Expose Scams," *USA Today*, December 5, 1997, p. 4B.

---

replace now-standard gas-burning vehicles. The automakers are pushing development of electric vehicles in response to government efforts to curb pollution. California regulators have mandated that, by 2003, 10 percent of the new cars and trucks sold in the state must be electric vehicles. New York and Massachusetts have enacted similar regulations, and ten other states plus the District of Columbia are considering similar laws.[32]

Another solution gaining acceptance among businesses is **recycling**—reprocessing used materials for reuse. Recycling could provide much of the raw material that manufacturers need, thereby conserving the world's natural resources and reducing the need for landfills. Several industries are experimenting on and developing ways to use recycled materials.

Take old tires like those shown in Figure 2.10, for example. At least one-third of the rubber in every tire comes from a tree, and with an estimated 800 million used tires in dumps across the United States, the importance of finding a use for them is two-fold: save trees and clean up the environment. Recently, entrepreneurs have been coming up with inventive new uses for recycled tires, from tarp anchors and planters to shoe soles and jungle gyms. In fact, uses

have been found for over 75 percent of all waste tires: Over 100 factories supplement coal fuel by burning tires; 150 million tires each year are used making cement, paper, electricity, lime, iron, and copper; the ground-rubber market consumes another 12 million tires a year; and tire fuel is expected to gain wider acceptance in the near future.[33]

Developing the Quality of the Work Force In the past, a nation's wealth has often been based on its money, production equipment, and natural resources. A country's true wealth, however, lies in its people. An educated, skilled work force provides the intellectual know-how required to develop new technology, improve productivity, and compete in the global marketplace. It is becoming increasingly clear that in order to remain competitive, U.S. business must assume more responsibility for enhancing the quality of its work force. Since 1991, hotel chain Marriott Corp. has trained over 600 former welfare recipients as entry-level employees. The following Business Hall of Fame box

Business Directory

recycling reprocessing of used materials for reuse.

Figure 2.9 FTC Guidelines for Environmental Claims in Green Marketing

In July 1992, the Federal Trade Commission spelled out exactly how various terms should be used in marketing and advertising to avoid misleading consumers about a product's environmental friendliness.

If a business says a product is...	The product or package must...
Biodegradable	break down and return to nature in a reasonably short period of time.
Recyclable	be entirely reusable as new materials in the manufacture or assembly of a new product or package.
Refillable	be included in a system for the collection and return of the package for refill. If consumers have to find a way to refill it themselves, it is not *refillable.*
Ozone Safe/Ozone Friendly	must not contain any ozone-depleting ingredient.

with Pacific Enterprises, it faced strong questioning about its ethnic diversity record. Minority advocacy groups argued that the firm had lagged far behind other utilities in diversifying the ethnic makeup of its management and in supporting economic development efforts for low-income communities.[35]

Oil giant Texaco had its own diversity crisis. When top company executives were exposed for using derogatory terms when referring to African Americans, the firm faced public outrage and threats of boycotts. Several employees filed a class-

reveals how successful corporate-sponsored training and employment programs can be.

Most new jobs require college-educated workers. Many professions demand as much as 10 years of study beyond high school, and even the least-skilled jobs require certain levels of reading, computing, and thinking abilities. Business must encourage students to stay in school, continue their education, and sharpen their skills. Companies must also encourage employees to learn new skills and remain competitive.

An added benefit of supporting educational initiatives may be a more positive image in the eyes of customers. How can a company improve its image? According to a recent survey, over 70 percent of respondents recommended donating school materials and equipment, supporting literacy programs for children and adults, and supporting part-time work programs for kids.[34]

Organizations also face enormous responsibilities for helping women, members of various cultural groups, and those who are physically challenged to contribute fully to the economy. Failure to do so is not only a waste of over half of the nation's work force, but it can also have a devastating impact on a firm's public image. Firms such as Lockheed Martin use messages like the one in Figure 2.11 to communicate the importance of diversity to continued leadership in cutting-edge technologies.

However, newspaper and television news reports all too often include stories of firms facing negative consequences from diversity issues. When West Coast electric utility Enova Corp. recently proposed a $4.3 billion merger

Figure 2.10 Recycling Old Tires for New Uses

Tire Dump
California
5 October
1600 hrs

DUMP THEM, YOU BREAK THE LAW. RECYCLE IMPROPERLY, YOU BREAK THE LAW. MEANWHILE, MORE TIRES JUST CAME IN.

Whether your company produces waste, tries to recycle or depends on a steady supply of raw materials, your business is bound to be affected by environmental controls.

There are thousands of regulations, both in the U.S. and overseas, designed to protect the environment. These environmental standards are in a constant state of flux, and can have far-reaching risk implications for all kinds of businesses.

Fortunately, AIG specializes in designing the kind of custom coverages you need to cope successfully with changing conditions. In fact, AIG is the only worldwide insurance and financial organization that helps manage your business risks with a broad range of customized services. Services like cleanup cost cap, hedging and market-making in commodities and stop-loss protection. And we've got the top financial ratings to back us up. So we'll be there to help keep your business rolling along.

AIG

WORLD LEADERS IN INSURANCE AND FINANCIAL SERVICES
American-International Group, Inc., Dept. A, 70 Pine Street, New York, NY 10270

Figure 2.11 **Lockheed Martin: Offering Career Opportunities as Diverse as Its Employees**

IMAGINE IF IT HAD BEEN PAINTED IN ONLY ONE COLOR.

Monet's art celebrated color, fresh perspectives and striking diversities. At Lockheed Martin, we believe wholeness comes from diversity. And in diversity, a range of insights and viewpoints that leads to creative solutions. Solutions that set Lockheed Martin apart. To continue our leadership role in cutting edge technologies, we're committed to having a diverse work force. ♦ Positions are available for experienced personnel. The corporation also has more than 1,000 entry-level career opportunities for recent college graduates in engineering. If you'd like to work for a company where the opportunities are as diverse as the employees, fax or send your resume to Lockheed Martin listed below.

LOCKHEED MARTIN

©1997 Lockheed Martin Corporation

♦ Manager Internal Audit	♦ Senior Accountant	♦ Senior Accountant
♦ Senior Internal Auditors	of Financial Reporting	of Consolidation and Analysis
♦ Information Technology Auditors (IT)	♦ Associate Benefits Analyst	♦ Executive Secretary

Please fax your resume to Dept. 0A9704b, (800) 461-5789, or mail to
Lockheed Martin Corporation, Box 8048, Dept. 0A9704b, Bldg. 10/Rm. 1019, Philadelphia, PA 19101

action lawsuit against Texaco, alleging that the company discriminated against African American employees in its promotion and performance appraisal practices.

Corporate Philanthropy As pointed out in Chapter 1, not-for-profit organizations play an important role in society by serving the public good. They provide the human resources that enhance the quality of life in communities around the world. In order to fulfill this mission, however, many not-for-profit organizations rely on financial contributions from the business community. Businesses receive substantial pressure from government and consumers to lend this support. They respond by donating over $8 billion each year to not-for-profit organizations. This **corporate philanthropy** includes cash contributions, donations of equipment and products, and supporting the volunteer ef-forts of company employees.[36] Local cultural organizations are likely to be the most frequent recipients of corporate generosity. The most recent data indicate that 61 percent of surveyed companies reported such contributions. Adopt-a-school programs were a close second in popularity, followed by community development and housing and job training programs.[37] As Table 2.3 shows, the range of programs supported by corporate giving is very broad.

Corporate philanthropy can have many positive benefits beyond the purely altruistic rewards of giving. Among the benefits are higher employee morale, enhanced image, and improved customer relationships.[38] Hanna Andersson, a mail-order children's wear firm, donates 5 percent of its profits to charity, far above the national corporate giving average of 1 percent. Additionally, the firm invites customers to send back outfits that their children have outgrown. The company then donates the clothing to needy families. In return, the customer gets a 20 percent discount on the next purchase. More than 3,000 "Hannadowns" pour into corporate headquarters each month.[39]

In an effort to maximize the benefits of corporate giving in an era of downsizing, businesses have become more selective of the causes and charities they choose to support. Many seek to align their marketing efforts with their charitable giving. This is known as *cause-related marketing*. Boston Market, for example, conducted a great deal of research before giving its financial support to Y-Me's hotline number at all of its stores and providing free meals for chemotherapy patients. "We chose this because breast cancer affects the whole family. . . . Our business is about families, and we want to do something to help them," says Robin Showdeir, Boston Market's director of cultural relations.

Working Assets, a San Francisco provider of credit cards and long-distance phone service, asks its customers to decide which causes are important to them. Each of the firm's 260,000 customers votes on how much the company should give each of the 200 not-for-profit organizations that Working Assets supports. Last year, Working Assets contributed $2.5 million to not-for-profit organizations and causes chosen by its customers.

Another form of corporate philanthropy is volunteerism. In their roles as corporate citizens, thousands of businesses encourage their employees to contribute their efforts to projects as diverse as Habitat for Humanity, local literacy programs, and Red Cross blood drives. In addition

BUSINESS HALL OF FAME

Bill Strickland: Modeling the Future with Education, Training, and Hope

At 17, Andy Karaman is thinking about college. Typical for someone at that age, right? Not necessarily. Andy will be the first in his family to attend college, the first to dream of a career in art.

Janine Johnson is planning on owning her own restaurant. A single mother of four on welfare, she will soon complete a course in culinary arts. Commuting two hours each way, she spends her days studying to become a chef.

What inspires these people to follow their dreams? Bill Strickland says, "You start with the perception that the world is an unlimited opportunity." And that's just what he did. When he began the Manchester Craftsmen's Guild (MCG) and took over the Bidwell Training Center (BTC), Strickland began reshaping the business of social change. With a combined staff of 110 and a budget over $6 million, both programs offer support, training, and hope—all free of charge.

Strickland knows what it's like to feel hemmed in by life. A 16-year-old black kid in a decaying neighborhood, he wanted out but couldn't find the way. Then opportunity knocked one day as he looked from a dark hallway through a doorway into a sunlit classroom and saw a man absorbed in shaping a vessel out of a rotating mound of clay. That doorway led to a "whole range of possibilities and experiences I had not explored." He walked in and introduced himself to ceramics teacher Frank Ross, who became his mentor for the next 20 years. Ross taught Strickland about pottery—and much more. Strickland remembers, "He said, 'You have the talent and the resources to take control of your life,' and I believed him. I saw a radiant, hopeful image of how the world ought to be."

Two years later, Strickland entered college, where in 1968—before he had even graduated—he decided to do something to bring hope back to the streets. He opened MCG, and after-school program that uses art to teach life skills to at-risk school kids—the same program that Andy Karaman attends. In 1971, Strickland was asked to take over BTC, a partnership program with local companies that trains adults for real work in real jobs—the same program that offers Janine Johnson training and support.

Using these two programs, Strickland is rebuilding his community from two directions: getting troubled kids into college and giving adults career training. In 1983, with only $112 in the bank, Strickland launched a fundraising drive to construct an $8-million building to house these rapidly growing programs. The effort took three years, but the contacts he made have lasted much longer.

Strickland's loyal supporters include former president George Bush (who named Strickland to the board of the National Endowment for the Arts), Hillary Clinton, Harvard Business School, Harvard Graduate School of Education (where Strickland serves as an adjunct faculty member), San Francisco Mayor Willie Brown and jazz musician Herbie Hancock (who are replicating Strickland's programs in San Francisco), and the MacArthur Foundation (that awarded Strickland a $295,000 "genius" grant in 1996).

to making tangible contributions to the well-being of fellow citizens, such programs generate considerable public support and goodwill for the companies and their employees. In some cases, the volunteer efforts occur mostly during off-hours for employees. In other instances, the firm permits its work force to volunteer during regular working hours. Chemical giant Hoechst Celanese executives are shown taking time off from a meeting to help renovate a North Carolina facility for adults with special needs in Figure 2.12.

Table 2.3	Favorite Charities of Selected Companies	
Company and Date Program Started	**Cause**	**Total Amount Donated**
Avon (1993)	Breast cancer awareness	$22 million
American Express (1993)	Hunger relief and prevention	$20 million
Chevrolet (1989)	Tree planting and urban forestry	$5 million
Ralston Purina (1990)	Endangered species preservation	$3.5 million
Estée Lauder (1993)	Breast cancer research	$2.2 million
Visa USA (1996)	Children's literacy	$1 million
Sterling Vineyards (1992)	Public land conservation	$400 thousand
Quaker (1996)	Breast cancer research	$160 thousand

Both MCG and BTC are success stories. Over the past five years, 75 to 80 percent of the kids in the MCG program have gone on to college, and 78 percent of the adults who graduate from BTC find jobs. Strickland continues to strengthen these programs by never losing sight of the possibilities and expanding on them. For example, he oversees a jazz concert hall, a Grammy Award–winning record label, and a food-services company, and he has begun a new national effort to teach not-for-profit leaders how to think like entrepreneurs. As he pursues diverse directions such as fund-raising, franchising, and real-estate development, Strickland shows his flair for mixing profit and not-for-profit goals to shape social miracles for folks like Andy Karaman and Janine Johnson.

QUESTIONS FOR CRITICAL THINKING

1. **Do you agree with Bill Strickland's suggestion that self-perception controls what people do in life by determining what opportunities they choose or refuse? Defend your answer.**

2. **Strickland successfully recruits profit-seeking companies to work with not-for-profit organizations. Beside the good feelings they get from helping others, what benefits do the for-profit companies receive from these joint efforts?**

3. **As Mayor Willie Brown and jazz musician Herbie Hancock try to replicate Strickland's programs in San Francisco, can they expect their programs to be as successful as the original without the inspiration of Strickland himself? In other words, can they replicate Strickland's vision and enthusiasm as well as his programs? Explain your answer.**

Sources: Ryan Rhea, "Social Visionary and Entrepreneur Bill Strickland to Deliver an Address as Part of Washington University's Assembly Series," News & Information, Office of Public Affairs, accessed at wupa.wustl.edu, February 9, 1999; Bidwell Training Center home page, accessed at www.realpittsburgh.com, February 23, 1999; and Sara Terry, "Genius at Work," *Fast Company*, September 1998, pp. 170–181.

Responsibilities to Customers

Businesspeople share a social and ethical responsibility to treat their customers fairly and act in a manner that is not harmful to them. Auto-safety advocate Ralph Nader first pioneered this idea in the late 1960s. Since then, **consumerism**—the public demand that a business consider the wants and needs of its customers in making decisions—has gained widespread acceptance. Consumerism is based on the belief that consumers have certain rights. The most frequently quoted statement of consumer rights was made by President John F. Kennedy in 1962; it included the rights to be safe, to be informed, to choose, and to be heard. Numerous state and federal laws have been implemented since then to protect these rights.

The Right to Be Safe Contemporary businesspeople must recognize obligations, both moral and legal, to ensure the safe operation of their products. Consumers should feel assured that the goods and services they purchase will not cause injuries in normal use. *Product liability* refers to the responsibility of manufacturers for injuries and damages caused by their products. Products that lead to injuries, either directly or indirectly, can have disastrous consequences for their makers. Dow Corning, for instance, was ordered to pay millions of dollars in damages for injuries to women from the silicone in breast implants it manufactured. The company eventually had to declare bankruptcy. Dow Corning's parent company, Dow Chemical, was also held liable for damages from the breast implants, even though the parent company argued that it had never made silicone, tested it for human use, or claimed it was safe.[40]

Many companies put their products through rigorous testing to avoid safety problems. Still, testing alone cannot foresee every eventuality. Companies must consider all possibilities and provide adequate warning of potential dangers. Although Mattel has a strict testing program for its toys, the company did not recognize the real-world threat one doll would pose. The Cabbage Patch Snacktime dolls were designed to gobble meals of fake carrots and French fries, but they ended up chewing on children's hair, as well. After reports of 35 hair-eating episodes, the Consumer Product Safety Commission urged Mattel to issue a warning about the danger, along with instructions for disabling the dolls, on packages.[41]

When a product does pose a threat to customer safety, a responsible manufacturer responds quickly to either repair the problem or recall the dangerous product. For example, when defective cranks on mountain bikes made by Shimano American Corp. caused 22 injuries, the 76-year-old company voluntarily recalled millions of mountain bikes worldwide.[42]

Safety planning is now a vital management issue for many businesses. Companies and industry associations have sponsored voluntary improvements in safety standards. Consider Jack-in-the-Box. After an outbreak of food-related illnesses and deaths was linked to undercooked hamburgers in its restaurants, the firm aggressively sought to tighten internal safety measures. The company also pushed for new state and federal laws to improve food-handling safety throughout the restaurant industry.[43]

The Right to Be Informed Consumers should have access to enough education and product information to make responsible buying decisions. In their efforts to promote and sell their goods and services, companies can easily neglect consumers' right to be fully informed. The Federal Trade Commission and other federal and state agencies have established rules and regulations that govern advertising truthfulness. These rules prohibit businesses from making unsubstantiated claims about the performance or superiority of their goods or services. They also require businesses to avoid misleading consumers. Businesses that fail to comply face scrutiny from the FTC and consumer protection organizations.

A television ad for General Motors' Chevrolet S-Blazer, for example, promoted a 2-year lease for $1,360 down and $299 a month. Further information about costs

Figure 2.12	**Volunteerism: A Growing Form of Corporate Philanthropy**

and restrictions was shown in light-colored fine print that appeared on the television screen for just 5 seconds. The FTC said this ad was misleading, because consumers were not adequately informed about the full costs associated with leasing the vehicle. GM wasn't the only automobile company to experience the FTC's wrath, which labeled the industry "deplorable."[44]

The Food and Drug Administration (FDA), which sets standards for advertising conducted by drug manufacturers, recently eased restrictions for prescription drug advertising on television. In print ads, drug makers are required to spell out potential side effects and the proper uses of prescription drugs. Because of the requirement to disclose this information, prescription drug television advertising was limited. Now, however, the FDA says drug ads on radio and TV can directly promote a prescription drug's benefits if they provide a quick way for consumers to learn about side effects, such as displaying a toll-free number or Internet address.[45]

The ad for Prozac shown in Figure 2.13 includes over six paragraphs of information—considerably less than the pageful of tiny type that was once required. Recently, however, the Food and Drug Administration reduced the amount of information that prescription drug advertisers must provide in all ads for potential patients about the medical effects of using certain drugs.

The responsibility of business to preserve consumers' right to be informed extends beyond avoiding misleading advertising, however. All communications with customers—from salespeople's comments to warranties and invoices—must be controlled to clearly and accurately inform customers. Sears recently agreed to refund at least $100 million to customers who were pressured to pay off their credit card debts even though they were protected by bankruptcy laws. When a person declares bankruptcy, the companies to which they owe money must work through the bankruptcy court to arrange payment. Instead, Sears went directly to its 200,000 customers who had declared bankruptcy and demanded payment, failing to inform them that they did not legally have to pay.[46]

The Internet raises new issues about the right to be informed. The online world is ripe for misleading or deceptive marketing claims. The National Consumers League, a consumer protection organization, notes that complaints against Internet marketers more than tripled in 1997. The most common complaints are extravagant promises, suspiciously low prices, or undelivered merchandise. The league has set up a Fraud Watch Web site to warn Internet users of marketing scams.[47] In one case, customers paid for reconditioned phone equipment purchased through the Internet from KRW Internet Sales & Marketing, but they never received the products. The Denver street address displayed by the firm on its Internet site turned out to be a private mail drop, and phone numbers listed there were disconnected local numbers.[48]

www. **www.fraud.org**

Despite strict product testing by Mattel, the company was forced to issue a public warning about the Cabbage Patch Snacktime Kids doll, which nibbles on plastic French fries, as shown here, as well as on children's hair.

To protect themselves against claims of insufficient disclosure, businesses often include warnings on products. As Figure 2.14 shows, sometimes these warnings go far beyond what a reasonable consumer would expect.

The Right to Choose Consumers have the right to choose which goods and services they need and want to purchase. Socially responsible firms attempt to preserve this right, even if they reduce their own sales and profits in the process. Other companies, however, are not as ethical about protecting a consumer's right to choose.

Consider, for example, what happened to Louis Poggi, who had an account with the stock brokerage firm Investors Associates. When he received a telephone call from a salesperson at Investors Associates trying to sell him stock, Poggi turned down the offer. A few weeks later he was surprised to learn that the salesperson had purchased 1,000 shares of the

| Figure 2.13 | Informing Consumers about the Side Effects of Prescription Drugs |

Depression hurts.

Depression isn't just feeling down. It's a real illness with real causes. Depression can be triggered by stressful life events, like divorce or a death in the family. Or it can appear suddenly, for no apparent reason.

Some people think you can just will yourself out of a depression. That's not true. When you're clinically depressed, one thing that can happen is the level of serotonin (a chemical in your body) may drop. So you may have trouble sleeping. Feel unusually sad or irritable. Find it hard to concentrate. Lose your appetite. Lack energy. Or have trouble feeling pleasure. These are some of the symptoms that can point to

depression—especially if they last for more than a couple of weeks and if normal, everyday life feels like too much to handle.

To help bring serotonin levels closer to normal, the medicine doctors now prescribe most often is Prozac.® Prozac isn't a "happy pill." It's not a tranquilizer. It won't take away your personality. Depression can do that, but Prozac can't.

Prozac has been carefully studied for nearly 10 years. Like other antidepressants, it isn't habit-forming. But some people do experience mild side effects, like upset stomach, headaches, difficulty sleeping, drowsiness, anxiety and

nervousness. These tend to go away within a few weeks of starting treatment, and usually aren't serious enough to make most people stop taking it. However, if you are concerned about a side effect, or if you develop a rash, tell your doctor right away. And don't forget to tell your doctor about any other medicines you are taking. Some people should not take Prozac, especially people on MAO inhibitors.

As you start feeling better, your doctor can suggest therapy or other means to help you work through your depression. Remember, Prozac is a prescription medicine, and it isn't right for everyone. Only your doctor can decide if Prozac

is right for you—or for someone you love. Prozac has been prescribed for more than 17 million Americans. Chances are someone you know is feeling sunny again because of it.

Prozac can help.

pr·zac
fluoxetine hydrochloride

Welcome back.

Please see important information on following page. *Lilly*

Figure 2.14 **Wacky Warning Labels**

The number of product liability lawsuits has skyrocketed in the past decade. To protect themselves, businesses have become more careful about including warnings on products. However, some companies may go overboard, as demonstrated by these actual product warning labels:

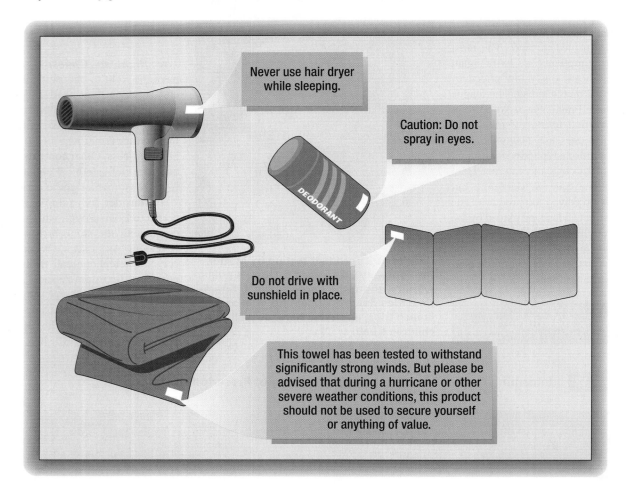

Never use hair dryer while sleeping.

Caution: Do not spray in eyes.

Do not drive with sunshield in place.

This towel has been tested to withstand significantly strong winds. But please be advised that during a hurricane or other severe weather conditions, this product should not be used to secure yourself or anything of value.

stock in Poggi's name and was demanding payment. State regulators, who canceled Poggi's "purchase" and other unauthorized transactions, estimate that over a 2-year period, Investors Associates used similar tactics to relieve unsuspecting customers of more than $10 million.[49]

Since the long-distance telephone industry has been deregulated, many customers have also been the victims of fraud. Several unscrupulous long-distance carriers have duped customers into switching their service through an unsavory practice called *slamming*. The firms induce customers to sign contest-entry forms that contain less-than-obvious wording saying they agree to be switched. In other cases, long-distance companies have switched customers without their consent after making telemarketing calls to them.

The Right to Be Heard Consumers should be able to express legitimate complaints to appropriate parties. Many companies exert considerable effort to ensure full hearings for consumer complaints. Ford Motor Co., for example, has set up a consumer appeals board to resolve service complaints. Similarly, The Custom Foot, a men's and women's shoe store chain, places high value on satisfying customers. Each pair of Custom Foot shoes is made to order according to individual customer preferences and measurements. After every sale, a store representative calls each customer to make certain that no problems or complaints have arisen since he or she received the products. The Custom Foot then uses this feedback to fine-tune its sales and production processes.[50]

Responsibilities to Employees

As Chapter 1 explained, one of the most important business resources is an organization's work force. Companies that are able to attract skilled and knowledgeable employees are better able to meet the challenges of competing on a global basis. However, in return, businesses have wide-ranging responsibilities to their employees. These include workplace safety, quality of life issues, avoiding discrimination, and preventing sexual harassment and sexism.

Workplace Safety In the earliest part of the 20th century, few businesses paid much attention to the safety of their workers. In fact, most business owners viewed employees as mere cogs in the production process. Workers, often very young children, toiled in frequently dangerous conditions. In 1911, 146 people, mostly young girls, died in a fire at the Triangle Shirtwaist Factory in New York City. Contributing to the massive loss of life were the sweatshop working conditions at the factory, including overcrowding, blocked exits, and a lack of fire escapes. The horrifying tragedy forced businesses to begin to recognize their responsibility for their workers' safety.

The safety and health of workers while on the job is now an important business responsibility. The Occupational Safety and Health Administration (OSHA) is the main federal regulatory force in setting workplace safety and health standards. These mandates range from broad guidelines on storing hazardous materials to specific standards for worker safety in industries like construction, manufacturing, and mining. OSHA tracks and investigates workplace accidents and has the authority to fine employers who are found liable for injuries and deaths that occur on the job. While businesses are required to comply with many OSHA regulations, ultimately each company's management must set standards and implement programs to ensure that workers are kept safe in the workplace.

Executives at Georgia-Pacific, for example, had a serious safety problem. Accident rates in the forest-products company's paper mills, sawmills, and plywood factories were high, averaging nine serious injuries per 100 employees each year. Twenty-six workers died on the job between 1986 and 1990. To reduce accidents among the company's 47,000 workers, Georgia-Pacific launched a safety crusade.

One of the first changes executives sought was a transformation in employee and management attitudes. Previously, employees took dangerous risks in operating machinery, because they felt pressured by management to get products out at any cost. Management made it clear that safety would begin to take priority. Workers who spot a potential safety problem can now shut down production lines. Intensive training sessions are held throughout the company on a regular basis, reinforcing the message that safety comes first. Managers are held accountable for the safety records of their departments, and safety success stories are beamed via the company's SafeTV cable network to 350 Georgia-Pacific sites around the United States. The result? By 1996, nearly 80 percent of the company's plants operated without injuries, and no employees died on the job. The company's sawmills are now about 70 percent safer than the industry average.[51]

Quality of Life Issues Balancing work and family is becoming harder for many employees. They find themselves squeezed between working long hours and handling child-care problems, caring for elderly parents, and solving other family crises. In a recent survey of 12,000 workers, only 49 percent said they could have a good family life and still get ahead at work.[52] Those juggling work with life's other demands aren't just working mothers. Childless couples, single people, and men all expressed frustration with the pressures of balancing work and family. Helping workers find solutions to these quality of life issues has become an important concern of many businesses, but finding answers isn't always easy. A recent *Business Week* survey ranked five firms at the top of the "family friendly" ranking. Table 2.4 lists the most family-oriented firms and their strongest family-friendly characteristics.

Some companies offer flexible work arrangements to support employees. Hewlett-Packard Co. has redesigned jobs in several units in order to allow employees to work from home, work part-time, or work shortened work weeks. All managers at First Chicago NBD Corp. are required to submit written plans specifying how employee job flexibility can be increased. At Baxter Export, the international shipping division of medical equipment maker Baxter International, 30 percent of workers telecommute, share jobs, or work part-time.[53]

Table 2.4	Top Five Family-Friendly Firms	
Company	**Grade**	**What It Does Right**
MBNA America	A	Strong family friendly culture and programs
Motorola	A−	Continuous communication through Intranet
Barnett Banks (now Nationsbank)	A−	On-site primary school, car cleaning
Sequent Computer Systems	A−	On-site kindergarten, first grade
First Tennessee Bank	A−	Measures effect of work-family strategies on profits

Table 2.5	Laws Designed to Ensure Equal Opportunity
Law	**Key Provisions**
Title VII of the Civil Rights Act of 1964 (as amended by the Equal Employment Opportunity Act of 1972)	Prohibits discrimination in hiring, promotion, compensation, training, or dismissal on the basis of race, color, religion, sex, or national origin.
Age Discrimination in Employment Act of 1968 (as amended)	Prohibits discrimination in employment against anyone aged 40 or over in hiring, promotion, compensation, training, or dismissal.
Equal Pay Act of 1963	Requires equal pay for men and women working for the same firm in jobs that require equal skill, effort, and responsibility.
Vocational Rehabilitation Act of 1973	Requires government contractors and subcontractors to take affirmative action to employ and promote qualified disabled workers. Coverage now extends to all federal employees. Coverage has been broadened by the passage of similar laws in more than 20 states, and through court rulings, to include persons with communicable diseases, including AIDS.
Vietnam Era Veterans Readjustment Act of 1974	Requires government contractors and subcontractors to take affirmative action to employ and retain disabled veterans. Coverage now extends to all federal employees and has been broadened by the passage of similar laws in over 20 states.
Pregnancy Discrimination Act of 1978	Requires employers to treat pregnant women and new mothers the same as other employees for all employment-related purposes, including receipt of benefits under company benefit programs.
Americans with Disabilities Act of 1990	Makes discrimination against the disabled illegal in public accommodations, transportation, and telecommunications; stiffens employer penalties for intentional discrimination on the basis of an employee's disability.
Civil Rights Act of 1991	Makes it easier for workers to sue their employers for alleged discrimination. Enables victims of sexual discrimination to collect punitive damages; includes employment decisions and on-the-job issues such as sexual harassment, unfair promotions, and unfair dismissal. The employer must prove that it did not engage in discrimination.
Family and Medical Leave Act of 1993	Requires all businesses with 50 or more employees to provide up to 12 weeks of unpaid leave annually to employees who have had a child or are adopting a child, or are becoming foster parents, who are caring for a seriously ill relative or spouse, or who are themselves seriously ill. Workers must meet certain eligibility requirements.

Other firms offer benefits such as subsidized child care or on-site education and shopping to assist workers trying to balance work and family. At MBNA, bank employees can bring their children to the company's on-site day-care center, get their clothes tailored in the office, and work out in the firm's fitness center.[54]

Another solution has been to offer **family leave** to employees who need to deal with family matters. The Family and Medical Leave Act of 1993 requires every business with 50 or more employees to provide up to 12 weeks of unpaid leave annually for an employee who has a child or is adopting a child, who is becoming a foster parent, caring for a seriously ill relative or spouse, or who is seriously ill. Workers must meet certain eligibility requirements. Employers must continue to provide health benefits during the leave and guarantee that employees will return to equivalent jobs. The issue of who is entitled to health benefits can also create a dilemma as companies struggle to balance the needs of their employees against the staggering costs of health care.

> ## They said it
>
> "It doesn't matter if a cat is black or white, so long as it catches mice."
>
> Deng Xiaoping (1904-1997)
> Chinese premier

Ensuring Equal Opportunity on the Job Business-people face many challenges managing an increasingly diverse work force in the 21st century. By 2050, ethnic minorities and immigrants will make up nearly half of the U.S. work force. Businesses will also need to find ways to responsibly recruit and manage older workers, disabled workers, and workers with varying lifestyles. All of these groups deserve the right to work in an environment that is nondiscriminatory.

An effective diversity effort requires commitment from top management and the involvement of employees at all levels. One firm that has actively sought to manage and benefit from diversity is CoreStates. The bank's CEO, Terrence A. Larsen, initiated the effort after he noticed problems with interactions between various employee groups. At the company's annual employee meeting, he announced he would no longer tolerate bigotry, sexism, or infighting between employees with different backgrounds. He appointed a senior vice president in charge of diversity and change management, tasking her with encouraging awareness of diversity issues. For example, all CoreStates managers must attend a 5-day training program that helps them understand how individual, group, and organization attitudes and expectations affect relationships and communications between diverse groups. The company also encourages employees to establish networks based on their diverse interests and concerns. Currently, there are networks for senior-level women, people of color, gays and lesbians, and white males.[55]

To a great extent, efforts at managing diversity are regulated by law. The Civil Rights Act (1964) outlawed many kinds of discriminatory practices, and Title VII of the act specifically prohibits discrimination in employment. As shown in Table 2.5, other nondiscrimination laws include the Equal Pay Act (1963), the Age Discrimination in Employment Act (1967), the Equal Employment Opportunity Act (1972), the Pregnancy Discrimination Act (1978), the Civil Rights Act of 1991, and numerous executive orders. The Americans with Disabilities Act (1990) protects the rights of physically challenged people. The Vietnam Era Veterans Readjustment Act (1974) protects the employment of veterans of the Vietnam war.

The **Equal Employment Opportunity Commission (EEOC)** was created to increase job opportunities for women and minorities and to help end discrimination based on race, color, religion, disability, sex, or national origin in any personnel action. The EEOC can help employers set up programs to increase job opportunities for women, minorities, the disabled, and people in other protected categories. Part 3 takes a closer look at diversity and employment discrimination issues as part of a discussion of human resource management.

Sexual Harassment and Sexism Every employer has a responsibility to ensure that all workers are treated fairly and are safe from sexual harassment. **Sexual harassment** refers to unwelcome and inappropriate actions of a sex-

The Women's Bureau of the U.S. Department of Labor publishes information and offers a toll-free number and regional centers to help employees deal with sexual harassment at work. The brochure shown describes sexual harassment and explains how to handle it.

ual nature in the workplace. It is a form of sex discrimination that violates the Civil Rights Act of 1964, which gave both men and women the right to file lawsuits for intentional sexual harassment.

Over 10,000 sexual harassment complaints are filed with the Equal Employment Opportunity Commission each year, and thousands of other cases are either handled internally by companies or never reported. Research shows that 90 percent of *Fortune* 500 firms have dealt with complaints about sexual harassment, more than one-third of them have been sued at least once, and a quarter of them have been sued repeatedly.[56] In another study, 88 percent of 9,000 women surveyed said they had been sexually harassed on the job one or more times.[57]

Sexual harassment is divided into two types. The first category occurs when an employee is pressured to comply with unwelcome advances and requests for sexual favors in return for job security, promotions, and raises. Sexual harassment can also result from a hostile work environment in which an employee feels hassled or degraded because of unwelcome flirting, lewd comments, or obscene jokes. The

Business Directory

sexual harassment inappropriate actions of a sexual nature in the workplace.

SOLVING AN ETHICAL CONTROVERSY

Should Whistle-Blowers Get a Share of the Money They Help Recover?

Few on-the-job ethical dilemmas are more gut wrenching than the issue of what an employee can do about a company engaged in illegal, immoral or unethical practices—especially when the infractions are ongoing and the company refuses to change. For some employees, the potential damage to the public good outweighs their loyalty to the organization, and they turn to the media or government authorities to expose the wrongdoing and correct it. But the act of whistle-blowing often exerts a steep price for the person who actually blows the whistle—ostracism by fellow workers and, frequently, dismissal when the employer finds out.

Rob Merena, a SmithKline Beecham billing analyst in Collegeville, Pennsyl-

vania, got nowhere in reporting improper charges being billed to the U.S. government. When he called the government fraud hot line, he was referred to the office of the U.S. Attorney in Philadelphia. He agreed to continue working undercover for another 18 months and then assist the FBI and other government agencies in reviewing subpoenaed SmithKline Beecham documents and computer files. All the while, he was sworn to secrecy, and all the while he paid a high price for his cooperation.

Once Merena's role in the investigation became known to his superiors, he lost his $60,000-a-year job. He fell deeply into debt and had trouble supporting his family. And friends from SmithKline began to shun him. The stress became overwhelming. He suffered panic attacks, and his wife often cried herself to sleep.

Then the nearly-broke Merena dis-

covered something about whistle-blowers that he had not known before. In cases involving the federal government, whistle-blowers can receive as much as 30 percent of recovered funds. Merena asked for his share of the settlement, but the Justice Department said no—he didn't deserve the money because his contribution wasn't all that helpful and only added to a case that was already in progress. So Merena went back to court, this time to fight his former ally—the U.S. government.

Ultimately, Merena prevailed and received an award of $52 million. Although the federal government paid $9.7 million, its attorneys appealed the rest. But Merena joined the ranks of millionaires and could potentially receive millions more. However, he is still having trouble finding a job, because he has to tell prospective employers why he left SmithKline.

When asked about regrets, Merena

---

courts have ruled that allowing sexually oriented materials like pinup calendars and pornographic magazines at the workplace can create a hostile atmosphere that interferes with an employee's ability to do the job. Employers are also legally responsible to protect employees from sexual harassment from customers and clients.[58] The EEOC's Web site informs employers and employees of criteria for identifying sexual harassment and how it should be handled in the workplace.

In one highly publicized case, female workers at Mitsubishi Motors Corp.'s Illinois factory charged that male co-workers routinely groped and grabbed at them. Some women said they were forced to have sex in order to win jobs. Pornographic drawings with the women's names on them were passed among workers on the assembly line. The company had no formal mechanism in place to allow employees to complain about sexual harassment. Those who objected informally found themselves shut out of job opportunities. To settle the resulting lawsuit, the company agreed to pay an estimated $9.5 million in damages to 23 female workers. Lawsuits filed by other female Mitsubishi workers could cost the company as much as $5 million more.[59]

www www.eeoc.gov

To avoid sexual harassment problems, many firms have established policies and employee education programs aimed at preventing such violations. An effective harassment prevention program should include:

▼ Issuing a specific policy statement prohibiting sexual harassment

▼ Developing a complaint procedure for employees to follow

▼ Creating a work atmosphere that encourages sexually harassed staffers to come forward

▼ Investigating and resolving complaints quickly, and taking disciplinary action against harassers

Unless all of these components are supported by top management, sexual harassment is difficult to eliminate.

Sexual harassment is often part of the broader problem of **sexism**—discrimination against members of either sex,

takes his time before responding: "No, I want to see this through to the end now. I'm thankful, though, that I didn't know the process before going into this."

Should Whistle-Blowers Benefit Financially from Their Actions?

PRO

1. When whistle-blowers report their employers to the media or government agencies, they pay a high price emotionally, financially, and professionally. They deserve a generous reward for their courage.

2. Even though employers, media firms, and government agencies have funds to cover the soaring legal expenses, whistle-blowers have no means of recovering their legal fees unless they receive a share of the settlement.

3. Without some fallback protection from the employer's retribution, the loss of income and security, and the anger and cruelty of fellow workers, honest workers may be forced to close their eyes and refuse to speak out against illegal or unethical practices on the job.

CON

1. The federal government should not have to pay significant amounts to whistle-blowers whose assistance is limited in scope or usefulness.

2. Adding jackpot payoffs for actions traditionally associated with good citizenship could turn otherwise honest, hard-working people into greedy bounty hunters who waste everyone's time with undeserving or unimportant cases.

3. It isn't fair to the American people for whistle-blowers to become millionaires for simply telling the truth about a company's questionable business practices. People should not need a reward for doing the right thing.

SUMMARY

Do large case awards help whistle-blowers weather the storm? Or does the money actually encourage employees to blow the whistle on their employers when the issue could have been resolved through internal channels? Whistle-blowers helped the government recover more than $1 billion during the past decade. Surely the emotional, financial, and professional price they endure is worth some kind of recompense. But should that reward make whistle-blowers rich beyond their dreams?

Sources: "Blue Cross Whistle-Blower Gets $29M," *The Associated Press*, January 27, 1999; Tom Lowry, "Whistle-Blower Now Fighting Former Allies," *USA Today*, November 9, 1998, p. 15B; and "Expert Says Georgia Law a 'Cardboard Shield,'" *Atlanta Journal*, April 12, 1998, accessed at www.accessatlanta.com.

---

but primarily affecting women. Some examples of sexism are blatant, as when a woman earns less than a male colleague in the same job, or when a male employee gains a promotion over a better-qualified female. Other instances are more subtle; the only female in a work group may not be introduced to a client or may not get a work assignment.

One important sexism issue concerns equal pay for equal work. On average, women in the United States earn 71 cents for every dollar earned by men. In the course of a working lifetime, this disparity adds up to a gap of $420,000. This data actually represents an improvement; in 1980, women's wages averaged 64 percent of men's. The gap is closing only partly because of gains in women's salaries; the rest is due to a decline in men's earnings. Female high-school graduates still earn less than men who quit school before the ninth grade.[60]

Responsibilities to Investors and the Financial Community

Although a fundamental goal of any business is to make a profit for its shareholders, investors and the financial community demand that businesses behave ethically as well as legally in handling their financial transactions. When businesses fail in this responsibility, thousands of investors and consumers can suffer.

For example, in the early 1990s, banks and savings and loan institutions (S&Ls) were failing at the highest rate since the Great Depression of the 1930s. All too often, the problems resulted because bank executives approved too many high-risk investments. The banks used their deposits to finance real estate developers, third-world governments, and corporate buyouts. When the borrowers couldn't repay the loans, the banks failed. Federal deposit insurance covered most depositors' losses at the failed banks and S&Ls. However, these payments cost the government, and ultimately taxpayers, billions of dollars.

Both state and federal government agencies currently protect investors from abuses such as land fraud. As Figure 2.15 points out, personal finance magazines such as *Kiplinger's* also play an important role in alerting investors to such abuses.

The Securities and Exchange Commission is the federal agency responsible for investigating suspicions that publicly traded firms engaged in unethical or illegal finan-

| Figure 2.15 | **Protecting Investors from Unethical Practices** |

cial behavior. Often investigations arise when a business uses faulty accounting practices that inaccurately portray its financial resources and profits to investors. For example, Pinnacle Micro, a maker of computer storage devices, suffered from falling profits for several years. The SEC found that the company tried to hide its losses by counting sales that were actually made the following year in its current-year sales figures. This maneuver made it appear that the firm had met its annual sales goals when it really hadn't. As a result of these and other accounting problems, the SEC fined the company and ordered it to release revised accounting records that correctly showed its weak profits. Three of the company's officers were also fined for their role in the situation. Chapter 19 discusses accounting practices further.

Businesses also behave unethically when they mislead investors about potential opportunities. Consider Bre-X Minerals. The company claimed that it had found a deposit of 71 million ounces of gold, worth $24 billion, in a rain forest in Indonesia. Hearing the news, investors drove the stock price for Bre-X to record levels. However, reports soon revealed that the company had actually placed 60

ounces of gold into a sample taken at the mining site in order to support its discovery claims. In reality, exploration had found no gold. Bre-X became the focus of a criminal investigation, and shareholders sued the company for providing false information to investors.

Bre-X is not the only business to face charges in court. As this chapter's Solving an Ethical Controversy described, SmithKline Beechan was placed under investigation for Medicare fraud. The company eventually settled with the Justice Department for $325 million, which was the largest award ever in a whistle-blower case.

ETHICS AND SOCIAL RESPONSIBILITY IN THE GLOBAL MARKETPLACE

Expanding globally can open new dilemmas about a firm's ethics and social responsibility. Global corporations need to carefully evaluate the cultures of the countries where they do business. Individual cultures may not only have different standards of right and wrong but also different conceptions of how misdeeds should be treated. In many countries, bribes and kickbacks are considered part of doing business. Solving ethical problems in foreign countries may require flexibility and creativity.

Consider the ethical dilemma Jerry Torma faced. Torma spent 4 years working in the Middle East as director of international compensation for Nordson Corp. Local officials demanded that he provide "facilitating payments" before they would process work permits for the company. Other foreign firms had agreed to pay these bribes. Torma, however, took a different approach. He explained to the officials that he wasn't permitted to pay bribes and suggested they work together to find a different solution. In talking with one official, Torma discovered that a monumental backlog of paperwork awaited the official's staff. Torma suggested that he provide the assistance of a secretary to help clear the backlog instead of paying a bribe. This solution was legal, ethical, and satisfactory to both parties.[61]

Global firms also face quandaries about their responsibilities to workers in countries where commitments to social responsibility for employees are often weaker than those of domestic firms. In many countries, government agencies and others exert little or no control over the conditions in which workers toil. The average worker may only earn a few dollars a week, and child labor is considered an acceptable practice. When U.S. manufacturers do business in these countries, or purchase products manufactured in them, they can violate the social responsibility expectations of U.S. consumers. These firms must balance their needs for low-cost labor with their responsibilities toward human rights.

For example, the U.S. Department of Labor reports that 80 percent of the soccer balls sold in the United States were made with child labor in Pakistan. Reebok, a major importer of soccer balls from Pakistan, has vowed that it will purchase soccer balls made only in factories that use adult labor. To verify this position, Reebok has hired an accounting firm to audit factory records. The company also invited human rights observers to visit and interview workers on a regular basis. Finally, Reebok has also committed to support training programs for children who were previously employed in Pakistani soccer ball factories. In the United States, the company's soccer balls will carry a label reading, "Human rights guarantee: No child labor used."[62]

Nike was also forced to confront this dilemma recently when reports revealed that most of the company's products were manufactured in foreign factories where workers were paid only pennies a day. Nike issued requirements for wages and working conditions in factories wishing to do business with the company. The company severed ties with several Asian factories that failed to meet these standards. Critics still contend, however, that Nike should pay its foreign workers wages comparable to those earned by workers in the United States.[63]

To confront these issues, the Council on Economic Priorities (CEP), a public-interest group based in New York, has joined with a group of influential companies including Avon, Toys 'R' Us, and Eddie Bauer to launch a program called *Social Accountability 8000* (SA 8000). The group has outlined standards for employers to follow in hiring workers abroad. Among the proposed labor standards, participating companies would agree to:

- ▼ Avoid using child or forced labor
- ▼ Provide safe working environments
- ▼ Respect workers' rights to unionize
- ▼ Require no more than 48-hour work weeks
- ▼ Pay wages sufficient to meet workers' basic needs[64]

WHAT'S AHEAD

As this chapter has shown, the decisions and actions of businesspeople are often affected by outside forces such as the legal environment and society's expectations about business responsibility. Firms also are affected by the economic environments in which they operate. The next chapter discusses the broad economic issues that influence businesses around the world. Our discussion will focus on how factors such as supply and demand, unemployment, inflation, and government monetary policies pose both challenges and opportunities for firms seeking to compete in the global marketplace.

SUMMARY OF LEARNING GOALS

1. Explain the concepts of business ethics and social responsibility.

Business ethics refers to the standards of conduct and moral values that govern actions and decisions in the workplace. Businesspeople must take a wide range of social issues into account when making decisions. *Social responsibility* refers to management's acceptance of the obligation to consider profit, consumer satisfaction, and societal well-being of equal value in evaluating the firm's performance.

2. Describe the factors that influence individual ethics and common ethical dilemmas in the workplace.

Among the many factors shaping individual ethics are past experience, peer pressure, and organizational culture. Individual ethics are also influenced by family, cultural, and religious standards. Additionally, the culture of the organization where a person works can be a factor. Common on-the-job ethical situations faced by individuals include conflicts of interest, loyalty to one's employer, bribery, and whistle-blowing.

3. Explain how organizations shape ethical behavior.

Employees are strongly influenced by the standards of conduct established and supported within the organizations where they work. Businesses can help shape ethical behavior by developing codes of conduct that define their expectations. Organizations can also use this training to develop employees' ethics awareness and reasoning. Executives must also demonstrate ethical behavior in their decisions and actions in order to set examples for employees to follow.

4. Relate the ways in which government regulation affects business ethics and social responsibility.

Because businesses sometimes fail to regulate their own actions, federal, state, and local governments may step in to regulate business activity. The federal government regulates competition and commercial activities. In a regulated industry, competition is either limited or eliminated, substituting close government control for free competition. Laws have also been enacted to protect against unfair competition and to protect consumers. Deregulation has significantly reshaped the legal environments in many industries in the last two decades.

5. Describe the responsibilities of business to the general public, customers, and employees.

The responsibilities of business to the general public include dealing with public-health issues, protecting the environment, and developing the quality of the work force. Additionally, many would argue that businesses have a social responsibility to support charitable and social causes in the communities in which they earn profits.

Business also has a social and ethical responsibility to treat customers fairly and act in a manner that will not harm them. Ultimately, businesses themselves are responsible for protecting consumers' rights. Among the rights of consumers that businesspeople should uphold are the rights to be safe, to be informed, to choose, and to be heard.

A firm's employees are an important resource, and businesses have wide-ranging responsibilities to their workers. They must make sure that the workplace is safe for employees. Businesses must also address quality of life issues by helping workers find solutions to problems such as how to balance work and family requirements. Employees also deserve the right to work in nondiscriminatory environments, so businesses must manage diversity. Finally, employers have a responsibility to ensure that all workers are treated fairly and are safe from sexual harassment.

6. Explain why investors and the financial community are concerned with business ethics.

Investors and the financial community demand that businesses behave ethically as well as legally in handling their financial transactions. They must be honest in reporting their profits and financial performance in order to avoid misleading investors. The Securities and Exchange Commission is the federal agency responsible for investigating suspicions that publicly traded firms have engaged in unethical or illegal financial behavior.

7. Describe the ethical and social responsibility issues facing businesses in the global marketplace.

Global expansion opens new dilemmas about a firm's ethics and social responsibility. Individual cultures may not only have different standards of right and wrong but also different concepts of how misdeeds should be treated. Bribes and kickbacks are considered part of doing business in many countries. Other countries may have different expectations of a firm's social responsibilities. Solving ethical problems in foreign countries may require flexibility and creativity.

TEN BUSINESS TERMS YOU NEED TO KNOW

business ethics	deregulation
conflict of interest	social responsibility
whistle-blowing	recycling
code of conduct	corporate philanthropy
regulated industry	sexual harassment

Other Important Business Terms

integrity	family leave
social audit	Equal Employment Opportunity Commission (EEOC)
pollution	
consumerism	sexism

REVIEW QUESTIONS

1. What do the terms *social responsibility* and *business ethics* mean? Cite an example of each. Discuss the current status of social responsibility and business ethics practices in U.S. industry.
2. Explain how individuals' actions can be shaped by an organization's traditions and expectations. Do you agree or disagree that a company where ethical behavior is expected tends to have fewer problems with employee misconduct than firms with other expectations? Why or why not?
3. Does self-regulation deter government regulation in matters of social responsibility and business ethics? Why or why not?
4. How does government regulate both competition and specific business practices? Describe specific regulations with which businesspeople should be familiar. What is deregulation? What are its advantages and disadvantages?
5. What are the responsibilities of business to the general public? Cite specific examples.
6. What basic consumer rights does the consumerism movement try to assure? How has consumerism improved the contemporary business environment?
7. What is meant by discrimination? How can organizations ensure equal opportunity on the job?
8. Distinguish between sexual harassment and sexism. Cite examples of each. How can firms avoid these problems?
9. What are a firm's responsibilities to its investors and the financial community? What can happen when a firm fails to meet these responsibilities?
10. List some of the ethical dilemmas that people in international businesses may encounter.

QUESTIONS FOR CRITICAL THINKING

1. Al "Chain Saw" Dunlap made most businesspeople's "Bosses from Hell" list for his willingness to eliminate thousands of jobs in pursuit of corporate profit. When Dunlap was CEO of Kimberly Clark's Scott Paper division, he eliminated the company's $5 million annual corporate philanthropy budget as part of his efforts to cut costs and boost the company's profits. Before the Sunbeam Corp. board of directors fired him from his next job, Dunlap vetoed that company's $1 million annual giving program, too. His explanation: "The purest form of charity is to make the most money you can for shareholders and let them give to whatever charities they want."
   a. Do you agree with Dunlap's point of view? Why or why not?
   b. What positive and negative effects might Scott Paper and Sunbeam experience from eliminating their corporate philanthropy budgets?
   c. Are most consumers aware of the corporate contributions of specific companies?
2. "Everybody exaggerates when it comes to selling products, and the consumer ought to take that with a grain of salt," said one advertising executive recently in response to a complaint filed by the Better Business Bureau about misleading advertising. "Don't we all have a brain, and can't we all think a little bit?"
   a. Discuss the consumer's responsibility in sorting the information provided by businesses seeking to market their products. If a consumer fails to carefully read an instruction manual and is injured, who do you think should be responsible?
   b. Do you agree or disagree with the statement that all businesses exaggerate when selling, advertising, and marketing products? Find at least two advertisements that support your argument.
3. Write a personal code of ethical conduct that details your own feelings about ethical issues such as lying, stealing, taking bribes, and hurting others. How will you handle situations where the ethics are not clear-cut? Do you think your code of conduct will be different 5 years from now? In 10 years? In 20 years? Would you take action that didn't fit with your code of conduct if your employer made it a requirement for advancing in your job? If you were offered a large sum of money? What role will your personal ethics play in deciding your choice of career and acceptance of a job?
4. Suppose that you own a small company with 12 employees. One of them tells you in confidence that he has just found out he has AIDS. You know that health-care costs for AIDS patients can be disastrously high, and this expense could drastically raise the health insurance premiums that your other employees must pay. What are your responsibilities to this employee? To the rest of your staff? Explain.
5. Evaluate the potential ethical and social issues facing the listed organizations. If possible, make recommendations for how the organizations should handle or avoid specific issues.
   a. Ford Motor Company
   b. Real estate developers
   c. the American Heart Association and the American Lung Association
   d. Jenny Craig Weight Loss Centers
   e. IBM

Experiential Exercise

Directions: At the end of the chapter section titled *Ethical Reasoning,* you learned about Lockheed Martin's ethics training program, "The Ethics Challenge," based on the popular comic-strip characters Dilbert and Dogbert. The following exercise provides a sampling of the complete board game by beginning with an overview of the game's *Ethical Decision Making Model* and giving you two of the fifty case studies to solve. Either work alone or as a member of a group to complete this exercise. (If you were involved in the ethics training sessions at Lockheed Martin, you would probably be one member in a group of five to seven individuals.)

1. Use the *Ethical Decision Making Model* to help you select the best option in the two case studies presented below. In addition to answers designated A, B, C, and D, each case includes a Dogbert answer, which is worth zero points, since it usually is the worst thing you could possibly do. Some answers are better than others and will rate point values between 0 and 5. Circle your choices after you have read the case studies.

2. Following the second case study is a section titled *Leader's Comments*. Read this section after you've selected your answers because it will explain the rationale for each potential answer and provide the points assigned to each response.

Ethical Decision Making Model
1. Evaluate information.
2. Consider how your decision might affect stakeholders (employees, customers, communities, shareholders, suppliers).
3. Consider what ethical values are relevant to the situation (honesty, integrity, respect, trust, responsibility, citizenship).
4. Determine the best course of action that takes into account relevant values and stakeholders' interests.

CASE FILE NUMBER: 18
Category: Quality Assurance
Setting the Standard: Responsibility

You work in Quality Assurance. You rejected some parts as not conforming to specifications, but your manager told you to accept the parts "as is." You don't agree with the decision. What do you do?

Potential Answers:
A. Do nothing. It's the manager's decision to make.
B. Discuss it with your manager.
C. Call the Ethics HelpLine.
D. Ask the engineers who are responsible for the specification to clarify the situation.
Dogbert: Gripe about it to everybody in the cafeteria.

CASE FILE NUMBER: 39
Category: Employee Recognition Program
Setting the Standard: Honesty

A work team submits a suggestion to the suggestion program. In the meantime, some employees on the team are laid off. The suggestion has been adopted. How do you distribute the award payment?

Potential Answers:
A. Divide it equally among the members of the team still employed.
B. Divide it among all former team members, whether they're still working or not.
C. If the remaining team members agree, donate the check to a charity.
D. Divide the check among all the current employees. If the former employees find out about the award, they can call and request their share.
Dogbert: Declare yourself the winner.

Leader's Comments: Case File Number 18
A. 0 points. If you have a concern, don't ignore it.
B. 5 points. This is your opportunity to explain your concern to your manager. The manager may have justification for accepting the part—some decisions are based on judgment or experience. Then, if you're still concerned, call the Ethics HelpLine.
C. 4 points. This is always a good idea, especially if you are uncomfortable resolving the situation with your manager.
D. 3 points. The engineers may give you technical information that resolves your concern.

Leader's Comments: Case File Number 39
A. 0 points. This deliberately cheats the former employees out of their share of the award.
B. 5 points. This is the only fair solution. This way everyone who earned a share gets a share.
C. 2 points. Better than A, but it still excludes the laid-off workers.
D. 0 points. Put yourself in the shoes of the laid-off workers. How would you feel if you were excluded?

Source: Lockheed Martin's 1997 ethics awareness training module, *The Ethics Challenge.*

Nothing but Net

1. **Social Responsibility.** The Business for Social Responsibility (BSR) is an organization for companies of all sizes and sectors. BSR's mission is to help its members achieve long-term commercial success by implementing ethical policies and practices and meeting their responsibilities to all who are affected by their decisions. Visit BSR's fact sheet at

   www.bsr.org/bsrfacts.htm

   and answer the following questions:
   (a) How many member companies belong to BSR?
   (b) What are BSR's areas of expertise?
   (c) What benefits do member companies receive for their BSR dues?
2. **Ethics.** Select a topic, such as whistle-blowing at Archer Daniels Midland

   condor.depaul.edu/ethics/adm.html

   or The Body Shop's ethics controversy

   www.arq.co.uk/ethicalbusiness/archive/bodyshop/index.htm

   then use your search engine to find information to write a 1- to 2-page analysis of your selected topic. Another source for topic ideas is DePaul University's Institute for Business & Professional Ethics at

   condor.depaul.edu/ethics/prob1.html

   which provides links regarding specific issues or problem areas.
3. **Protecting the Environment.** Visit a Web site of a company committed to protecting the environment. Two such sites are Goodyear and The Gap:

   www.goodyear.com/about/enviro/balance.html

   www.gap.com/company/comm.env.policy.asp

   Identify (a) the specific challenges facing the company you have chosen and (b) the strategy and accomplishments of the company regarding its efforts to protect the environment.

Note: Internet Web addresses change frequently. If you do not find the exact sites listed, you may need to access the organization's or company's home page and search from there.

CONTRIBUTING TO THE COMMUNITY—
LA MADELEINE

What is a socially responsible corporation? How do the concepts of corporate vision and community contribution fit? Patrick Esquerré states that his French bakeries are not part of a restaurant chain. Rather he describes each of them as "a French bakery on the corner" that provides a homey place to eat for its "guests."

Esquerré's vision of la Madeleine is "to be as close as possible to our guests, and to our associates—the people working inside the company—in order to inspire whatever needs to be done to make them feel good, to make each person feel special." What does this mean in terms of actions? Esquerré actually designed the first la Madeleine bakery and restaurant by listening to people who walked by as construction began. When they commented that they hoped there would be a wood burning stove, he made sure there was. When he asked passersby about what they thought a French bakery should have and they answered "wood beams in the ceiling," these were installed as well.

Esquerré sees his guests as the leaders of the organization. His customers decide what they want, how they want it, and even at what price. How does he view his own job? "My job is to listen to these leaders; to adapt to their tastes as much as I can without compromising on key issues; and, to surprise them by going beyond what they expect."

This unique leader sees his "guests" and associates (employees) as part of his family. One of Esquerré's priorities is to make sure that his associates are recognized for their good work as often as possible. It is important to him, for example, that associates know there is a chance for advancement and promotion within their firm. In addition, he uses a bonus plan to reward excellent performance and to increase motivation. Perhaps even more important is the fact that as part of the "orientation" program, all managers who begin a career at la Madeleine are taken to France to be given an opportunity to experience French life. This experience helps to guide them in their jobs. Managers-of-the-Year are rewarded with a free trip to France with their spouses. The managers at la Madeleine are those very people who must listen, adapt, and surprise their guests!

Esquerré also pays attention to the needs of the communities in which the bakeries are located. He and his associates regularly participate in local fundraising activities. Bill Buchanan, one of Esquerré's managers, commented, "The environment that Patrick Esquerré provides for everyone is one in which you can be successful, care for others, and give back to the community in particular—this has made an impact on my own management style, as well as how I conduct my life."

One of the company's programs is a joint effort between the local Public Broadcasting Service station, la Madeleine, and the local food bank. Esquerré makes a fresh food donation to the neighborhood food bank equivalent to 50 percent of total PBS pledges. This tends to increase overall giving to PBS as people understand that the value of their donations is increased through the program. The company has donated over $200,000 of food in a given year.

Contributions, however, are not the only way that la Madeleine is involved in community efforts. Esquerré, along with other managers, frequently takes truckloads of baked goods into the streets to feed the homeless. One manager noted that he had gone with Patrick Esquerré on a weekend to the parking lot right behind City Hall in Dallas to hand out food, coffee, and orange juice to people "who have no other means."

Does la Madeleine have no concern about its bottom line? The corporate philosophy is that you worry about the bottom line by focusing on the top—building sales and maintaining strong involvement with the community, making sure that people want to come to your bakery. Rather than focusing on the short run, la Madeleine and Patrick Esquerré focus on community and the long run—in doing so, he has developed a highly successful and growing enterprise.

Questions

1. Describe the ways that la Madeleine shows the philosophy of community social responsibility. What other responsibilities to the general public may be appropriate for la Madeleine?

2. How does la Madeleine show its responsibility to its customers? To its employees? Explain.

3. Give an example of a firm in your own community that you feel is socially responsible. How has this affected their success in their location?

Sources: L. Stones and K. Lynn, "Entrepreneurism + Customer Service = Success," *Management Review* (November 1993), 38–44.

chapter **3**

Economic Challenges Facing Global and Domestic Business

LEARNING GOALS

1. Distinguish between microeconomics and macroeconomics.

2. List each of the factors that collectively determine demand and those that determine supply.

3. Compare supply and demand curves and explain how they determine the equilibrium price for a good or service.

4. Contrast the three major types of economic systems.

5. Identify the four different types of market structures in a private enterprise system.

6. Identify the major factors that guide an economist's evaluation of a nation's economic performance.

7. Compare the two major tools used by a government to manage the performance of its national economy.

8. Describe the major global economic challenges of the 21st century.

UPS Improves Worker Skills and Its Workforce

Package-handling giant United Parcel Service (UPS) has reaped the benefits of recent economic prosperity in the form of strong demand. At the same time, UPS has been forced to find innovative ways to attract and retain the human resources it needs. With unemployment rates below 4.5 percent and Help Wanted signs everywhere, UPS discovered that above-average compensation and an attractive benefits package was not sufficient to attract the people needed to service the firm's growing business. Then UPS management chose a new approach aimed at accomplishing more than simply filling its personnel roster. It became a founding member of the Welfare to Work Partnership, a federal program aimed at reducing the nation's welfare rolls.

Susan Miller represents one of many success stories. Hired on a part-time basis as a package handler, Miller worked hard to leave the welfare rolls and return to work—something she sees as an important example for her three small children. She quickly earned the respect and trust of both management and her coworkers. Promotion to supervisor soon followed, and today she is responsible for training new-hires at the Atlanta hub.

But the Welfare to Work Partnership has not been problem free. When participants couldn't find public transportation to the UPS distribution center near Philadelphia International Airport, the firm arranged for two school buses to carry workers back and forth. Later it convinced the metro bus system to extend routes directly to the terminal by agreeing to subsidize any bus that didn't break even. Today, 53 buses make the trip 24 hours a day, and all of them are profitable.

The buses aid UPS employees in nonwork activities. For example, Tiffany Smith, a 21-year-old package sorter, rides the bus to the terminal to take classes for her general equivalency diploma. Taught at the airport by local college professors, these classes are paid for by UPS.

Nowhere was worker education more important to UPS than at its Louisville hub in Kentucky. The company needed to hire 6,000 more workers to fill the midnight shift, but Louisville's unemployment rate was already so low that consideration was being given to relocating the facility to a place with a larger applicant pool. Then someone came up with a unique employee benefit: night-shift workers would receive free tuition at their choice of three local colleges. Although it cost the employer approximately $1,500 per semester for each participant, the offer proved a real crowd-pleaser. The following semester began with 700 UPS workers participating.

www.ups.com

The welfare-to-work effort is great for the employee participants but it also produces hundreds of capable workers for the employers. "I have been pleasantly surprised," says UPS CEO James P. Kelly. In just the first six months, UPS retained 88 percent of its welfare employees (compared with a previous rate of 60 percent) in Philadelphia. Of equal importance is the fact that UPS experienced no decline in productivity.

Much of the additional recruitment and training costs are covered in the form of federal tax credits of up to $8,500 for each welfare recipient hired. But the payoff comes in many ways. The nation's welfare caseload has plummeted more than 30 percent over the past four years. Companies like UPS have gained productive employees, and former welfare recipients have acquired skills capable of freeing them from the cycle of poverty. As Pamela Brown, one of UPS's many success stories, puts it, "Moving off welfare is like climbing a mountain with your head held high."[1]

CHAPTER OVERVIEW

At UPS, the training and assistance that workers receive benefit both the company and society in general. Employees are a resource that a company uses to produce its goods and services. In return, empoyees gain wages, skills, and—in the Welfare to Work Partnership program—education that improves individuals' lives and raises the overall quality of the workforce.

Looking at the exchanges that companies and societies make as a whole, we are speaking of their **economic sys-**

clothing supplier, he is particularly attracted to the suit shown in Figure 3.1. This one person with a single purchase has involved himself in international trade by choosing the Italian-made Ermenegildo Zegna suit over the U.S.-made Hilfiger brand. Businesses also make economic decisions when they choose how to use human and natural resources, invest in machinery and buildings, and form partnerships with other firms.

Economists refer to the study of small economic units, such as individual consumers, families, and businesses, as

---

Figure 3.1   **Making Economic Choices between Domestic and Imported Products**

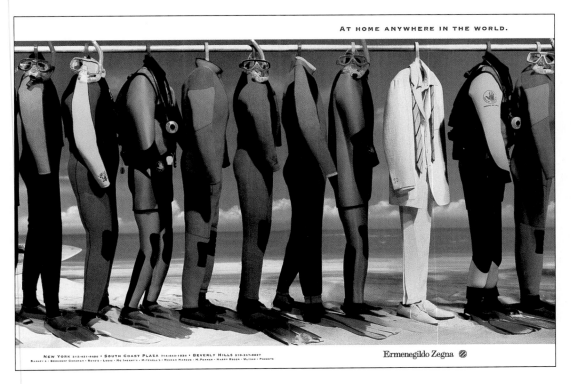

AT HOME ANYWHERE IN THE WORLD.

NEW YORK 212-421-4488 • SOUTH COAST PLAZA 714-545-1234 • BEVERLY HILLS 310-247-8827

Ermenegildo Zegna

---

tems, that is, the combination of policies and choices a nation makes to allocate resources among its citizens. Countries vary in the ways they allocate scarce resources.

Economics, the social science analyzing the choices made by people and governments in allocating scarce resources, affects each of us, since everyone is involved in producing, distributing, or simply consuming goods and services. In fact, your life is affected by economics every day. When you decide what goods to buy, what services to use, or what activities to fit into your schedule, you are making economic choices.

The choices you make often are international in scope. Consider, for example, a man who decides to buy a new suit. Even though he has leaned toward Tommy Hilfiger as his

microeconomics. On a broader level, however, government decisions about the operation of the country's economy also affect you, your job, and your financial future. When the U.S. Congress decided to reduce military spending in the early 1990s, for example, many military bases were closed, affecting the financial well-being of businesses and individuals in surrounding communities. The study of a country's overall economic issues is called **macroeconomics.** (*Macro* means *large*.) This discipline addresses such issues as how an economy maintains and

Business Directory

economics social science analyzing the choices made by people and governments in allocating scarce resources.

allocates resources and how government policies affect people's standards of living.

Chapter 1 explained the increasing interdependence of the world's nations and their economies. As a result, macroeconomics also examines not just the economic policies of individual nations, but the ways in which those individual policies affect the world's economy overall. Remember, though, that microeconomics and macroeconomics are interrelated disciplines—large macroeconomic issues reflect the small decisions made every day by individuals, families, and businesses.

This chapter introduces economic theory and the economic challenges facing individuals, businesses, and governments seek to manage economies in order to create stable business environments in their countries. The final section in the chapter looks at some of the driving economic forces that will affect people's lives in the early years of the 21st century.

MICROECONOMICS: THE FORCES OF DEMAND AND SUPPLY

A good way to begin the study of economics is to look at the economic activities and choices of individuals and small economic units such as families and firms. These economic actions determine both the prices of goods and services and the amounts sold. Microeconomic information is vital for a business, because its survival depends on selling enough of its products at prices high enough to cover expenses and earn profits. This information is also important to consumers, whose well-being may depend on the prices and availability of needed goods and services.

At the heart of every business endeavor is an exchange between a buyer and a seller. A buyer recognizes that he or she has a need or wants a particular good or service and is willing to pay a seller in order to obtain it. The seller is motivated to participate in the process by the anticipated financial gains from selling the good

| **Figure 3.2** | **Consumer Preferences, Incomes, and the Prices of Substitute Products: Factors Affecting Demand for Automobiles** |

ernments in the global marketplace. This discussion begins with the microeconomic concepts of supply and demand and their effect on the prices people pay for goods and services. Next, the various types of economic systems are explained along with tools for comparing and evaluating their performance. The chapter then examines the ways in which

or service. The exchange process, therefore, involves both demand and supply. **Demand** refers to the willingness and ability of buyers to purchase goods and services at different prices. The other side of the exchange process is **supply,** the willingness and ability of sellers to provide goods and services for sale at different prices.

Understanding the factors that determine demand and supply, as well as how the two interact, can help you to understand many of the actions and decisions that individuals, businesses, and government make. This section takes a closer look at these concepts.

Business Directory

demand willingness and ability of buyers to purchase goods and services.

supply willingness and ability of sellers to provide goods and services for sale.

Factors Driving Demand

For most people, economics amounts to a balance between unlimited wants and limited financial means. Because of this dilemma, each person must make choices about how much available money to save and how much to spend, as well as how to allocate that spending among all the goods and services competing for attention. This continuing effort to overcome the unlimited wants/limited means dilemma caused one writer to refer to economics as *the dismal science*.

Even though you may be convinced that the Jeep Wrangler shown in Figure 3.2 is the perfect answer to your automotive needs, a quick perusal of the required monthly payments may force you to compromise with a less expensive Suzuki Samurai. Even if you can afford the monthly payments on the Jeep, you may still select the more economical Samurai and spend the money you save on new clothes, a trip to Disney World, or a more expensive apartment with an extra bedroom. Demand, therefore, is driven by a number of factors that influence how people decide to spend their incomes.

Price is one of the most important factors influencing demand. In general, as the price of a good or service goes up, people buy diminishing amounts. In other words, as price rises, the quantity demanded declines. At lower prices, consumers are generally willing to buy more of a good. A **demand curve** is a graph of the amount of a product that buyers will purchase at different prices. These curves typically slope downward, reflecting the fact that lower and lower prices typically attract larger and larger purchases.

If you have shopped for a personal computer in recent months, you have encountered the steep decline in prices for these products—and the resulting impact on sales. Tumbling component costs allowed manufacturers like Compaq, Dell, Gateway, and Hewlett-Packard to offer ultra-cheap PCs with expanded power and features. As consumers discovered that

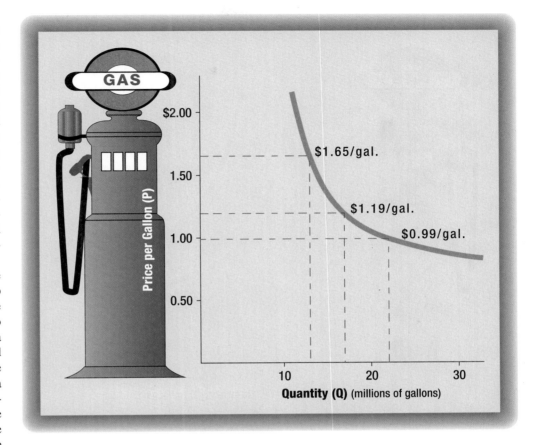

Figure 3.3 **Demand Curve for Gasoline**

for around $800 they could get a computer with Intel's latest Pentium chip, the Windows 95 operating system, a speedy modem, and CD-ROM drives, they rushed into the market. Currently, two of every five PCs sold in the United States carry retail prices below $1,000. By 2000, prices for basic PCs had dropped below $500, making it possible for over 50 percent of the nation's households to own at least one.[2]

Gasoline provides another good example of how demand curves work. Figure 3.3 shows a possible demand curve for the total amount of gasoline that people will purchase at different prices. When gasoline is priced at $1.19 a gallon, for example, drivers may fill up their tanks once or twice a week. At $1.65 a gallon, however, many of them may start economizing. They may make fewer trips, start carpooling, or ride buses to work. The quantity of gasoline demanded at $1.65 a gallon, therefore, is lower than the amount demanded at $1.19 a gallon. The opposite happens at $0.99 a gallon. Some drivers may decide to top off their tanks more often than they would at a higher price; they may also decide to take cross-country motoring vacations or drive to school

They said it

"You can make even a parrot into a learned economist by teaching him two words: supply and demand."

Anonymous

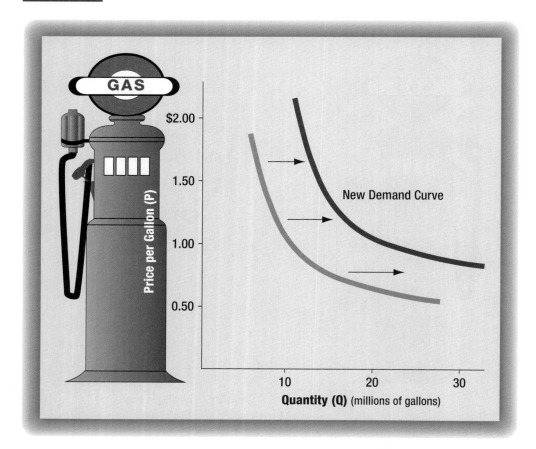

Figure 3.4 Shift in the Demand Curve for Gasoline

For example, record amounts of gasoline were consumed last year. As the popularity of gas-guzzling vehicles like sport-utility vehicles grew, Americans used more gasoline. In addition, many consumers in developing countries like India and China found themselves able to afford to buy cars for the first time, increasing the demand for gasoline at all prices. Figure 3.4 shows how the increased demand for gasoline worldwide has created a new demand curve. The new demand curve shifts to the right of the old demand curve, indicating that overall demand has increased at every price. A demand curve can also shift to the left when the demand for a good or service drops.

While price is the underlying cause of movement along a demand curve, many factors can combine to determine the overall demand for a good or service. These include customer preferences and incomes, the prices of substitute and complementary products, the number of buyers in a market, and the strength of their optimism regarding the future. Changes in any of these factors will produce a new demand curve.

instead of taking the bus. As a result, more gasoline is sold at $0.99 a gallon than at $1.19 a gallon.

Economists make a clear distinction between changes in the quantity demanded at various prices and changes in overall demand. A *change in quantity demanded,* such as the change that occurs at different gasoline prices, is simply movement along the demand curve. A *change in overall demand,* on the other hand, results in an entirely new demand curve.

Take a change in income as an example. Rising incomes are likely to permit firms to sell more products at every price, causing the demand curve to shift to the right. By contrast, a significant increase in film prices may re-

Table 3.1 Expected Shifts in Demand Curves

Factor	Demand Curve Shifts to the Right IF:	to the Left IF:
Customer preferences	increase	decrease
Number of buyers	increases	decreases
Buyers' incomes	increase	decrease
Prices of substitute goods	increase	decrease
Prices of complementary goods	decrease	increase
Future expectations become more	optimistic	pessimistic

duce overall demand for complementary goods like cameras. Table 3.1 describes how a demand curve is likely to respond to each of these changes.

For a business to succeed, management must carefully observe the factors that may affect demand for the goods and services it hopes to sell. In setting prices, for example, firms often try to predict how the chosen levels will influence the amounts they sell. Businesspeople also try to influence overall demand through advertising, sales calls, product enhancements, and other marketing techniques.

Factors Driving Supply

Important economic factors also affect supply, the willingness and ability of businesses to provide goods and services at different prices. Just as consumers must make choices about how to spend their incomes, businesses must also make decisions about how to use their resources in order to obtain the best profits.

Obviously, sellers would prefer to command high rather than low prices for their goods or services. A **supply curve** graphically shows the relationship between different prices and the quantities that sellers will offer for sale, regardless of demand. Movement along the supply curve is the opposite of movement along the demand curve. That is, as price rises, the quantity sellers are willing to supply also rises. At progressively lower prices, the quantity supplied decreases. In Figure 3.5, for example, a possible supply curve for gasoline shows that increasing prices for gasoline should bring increasing supplies to market, as oil companies are motivated by the possibility of earning growing profits.

Businesses require certain inputs in order to operate effectively to produce their goods and services. These inputs, called **factors of production,** include natural re-

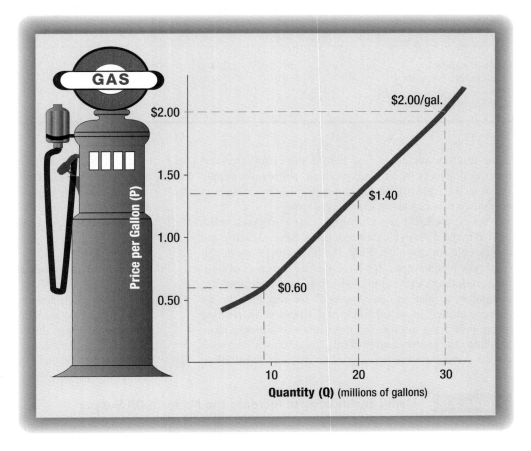

Figure 3.5 **Supply Curve for Gasoline**

sources, capital, human resources, and entrepreneurship. *Natural resources* include everything that is useful in its natural state. Examples of natural resources include land, building sites, forests, and mineral deposits. *Human resources* include the physical labor and intellectual inputs contributed by workers. *Capital* refers to resources such as technology, tools, information, physical facilities, and financial capabilities. Finally, the fourth factor of production, *entrepreneurship,* is the willingness to take risks to create and operate a business.

Factors of production play a central role in determining the overall supply of goods and services. A change in the cost or availability of any of these inputs can shift the entire supply curve, either increasing or decreasing the amount available at every price. For example, if the cost of raw materials (natural resources) rises, producers may respond by lowering production levels, shifting the supply curve to the left. On the other hand, if an innovation in the production process allows them to turn out more products

DID YOU KNOW?

How long it takes to manufacture a: McDonald's Big Mac, 21 seconds; Chevrolet Corvette, 40 hours; commuter airplane, 18,000 hours.

Table 3.2	Expected Shifts in Supply Curves		
		Supply Curve Shifts	
Factor	to the Right IF:		to the Left IF:
Costs of inputs	decrease		increase
Costs of technologies	decrease		increase
Taxes	decrease		increase
Number of suppliers	increases		decreases

using less raw materials than before, the change reduces the overall cost of the finished products, shifting the supply curve to the right. Table 3.2 summarizes how changes in various factors can affect the supply curve.

As Figure 3.6 shows, the supply curve for gasoline has shifted to the right in the past few years. Several factors are responsible for this shift. First, the oil industry has developed new technologies that have slashed the costs of finding, producing, and refining oil. Engineers can now use computers to plan the best methods for reaching the resources hidden in an oil field, and advances in refining technology have allowed oil companies to squeeze more gasoline out of every barrel of oil. These innovations have cut the average cost of finding and producing a barrel of oil

by about 60 percent over the past 10 years. At the same time, new sources of oil are opening up. Special sensors use magnetic imaging to peer ahead of drills as they move underground, finding the least expensive routes to new oil sources both underground and under the sea.[3]

How Demand and Supply Interact

Separate shifts in demand and supply have obvious effects on prices and the availability of products. In the real world, however, changes do not alternately affect demand and supply. Several factors often change at the same time— and they keep on changing. Sometimes such simultaneous

Figure 3.6 Using Technology to Increase the Nation's Oil Supply

Using the Laws of Supply and Demand to Purchase a Car

Looking for a great deal on a car? You can save thousands of dollars by applying the laws of demand and supply when shopping the car lots. Here are three ways to save:

1. *Buy a model that is out of season.* Demand for four-wheel-drive vehicles tends to drop in the summer months in northern regions of the country. As soon as the snow starts to fall, prices typically rise 5 percent to 10 percent. On the other hand, if your heart is set on a convertible, shop in the winter when demand has declined. Once spring arrives, demand for convertibles will rise, driving up prices.

2. *Shop during times of high supply.* Dealers are much more willing to negotiate especially if their lots are overstocked. Avoid the most popular models if you want to save money. Another trick is to shop in early fall, right after next year's models arrive in dealer showrooms. Many dealers still have plenty of the current models on their lots, and they bargain vigorously about price to sell them.

3. *Consider used cars from expired leases.* An increasingly common response to sticker shock is to lease, rather than purchase, new autos. A typical 36-month lease includes an annual 12,000-mile limit with stiff financial penalties for drivers who exceed these limits. As a result, the used-car market is often flooded with relatively low-mileage, well-maintained used cars. The availability of thousands of such cars has driven down used-car prices 5 percent to 10 percent over the past year in several models.

changes in multiple factors cause contradictory pressures on prices and quantities. In other cases, the final direction of prices and quantities reflects the factor that has changed the most.

Figure 3.7 shows the interaction of both supply and demand curves for gasoline on a single graph. Notice that the two curves intersect at *P.* The law of supply and demand states that prices *(P)* are set by the intersection of the supply and demand curves. The point where the two curves meet identifies the **equilibrium price,** the prevailing market price at which you can buy an item.

If the actual market price differs from the equilibrium price, people tend to make economic choices that restore the equilibrium level. For instance, if oil companies lower their prices below equilibrium, drivers are likely to increase their gasoline use and quickly snap up all of the available supply. As sellers renew their stocks, they are likely to mark up the price so they can increase their profits. On the other hand, if merchants mark their

prices too high, some buyers will drop out of the market entirely, and others will reduce their purchases of the product. Sellers must then compete with each other for

| Figure 3.7 | **Law of Supply and Demand** |

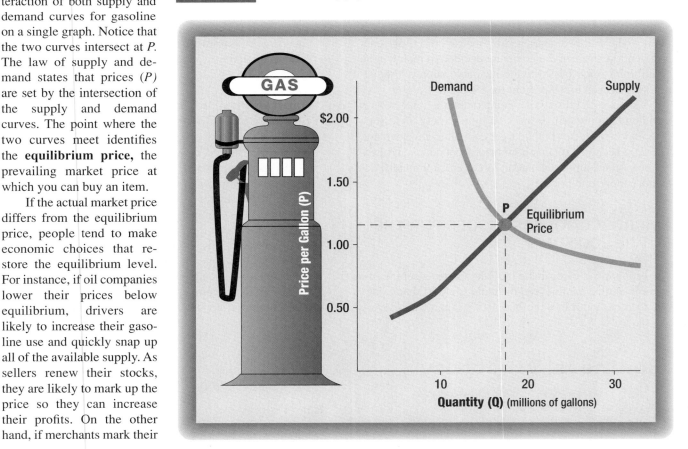

Table 3.3	Types of Competition

	Types of Competition			
Characteristics	**Pure Competition**	**Monopolistic Competition**	**Oligopoly**	**Monopoly**
Number of competitors	Many	Few to many	Few	No direct competition
Ease of entry into industry by new firms	Easy	Somewhat difficult	Difficult	Regulated by government
Similarity of goods or services offered by competing firms	Similar	Different	Similar or different	No directly competing products
Control over price by individual firms	None	Some	Some	Considerable in a pure monopoly; little in a regulated monopoly
Examples	Small-scale farmer in Mississippi	Hallmark card shop	McDonnell Douglas	De Beers

customers by lowering their prices to the point at which they can sell all of their supplies, which is the equilibrium price.

General Motors' Saturn automobile division recently faced a supply-demand imbalance that required management's attention. A 10 percent sales decline during 1997 left Saturn dealers with an 84-day supply of unsold models, far more than the desired 65-day supply. One option management considered, but quickly rejected, was a price reduction. Executives feared a backlash from existing customers who had been attracted by the Saturn no-discount price policy. Instead, the company decided to maintain an equilibrium price by shrinking available supply. Production was slashed by 19 percent for 1998.[4]

As the earlier discussion pointed out, the forces of demand and supply can be affected by a variety of factors. One important factor is the larger economic environment. The next section explains how macroeconomics and economic systems influence market forces and, ultimately, demand, supply, and prices.

MACROECONOMICS: ISSUES FOR THE ENTIRE ECONOMY

The economic choices made by Fidel Castro's communist government have influenced the daily life of Cubans since Castro took control in the late 1950s. Like Cuba, every country faces decisions about how to best use the four basic factors of production. Each nation's policies and choices help to determine its economic system.

The political, social, and legal environments differ in every country. Therefore, no two countries have exactly the same economic system. In general, however, economic systems can be classified into three categories: private enterprise systems, planned economies, or combinations of the two referred to as *mixed economies*. As business becomes an increasingly global undertaking, it is important to understand the primary features of the various economic systems operating around the world.

Capitalism: The Private Enterprise System and Competition

Most industrialized nations operate economies based on the **private enterprise system**, also known as *capitalism* or a *market economy*. A private enterprise system rewards businesses for meeting the needs and demands of consumers. Government tends to favor a "hands off" attitude toward controlling business ownership, profits, and resource allocations. Instead, competition regulates economic life, creating opportunities and challenges that businesspeople must handle in order to succeed.

The relative competitiveness of a particular industry is an important consideration for every firm, because it determines the ease and cost of doing business within that industry. Four basic degrees of competition take shape in a private enterprise system: pure competition, monopolistic competition, oligopoly, and monopoly. Table 3.3

Business Directory

private enterprise system economic system in which business success or failure depends on how well firms match and counter the offerings of competitors; also known as *capitalism* or a *market economy*.

highlights the main differences between these types of competition.

Pure competition is a market structure, like that of small-scale agriculture, in which large numbers of buyers and sellers exchange homogeneous products so no single participant has a significant influence on price. Instead, prices are set by the market itself as the forces of supply and demand interact. Firms can easily enter or leave a purely competitive market, because no single company dominates. Also, in pure competition, buyers see little difference between the goods and services offered by competitors.

Agriculture is probably the closest modern example of pure competition. The grain grown and sold by one farmer is virtually identical to that sold by others. Over the next few years, U.S. agriculture is expected to move even closer to pure competition as Congress phases out federal price guarantees and subsidies. Farmers will now need to pay even closer attention than they have in the past to actual market demand in deciding which products to grow. Even though Harry Stephens' family has raised cotton in Arkansas since before the Civil War, he switched to growing corn on part of his property last year. Stephens decided to respond to a shortage of corn that drove up the commodity's price.[5]

Monopolistic competition is a market structure, like that for retailing, in which large numbers of buyers and sellers exchange relatively well-differentiated (heterogeneous) products, so each participant has some control over price. Products can be differentiated from competing offerings on the basis of price, quality, or other features. A firm can relatively easily begin or stop selling a good or service in an industry that features monopolistic competition. Indeed, the success of one seller often attracts new competitors to such a market. Individual firms also have some control over how their individual goods and services are priced.

The market for beer is an example of monopolistic competition. Consumers can choose from hundreds of beer brands. Brewers try to make their products stand out using advertising, pricing, packaging, and different brewing techniques. Jim Koch, founder of Samuel Adams Brewery, built his company by persuading beer drinkers to pay a premium price for a high-quality, American-brewed beer. To convince consumers of the beer's superiority over competing offerings, the company's Web site explains how Samuel Adams is brewed and highlights its high standards of product freshness. The site also educates visitors about the different tastes of the firm's 15 beer varieties. The brand's success has produced a host of imitators, as competitors have rushed to introduce their own beers.[6]

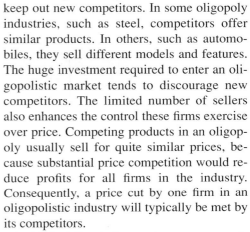

www. **www.samadams.com**

An **oligopoly** is a market situation, like those in the steel and airline industries, in which relatively few sellers compete, and where high start-up costs form barriers to keep out new competitors. In some oligopoly industries, such as steel, competitors offer similar products. In others, such as automobiles, they sell different models and features. The huge investment required to enter an oligopolistic market tends to discourage new competitors. The limited number of sellers also enhances the control these firms exercise over price. Competing products in an oligopoly usually sell for quite similar prices, because substantial price competition would reduce profits for all firms in the industry. Consequently, a price cut by one firm in an oligopolistic industry will typically be met by its competitors.

Consider the U.S. airline industry. A recent competitive move by Delta Air Lines is illustrated in Figure 3.8. Delta's management realizes that if it were to reduce its fares for flights from Atlanta to Toronto, other competitors such as American and United would quickly match the new

fares. Most airlines offer quite similar services, so Delta tries to differentiate itself by offering passenger convenience in the form of nonstop flights to cities like Montreal, Toronto, and Vancouver. In addition, the airline provides 1,339 Canadian one-stop connections from over 160 U.S. cities.

The sizes of current competitors and the financial investment required to join them pose extremely difficult obstacles for new airlines trying to break into the industry. Passage of the Airline Deregulation Act of 1978 has prompted more than 200 fledgling airlines to try to take on the established industry players, but only a handful have survived. One exception is Reno Air, which benefited by forming a strategic partnership with American Airlines to take over several of its shortest routes. Even though Reno has been operating for more than 5 years, it continues to get by with razor-thin profit margins, as its management struggles to build an expensive infrastructure of planes, airport facilities, skilled personnel, and reservation centers.[7]

www. **www.renoair.com**

The final type of market structure is a **monopoly,** in which a single seller dominates trade in a good or service for which buyers can find no close substitutes. A *pure monopoly* occurs when a firm possesses unique characteristics so important to competition in its industry that they serve as barriers to prevent entry by would-be competitors. Many firms create short-term monopolies when research breakthroughs permit them to receive exclusive patents on new products. In the pharmaceuticals industry, drug giants like Merck, Pfizer, and Pharmacia & Upjohn invest billions in research and development programs. Their successful efforts are rewarded through temporary monopolies created by patent laws. The Business Hall of Shame discusses how prices and supply can be controlled by a cartel—specifically the Organization of Petroleum Exporting Countries. Cooperation is central to control, however.

Other than temporary monopolies granted through patents, most pure monopolies are prohibited in the United States through antitrust legislation such as the Sherman Act and the Clayton Act. Much more common are *regulated monopolies,* in which a local, state, or federal government grants exclusive rights in a certain market to a single firm. Public utilities, such as the power company advertised in Figure 3.9, are included in this category. Pricing decisions—particularly rate-increase requests—are subject to control by regulatory authorities such as state public service commissions. In recent years, governments have adopted a policy of encouraging increased competition in industries previously considered to be regulated monopolies. Long-distance telephone service, cable television, cellular phones, even local telephone service and electrical service have been deregulated, and entry barriers have been removed to encourage new competition.

Planned Economies: Communism and Socialism

In a **planned economy,** strict government controls determine business ownership, profits, and resource allocation to accomplish government goals rather than those set by individual businesses. Communism and socialism are both forms of planned economies.

The writings of Karl Marx in the mid-1800s formed the basis of communist theory. Marx believed that private enterprise economies created unfair conditions and led to worker exploitation, because business owners controlled most of society's resources and reaped most of the economy's rewards. Instead, he suggested an economic system where all property would be shared equally by the people of a community under the direction of a strong central government. Thus, **communism** is an economic system in which private property is eliminated, goods are owned in common, and factors of production and production decisions are controlled by the state.

Marx believed that elimination of private ownership of property and businesses would ensure the emergence of a classless society that would benefit all. Each individual would contribute what

Figure 3.8   **Competing in the Oligopolistic Airline Industry by Offering Nonstop Service to Seven Canadian Cities**

Heading North For Canada With 58 Nonstops Every Day.

The next time business takes you to Canada, fly the airline that has dozens of nonstops leaving for seven cities north of the border every day. And with 1,339 daily one-stop connections, from over 160 cities in the U.S., Delta's extensive hub system can get you to Canada with ease. From the U.S. to Toronto, Montreal, Vancouver, Calgary, Edmonton, Ottawa and Quebec City, chances are Delta has a flight leaving whenever you'd like to go. ▲ **Delta Air Lines**
You'll love the way we fly

Visit our web site at http://www.delta-air.com

he or she could, and resources would be distributed according to each person's needs. Under communism, the central government owns the means of production, and the people work for state-owned enterprises. The government determines what people can buy, because it dictates what is produced in the nation's factories and farms.

Many nations adopted communist economic systems during the 20th century in an effort to improve quality of life for their citizens. In practice, however, communist governments often give people little or no freedom of choice in selecting jobs, purchases, or investments. Communist governments often make mistakes in planning the best uses of resources in order to compete in the growing global marketplace. Government-owned monopolies often suffer from inefficiency.

Consider the former Soviet Union, where large government bureaucracies controlled nearly every aspect of daily life. Shortages became chronic, because producers felt little or no incentive to satisfy customers. The quality of goods and services also suffered for the same reason. When Mikhail Gorbachev was selected as the last prime minister of the dying Soviet Union, he took strides to improve the quality of Soviet-made products. Gorbachev authorized an exhibition of shoddy and defective goods produced by the Soviet workers, including a whole consignment of boots with high heels attached to the toes.

Effectively shut out of trading in the global marketplace and caught up in a treasury-depleting arms race with the United States, the Soviet Union faced severe financial problems. Eventually these economic crises led to the collapse of Soviet communism and the breakup of the Soviet Union itself.

A second type of planned economy, **socialism,** is characterized by government ownership and operation of all major industries. This system shares some common beliefs with communism, in that socialists assert that major industries are too important to a society to be left in private hands and that government-owned businesses can serve the public's interest better than can private firms. However, socialism also allows private ownership in industries considered less crucial to social welfare, like retail shops, restaurants, and certain types of manufacturing facilities.

What's Ahead for Communism? Many formerly communist nations have undergone dramatic changes in recent years. Some of the most exciting developments have occurred in the republics that formerly composed the Soviet Union. These new nations have restructured their economies by introducing Western-style private enterprise systems. By decentralizing economic planning and sweetening incentives for workers, they are slowly shifting to market-driven systems.

Economic reforms in these countries haven't always shown smooth progress. Although many have opened their arms to Western entrepreneurs and businesses, these investors have often encountered difficulties such as official corruption, crime, and the persistence of bloated bureaucracies. Reducing the power of government-operated monopolies has also proved a difficult challenge. In Russia, for example, three sprawling monopolies still control the gas, electricity, and rail industries. Close links to government officials and preferential tax breaks obstruct plans for new competitors to enter these markets. The power of these monopolies gives them a stranglehold on prices that critics say is blocking free-market capitalism in Russia. Reformers are pushing for changes that would force these

Figure 3.9 **The Utility Industry: Evolving from Regulated Monopoly to Competitive Marketplace**

IN ALABAMA, WE HAVE THE POWER TO BUILD A BETTER FUTURE FOR EVERYONE.

All things being equal, most opportunities aren't. But one state that works most aggressively to create equal opportunities for everyone is Alabama. We do it by helping to create as many jobs, in as many fields, as possible. In the past few years alone, Alabama Power has worked with other state agencies to help approximately 3,800 companies relocate here, creating almost 100,000 new jobs and training opportunities for Alabama citizens. In the same spirit, Alabama Power is especially proud to lend additional support to minority businesses. Our Mentorship Program and Minority/Female Business Development Program are among the most lauded in the nation.

So, the possibilities should seem clear. In moving or expanding your business to Alabama, you'll not only enjoy some of the lowest electric prices in the nation, you'll help us create an environment where everyone can rise to their best. There's only one way to provide that kind of opportunity. And that's by working together to create it. We invite you to join us. If you are interested in relocating or expanding your business, call Alabama Power, 1-800-990-APCO.

ALABAMA POWER
A SOUTHERN COMPANY

Business Directory

communism planned economic system in which private property is eliminated, goods are owned in common, and factors of production and production decisions are controlled by the state.

socialism planned economic system characterized by government ownership and operation of all major industries.

and other Russian companies to improve efficiency and respond to market demands. For example, Unified Energy Systems, which controls all electricity transmission in Russia, has recently been forced to reduce its prices and open up its market to competitors.[8]

Today, communism remains firmly entrenched in just a few countries, like the People's Republic of China, North Korea, and Cuba. Even these staunchly communist countries, however, show signs of growing openness toward some of the benefits of private enterprise as possible solutions to their economic challenges.

In China, for example, about half of the 118,000 state-run manufacturing enterprises lost money last year. China's 123 auto assembly plants produce about 1.5 million vehicles a year, less than one-sixth the number of vehicles manufactured in the United States by the Big Three automakers. Other Chinese industries face enormous overcapacity, because too many factories make the same goods.

To solve these problems, China's President Jiang Zemin hopes to sell thousands of government-owned factories to private investors. A bankrupt rubber plant, for example, was recently sold for $12 million to a private Shanghai investment group. In addition, Jiang plans to set up national health and retirement programs that would release state companies from the high costs of providing health care, pensions, and housing. The government is also simplifying the process for Chinese citizens to buy their own homes.[9]

Another symbol of China's changing economic strategy has accompanied the 1997 return of Hong Kong to Chinese rule. Jiang's government has promised that Hong Kong's businesses will continue to operate in a private enterprise economic system.

The dramatic end of the Soviet Union in the early 1990s is symbolized by the removal of the statue of Vladimir Lenin, leader of the Russian Revolution of 1917 and the first Soviet premier.

Mixed Market Economies

Private enterprise systems and planned economies adopt basically opposite approaches to operating economies. In practice, however, most countries implement **mixed market economies,** economic systems that display characteristics of both planned and market economies in varying degrees. For example, government-owned firms sometimes operate alongside private enterprises.

France has blended socialist and free enterprise policies for hundreds of years. The country's banking, automobile, utility, aviation, steel, and railroad industries have traditionally been run as nationalized industries, controlled by the government. Meanwhile, a market economy flourishes in other industries. Over the past two decades, the French government has loosened its reigns on state-owned companies, inviting both competition and private investment into industries previously operated as government monopolies.[10]

The proportions of private and public enterprise can vary widely in mixed economies, and the mix frequently changes. Like France, over 50 countries have converted government-owned companies into privately held firms in a trend known as **privatization.** Governments may privatize state-owned enterprises to improve their economies, believing that private corporations can manage and operate the businesses more cheaply and efficiently than government units can. Selling these enterprises also helps governments to raise badly needed funds.

For example, the Brazilian government recently privatized its railroad system, selling the 2,760-mile network to a consortium of industrial and mining companies for $146 million. The new owners plan to invest an additional $136 million in the railway, boosting its competitive strength against the trucking and inland waterway systems and benefiting the entire Brazilian economy. During the last decade, Brazil has also sold its five biggest government-run steel mills to private investors, generating a cash infusion of $5.6 billion in the process.[11]

Table 3.4 compares the three alternative economic sys-

Business Directory

mixed market economy economic system that combines characteristics of both planned and market economies in varying degrees, including the presence of both government ownership and private enterprise.

Table 3.4	Comparison of Alternative Economic Systems

| System Features | Capitalism (Private Enterprise) | Planned Economies | | Mixed Economy |
		Communism	Socialism	
Ownership of enterprises	Businesses are owned privately, often by large numbers of people. Minimal government ownership leaves production in private hands.	The government owns the means of production with few exceptions, like small plots of land.	Basic industries are owned by government, but private owners operate some small-scale enterprises.	A strong private sector blends with public enterprises. The private sector is larger than that under socialism.
Management of enterprises	Each enterprise is managed separately, either by its owners or by people who represent the owners, with minimal government interference.	Centralized management controls all state enterprises in line with 3- to 5-year plans. Planning now is being decentralized.	Significant government planning pervades socialist nations. State enterprises are managed directly by government bureaucrats.	Management of the private sector resembles that under capitalism. Professional managers are also common in state enterprises.
Rights to profits	Entrepreneurs and investors are entitled to all profits (minus taxes) that their firms earn. However, they are expected to operate in a socially responsible manner.	Profits are not acceptable under communism.	Only the private sector of a socialist economy generates profits.	Entrepreneurs and investors are entitled to private-sector profits, although they of must pay high taxes. State enterprises also typically are expected to break even or to provide financial returns to the government.
Rights of employees	The rights to choose one's occupation and to join a labor union have long been recognized.	Employee rights traditionally were limited in exchange for promised protection against unemployment.	Workers have the right to choose their occupations and to join labor unions. However, the government influences career decisions for many people.	Workers have the right of job choice and labor-union membership. Unions often become quite strong in these countries.
Worker incentives	Considerable incentives motivate people to perform at their highest levels.	Incentives are emerging in communist countries.	Incentives usually are limited in state enterprises, but do motivate workers in the private sector.	Capitalist-style incentives operate in the private sector. More limited incentives influence public-sector activities.

tems on the basis of ownership and management of enterprises, rights to profits, employee rights, and worker incentives.

EVALUATING ECONOMIC PERFORMANCE

Ideally, an economic system should provide two important benefits for its citizens: a stable business environment and sustained growth. In a stable business environment, the overall supply of all goods and services is aligned with the overall demand for all goods and services. No wild fluctuations in price or availability complicate economic decisions. Consumers and businesses not only have access to ample supplies of desirable goods and services at affordable prices, but they also have money to buy the items they demand.

Growth is another important economic goal. An ideal economy incorporates steady change directed toward continually expanding the amount of goods and services

BUSINESS HALL OF SHAME

Global Market and Local Greed Give OPEC Gas Pains

Oil has long been considered black gold the world over. Indeed, in the early 1970s, U.S. consumers were paying exorbitant prices at the gas pump for the precious commodity. Why? Because the Organization of Petroleum Exporting Countries (OPEC), an oil cartel of 11 countries formed in 1960, restricted oil production to increase profits. For years, OPEC regulated the production, pricing, and marketing of oil and too often used its power unfairly. More recently, however, OPEC has lost some of its control over the oil market, and Americans have enjoyed some of the lowest gas prices at the pump in a quarter century.

Currently, OPEC members include Iran, Iraq, Kuwait, Saudi Arabia, Venezuela (the founding five), and six others: Algeria, Indonesia, Libya, Nigeria, Qatar, and the United Arab Emi-

rates. OPEC's stated mission is to coordinate and unify member petroleum policies to ensure (1) the prosperity of petroleum producers, (2) the availability of oil to consumers, and (3) the fair return on capital to investors. Twice a year, OPEC ministers meet to analyze the oil market and review predictions for world conditions. From this information, they determine whether oil production should be decreased or increased.

The world runs on energy, and oil remains the most popular fuel. Oil prices affect the price of transportation, the cost of producing goods and services, and the availability of food, water, and shelter. OPEC's member countries currently produce about 40 percent of the world's crude oil. Although the cartel doesn't fully control the oil market, its exports make up roughly 60 percent of the oil traded internationally.

But the market is changing as oil gushes from new suppliers all over the world. If OPEC were to cut production now, consumers would simply turn to

other suppliers for their energy needs. The oil market has been greatly enhanced by today's information technologies such as computer visualization to reveal potential reserves deep underground. This makes finding oil easier, lowers research and exploration costs, and increases the amount of oil available.

As oil producers recognize the wealth that lies in oil revenues, they are focusing more than ever before on finding oil. Suddenly, countries formerly closed to outside companies now are inviting foreigners to join in exploration and production efforts. Saudi Arabia recently asked seven U.S. oil companies to bid on new oil and gas projects. Iranians and Kuwaitis have also been talking with foreign investors—and promising long-terms access to oil reserves.

Although today's swiftly changing environment should encourage OPEC members to cooperate more than ever, many members continue to make decisions dictated by self-interest and

---

produced from the nation's resources. Growth leads to expanded job opportunities, improved wages, and a rising standard of living.

Flattening the Business Cycle

In reality, however, a nation's economy tends to flow through various stages of a business cycle, including prosperity, recession, depression, and recovery. No true economic depressions have occurred in the United States since the 1930s, and most economists believe that society is capable of preventing future depressions through effective economic policies. Consequently, they would expect a recession to give way to a period of economic recovery.

Both business decisions and consumer buying patterns differ at each stage of the business cycle. In periods of economic *prosperity* such as the late 1990s, unemployment remains low, strong consumer confidence

They said it

"It's a recession when your neighbor loses his job; it's a depression when you lose your own."

Harry S. Truman (1884–1972)
33rd president of the
United States

about the future lead to record purchases, and businesses expand to take advantage of marketplace opportunities. During *recessions*—cyclical economic contractions that last 6 months or longer—consumers frequently postpone major purchases and shift buying patterns toward basic, functional products carrying low prices. Businesses mirror these changes in the marketplace by slowing production, postponing expansion plans, and reducing inventories. Should the economic slowdown continue in a downward spiral over an extended period of time, the economy falls into *depression*. Many Americans grew up hearing stories from their grandparents who lived through the 1930s haunted by the specter of joblessness (a 25 percent unemployment rate at one point), idle factories, and despair about the future.

In the *recovery* stage of the business cycle, the economy emerges from recession and consumer spending picks up steam. Unemployment begins to decline, as business ac-

greed. For example, as the world's largest producer, Saudi Arabia doesn't relish cutting production as a means of increasing world prices when such action would merely encourage some other country to seize the business it turns down. In fact, many observers feel that the Saudis would rather increase production. Although this would drive down world prices and hurt the Saudis, it could ruin the new high-cost competitors from the Caspian Sea and West Africa. And despite OPEC agreements to cut production, the temptation for cash-strapped members is to ship more oil, further weakening the cartel.

Oil's role in the energy market may shrink, but it will long remain the world's largest source of energy. And OPEC will continue to wield its power simply because it controls over three-fourths the world's crude oil reserves. The oil cartel is no longer polishing its cache of black gold as the oil market becomes glutted with new competitors. Experts point out that the

market—not OPEC—is finally gaining power in an energy-starved world.

www. www.opec.org

QUESTIONS FOR CRITICAL THINKING

1. Iraq is sitting on nearly as much oil as Saudi Arabia. Some analysts think that once political sanctions are ended, Iraq's fields will be rebuilt and could start producing between 6 million and 8 million barrels a day—rivaling Saudi Arabia. What effect do you think such a development might have on the OPEC cartel?

2. Some observers think that survival among OPEC members depends on a "careful balancing of interests." What do experts mean by this phrase? Relate your answer to the way the oil cartel must operate to secure agreement from its members.

Sources: "A Brief History of OPEC," OPEC Web site, accessed at www.opec.org, February 9, 1999; "Growing Economic Malaise to Shrink Oil Demand—IEA," Reuters Limited, February 9, 1999; "UAE: Include Iraq in OPEC Decision," The Associated Press, February 7, 1999; David Ignatius, "Where the Oil Is," *Washington Post*, February 7, 1999, p. B7; and Daniel Yergin and Joseph Stanislaw, "How OPEC Lost Control of Oil," *Time.com*, April 6, 1998, accessed at cg.pathfinder.com/time/magazine.

tivity accelerates and firms seek additional workers to meet growing production demands. Gradually, the concerns of recession begin to disappear, and consumers begin to purchase more discretionary items such as vacations, new automobiles, and other extravagances.

Economists observe several indicators to measure and evaluate how successfully an economic system provides both stability and growth. These variables include productivity as measured by gross domestic product (GDP), rate of inflation or deflation, employment levels, and relative economic freedom.

Productivity and the Nation's Gross Domestic Product (GDP)

An important concern for every economy is **productivity,** the relationship between the goods and services produced in a nation each year and the human work and other production inputs necessary to produce them. In general, as productivity rises, so does an economy's growth and the

wealth of its citizens. In a recession, productivity declines or stagnates.

Chapter 1 explained that a commonly used measure of productivity is a country's **gross domestic product (GDP),** the sum of all goods and services produced within a nation's boundaries each year. Economists calculate per-capita GDP by summing the total output of all goods and services produced within a country and then dividing that output by the number of citizens. GDP is an important indicator for measuring a country's business cycle, since a shrinking GDP indicates a recession. As the economy again begins to expand, GDP reflects this growth.

GDP in the United States is tracked by the Bureau of Economic Analysis, a division of the U.S. Department of Commerce. Current updates and historical data on the GDP are available at the BEA's Web site.

www. www.bea.doc.gov/

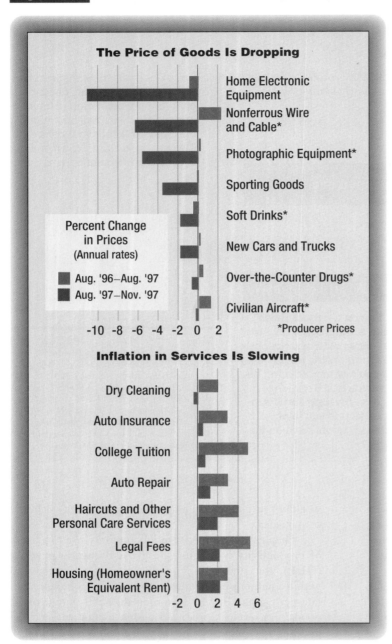

Figure 3.10 New Patterns in Price Changes

In extreme cases, **hyperinflation** occurs—an economic situation characterized by soaring prices. In 1993, for example, Ukrainian consumers suddenly saw the price of food, clothes, and housing rise 5,000 percent![12]

Inflation devalues money as persistent price increases reduce the amount of goods and services people can purchase. The most severe inflationary period in the United States in the last half of the 20th century peaked in 1980 when general price levels rose 13.6 percent. In recent years, however, inflation worries have gradually been replaced with a phenomenon of falling prices. In fact, goods prices, excluding food and energy, have actually declined since mid-1997. As Figure 3.10 shows, shoppers are discovering big price reductions in products ranging from home electronic equipment and sporting goods to a six-pack of Cokes and a new Nissan Altima. Even services, long characterized by relatively high rates of inflation, are experiencing slowing price hikes.

Increased productivity that results in falling prices can have a major positive impact on an economy. In a low-inflation environment, businesses can make long-range plans without the constant worry of sudden inflationary shocks. Low interest rates encourage them to invest in research and development and capital improvements, both of which are likely to produce productivity gains. Consumers can purchase growing stocks of goods and services with the same amount of money, and low interest rates encourage major acquisitions like new homes and autos.[13]

In the United States, changes in price levels are tracked by the **Consumer Price Index (CPI),** which measures the monthly average change in prices of goods and services. The federal Bureau of Labor Statistics (BLS) calculates the CPI monthly based on prices of a *market basket*—a compilation of the goods and services most commonly purchased by urban consumers. Figure 3.11 shows the categories included in the CPI market basket.[14]

Price-Level Changes

The general level of prices is another important indicator of an economy's stability. For most of the 20th century, economic decision makers have concerned themselves with **inflation,** rising prices caused by some combination of excess consumer demand and increases in the costs of raw materials, component parts, human resources, and other factors of production. The first type is referred to as *demand-pull inflation;* the second is called *cost-push inflation.*

Each month, BLS representatives visit thousands of stores, service establishments, rental units, and doctors' offices all over the United States to price the multitude of items in the CPI market basket. This data is then compiled to create the CPI. Thus, the CPI provides a running measurement of consumer price changes. Critics charge, however, that the CPI may actually overstate inflation by not fully accounting for changes in the goods that people buy. The *Producer Price Index (PPI)* is another economic indicator used to track the prices that business buyers pay for the goods their firms use in manufacturing.

Although falling prices might seem like a positive economic indicator, this is not necessarily true. Deflation resulting from productivity gains benefits both producers and consumers. For example, a wave of consumer pessimism about the future might induce people to postpone purchases, increase savings, and restrict spending to wait out the expected crisis. Businesses, stuck with inventories they are unable to sell, may respond by reducing prices in an effort to generate needed funds. Such a situation severely restricts profits, prompting management decision makers to scale back production plans. The result may be job layoffs, declines in the value of personal investments such as homes, and other problems of slow growth or even a recession.[15]

Employment Levels

Consumers need money in order to purchase the goods and services produced in an economy. Because most consumers earn the money they spend by working, the number of people in a nation who currently have jobs is an important indicator of both overall stability and growth. People who are actively looking for work but unable to find jobs are counted in unemployment statistics.

Economists refer to a nation's **unemployment rate** as an indicator of its economic health. The unemployment rate is usually expressed as a percentage of the total work force. The total labor force includes all people who are willing and available to work at the going market wage, whether they currently have jobs or are seeking work. The U.S. Department of Labor, which tracks unemployment rates, also includes so-called *discouraged workers* in the total labor force. These individuals want to work but have given up looking for jobs.

www.dol.gov

Unemployment can be grouped into the four categories shown in Figure 3.12: frictional, seasonal, cyclical, and structural unemployment. *Frictional unemployment* applies to members of the work force who are temporarily not working but are looking for jobs. This pool of potential workers includes new graduates, people who have left jobs

for any reason and are looking for others, and former workers who have decided to return to the labor force. *Seasonal unemployment* is the joblessness of workers in a seasonal industry. Construction workers, farm laborers, and retail clerks often must contend with bouts of seasonal unemployment.

Cyclical unemployment includes people who are out of work because of a cyclical contraction in the economy.

| Figure 3.11 | Consumer Price Index Market Basket |

Category	Examples
Food and Beverages	breakfast cereal, milk, coffee, wine, chicken, snacks
Housing	rent, fuel oil, furniture
Apparel	men's shirts, women's dresses, jewelry
Transportation	automobiles, airline fares, gasoline
Medical Care	prescription drugs, medical supplies, doctor's office visits, eyeglasses
Recreation	television, pets and pet products, sports equipment, movie tickets
Education	tuition, postage, telephone service, computers
Other Goods and Services	tobacco, haircuts

During periods of economic expansion, overall employment is likely to rise, but during economic slowdowns such as recessions, unemployment levels commonly rise. At such times, even workers with good job skills may face temporary unemployment.

Structural unemployment applies to people who remain unemployed for long periods of time, often with little hope of finding new jobs like their old ones. This situation may arise because these workers lack the necessary skills for available jobs or because the skills they have are no longer in demand.

Relative Economic Freedom

Some economists have suggested another way to measure and compare the world's economies. They advocate looking at the *relative economic freedom* enjoyed in each country.

The Fraser Institute, a Canadian economic think tank, recently developed a formula for comparing economic variables that combines inflation rates, government regulation, taxation, and restrictions on trade to determine final rankings. The most recent study ranked Hong Kong as highest in the world in relative economic freedom. Other countries in the top ten included, in order, Singapore, New Zealand, the United States, the Indian Ocean island of Mauritius, Switzerland, the United Kingdom, Thailand, Costa Rica, and Malaysia. Singapore's second-place ranking is evidence of the statistic's focus on economic—rather than political—freedoms. The Business Hall of Fame examines Dole's foothold in Japan's tightly restricted agricultural industry.

In last place among 115 nations ranked in the study is Algeria. Other nations at the bottom of the list are Croatia, Ukraine, and Albania. A country's per-capita income and its economic growth appear to be closely related to economic freedom. For example, Hong Kong, the highest ranked nation, also has the highest per-capita GDP.[16] To determine the rankings of countries you have visited or plan to visit, contact the Fraser Institute Web site.

www.fraserinstitute.ca/

MANAGING THE ECONOMY'S PERFORMANCE

Besides just measuring economic growth and evaluating stability, economists provide tools that governments use to manage their countries' economic performance. A national government can use both monetary policy and fiscal policy to fight inflation, increase employment levels, and encourage growth.

Monetary Policy

A common method of influencing economic activity is **monetary policy,** government action to increase or decrease the money supply and change banking requirements and interest rates to influence spending by altering

Figure 3.12   **Four Types of Unemployment**

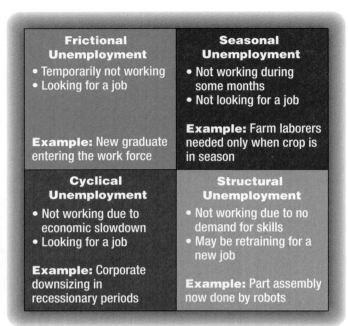

bankers' willingness to make loans. An *expansionary monetary policy* increases the money supply in an effort to cut the cost of borrowing, which encourages business decision makers to make new investments, in turn stimulating employment and economic growth. By contrast, a *restrictive monetary policy* reduces the money supply to curb rising prices, overexpansion, and concerns about overly rapid economic growth.

In the United States, the Federal Reserve System ("the Fed") is responsible for formulating and implementing the nation's monetary policy. It is headed by a chairman (currently Alan Greenspan) and a Board of Governors, each of whom is appointed by the president. All national banks must be members of this system and keep some percentage of their checking and savings funds on deposit at the Fed.

The Fed's Board of Governors uses a number of tools to regulate the economy. By changing the required percentage of checking and savings accounts that banks must deposit with the Fed, the governors can expand or shrink funds available to lend. The Fed also lends money to member banks, which, in turn, make loans (at higher interest rates) to business and individual borrowers. By changing the interest rates charged to commercial banks, the Fed affects the interest rates charged to borrowers, and consequently their willingness to borrow.

The Federal Reserve has a number of other monetary policy tools at its disposal. Each of these is described in detail in Chapter 20, where Table 20.4 indicates the effect of a change in each tool on the economy.

Fiscal Policy

Governments also influence economic activities through taxation and spending decisions. Through revenues and expenditures, the government implements **fiscal policy,** the second technique that officials use to control inflation, reduce unemployment, improve the general welfare of citizens, and encourage economic growth. Increased taxes may restrict economic activities, whereas lower taxes and increased government spending usually boost spending and profits, cut unemployment rates, and fuel economic expansion.

Each year the president prepares a budget for the federal government, a plan for how it will raise and spend money during the coming year, and presents it to Congress for approval. A typical federal budget proposal undergoes months of deliberation and numerous modifications before receiving approval. The major sources of federal revenues and categories of expenditures are shown in Figure 3.13.

The federal budget includes a number of different spending categories, ranging from defense and social security to interest payments on the national debt. The decisions about what to include in the budget have a direct effect on various sectors. During a recession, the federal government may approve major spending on interstate highway repairs to improve transportation and increase employment in the construction industry. A decision to invest new federal funds in job-training programs often pays off in productivity gains produced by enhancing the skills of the workforce.

As Malaysia develops from a small, agricultural economy to a newly industrialized nation, its government is taking steps to ensure that the country's infrastructure components of transportation, power generation, and communications keep pace. As Figure 3.14 describes, YTL Corp. feels the direct effects of government spending decisions aimed at infrastructure improvements. Since 1955, the company, based in Kuala Lumpur, has participated in major projects in construction, hotels and resorts, manufacturing, and power generation.

Taxes, fees, and borrowing are the primary sources of government funds to cover the costs of the annual budget. Both the overall amount of these funds and the specific combination of them have major effects on the economic well-being of the nation. One way governments raise money is to impose taxes on

Ranked first in economic freedom, both business managers and tourists have long included Hong Kong among the world's great cities. Blessed with free trade, one of the world's great harbors, and a new state-of-the-art international airport, Hong Kong is the premier gateway to business in China and Southeast Asia.

sales and income. Increasing taxes reduce people's incomes, leaving them with less money to spend. Such a move can reduce inflation, but overly high taxes can also slow economic growth.

Taxes don't always generate enough funds to cover every spending project the government hopes to undertake. When the government spends more than the amount of money it raises through taxes, it creates a **budget deficit**. To cover the deficit, the U.S. government has borrowed money by offering Treasury bills, Treasury notes, and Treasury bonds for sale to investors. All of this borrowing comprises the **national debt.** Currently, the U.S. national debt is about $5.5 trillion, or approximately $20,000 for every U.S. citizen.[17]

In recent years, both citizen groups and politicians have called for a halt to the long-time practice of borrowing to fund government spending in excess of its income. Instead, a growing commitment has targeted a **balanced budget,** in which the total revenues raised by taxes equal total proposed spending for the year. Even though the federal government spent more money than it received from taxes and fees during every year of the 1970s, 1980s, and most of the 1990s, over half of the nation's state governments are required by their constitutions to balance their annual budgets. By 1999, the federal government accomplished a feat not experienced since 1969—a balanced

Business Directory

monetary policy   government action to increase or decrease the money supply and change banking requirements and interest rates to influence bankers' willingness to make loans.

fiscal policy   government spending and taxation decisions designed to control inflation, reduce unemployment, improve the general welfare of citizens, and encourage economic growth.

budget deficit   funding shortfall that results when the government spends more than the amount of money it raises through taxes and fees.

Figure 3.13 The Federal Budget: Where the Money Comes From and Where It Goes

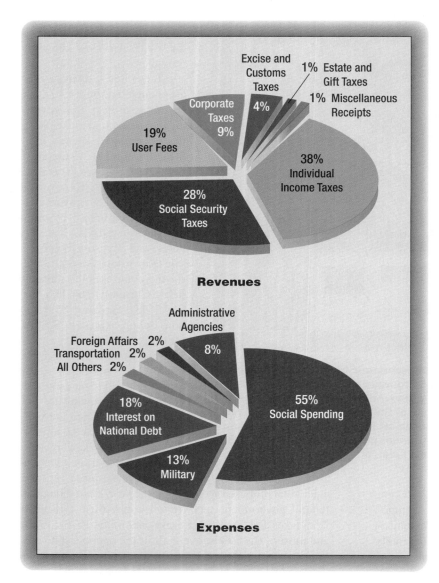

Revenues

Expenses

nomic indicators painted a very positive picture of sustained growth and relative economic stability.

Continuing Growth The U.S. GDP is enjoying a strong cycle of growth. Fueling much of this growth is the continuing expansion of companies in high technology industries, such as software publishers and computer manufacturers. Corporate profits rose 14 percent last year, signaling not only an increase in productivity but strong payoffs from investments in expansion programs. Investors have responded by pushing the U.S. stock market to historic highs.[18]

For individual businesses, the continued growth of the economy opens new doors. Consider the experience of Bobbi's Sweet Surrender, a small baker of gourmet cookies, cakes, and brownies in southern California. When economic growth slowed early in the decade, the company had trouble selling its fancy baked goods. "Things were really tight and people weren't buying gourmet products," explains owner Bobbi Cameron.

In today's economic climate, however, sales have exploded as consumers once again have enough disposable income to splurge on premium-priced baked goods. The company's overall cookie production grew to 400,000 pounds last year, and Cameron expects next year to be her biggest ever. "Before, we were trying to get business," she says. "But what's nice is people are now calling us about our products."[19]

Inflation in Check In recent years, both the CPI and PPI have reported little or no inflation in the U.S. economy. The CPI rose just 1.8 percent in 1998, compared with 3.3 percent the year before and 6.0 percent in 1990. The PPI actually dropped 1.2 percent, as energy costs declined. Given suggestions that the CPI may actually overstate inflation by not fully accounting for changes in the goods people buy, the U.S. inflation rate in 1997 may actually have been close to zero with deflation a reality in 1998.[20]

budget. This goal was reached through a combination of healthy tax-income driven by a prosperous economy and significant spending cuts in such areas as defense and welfare payments.

The U.S. Economy: These Are the Good Old Days

For most of the 1990s, the U.S. economy has experienced the strongest wave of prosperity in nearly a quarter-century. For many individuals and businesses in America, these *are* the good old days, ripe with economic opportunity. As *Contemporary Business* went to press, current eco-

Strong Employment U.S. firms employ more people now than at any time in the last 25 years. In recent years, the national unemployment rate has remained below 5 percent. However, some companies and industries are still making structural changes to their employment practices. Eastman Kodak, AT&T, and JCPenney are just three of several U.S. businesses that have recently announced major job cutbacks reducing each firm's workforce by at least 4,000 employees. Toymaker Hasbro also recently announced plans to cut 20 percent of its worldwide workforce and close several factories. Industry analysts noted that the toy industry is changing as children's interests shift toward computer games. As a result, Hasbro is reevaluating its human resource needs and eliminating numerous manufacturing positions through automation.[21]

Shrinking Budget Deficit

The strong economy also helped the federal government to accomplish its goal of balancing the budget. Three decades passed between the 1969 balanced budget and the slight budget surplus of 1999. As Figure 3.15 indicates, several factors contributed to this achievement. First, the Clinton administration has reduced government spending, slashing the deficit by more than $400 billion over 5 years. The strong economy has helped, too. As businesses' earnings grow, they pay increasing tax bills. In fact, estimates suggest that the federal government will collect an extra $225 billion in tax revenues over the next 5 years.[22]

All these indicators show that, at present, the U.S. economy retains its recent strength. However, future prosperity is not guaranteed. With inflation levels near zero, some analysts worry about deflationary pressures that might force businesses to charge lower prices than they can justify by savings from increasing productivity. At the same time, the low unemployment rate is pressuring employers to raise wages in order to attract and keep workers. Proposals to increase the minimum wage above the $5-per-hour level are favored by many economists and government officials as one means of reducing the growing gap between rich and poor. Critics of the proposal worry that raising human resource costs would cause profits to drop, forcing firms to lay off workers and slowing overall economic growth. The final section of this chapter examines some other economic challenges that may lie ahead.

Figure 3.14 **Government Spending Aimed at Infrastructure Improvements**

Over the next decade, Asia will spend over US$273 million a day on infrastructure projects. (How can you get an overview of the latest developments?)

YTL's home is in Malaysia, a country whose government targets the economy to grow 7% annually until the year 2020. That growth is being made possible largely by the continuing development of the country's modern infrastructure.

YTL's skills have grown in step with Malaysia's development from a small agricultural economy to a newly industrialised nation.

From a modest construction start-up in 1955, we have since participated in many infrastructure projects in Malaysia, culminating in our recent appointment as the country's first Independent Power Producer.

Since 1955, the YTL Group has been a leader in the development of the infrastructure so necessary for the continued successful expansion of Malaysia's economy; in construction contracting, property development, hotels and resorts, manufacturing and power generation.

Newly emerging economies throughout Asia are destined to replicate Malaysia's economic success. Ambitious nations need companies with local knowledge.

If you want an experienced partner in your quest to help build the rest of the Asian region, talk to us.

Working for the advancement of infrastructure since 1955

YTL Corporation Berhad, 55 Jalan Bukit Bintang, 55100 Kuala Lumpur, Malaysia. Fax: 603-2421477

GLOBAL ECONOMIC CHALLENGES OF THE 21ST CENTURY

Businesses face a number of important economic challenges in the coming century. As the economies of countries around the globe become increasingly interconnected, governments and businesses must compete throughout the world. Although no one can predict the future, both governments and businesses will likely need to successfully meet several challenges to maintain their global competitiveness. This section overviews challenges such as the continuing shift toward a global information economy, the aging of the world's population, continuing emphasis on improving quality and customer service, and efforts to enhance the competitiveness of every country's workforce.

The Shift toward a Global Information Economy

The economic growth that began in the industrial revolution of the late 1700s was driven by manufacturing advances that enabled businesses to speed mass production of goods. The economic growth of the 21st century, however, will be propelled by technological advances that enable businesses to enhance the effectiveness of their use, management, and control of information. In the information economy, businesses are working smarter than before, using brains, not brawn, to push economic growth.

American companies are leading the information revolution. Nearly 60 percent of U.S. workers are employed in information-intensive jobs, rather than in traditional labor-intensive positions.[23] Computers enhance productivity in sectors from agriculture to factories. In fact, U.S. businesses and consumers spent an average of $850 per person

BUSINESS HALL OF FAME

Dole Japan Delivers Fresh Produce and Lower Prices

If you like apples and you happen to live in Japan, you'd better be prepared to pay dearly. In Tokyo, an apple costs $5. "Why so much?" you ask. The primary reason is the large number of middlemen who operate between the orchard and the Japanese consumer, each of them receiving a share of the final price. The system is both inefficient and expensive, but it has remained impenetrable for hundreds of years. But Dole Japan, a subsidiary of Dole Foods, has broken through the layers of intermediaries and lowered the price of fresh produce in the Land of the Rising Sun.

Both retailers and Japanese consumers are benefitting from Dole's streamlined distribution system. Prices on locally grown fresh produce have been slashed 25 percent.

Agricultural deregulation played a major role in the price cuts. It permitted Dole to introduce contract growing to local producers of broccoli, tomatoes, cabbage, radishes, carrots, lettuce, and melons. Prior to deregulation, growers had to sell their output to their cooperatives. In fact, when tomato farmer Chikashi Matsunaga tried to sell his output on his own, the co-op kicked him out, making it virtually impossible for him to find a buyer. Since deregulation, he has been able to sell all the tomatoes he can grow to Dole Japan. Says Matsunaga, "We just deliver tomatoes in large containers and Dole does the rest of the work. Dole also sets prices in advance so we know we can cover costs and earn a living."

Dole Japan has been working at removing unnecessary links in Japan's food chain for over a decade. In addi-

tion to reducing prices, slashing the number of middlemen in the distribution channel gives Dole greater quality control of the produce it distributes to supermarket shelves. With some 15 fresh-cut fruit and vegetable centers in Japan, the company can deliver items such as precut salads to any store in the country within three hours.

The Japanese government traditionally has protected its farmers, distributors, and retailers with regulation, import restrictions, and numerous other barriers to open competition—even though it knew that Japanese consumers paid more for products than their counterparts in other nations. But times are changing and since Japan grows only 42 percent of its food—the lowest ratio among large industrial nations—it is imperative that it have access to food sources located outside the country. In addition, 40 percent of Japanese farmers are now 65 or older, adding to concerns that the Japanese government must take action to secure a strong food industry. Observers expect a revision in the government's Agriculture Basic Law to permit corporations to till the land. Rules governing retail operations have already been relaxed.

With more deregulation likely in the near future, Dole is in a great position to supply Japan's increasing need for affordable and available produce. The firm's goal has been stated as "to have the industry's finest distribution system deliver the highest quality product at the most efficient cost structure." In short, Dole is committed to providing more efficient food distribution in Japan and around the world.

www.dole.com

QUESTIONS FOR CRITICAL THINKING

1. The falling barriers against foreign competitors are likely to encourage other non-Japanese companies to enter the market to compete not only with the Japanese firms but also with Dole. Is this influx of non-Japanese producers likely to hurt Dole's position? Explain your answer.

2. In today's global economy, how are each of the following likely to affect Dole's operations in Japan?

   a. the recent Russian economic collapse, which reduced demand for bananas

   b. Hurricane Mitch, which devastated Dole's Central American fruit-farming operations.

Sources: "Dole Asia," Dole's Web site, accessed at www.dole.com, February 9, 1999; and Neil Weinberg, "Upsetting the Apple Cart," *Forbes*, December 14, 1998, pp. 210, 212.

How to Survive an IRS Tax Audit

The federal agency most responsible for collecting funds that finance government expenditures is the Internal Revenue Service (IRS). Although your chance of the IRS auditing your tax return is about 1 in 100, just the thought of an audit is enough to make taxpayers shudder. President Clinton and both houses of Congress support an IRS reform law designed to shift the agency's focus to improving the government's understanding and problem-solving ability from the taxpayer's point of view. Even so, tax audits rank among life's least pleasant events.

If you are called for an audit, the IRS will thoroughly examine your tax return to evaluate the accuracy of all information you have provided. These five tips will help you to survive an IRS audit:

1. *Be prepared.* The IRS will give you time to gather relevant records. Go through your tax file and find proof of the information you used to prepare the tax return being audited. In general, you should save this information for at least 3 years. If, during the audit, you find you don't have needed information, you have the right to postpone the audit in order to complete further preparations.

2. *Ask for a correspondence audit.* Not all audits need to be conducted face-to-face. Many taxpayers reduce the stress of their dealing with IRS auditors by exchanging information via the mail. This is called a *correspondence audit.*

3. *Don't volunteer any additional information.* Most audits look at specific areas of your tax return. If, however, you raise another issue during the audit, the auditor can investigate it. Therefore, keep your answers as brief and specific as possible.

4. *Everything is negotiable.* If the audit shows that you owe additional taxes, along with penalties and interest, ask the auditor if the IRS will accept less than the full amount. The IRS also frequently waives or reduces penalties.

5. *Never sign when you don't agree.* The auditor will ask you to sign a form after completion of the audit. If you don't agree with the auditor's findings, you don't have to sign the form. Signing the form may limit your rights to future appeals.

Source: "IRS Head Proposes Major Overhaul," *USA Today,* January 28, 1998, p. B1; and Louis E. Boone, David L. Kurtz, and Douglas Hearth, *Planning Your Financial Future* (Fort Worth, Tex.: Dryden Press, 1997), p. 180.

on information technology in a recent year—eight times the global average of $98.[24] That trend adds up to some $420 billion a year, $282 billion on computer hardware alone.[25]

Investments in information technology have paid off for U.S. businesses by increasing their global competitiveness. Worker productivity is rising, customer service is improving, and production costs in many industries are shrinking or remaining constant. Consider Bethlehem Steel's experience. Through the 1980s, the steel manufacturer struggled to compete with foreign competitors with lower production costs—especially labor costs. Since then, Bethlehem Steel has invested almost $6 billion to modernize its facilities. Much of this amount paid for new technologies to reduce the amount of human labor required to produce steel. The firm needed 7 worker-hours of labor to produce a ton of steel 10 years ago. Today, thanks to its modernization investments, Bethlehem Steel can produce a ton of steel with only 3 hours of human resource inputs.[26]

The growth of information technology has fueled U.S. economic growth in another way. During the past 3 years, 27 percent of America's GDP growth came from such high-technology sectors as computer manufacturers, software designers, and telecommunications firms.

Figure 3.15 **How the Federal Government Reduced Budget Deficits by $534 Billion over 5 Years and Balanced the Budget**

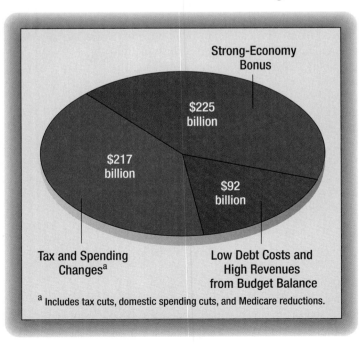

SOLVING AN ETHICAL CONTROVERSY

The Growing Gap between Rich and Poor

Framingham, Massachusetts, is a town with a split personality. Residents on the town's north side, many employed by the area's growing high-technology industries, live in relative affluence in colonial-style homes on attractive, tree-lined streets.

Venture into Framingham's south side, however, and a different picture emerges. The area was once home to generations of blue-collar workers employed by the town's manufacturing plants, but most of these employers have moved or simply gone out of business. Now the south side is filled with decaying buildings occupied by families barely scraping by on low-paying jobs or welfare. Most south-side

residents see little chance of bettering their lives.

"Framingham was one of the places where we always saw people moving up the rungs on the ladder," explains Robert Reich, former U.S. labor secretary. "The reality today is that those rungs are much farther apart. And what is happening in Framingham is happening across the country."

Despite strong U.S. economic growth, the gap between the 20 percent of U.S. families with the highest incomes and the 20 percent at the lowest income levels has widened significantly over the last 20 years. Families at the top level saw their incomes increase 30 percent during this time, from $27,000 to $117,000. Meanwhile, wages among the bottom 20 percent dropped 21 percent, to an annual average of just $9,250.

The government could implement several policy options to narrow the gap, such as offering tax breaks to those at lower-income levels or tightening trade agreements with other countries in order to keep low-end manufacturing jobs from moving to foreign facilities. The government could also raise the minimum wage again or increase welfare benefits. As the income gap widens, the controversy grows over whether the government should take these or other actions to close it.

 Should the Government Intervene to Narrow the Income Gap?

PRO

1. An economic system owes its members some share in its prosperity. Those without skills should not

---

This contribution to the nation's economic growth is seven times greater than GDP gains coming from the U.S. auto industry.[27]

Even though the United States leads the world in information technology, several emerging trends may threaten the benefits the country derives from this leadership position. First, other countries are adapting these information technology advances in their own industries, which may reduce the competitive advantage currently enjoyed by the United States. Also the U.S. economy is becoming increasingly dependent on the continued growth of high-technology industries. A downturn in demand for these goods and services could negatively affect the entire economy. This dependence puts added pressure on U.S. companies to stay on top of technology development.[28]

Effect of an Aging Population

Most nations are experiencing some graying of their populations. In the United States, the median age has reached 35, and the baby boomers, people born between 1946 and 1965, comprise the largest population

They said it

"The factory of the future will have only two employees, a man and a dog. The man will be there to feed the dog. The dog will be there to keep the man from touching the equipment."

Warren G. Bennis (1925–)
American business writer

group. These people will approach retirement age over the next two decades. By 2025 over 62 million Americans will be 65 or older—nearly double today's number.

First, as this huge group ages, the need for health care, social security, and other support services is likely to grow. This trend could put budgetary pressure on governments, as they struggle to meet these changing demands.

Employers will also have to deal with pressing issues due to the aging of their workforces: retirement, worker disabilities, and insurance. As the baby boomers begin to retire, U.S. businesses will also need to find ways to replace their skills in the workplace. Generation Xers, people born between 1966 and 1976, are a much smaller population group, so employers face the possibility of significant labor shortages early in the 21st century.

Demand for many goods and services will also change as the baby boomers age. Retired consumers will probably demand fewer large homes, sport-utility vehicles, child-care services, and bank loans. They will, however, have a growing need for medical care, insurance, travel services, and retirement housing. As Figure 3.16 illustrates, successful

be sacrificed to increase business firms' profits. Instead, a fair economic system trades some growth for economic fairness among all members. "The widening income gap shows that the distribution of the benefits of economic growth has gone awry," says Harvard University economics professor Richard Freeman.

2. Income inequality is a form of discrimination. Wages paid to minority groups and women tend to be significantly lower than those earned by white males.

CON

1. Income inequality is not an inherent problem. Rather, it is capitalism's way of rewarding those who have invested time and effort to develop skills and knowledge. "Rich people are becoming richer because they have some special talent in a global economy," says

Dan Mitchell of the Heritage Foundation.

2. Cutting income inequality through programs like welfare is not fair to those who have worked their way up the economic ladder. Why should their tax dollars support people who have not made the same effort?

SUMMARY

In Framingham, social service agencies dispense benefits like subsidized housing, welfare, food stamps, and Medicaid to the city's south-side poor. Meanwhile, in the kitchen of their large house on the north side, David Walsh and his wife mourn the changes in the town where they have lived for 25 years. "Framingham has become two towns," says Walsh. "Where we live is a wonderful, safe, suburban neighborhood. The south side used to be for people on the lower rungs of the ladder, climbing up. That's not true

anymore. When you go over there now, there's prostitution, drugs, crime, families that are broken. These are people who are falling off the ladder, not climbing up."

Sources: Alice Ann Love, "Social Security Narrows Income Gaps," The Associated Press, April 9, 1999; Del Jones, "Family Income Disparity Increases: Gap Broadens between Richest, Poorest," *USA Today*, December 17, 1997, p. 4B; Gene Koretz, "Economic Trends: The Unhealthy U.S. Income Gap," *Business Week*, November 10, 1997, p. 22; and Charles M. Sennott, "Framingham USA: The Income Gap," *Boston Globe*, special series, July 20–22, 1997.

businesses will respond to these changing marketing opportunities.

Companies that currently offer goods and services geared toward the needs of young consumers aren't likely to disappear, of course, but they may need to adjust their strategies. They may, for example, shift their focuses toward overseas markets to find continued growth. Many Asian countries have relatively large numbers of young consumers who could fill the gap left by the aging U.S. baby boom generation.

Improving Quality and Customer Service

Ongoing improvements in product quality and customer service will continue to require close attention by companies hoping to compete in the global economy of the 21st century. Although technology can help firms to develop exciting new products, poor quality can cause failures when the products hit the market. For example, Seattle-based Virtual i-O Corp. developed a new technology for virtual reality headsets, the computer output systems that give customers three-dimensional virtual reality journeys. The new technology received high marks and attracted millions of dollars from investors. But Virtual i-O eventually declared bankruptcy because poor product quality limited the value

of its products to consumers. "It didn't stand up to the abuse that happens on the retail floor, so a lot of demos didn't work," explained one industry analyst.[29]

On the other hand, Kirk Perron's obsession with product quality made his Jamba Juice business flourish. Perron launched the first store selling his nutritious milkshake-like fruit drinks in 1990. Even though the new venture exceeded his highest expectations, he purposely limited the number of stores the company opened so he could personally monitor product quality. "I just could not see a future with, say, 100 stores," Perron says. "It would have been total chaos." Perron acknowledges that preserving high quality also requires "leveling out Mother Nature's uncontrolled inconsistencies." To accomplish this, the company buys the best fruit at the peak of the season and then freezes the ingredients for future use. When a particularly tasty variety of red peach became available, for example, Perron bought the entire crop.[30]

Customer service is the crucial aspect of a competitive strategy that defines how a firm treats its customers. Businesses show that they value exceptional customer service when they create the easiest possible systems for customers to order and receive their products. They also design systems such as customer-service hot lines to resolve product-related customer complaints. Even marketers of such basic products as Pizza Hut pizzas list toll-free

| Figure 3.16 | AIG Financial Services: Responding to an Aging Population |

SOME SEE SENIOR CITIZENS. WE SEE A BOOM IN CONDO CONSTRUCTION, NEW BUSINESS START-UPS AND INCREASED DEMAND FOR THE WEATHER CHANNEL.

The demographics in many parts of the world are changing rapidly. And along with those changes come unexpected risks and opportunities for all kinds of industries.

Fortunately, AIG is a business partner with expertise in managing total marketplace risk. We specialize in designing the kinds of custom coverages that corporations must have to cope successfully with emerging conditions. Whether your company is actively meeting the demands of aging baby boomers or is a business likely to be affected by shifts in population, AIG has the insurance and financial services you'll need. Services like contractors' liability insurance, asset management and even satellite interruption coverage. And we've got the top financial ratings to back us up.

So when you're ready to deal with change, we'll be willing and able. **WORLD LEADERS IN INSURANCE AND FINANCIAL SERVICES** AIG

American International Group, Inc., Dept. A, 70 Pine Street, New York, NY 10270

customer satisfaction numbers on their packages as communication channels for customer complaints and problems needing management attention.

When Harold Lewis assumed the reins as CEO of Childtime Children's Centers in 1991, the chain of child-care facilities was teetering on the edge of failure. Childtime's problem did not result from a shortage of potential customers; Americans spend $40 billion a year on child care. But the firm's financial statements showed losses or scant profits at most of the centers.

Lewis decided to emphasize customer satisfaction through a combination of quality improvements and enhanced communications with parents. A team of specialists strengthened the Childtime curriculum, and parents received information documenting the changes. Employees working with infants were required to wear disposable hospital booties over their shoes, a visible evidence of the sanitary environments provided at the child-care centers. Communications with parents increased in frequency and information content, and staff members issued report cards for children several times a year. By stressing customer service through these and other methods, Childtime has reached annual sales of $95 million, added new centers, and almost freed itself of debt.

Software designer PeopleSoft is another company benefiting from its management decision to organize operations around providing exceptional service. The firm's 300 account executives act as liaisons between business customers and internal staff members. They aren't paid commissions for the number of products they sell to customers. Instead, their performance evaluations and pay are tied to measures of customer happiness and loyalty. Their primary goal is to establish easy ways for customers to install and use PeopleSoft products. Account executives strive to understand every aspect of their customers' businesses so they can quickly solve problems that those firms face. They act as the customers' voices within the company. "The account manager is really our differentiator," says PeopleSoft's vice president of customer services. "It's the glue that holds PeopleSoft and the customer together."[31]

Maintaining the Competitiveness of the Workforce

Like PeopleSoft, thousands of businesses have discovered that human resources are replacing factories and machines as a decisive competitive factor. "The only way we can beat the competition is with people," notes Chrysler CEO Robert Eaton. "That's the only thing anybody has. Your culture and how you motivate and empower and educate your people is what makes the difference." Success hinges on whether or not a company creates an environment that encourages employees to innovate and follow up on new ideas. Internal systems must then quickly move new ideas through product development and into the marketplace.

Just adding new equipment is not enough. Workers must be trained in effective use of these resources. Employees must have the skills to control, combine, and supervise work operations, and they must be motivated to provide the best-quality products and highest levels of customer service.

The skills and education levels that businesses demand of their workforces are changing in the information economy. Effective workers must now be able to ask appropriate questions, define problems, combine information from many different sources, and deal with topics that stretch across disciplines and cultures. Companies are investing in training programs in order to develop the worker skills they need. U.S. employers spent an estimated $55 billion on formal employee training programs in 1995, and 69 percent of U.S. firms with 65 or more employees reported in a recent study that they are substantially increasing spending on employee training.[32]

The RJ Lee Group is a Pennsylvania company that uses computer-controlled scanning microscopes and other high-tech devices to analyze crime-scene materials for police departments. The company is expanding, but so are its competitors. "The only way to survive is to make your people work smarter and make them more productive," says owner Richard J. Lee. To accomplish that goal, Lee requires all of his technical people to be trained to handle the tasks of jobs other than their own. He also expects computer literacy of everyone in the company, so they can understand and use the company's state-of-the-art internal computer network.[33]

Other companies are joining forces to improve the competitive strength of their workforces. When phone giant Ameritech had trouble finding qualified workers in Cleveland, the company formed a coalition called the Jobs & Work Force Initiative. The task force has involved more than 100 companies in activities aimed at raising the skill levels of Cleveland's workforce. Ameritech's executives are also backing a statewide School-to-Work Program throughout Ohio that makes sure real-world training is part of the curricula at all 2-year and 4-year colleges in the state. The schools are encouraged to include instruction in computer use and customer service in their course offerings.[34]

But business efforts alone are not sufficient to ensure a skilled workforce. As the Business Hall of Fame demonstrated, Ireland's economic success is largely tied to government investment in education and training. In today's global marketplace, similar government initiatives may be required from other countries seeking to develop competitive workforces.

Education levels in the United States have grown over the past two decades. Between 1984 and 1994, the number of people enrolled in both 2-year and 4-year colleges rose 17 percent. By 2005, nearly 4 million more students will be graduating each year than in 1985. Increasingly, education is a critical requirement for any high-paying job. Workers with high-school diplomas, for example, now earn an average of $31,081 a year, while college graduates receive nearly twice as much, $61,008. As Table 3.5 shows, the fastest-growing jobs in the United States demand postsecondary education.

CREATING A LONG-TERM GLOBAL STRATEGY

No country is an economic island in today's global economy. Not only has an ever-increasing stream of goods and services crossed national borders, but many businesses have become true multinational firms, operating manufacturing

Table 3.5	Jobs on the Fast Track			
Career	Description	Entry Salary	Top Salary	Minimum Education
Accounting Business Valuator	Determine the value of business assets	$30,000	$200,000	Bachelor's in accounting, CPA certification
Bank Financial Planner	Recommend investments, manage portfolios	20,000+	175,000	Bachelor's in finance, MBA preferred
Communications Crisis Specialist	Public relations for handling corporate crises	23,000	76,000	Bachelor's in P.R., journalism, or communications
Computer Engineer	Design computer hardware	55,000	79,000+	Bachelor's in software systems, computer engineering, or math
Human Resources Training Specialist	Train workers	31,400	73,900	Bachelor's or master's in business, computers, education, or psychology

plants and other facilities around the world. As global trade and investments grow, the economic events in one country can reverberate around the globe.

Consider, for example, how Asia's recent economic woes may affect business in the United States. Starting in mid-1997, financial markets in Thailand, Indonesia, South Korea, and Japan tumbled. The U.S. stock market reacted with a drop of its own amid fears of shrinking revenues for companies that had invested heavily in Asia. Although the U.S. stock market quickly rebounded, analysts predict that ongoing problems in Asia will continue to affect U.S. businesses by weakening the Asian market for U.S.-made goods such as computers, electronics, and consumer goods. U.S. manufacturers that have built up manufacturing capacity in expectation of growth in Asian markets may find themselves oversupplied, eventually forcing layoffs.[35]

Still, global expansion can offer huge opportunities to U.S. firms. As mentioned in Chapter 1, U.S. residents account for only 4 percent of the world's 6 billion people.

Growth-oriented companies can't afford to ignore the world market outside their native countries. Other U.S. businesses are benefiting from the lower labor costs in other parts of the world, and some are finding successful niches importing goods made by foreign manufacturers. The biggest challenge for U.S. businesses in the 21st century is to develop long-term strategies for global competitiveness that minimize risk while maximizing these opportunities.

WHAT'S AHEAD

Chapter 4 will focus on the global dimensions of business. The chapter will review the key concepts of doing business internationally and examine how nations can position themselves to benefit from the global economy. Then, it will describe the specific methods used by individual businesses to expand beyond their national borders and compete successfully in the global market.

SUMMARY OF LEARNING GOALS

1. Distinguish between microeconomics and macroeconomics.

Microeconomics is the study of economic behavior among individual consumers, families, and businesses whose collective behavior in the marketplace determines the quantity of goods and services demanded and supplied at different prices. By contrast, macroeconomics is the study of the broader economic picture and how an economic system maintains and allocates its resources; it focuses on how a government's monetary and fiscal policies affect the overall operation of an economic system.

2. List each of the factors that collectively determine demand and those that determine supply.

Demand is the willingness and ability of buyers to purchase goods and services at different prices. Factors that collectively determine overall demand for a good or service include customer preferences, number of buyers and their incomes, the prices of substitute goods, the prices of complementary goods, and consumer expectations about the future. Supply sums up the willingness and ability of businesses to offer goods and services for sale at different prices. Overall supply is determined by the costs of inputs (natural resources, capital, human resources, and entrepreneurship), costs of technology resources, taxes, and the number of suppliers operating in the market.

3. Compare supply and demand curves and explain how they determine the equilibrium price for a good or service.

A demand curve is a graph showing the amount of a good or service buyers will purchase at different prices. Since buyers likely will demand increasing quantities of a good at progressively lower prices, demand curves usually slope downward as they move to the right. By contrast, a supply curve is a schedule of the amounts of a good or service that businesses will offer for sale at different prices. Since sellers will likely make progressively more goods and services available as prices rise, supply curves usually slope upward as they move to the right. The interaction of the supply and demand curves determines the equilibrium price, the price at which the quantity supplied by sellers is precisely equal to the quantity demanded.

4. Contrast the three major types of economic systems.

Each of the world's national economies can be classified as either a private enterprise economy, a planned economic system such as communism or socialism, or a mixed market economy. A private enterprise system is characterized by individuals and private businesses pursuing their own interests without undue governmental restriction; by private ownership of factors of production; by investment decisions made by private industry rather than by government decree; and by determination of prices, products, resource allocation, and profits through competition in a free market. In a planned economy, the government exerts stronger control over business ownership, profits, and resources in order to accomplish government—rather than individual—goals. Communism is an economic system without private property; goods are owned in common, and factors of production and production decisions are controlled by the state. Socialism, another type of planned economic system, is characterized by government ownership and operation of all major industries. The final type of economic system, a mixed market economy, blends government ownership and private enterprise, combining characteristics of both planned and market economies.

5. Identify the four different types of market structures in a private enterprise system.

Four basic models characterize competition in a private enterprise system: pure competition, monopolistic competition, oligopoly, and monopoly. Pure competition is a market structure, like that in small-scale agriculture, in which large numbers of buyers and sellers exchange homogeneous products, so no single participant has a significant influence on price. Monopolistic competition is a market structure, like that in retailing, in which large numbers of buyers and sellers exchange relatively well-differentiated (heterogeneous) products, so each participant has some control over price. Oligopolies are market situations, like those in the steel and airline industries, in which relatively few sellers compete, and where high start-up costs form barriers to keep out new competitors. The final market structure is a monopoly, in which only one seller dominates trade in a good or service, for which buyers can find no close substitutes. Local water utilities and firms that hold exclusive patent rights on significant product inventions are examples.

6. Identify the major factors that guide an economist's evaluation of a nation's economic performance.

Economists consider several economic indicators to measure and evaluate the success of an economic system in providing a stable business environment and sustained growth. A nation's productivity is evidence of its economic strength and competitiveness. Gross domestic product (GDP), the market value of all goods and services produced within a nation's boundaries each year, is a commonly used measure of productivity. Changes in general price levels—inflation, price stability, or deflation—are important indicators of an economy's general stability. The U.S. government measures price-level changes by the Consumer Price Index (CPI). A nation's unemployment rate is an indicator of both overall stability and growth. The unemployment rate shows the number of people actively seeking employment who are unable to find jobs as a percentage of the total labor force. A final factor is the relative economic freedom enjoyed by individuals and private businesses in a nation.

7. Compare the two major tools used by a government to manage the performance of its national economy.

The various tools used by government officials to influence the economy can be categorized as elements of either monetary policy or fiscal policy. Monetary policy encompasses a government's efforts to control the size of the nation's money supply. Various methods of increasing or decreasing the overall money supply affect interest rates and therefore impact borrowing and investment decisions. By changing the size of the money supply, government can encourage growth or control inflation. Fiscal policy, the second government tool, involves decisions regarding government revenues and expenditures. Changes in government spending affect economic growth and employment levels in the private sector. However, government must also raise money, either through taxes or through borrowing, to finance its expenditures. Since tax payments represent funds that might otherwise have been spent by individuals and businesses, any taxation changes also affect the overall economy.

8. Describe the major global economic challenges of the 21st century.

Business in the 21st century is likely to be propelled by technological advances that enable businesses to enhance the effectiveness of their use, management, and control of information. A highly trained workforce is an essential requirement for businesses that want to take advantage of this change. A second important economic challenge involves dealing with the effects of an aging population. Both government and business must be prepared to accommodate changing demands in health care, social security, and other support services. Customer service and quality remain vital ingredients for competitive superiority in the global market. A final factor in gaining competitive advantage is a competitive workforce. Both government and business must formulate effective plans for developing the skills and knowledge of workers in the 21st century.

TEN BUSINESS TERMS YOU NEED TO KNOW

economics	socialism
demand	mixed market economy
supply	monetary policy
private enterprise system	fiscal policy
	budget deficit
communism	

Other Important Business Terms

economic system	planned economy
microeconomics	privatization
macroeconomics	productivity
demand curve	gross domestic product (GDP)
supply curve	inflation
factors of production	hyperinflation
equilibrium price	Consumer Price Index (CPI)
pure competition	unemployment rate
monopolistic competition	national debt
oligopoly	balanced budget
monopoly	

REVIEW QUESTIONS

1. Imagine that you own a donut shop. Draw a supply and demand graph that estimates what will

happen to demand, supply, and the equilibrium price if these events occur:

a. A major medical report states that eating donuts appears to reduce the likelihood of heart disease.

b. Consumer incomes decline.

c. The price of flour falls.

d. The government imposes a tax on donut production.

e. Four new donut shops open for business in your area.

f. The Consumer Price Index shows a sharp jump in prices.

2. Compare the three major types of economic systems: private enterprise system, planned economies, and mixed market economies. Discuss the current status of each of these economic systems in the world. What potential benefits does each system offer? What negatives are associated with each system?

3. The four basic types of competition are pure competition, monopolistic competition, oligopoly, and monopoly. What type of competition does each of these companies face in its industry?

a. Texaco

b. McDonald's

c. America Online

d. Fred and Susan Smith's 640-acre Iowa farm

e. Amtrak

f. Your local water utility

4. Distinguish between inflation and deflation. Explain the difference between cost-push inflation and demand-pull inflation. Evaluate the economic indicators used by the U.S. government to measure price-level changes. Is deflation always a positive development?

5. Match the following descriptions with the type of unemployment they represent: (a) frictional, (b) seasonal, (c) cyclical, and (d) structural unemployment.

_____ A factory worker suffers a temporary layoff because of slow sales.

_____ A steelworker loses his job when a mill permanently closes.

_____ An amusement park employee is laid off at the end of the summer.

_____ A recent graduate searches for an entry-level job.

6. Distinguish between monetary policy and fiscal policy. How does each operate to regulate the economy? Cite specific examples. Explain the effects of both monetary policy and fiscal policy on your daily life.

7. Define the term *information economy*. How do the concerns of business differ in an information economy from those in a manufacturing economy?

8. Explain the contributions of quality and customer service to a nation's economic health. How does each help a firm to differentiate itself from competitors?

9. Explain how the development of a competitive national workforce affects the economy. How can the U.S. government and U.S. firms contribute to the development of a competitive workforce?

10. Discuss the importance of developing a long-term global strategy.

QUESTIONS FOR CRITICAL THINKING

1. Economics has been called "this dismal science." Do you agree or disagree? Support your arguments. Identify at least five ways that economics affects your daily life.

2. Identify, as specifically as possible, the factors most likely to affect demand, supply, and equilibrium price in the listed industries. If you were an executive of a company in these industries, how would you monitor changes for each factor?

a. The personal computer industry

b. The fast-food restaurant industry

c. The automobile manufacturing industry

d. The banking industry

3. Must a small business owner whose firm only operates locally remain aware of overall supply and demand trends in the national market for the firm's goods or services? Why or why not? How can supply and demand principles help small business owners to identify potential business opportunities?

4. Review the economic indicators discussed in this chapter. If you were president of the United States, what would you consider the most important indicator of the economy's overall health? Why? Discuss how both monetary and fiscal policies could affect this indicator.

5. Assume that you are chief economic advisor to the president of the United States, and you are convinced that the economy is entering a period of recession. What economic indicators would you cite to support your belief? What actions would you recommend that the president take? Should the federal government always intervene in a recession? Why or why not?

Experiential Exercise

Background: The most phenomenal movie success in recent memory is *Titanic.* Its high-priced production, compelling story line, and string of awards quickly propelled it into first place as the biggest money-making film of all time. Within a matter of weeks following its release, *Titanic* passed longtime box-office leaders like *Star Wars, E.T. The Extra-Terrestrial,* and *Jurassic Park*—and revenue continues to pour in.

Directions: Assume you are a decision-maker at a local theater and must determine the ticket price your theater should charge for an evening showing of *Titanic.* Based on the following assumptions, plot your theater's supply curve on the graph provided in this exercise and label it "supply curve."

Quantity	Price
250	$4.00
325	$6.00
400	$8.00

Using the following assumptions, plot your customers' demand curve on the graph in this exercise and label it "demand curve."

Quantity	Price
450	$4.00
350	$6.00
225	$8.00

Determine the point at which the quantity of theater tickets your company is willing to supply equals the quantity of theater tickets the customers in your area are willing to buy, and label that point "equilibrium price."

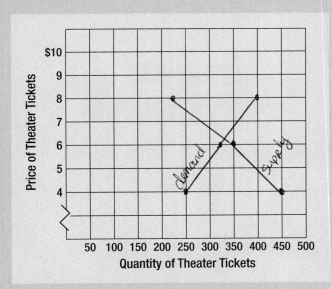

330 tickets $6.25 equl

Equilibrium Price of Theater Tickets

Nothing but Net

1. **Competition.** Assume you have a $2,000 budget to purchase any computer products you want. Visit

   www.zdnet.com/netbuyer/

   and conduct a search on the products you wish to purchase. After you key in information to define your requirements, this Web site will comparison shop for you at some 75 computer product vendors. The site provides you with a wealth of information about what competitors have to offer. Web sites such as these provide you with what you need to know to buy the best products at the best prices.

2. **Privatization.** Use any Web search engine and key in the word "privatization." Find a site that provides information related to an area of privatization that is of interest. For example,

   www.socialsecurity.org/

   is the Cato Institute's Web page on social security privatization. Once you've selected a specific privatization area, write a brief summary that includes at least three problems that are/were driving forces toward privatization and explain the privatization plan. If you select a privatization area that has not yet happened (e.g., social security), write your summary from the perspective of what problems exist that privatization could solve and how proponents suggest privatization should be implemented. On the other hand, if you choose an existing privatization plan (e.g., the Brazilian government's recent privatization of its railroad system), write from the perspective of why privatization was necessary and how privatization was implemented.

3. **Gross Domestic Product (GDP).** The Social Sciences Data Center of the University of Virginia provides NIPA (National Income and Product Accounts) data at

   www.lib.virginia.edu/ssdcbin/nipabin/level1.cgi

   Visit this site to submit a request for a line chart illustrating GDP in billions of dollars for any length of time from 1959 to the most recent quarter for which data is available.

Note: Internet Web addresses change frequently. If you do not find the exact sites listed, you may need to access the organization's or company's home page and search from there.

FOSSIL—KEEPING WATCH ON A GLOBAL BUSINESS

For being only a 14-year-old company, founded by a 23-year-old, Fossil, Inc., located in Richardson, Texas, has emerged as a leader of the fashion watch industry. In the early 1980s Tom Kartsotis was selling hard-to-get tickets for sporting events and concerts. This ticket-scalping business taught him important lessons in marketing. Tom's older brother Kosta, at the time a merchandise executive for a large Dallas department store chain, told him about the large profit margins being earned on importing retail goods from the Far East—in particular, the increasing trend of moderately priced watches pioneered by Swiss-owned Swatch. Taking Kosta's suggestion, Tom went to Hong Kong, where he hired a manufacturer to make 1,500 watches, which he sold to local department stores and boutiques. Fossil was born.

To carve his own niche in the fashion watch industry, Tom came up with a retro theme to differentiate his watches from Swatch or Guess. Inspiration for the watch designs comes largely from old magazines of the 1940s and 1950s.

Today Fossil designs, develops, markets, and distributes fashion watches, leather accessories, and sunglasses principally under the Fossil, FSL, and RELIC brand names. Fossil has sales and distribution centers in the United States, Germany, Italy, Japan, Spain, Hong Kong, Canada, Mexico, and the United Kingdom. This network of distributors offers Fossil products to over 50 countries.

Although Switzerland was known for watch manufacturing, Hong Kong has emerged as the center of the watch industry today. "The reason we picked Hong Kong is twofold," says Gary Bolinger, senior vice president of international sales and marketing. "One, the infrastructure is there. To be able to deliver and assemble goods, and get it out of the country in a timely manner. And secondly the mentality of the Hong Kong people that they can get anything done."

With Hong Kong's return to China in July 1997, there has been much speculation about its impact on businesses. "I have been back twice since the turnover and can safely say that from our business point of view in watch manufacturing there has been no change in that turnover," says Dermott Bland, senior vice president of watch products.

"There have been few changes with regards to exporting and importing, but in the majority, there have been improvements."

Fossil forges ahead with the challenges of anticipating fashion trends, managing product changes, taking the American image global, diversifying with other product lines. Recently, Fossil paired up with London Fog for the production and marketing of Fossil outerwear in the United States.

Questions

1. What type of market structure exists in the fashion watch industry? Explain.

2. How would you classify the economic systems of China? Hong Kong? What impact do you think the return of Hong Kong to China might have on companies like Fossil?

3. What global economic challenges do companies like Fossil and countries that Fossil does business with need to successfully meet to maintain their global competitiveness?

chapter 4

Competing in Global Markets

Beetlemania Revisited

As Yogi Berra would say, "It's *déjà vu* all over again." From "Love Bug" to retro-chic. From planned economy to affordable luxury. From Germany through Mexico—the Volkswagen Beetle has come a long way. It's back, and its brought with it all the magic and nostalgia from the past. The old Beetle of the 1960s and 1970s was more than a car. It was a trusted friend, a component of its owner's personality, and a link to youth that Baby Boomers still talk about with affection. The Beetle was the commuter car that offered solid transportation to an entire generation. It was simple, durable, and inexpensive. Its high gas mileage let owners survive gasoline shortages and soaring prices of the 1970s. By 1968, Americans had bought 399,674 Bugs, making it the leading import in the United States. But within a decade, the Beetle was being supplanted by a host of Japanese imports with names like Honda, Nissan, and Toyota, and the Volkswagen faded into obscurity.

Now it's back for the 21st century and U.S. car dealers can't keep the new Beetle in stock. A quick glance is all you need to recognize that it's the real deal. The body contains front and rear smiles, the dashboard sports a flower vase, and the interior still offers a large assist handle above the glove compartment.

The new model does contain a few basic differences. Front-wheel drive replaces the old rear-wheel approach. A new 2-liter 4-cylinder engine with 115 horsepower is a welcome improvement over the tiny original 48-horsepower version. The new Beetle is 3 inches taller, 4.6 inches longer, and the trunk has been moved from the front to the back. Perhaps the biggest change is the sticker price—$800 in 1949 to between $15,000 and $18,000 today.

www.vw.com

But the difference between the two generations extend beyond horsepower, inches, and price. Buyers won't overlook the up-to-date technology in new features such as standard air conditioning and optional CD player. In fact, the new Beetle is a thoroughly modern creation that is not only functional but also packed with plenty of creature comforts and the latest advancements in safety.

Standard features include such techno-comforts as a pollen and odor filter, a six-speaker stereo, an antitheft alarm system, halogen headlamps, and four-wheel disc brakes. State-of-the-art safety features include energy-absorbing crush zones, dual air bags, and front-seat-mounted side air bags. And for just a bit more cash, you can choose one-touch power windows, cruise control, fog lamps, a folding center armrest, 16-inch alloy wheels, leather seating with heatable front seats, and a three-spoke leather-covered steering wheel.

The old Beetle would rust with envy. Its new namesake is built to the highest standards with unmatched body rigidity. The new Beetle's bumpers and fenders are even made using a dent-resistant plastic. And, best of all, it is no slouch in road tests. The sporty little car rewards its driver with the performance and fun expected from a modern German-engineered car.

The Beetle's cute-as-a-bug image has U.S. consumers pressing their noses against showroom windows, eager for their 30-year-old friend who has come out of the past. True, the Bug now has a little less flower and a little more power. It promises to deliver Volkswagen's most advanced technology and a little more sunshine, along with 48 miles to the gallon. The original Beetle was designed by Ferdinand Porsche in 1935 Germany as a German car for the German masses. Now, designed in Germany and assembled in Mexico for U.S. and other car buyers, the Volkswagen Beetle is truly a product of international business.[1]

CHAPTER OVERVIEW

Consider for a moment how many products you used today that came from outside the United States. Maybe you drank Brazilian coffee with your breakfast, wore clothes manufactured in Honduras or Malaysia, drove to class in a German or Japanese car fueled by gasoline refined from Venezuelan crude oil, and watched a movie on a television set assembled in Mexico for a Japanese company like Sony. A fellow student in France may be wearing Levi's jeans, using an IBM or Compaq computer, and drinking Coca-Cola.

Figure 4.1 **The World of Coca-Cola**

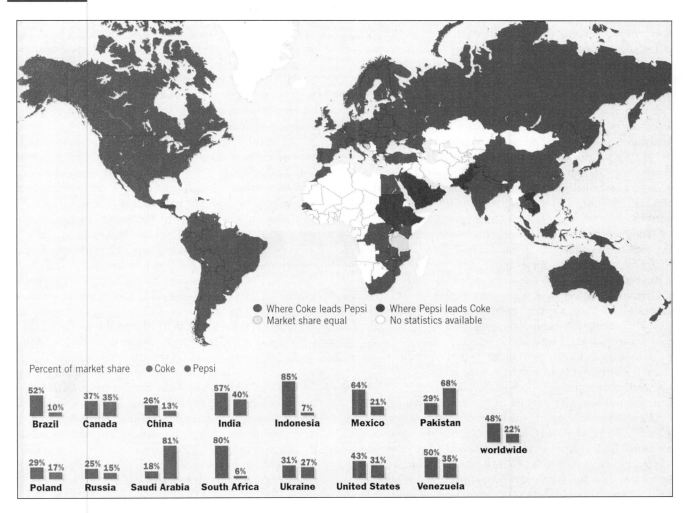

Like Volkswagen, Levi Strauss, IBM, Sony, and Coca-Cola, most U.S. and foreign companies recognize the importance of international trade to their future success. As Chapter 1 explained, economic interdependence is increasing throughout the world as companies seek additional markets for their goods and services as well as the most cost-effective locations for production facilities. No longer can businesses rely only on sales in domestic markets. Today, foreign sales are essential to U.S. manufacturing, agricultural, and service firms, providing new markets and profit opportunities. Foreign companies also seek out new markets.

Thousands of products cross national borders every day. The computers that U.S. manufacturers sell in France are **exports,** domestically produced goods and services

sold in markets in other countries. **Imports** are foreign-made products purchased by domestic consumers. International trade now accounts for almost 25 percent of the U.S. gross domestic product, compared with about 5 percent 25 years ago. U.S. exports exceed $925 billion each year, while annual imports total $1.3 trillion. That total amounts to three times the nation's imports and exports as recently as 1990.

For soft-drink giant Coca-Cola, global markets mean global profits. As Figure 4.1 shows, Coke is a dominant

Business Directory

exports domestically produced goods and services sold in markets in other countries.

imports foreign goods and services purchased by domestic consumers.

brand on every continent. Although its U.S. market share is an impressive 43 percent, it enjoys even better positions abroad, with virtual monopolies marked by market shares of 80 percent or higher in countries like South Africa and Indonesia. In fact, $4 of every $5 Coke earns come from overseas sales. By contrast, its major competitor Pepsi lags far behind in the international marketplace. With the exception of Canada, foreign sales don't produce a dime in profits for Pepsi. The chief reason for this difference in results appears to be Coca-Cola's continuing investment in distribution and other physical resources for getting its products within arm's reach of its customers; instead, Pepsi relies on creative promotions. One observer described soft-drink operations in emerging markets: "Soft drinks are much less about branding than logistics."[2]

Transactions that cross national boundaries may expose a company to an additional set of environmental factors—for example, new social and cultural practices, economic and political environments, and legal restrictions. Before venturing into world markets, companies must adapt their domestic business strategies and plans to accommodate these differences.

This chapter travels through the world of international business to see how both large and small companies approach globalization. First, it considers why nations trade, the importance and characteristics of the global marketplace, and how nations measure international trade. It then examines barriers to international trade that arise from cultural and environmental differences. To reduce these barriers, countries turn to organizations that promote international trade and multinational agreements designed to encourage trade. Finally, the chapter looks at the strategies firms implement for entering global markets and how they develop international business strategies.

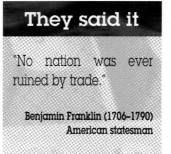

They said it

"No nation was ever ruined by trade."

Benjamin Franklin (1706–1790)
American statesman

WHY NATIONS TRADE

As domestic markets mature and sales growth slows, companies in every industry recognize the increasing importance of efforts to develop business in other countries. McDonald's opens restaurants in Latin America; Nike designs soccer shoes for Brazilians; Wal-Mart tempts Chinese shoppers with a wide selection of merchandise at discount prices. These and other U.S. companies are taking advantage of the interest shown by foreigners in their goods and services. Likewise, the U.S. market, with the world's largest purchasing power, attracts thousands of foreign companies to American shores. Large populations, substantial resources, and rising standards of living are boosting the attractiveness of many countries as targets for U.S. exports and imports.

International trade is vital to a nation and its businesses because it boosts economic growth. The economies of developing nations that encourage international trade grow at an average rate of 4.5 percent a year, compared to only 1 percent for those that resist trade with other countries. The same holds true for industrialized nations. Those that encourage trade saw their economies expand an average of 2.3 percent in a recent year, while business growth averaged only 0.7 percent in those with restrictive policies.

In addition, companies in nations that promote global trade can expand their markets, seek out growth opportunities in other nations, and achieve production and distribution economies. They also reduce their dependence on the economies of their home nations.

"The growth markets of the world are clearly overseas," believes John F. Smith, Jr., head of General Motors Corp., the world's largest automaker. As GM's share of the U.S. light-vehicle market has declined, its focus has shifted to overseas sales of models like the Opel Corsa. In an average year, Smith's firm sells 800,000 Corsas to drivers in 75 countries. In fact, one out of three GM vehicles is sold outside North America.[3]

GM is in the midst of implementing a $2.2 billion "four-plant strategy" for its operations in Argentina, Poland, China, and Thailand to take advantage of local sales opportunities. These new factories represent the company's largest international expansion. By concentrating its investments in the developing world, GM intends to establish 50 percent of its manufacturing capacity outside North America.[4]

www. **www.gm.com**

International Sources of Factors of Production

The General Motors global expansion strategy fits into a larger picture of why nations trade, and in particular, why they target partners in specific countries. Availability of comparably cheap or experienced labor and availability of natural resources, raw materials, and capital—the basic factors of production—influence a company's decision to invest in a foreign country. For example, expertise in titanium technology led Western manufacturers of golf equipment to Russia. Privately owned Metal-Park Co., a converted Soviet missile factory, now processes titanium to produce thousands of golf clubs for U.S. and Asian companies such as Taylor Made Golf Co. in Carlsbad, California.[5]

International trade also boosts employment and wages in the home country. More than 12 million U.S. workers—about one of every 10 members of the nation's workforce—produce goods or provide services for export. Rather than losing their jobs or taking wage cuts, domestic workers who hold export-related jobs earn an average of 15 percent more than the average wage. In the U.S. economy, every additional $1 billion of export sales supports an average of 20,000 jobs.[6]

Other key factors in choosing overseas markets include favorable regulatory conditions and healthy business climates. Trading with other countries also allows a company to spread risk; while the business cycle of a given market is at a low point, another may be enjoying brisk economic activity. For example, U.S. companies turned their attention to the Pacific Rim countries while Europe was in a recession, increasing exports to Europe again when economic activity there picked up. Later sections of the chapter discusses how these elements affect businesses.

Size of the International Marketplace

In addition to their pursuit of production factors such as human and natural resources, entrepreneurship, and capital, companies are attracted to international business by the sheer size of the marketplace. Of the world's 6 billion inhabitants, just over 20 percent live in relatively well-developed countries. The remaining 4.7 billion live on lower incomes in less-developed countries. The gap between these two groups will increase even more in the coming years due to significant differences in birth rates. Population growth in developed nations is only about 0.4 percent per year, five times slower than the 2 percent growth occurring in developing nations.

As developing nations expand their involvement in international trade, the potential for reaching new groups of customers dramatically increases. Firms looking for new sales are inevitably attracted to giant markets like China and India, with populations of 1.2 billion and 950 million, respectively. However, people alone are not sufficient to create a market. Purchasing power is also required. As Table 4.1 shows, population size is no guarantee of economic prosperity. Only two of the ten most populous countries appear on the list of those with the highest per-capita gross domestic product (GDP).

Even though people in the developing nations have lower per-capita incomes than those in the highly developed economies of North America and western Europe, their huge populations do represent lucrative markets. However, the high-income segments of those populations may amount only to small percentages of all households. For example, although India's people receive a low $330 per-capita income, that nation's growing middle class represents a huge potential target market for foreign businesses. An estimated 200 million Indians earn incomes comparable to those in the United States and Canada.[7]

Many developing countries have posted high rates of annual GDP growth, such as China with over 9 percent a year and India, Poland, and Turkey, each with over 6 percent. These markets represent opportunities for global businesses, even though their per-capita incomes lag behind those in more developed countries. Dozens of international firms are currently establishing operations in these countries to position themselves to benefit from local sales driven by rising standards of living.

Developing sophisticated systems of trade and industrial relations lifts the standard of living for a country's population, making it an even more desirable trading partner. A good example is Singapore. Once considered a developing nation, the tiny island country has used its newfound ability to produce competitively priced goods and services to earn industrialized nation status with a per capita gross domestic product of $22,900.[8]

Table 4.1	The World's Top Ten Nations Based on Population and Wealth		
Country	**Population (in millions)**	**Country**	**Per-Capita GDP[a]**
China	1,210	Luxembourg	$33,200
India	950	United States	28,500
United States	270	Japan	23,800
Indonesia	207	United Arab Emirates	23,600
Brazil	163	Switzerland	23,500
Russia	148	Norway	23,300
Pakistan	129	Singapore	22,900
Japan	126	Belgium	22,400
Bangladesh	123	Denmark	22,400
Nigeria	104	France	21,700

[a]Measured in U.S. dollars.

BUSINESS HALL OF FAME

Asian Sources: Changing the Way Asia Does Business

For years, a slow boat to China described the only option for international traders looking to import exotic products from the Far East. Too often, Asian business transactions depended on a company blindly trusting middlemen and go-betweens. Indeed, trade with these countries was often a dark business, reminiscent of Humphrey Bogart in *The Maltese Falcon*.

Fortunately, that is no longer the case. Although business travelers will agree that trips to Hong Kong, Singapore, or Beijing often are tiring and time consuming, they now have the resources of the Web to gain immedi-

ate access to companies in foreign markets without ever leaving home. In addition, cyber-companies now offer many specialized services that facilitate trade, such as providing Western buyers and Eastern suppliers a place to do business. Asian Sources does just that.

Acting as a gateway for electronic commerce, Asian Sources provides trade-matching services in an environment where differences in time, language, and physical distance present no barriers. Based in Hong Kong, Manila and Singapore, the company serves importers around the world and boasts of its unrivaled understanding of Asian business practices. After all, they will tell you, "Asia is our home."

Asian Sources gives practical advice to suppliers, suggesting which

computer systems to install and how to connect to the Internet. It has even negotiated special Internet deals for customers with AT&T in Hong Kong and IBM Global Network in Taiwan. CEO Sarah Benecke says the company's objective is to "help Asian companies meet the challenges of electronic commerce and emerge more efficient and competitive." She believes that e-commerce is no longer an option to be chosen or ignored. Companies that want global business have to get wired now.

Suppliers can also use the services of Asian Sources to create their Web sites. An Asian Sources account executive visits a company, enters product information into a notebook PC, and photographs the products with a digital camera. These data are then uploaded

MAJOR WORLD MARKETS

As Figure 1.6 showed, the major trading partners of U.S. firms are the country's northern and southern neighbors, Canada and Mexico. Other important global partners include Japan, China, Germany, and the United Kingdom.

More than coincidence ensures that these countries represent the world's major market regions: North America, western Europe, the Pacific Rim, and Latin America. These regions encompass not only western Europe and Japan, but also such emerging markets as India, Malaysia, and Vietnam. As Figure 4.2 shows, many of the world's most attractive emerging markets are located in Latin America and around the Pacific Rim.

North America With a combined population of about 400 million and a total GDP exceeding $9 trillion, this region represents one of the world's most attractive markets. The United States—

the single largest market in the world and the most stable economy—dominates North America's business environment. Home to less than 5 percent of the world popula-

Figure 4.2	Emerging Markets for the 21st Century

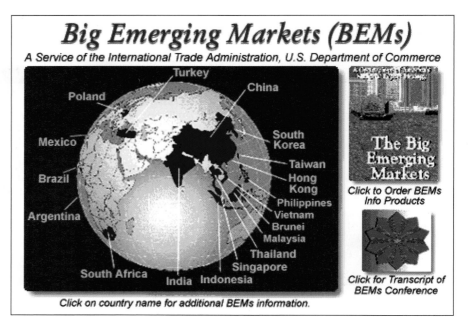

to Asian Sources and used to set up the supplier's virtual showroom. The site goes up on the Web overnight, faster than anyone has ever reached the world market before.

www.asiansources.com

In addition to its basic services, Asian Sources has introduced Private Buyer Catalogs that list the specific products an importer is interested in buying. When an Asian supplier advertises a new product through Asian Sources, the product specifications are automatically e-mailed to the appropriate buyer. The company targets big buyers, such as Ace Hardware, Toys 'R' Us, and Federated Department Stores (parent company to Bloomingdale's and Macy's). These large companies use the services of Asian Sources to find foreign products to stock in their domestic stores. Similarly, Asian suppliers look to Asian Sources to help them find outlets for their products.

Traditional product-sourcing techniques still rely on physical trips to Asia. Each year buyers congregate to meet new suppliers and check out their newest offerings. Asian Sources helps both buyers and sellers during these annual visits by initiating communication between all parties. This service strengthens ties and can even help eliminate the need for trips altogether.

By combining electronic commerce technology, the immediacy of the Internet, and the trust of strategic alliances, Asian Sources is easing business transactions around the globe. The company is doing more than just changing the way Asia does business—it is encouraging and increasing international business as a whole.

Sources: Asian Sources Web site, accessed at www.asiansources.com, February 9, 1999; and Carol Memmott, "Net Saves Time, Opens Door to Asian Market," *USA Today*, November 16, 1998, p. 8E.

QUESTIONS FOR CRITICAL THINKING

1. By using a Web site to advertise their products, suppliers are likely to get many small orders from small companies. Would this be a problem for suppliers? Explain.

2. Asian Sources is beginning to charge suppliers for sending product details to buyers. By paying, suppliers can post their products in a private environment to specific buyers—an improvement for suppliers. How will the new system help buyers? Explain your answer.

---

tion, the country's $8 trillion GDP represents about one-fifth of total world output. Major U.S.-based corporations like Citicorp., General Electric, and Disney maintain sizable investments both around the world and in North America.

Canada's business organizations, while often overshadowed by U.S. competitors, still have a major international presence, with companies like Bell Canada investing in Latin America.[9] Canada's international trade totals about $400 billion. Because trade with the United States now accounts for two-fifths of Canada's GDP, its economy is extremely vulnerable to events in the U.S. economy.[10]

South of the border, Mexico is another country moving from developing-nation to industrial-nation status, thanks to low-cost labor and the North American Free Trade Agreement (NAFTA). Stretching 2,100 miles from the Pacific Ocean to the Gulf of Mexico, the U.S.-Mexican border is home to 1,500 _maquiladoras,_ foreign-owned manufacturing plants that produce products for export. Tijuana has become the television manufacturing capital of the world. Sanyo Electric moved its North American headquarters from New York to San Diego to be close to its Tijuana plant. Cincinnati-based Baldwin Piano & Organ Co. employs 270 workers in its Juarez factory, across the border from El Paso.[11]

Mexican products are also competing effectively in the U.S. market. In 1998, U.S. sales of Corona surpassed those of long-time market leader Heineken making it the leading import brand of beer.

Western Europe Western Europe, particularly Germany, the United Kingdom, France, and Italy, is a sophisticated and powerful industrial region with a combined GDP comparable to that of the United States. The European Union, an economic community created in 1992 and discussed later in this chapter, has solidified the importance of this market. Royal Dutch Shell, Nestlé, Daimler Benz, and Glaxo Wellcome are international companies with headquarters in this region.

Significant investments from around the world are flowing into European nations, as foreign companies locate manufacturing and distribution facilities across the continent. In Britain, where traditional industries such as shipbuilding and coal mining have declined, foreign manufacturers are establishing themselves. Japan's Nissan Motor Co. set up an auto-assembly plant in the northeastern region of Sunderland to turn out 250,000 Primeras and Micras each year, making it one of Europe's three largest car-production facilities.

One growth industry currently making inroads in Britain is electronics. Scotland's equivalent of California's Silicon Valley, Silicon Glen, is located between Glasgow and Edinburgh. IBM, Compaq Computer, Hewlett-

Packard, and Sun Microsystems operate factories there, and Germany's Siemens is spending $1.8 billion on a new semiconductor plant that will employ 1,500 people.[12]

One of France's major economic assets is a large supply of well-trained, high-tech talent. French levels of formal education are second only to those in the United States, and France has supplied U.S. high-tech industries with such notable executives as 3Com CEO Eric Benhamou and Borland founder Philippe Kahn.[13] To attract foreign investors, the French government emphasizes the availability, expertise, and flexibility of its country's workforce in promotions such as the one shown in Figure 4.3.

Even the nearby countries of eastern Europe are considered excellent growth prospects for international businesses. Following the fall of communism, the former Soviet-bloc countries have opened their borders to international trade. They are also modifying their legal, political, and economic environments to improve conditions for development of market economies. A good example is Germany's eastern neighbor. Poland's GDP growth rate exceeds 6 percent per year, making it one of Europe's fastest-growing economies. U.S. exports to Poland have passed the $1 billion mark, up 56 percent since 1992.[14]

The Pacific Rim Australia, China (including Hong Kong), Indonesia, Japan, Malaysia, the Philippines, Singapore, South Korea, and Taiwan are the major nations of this large and growing region. As recently as 1996, the combined exports of Japan, China, and Hong Kong totaled $743 billion and U.S.-Asian trade was $210 billion. The industries that fuel Asian economies—electronics, automobiles, and banking—are strong competitors to U.S. companies.[15]

The euphoria once associated with rapid Asian growth rates faded in 1997, as the region faced what Singapore Prime Minister Goh Chok Tong called, "Asia's worst crisis since the Second World War." A combination of poorly regulated banking activities and an influx of investment dollars from westerners eager to participate in the region's economic growth led to a series

of bad loans for highly speculative real estate ventures. As business failures increased, nervous local and foreign investors began to pull their money out of banks, and real estate values plummeted, leaving the economies of Indonesia, Malaysia, South Korea, and Thailand in shambles.[16]

During the 5 years prior to this economic crisis, U.S. exports to Asia's ten largest markets had increased at an annual rate of 10 percent. This growth can be attributed to three factors:

▼ Asia's fast-growing economies created local markets where U.S. goods and services were in strong demand.

▼ Liberalized trade policies in the region removed many barriers to importing American products.

▼ Foreign investment in Asian countries accelerated, especially by U.S. companies.[17]

China is perhaps the most remarkable success story among a number of Pacific Rim nations with successes of their own. Until recently, China was known as a leading exporter of low unit-value goods like toy dolls and clothing. Today, however, it is challenging both the United States and Japan with its capabilities for low-cost production of high-tech products. Its exports of high-tech goods leaped 75 percent over the past 4 years, making China the world's second fastest-growing economy.[18]

Despite inevitable and periodic declines in the region's economies, Asia's technology-driven markets, rapid urbanization, and growing middle class make it a significant market for U.S. goods and services.

Latin America Latin American countries, in particular Brazil and Argentina, are attracting an unprecedented flow of foreign direct investment. Privatization of port facilities, railways, telecommunications, mining, and energy has contributed important motivation to attract new industry. Another stimulant is the 1995 formation of the MERCOSUR,

Figure 4.3 **Attracting Foreign Investments to France by Emphasizing Local Workforce Strengths**

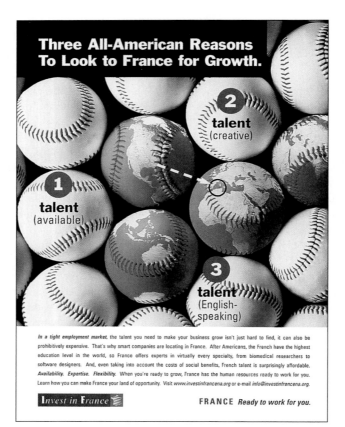

Three All-American Reasons To Look to France for Growth.

1 talent (available)

2 talent (creative)

3 talent (English-speaking)

In a tight employment market, the talent you need to make your business grow isn't just hard to find, it can also be prohibitively expensive. That's why smart companies are locating in France. After Americans, the French have the highest education level in the world, so France offers experts in virtually every specialty, from biomedical researchers to software designers. And, even taking into account the costs of social benefits, French talent is surprisingly affordable. *Availability. Expertise. Flexibility.* When you're ready to grow, France has the human resources ready to work for you. Learn how you can make France your land of opportunity. Visit *www.investinfrancena.org* or e-mail *info@investinfrancena.org*.

Invest in France

FRANCE *Ready to work for you.*

a cooperative attempt by Argentina, Brazil, Paraguay, and Uruguay to reduce trade barriers. The United States is the MERCOSUR's largest trading partner.

These moves to encourage international investment and trade are a dramatic change from the past, when foreign companies stayed away from Latin America, fearing its political and economic volatility. In addition, the area had compiled a poor record for innovation. Latin American firms spend very little on research and development and avoid active participation in new industries, due in part to difficulties in obtaining start-up capital.

Some of these conditions are changing, however. Pay television is gaining popularity, creating opportunities for local programming in Spanish and Portuguese. Privatization of telecommunications is creating some local technology companies. In Chile, Fundacio Chile, a technology transfer center, has developed new industries such as salmon farming (in which Chile now ranks second in the world), berry growing, and furniture making. The investment firm Cresud is investing in Argentina's farms and looking at growing activity in beef processing and marketing since U.S. restrictions on beef imports from the country have been lifted.[19]

Latin America is a big market for high-technology products. Microsoft sells $500 million in software in Latin America, and the total is soaring. "We are experiencing 30 to 40 percent growth every year," says Alessandro Annoscia, Microsoft's enterprise customer manager for Latin America. "We believe the region is underinvested still in the information technology business."[20]

As trade barriers slip away and governments and economies stabilize throughout the region, Latin America is becoming home to a growing contingent of multinationals and competing strongly in areas such as electric utilities. "Latin America is for big players now," says Ricardo Alvial Muñoz, investor relations director for the Chilean energy conglomerate Enersis. Enersis, Latin America's largest private-sector electricity firm, provides electric power to 32 million people in the region.[21]

Absolute and Comparative Advantage

Few countries can produce all the goods and services needed by their people. For centuries, trading has been the way that countries can meet those needs. If a country can focus on producing what it does best, it can export surplus domestic output and buy foreign products that it lacks or cannot efficiently produce. The potential for foreign sales of a particular good or service depends largely on whether the country has an absolute advantage or comparative advantage.

A country has an *absolute advantage* in making a product for which it can maintain a monopoly or that it can produce at a lower cost than any competitor. For centuries, China enjoyed an absolute advantage in silk production. This luxurious fabric was woven from fibers recovered from silkworm cocoons, making it a prized raw material in high-quality clothing such as the silk neckties shown in Figure 4.4. Demand among Europeans for silk led to establishment of the famous *silk road,* a 5,000-mile link between Rome and the ancient Chinese capital city of Xian.

Absolute advantages are rare these days. One good current example is the diamond-mining industry in Russia and South Africa. However, some countries manage to approximate absolute advantages in some products: Middle Eastern countries' control over oil can endanger U.S. supplies when a threat of war or political unrest emerges. The Brazilian and Colombian dominance in coffee production can create price surges when crop damage limits harvests.

By contrast, a nation can develop a *comparative advantage* in a product if it can supply it more efficiently and at a lower price than it can supply other goods, compared to the outputs of other countries. China has long held a comparative advantage in producing toys and clothing due to very low labor costs. On the other hand, Japan has maintained a comparative advantage in producing electronics by preserving efficiency and technological expertise. U.S. exports reflect the country's highly industrialized environment and variety of natural resources. U.S. firms export cars, computers,

Figure 4.4 **Silk: Source of Ancient China's Absolute Advantage**

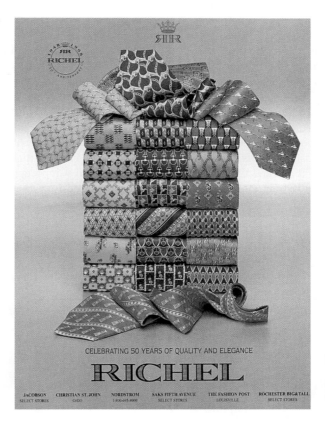

CELEBRATING 50 YEARS OF QUALITY AND ELEGANCE

RICHEL

JACOBSON SELECT STORES   CHRISTIAN ST. JOHN OHIO   NORDSTROM 1-800-695-8000   SAKS FIFTH AVENUE SELECT STORES   THE FASHION POST LOUISVILLE   ROCHESTER BIG&TALL SELECT STORES

and grain overseas, and they import clothing, oil, and television sets.

MEASURING TRADE BETWEEN NATIONS

Clearly, engaging in international trade provides tremendous competitive advantages to both the countries and companies involved. Any attempt to measure global business activity requires an understanding of the concepts of the balance of trade and balance of payments. Another important factor is currency exchange rates.

A country's **balance of trade** is the relationship between its exports and imports. If a country exports more than it imports, it achieves a favorable balance of trade, called a *trade surplus.* If it imports more than it exports, it produces an unfavorable balance of trade, called a *trade deficit.* The United States has run a trade deficit every year since 1976. Despite being the world's top exporter, the U.S. economy feels an even greater appetite for foreign-made goods. The trade deficit peaked in 1987 at $152 billion, dropped to $28 billion by 1991, and crept up to $114 billion in 1997.[22]

As Figure 4.5 shows, the export total for 1997 of $78 billion was more than offset by imports that topped the $1 trillion mark for the first time. Almost all of this deficit results from trade with Japan ($56 billion) and China ($50 billion). China is expected to surpass Japan prior to 2000 as the country with which the United States has its largest trade deficit. In addition, the trade deficit will continue to grow due to Asia's economic problems.[23]

A nation's balance of trade plays a central role in determining its **balance of payments**—the overall flow of money into or out of a country. Other factors also affect the balance of payments, including overseas loans and borrowing, international investments, profits from such investments, and foreign aid payments. Figure 4.6 illustrates the components of a country's balance of payments. A favorable balance of payments, or a *balance of payments surplus,* brings more money into a country than out of it. An unfavorable balance of payments, or *balance of payments deficit,* takes more money out of the country than enters it.

Major U.S. Exports and Imports

The United States, with combined exports and imports of $2 trillion, leads the world in international trade activity. Table 4.2 shows the top ten categories of goods exchanged by U.S. exporters and importers.

With $150 billion in annual imports from the United States, Canada is the largest single-country market for U.S. exports. The Pacific Rim countries as a region account for over $200 billion in annual U.S. imports.[24] While the United States imports more goods than it exports, the opposite is true for services. U.S. exporters sell more than $235 billion in annual service exports, about half of the total from travel and tourism—money spent by foreign nationals visiting the United States. U.S. service exports include business and technical services such as engineering, financial services, computing, legal services, and entertainment. Others involve technologies developed by U.S. firms that earn royalties and licensing fees from users abroad. Many service exporters are well-known companies, like American Express, American Airlines, America Online, AT&T, Citibank, Walt Disney, Allstate Insurance, and Federal Express, as well as retailers such as Foot Locker, The Gap, Office Depot, Toys 'R' Us, and PriceCostco warehouse clubs.

| **Figure 4.5** | **U.S. International Trade in Goods and Services** |

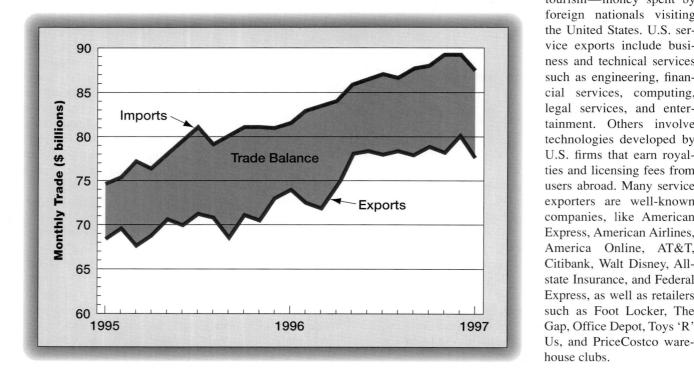

As developing nations industrialize, they often call on the expertise of U.S. financial and legal professionals. For example, when China's state-owned corporations needed to raise funds in international markets, accounting firm Arthur Andersen sent over 1,000 professionals to bring U.S. accounting standards to the country.[25]

Entertainment is a major growth area for U.S. service exports. "The North American market is basically saturated," says Daniel Friego, director of Buena Vista Studio's European distribution. Buena Vista, a Disney division, is not only exporting its U.S. movies to Europe and Asia, but it also produces feature films specifically for local audiences. "Internationally, we're seeing more people going to the movies," says Friego.[26]

The Discovery Channel also takes its TV shows worldwide to create a global television network. It reaches over 87 million subscribers in 90 countries, from New Zealand to Saudi Arabia. As Figure 4.7 indicates, the Discovery Channel's blend of science and technology, world cultures, nature, and adventure stories is a successful formula for attracting audiences around the globe, including 35 million Latin American viewers. Discovery's Cartoon Network is Asia's most popular children's network, seen in over 9 million homes and broadcast in three languages: English, Mandarin, and Thai. The Cartoon Network also has 5 million fans in Latin America and another 31 million in Europe.[27]

U.S. annual imports worth more than $1 trillion rank the country as the world's leading importer. American tastes for foreign-made goods, reflected by the huge trade deficits with the consumer-goods exporting nations of China and Japan, also extend to European products. Last year, the 15 EU countries shipped $6.5 billion of consumer-ready foods like cheese, liquor, and chocolate to U.S. buyers.[28]

U.S. economic growth is luring even more companies to try their luck in this market. "The U.S. market is huge, and we can't afford not to be there," says Mitsuo Hama, general manager of Rheon Automatic Machinery Co., a Japanese manufacturer of pasta-making machines. Rheon hopes to triple its exports to the United States by 2000. Similarly, another Japanese firm, Iris Ohyama Co., is exporting its flower pots, storage containers, and garbage bins to retailers like Staples and Target. The plastics company's $60 million in revenues from U.S. sales represent 10 percent of its total revenues, allowing it to survive in the face of Japan's economic downturn. "To survive," says owner Kentaroh Ohyama, "you have to succeed internationally."[29]

Exchange Rates

A nation's **exchange rate** is the rate at which its currency can be exchanged for the currencies of other nations. Each currency's exchange rate is usually quoted in terms of an-

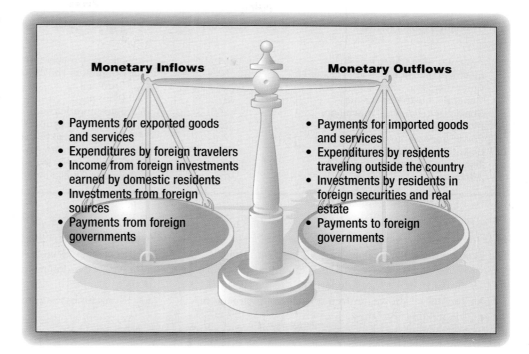

Figure 4.6 **Balance of Payments Components**

Monetary Inflows
- Payments for exported goods and services
- Expenditures by foreign travelers
- Income from foreign investments earned by domestic residents
- Investments from foreign sources
- Payments from foreign governments

Monetary Outflows
- Payments for imported goods and services
- Expenditures by residents traveling outside the country
- Investments by residents in foreign securities and real estate
- Payments to foreign governments

Business Directory

balance of trade surplus or deficit relationship between a nation's exports and imports.

balance of payments surplus or deficit flow of money into or out of a country.

exchange rate value of one nation's currency relative to the currencies of other countries.

Table 4.2	Top Ten U.S. Exports and Imports			
Major Export Product	**Amount (billions)**		**Major Import Product**	**Amount (billions)**
1. Agricultural products	$59		1. Electrical machinery	$76
2. Electrical machinery	57		2. Computers and office equipment	67
3. Computers and office equipment	36		3. Crude oil	51
4. General industrial machinery	27		4. Clothing	42
5. Specialized industrial machinery	26		5. Telecommunications equipment	34
6. Motor vehicle parts	25		6. Agricultural products	33
7. Power generating equipment	22		7. Cars produced in Canada	25
8. Scientific instruments	21		8. General industrial machinery	25
9. Telecommunications equipment	20		9. Power generating equipment	23
10. Airplanes	19		10. Cars produced in other countries (not Canada)	22

other important currency, for example, the number of Mexican pesos needed to purchase one U.S. dollar. Table 4.3 compares the values of several national currencies against the U.S. dollar over a 12-month period.

As the table shows, currency values fluctuate, or "float," depending on the supply and demand for each currency in the international market. In this system of *floating exchange rates,* currency traders create a market for the world's currencies based on each country's relative trade and investment prospects. In theory, this market permits exchange rates to vary freely according to supply and demand. In practice, exchange rates do not float in total freedom. National governments often intervene in the currency markets to adjust the exchange rates of their own currencies. Also, nations form currency blocs by linking their exchange rates to each other, and many governments practice protectionist policies that seek to guard their economies against trade imbalances. **Devaluation** describes a fall in a currency's value relative to other currencies or to a fixed standard. The dramatic changes in the value of the South Korean and Thai cur-

rencies shown in Table 4.3 are examples of devaluations. Each currency decreased to about half of its former value relative to the dollar due to the recent economic crisis in Asia.

Sometimes, national governments take deliberate action to devalue their currencies as a way to increase exports. Although devaluation may not change the price of a U.S.-made product, a buyer in Austria receives a de facto price cut due to a devaluation of the U.S. dollar, because he or she would gain more dollars for the same amount of Austrian schillings. Not only would U.S. goods sell for lower prices abroad, but foreign tourists would find that American vacations would cost less, too. At the same time, the U.S. currency devaluation would force U.S. consumers to pay more than before for imported products. American companies would also find foreign goods more expensive, while foreign firms would be attracted to cheaper U.S. products.

Exchange rate changes can quickly wipe out or create a competitive advantage, so they are important factors in decisions about whether or not to invest abroad. If the

Figure 4.7 **Entertainment: A Major U.S. Service Export**

We've got 35 million viewers in Latin America, but we're willing to share.

WORLD CULTURE · NATURE
HUMAN ADVENTURE · CURIOUS
SCIENCE & TECHNOLOGY
FUN · INTERACTIVE · SMART

Discovery Channel Latin America is one of the fastest growing networks in the region, now reaching over 6.7 million subscribers. Add the viewing audience for Discovery Kids Channel and you've got over a million more. Tack on the fact that we're #1 in viewer satisfaction for the second year in a row, and what have you got? The undivided attention of an entire continent. Care to borrow it for :30? If you've got something to sell, you've got somewhere to buy.

DISCOVERY CHANNEL
LATIN AMERICA/IBERIA

Discovery Kids CHANNEL

Miami: Call Cathleen Pratt at 305-461-4710 ext. 4401   New York: Call Chris Czarkowski at 212-751-2220 ext. 4933

dollar rises in price relative to the yen, for instance, a dollar will buy more yen. For example, in 1995, it took 84 yen to buy one U.S. dollar. By 1998, the value had dropped to almost 130 yen per dollar. As a result, Japanese products became less expensive than before the change. Japanese exports to the United States increased, and U.S. firms faced greater competition.[30]

Currencies that owners can easily convert into other currencies are called *hard* currencies. Examples include the U.S. dollar, British pound, Japanese yen, and Swiss franc. The Russian ruble and many eastern European currencies are considered *soft* currencies, because they cannot be readily converted. Exporters that trade with these countries often prefer to barter, accepting payment in oil, timber, or other commodities that they can resell for hard currency payments.

Table 4.3	Foreign Exchange Rates for Selected Currencies		
Country	Currency Unit	1997 Exchange Rate (per U.S. dollar)	1998 Exchange Rate (per U.S. dollar)
Canada	Dollar	1.3	1.4
China	Yuan	8.3	8.3
France	French franc	5.4	6.1
Germany	Deutsche mark	1.6	1.8
India	Rupee	36.0	39.0
Italy	Lira	1,568.0	1,790.0
Japan	Yen	118.0	127.0
Mexico	Peso	7.8	8.6
South Korea	Won	854.0	1,564.0
Switzerland	Swiss franc	1.4	1.5
Thailand	Baht	26.0	45.0
United Kingdom	Pound	0.59	0.63

BARRIERS TO INTERNATIONAL TRADE

All businesses encounter barriers in their operations, whether they sell only to local customers or trade in international markets. For example, national food chains distribute different products to rural U.S. stores than to large chain stores in major cities. These differences and difficulties are multiplied many times over for businesses with international operations. International companies may also have to reformulate their products to accommodate different tastes in new locations. Frito-Lay exports cheeseless Cheetos to Asia, while Domino's Pizza offers pickled ginger pizzas at its Indian fast-food restaurants.

In addition to social and cultural differences, companies engaged in international business also face economic barriers as well as legal and political ones. Some of the hurdles shown in Figure 4.8 are easily breached, while others require major changes in a company's business strategy. To successfully compete in global markets, companies and their managers must understand not only how these barriers affect international trade but also how to overcome them.

Social and Cultural Differences

Understanding and respecting social and cultural differences, ranging from language to customs to educational background to religious holidays, is a critical part of the process leading to international business success. Businesspeople armed with knowledge of host countries' cultures, languages, social values, and religious attitudes

Figure 4.8 Barriers to International Trade

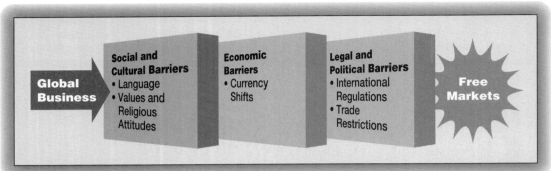

come well equipped to the negotiating table. Acute sensitivity to such elements as attitudes, forms of address and dress, body language, and timeliness also help them to win customers and achieve their business objectives. Without this knowledge, companies may discover that their goods and services will not appeal to customers in foreign countries. The Business Tool Kit provides advice on avoiding social and cultural blunders when doing business abroad.

Language Understanding a business colleague's local language is a critical factor in international business. Companies and their representatives must not only choose correct and appropriate words, but they must also translate words correctly to convey the intended meanings. Companies may need to rename products or rewrite slogans for foreign markets. Imagine the reaction in Japan when Microsoft's marketing tag line, "Where do you want to go today?" was translated, "If you don't know where you want to go, we'll make sure you get taken."[31]

Potential communication barriers include more than mistranslation. Companies may present messages through inappropriate media, overlook local customs and regulations, or ignore differences in taste. For example, *Good Housekeeping* does not try to export the same magazine it sells in the United States. "That would be cultural suicide," according to editor-in-chief Ellen Levine. For the Japanese market, *Good Housekeeping* changed the content to avoid articles about idealized

America and eliminated its Seal of Approval, which confused Japanese women. The magazine hired Japanese writers to produce stories that appealed to that country's readers, usually younger than its typical U.S. readers. In addition, *Good Housekeeping* needed to print the magazine on higher-quality paper than it used for the U.S. version to appeal to Japanese readers.[32]

Values and Religious Attitudes Even though today's world is shrinking in many ways, people in different countries do not necessarily share the same values or religious attitudes. Marked differences remain in workers' attitudes between traditionally capitalist countries and those adopting new capitalist systems and even among traditionally capitalist countries.

For example, U.S. society places a different value on the labor force than attitudes common in Europe. U.S. employees often receive no paid vacation benefits during their first year of employment and then get 2 weeks vacation, working up to 3 or 4 weeks over many years. In Europe, the standard vacation time is 5 to 6 weeks per year. A U.S. company that opens a manufacturing plant in Europe would not be able to hire any workers without offering vacations in line with local business practices.

U.S. culture promotes national unity tolerant of regional differences. The United States is viewed as a national market with a single economy. European countries that are part of the 15-member European Union are trying to create a similar marketplace. However, many resist the idea of being European citizens first and British, Italian, or French citizens second. British consumers differ from Italians in important ways, and U.S. companies that fail to recognize this variation will run into problems with brand acceptance.[33]

BUSINESS TOOL KIT

When in Rome . . . or Riyadh

When managers venture overseas, they are moving into mysterious cultural waters. Unless they research the customs of the countries they visit, they risk making major etiquette mistakes—and losing sales in the process. Here are some tips to help you avoid offending your international business colleagues, whether you are in Europe or the Middle East.

▼ *Gift giving* Some gifts that are commonly exchanged in the United States are associated with funerals elsewhere: flowers in Ghana and clocks in China, for example. If you express your admiration for a Ming vase while dining at the home of a Chinese colleague, the host will probably give it to you, as he believes it his responsibility to take care of your every wish. He will expect you to reciprocate in kind. In Latin America and throughout Asia, gifts of knives and handkerchiefs mean that the givers wish hardship on the recipients. Presenting gifts with the left hand in Moslem cultures is taboo, since it is believed to be the unclean hand.

▼ *Negotiating styles* In China, a signed contract is viewed as acknowledging an agreement to work together, not the final deal. A Chinese businessperson may want to change the terms. Indonesian and Japanese people desire to avoid confrontation and say *no* many ways, so understanding requires careful listening.

▼ *Scheduling* Don't arrive late for meetings in the Netherlands, as Dutch executives prize punctuality. In Russia, however, meetings often start late and run hours longer than expected, so allow flexibility in your schedule.

▼ *Gestures* The gesture of drawing a finger across one's throat means "I love you" in Swaziland, an interpretation far removed from its U.S. meaning. The gesture with the thumb and forefinger making a circle means "A-OK" in the United States, but it is considered obscene in Brazil.

▼ *Shaking hands* In Europe, businesspeople shake hands when they meet even after being apart for short periods, such as lunch breaks. The style of the handshake is also an important consideration. The French and Japanese expect one firm shake, and a Japanese handshake may include a slight bow. Arab and Latin American businesspeople typically favor lighter and more lingering handshakes. Ending the handshake too soon could be interpreted as a rejection.

Gifts bring particularly important risks, but what constitutes a good gift? Two general suggestions are gifts that reflect your home country—things like coffee-table books with photos of U.S. cities and landscapes and uniquely American fare such as maple syrup, Southern barbecue sauce, a baseball cap from a local team, a jacket from a well-known university, or a souvenir from the local golf course. (Just make sure that there are no "Made in Taiwan" labels on the bottom!) In Japan, difficult-to-find items like a basket of U.S.-grown citrus fruits make excellent gifts. A small, silver compass makes a wonderful gift for Muslim associates. No matter where in the world they may be, they can always locate Mecca and perform daily prayers.

Sources: Dean Foster, "The Gift that Keeps on Grating," *Brandweek*, February 23, 1998, p. 21; "Five Tips for International Handshaking," *Sales and Marketing Management*, July 1997, p. 90; and Nicole Crawford, "When in Ghana, Hold the Flowers," *Promo*, September 1997, p. 132.

Whirlpool, the U.S. appliance manufacturer, discovered that European value differences affected acceptance of its products. Company managers were surprised to learn that Scandinavians wanted washing machines that would spin-dry clothes much more thoroughly than those sold in southern Italy, where consumers prefer to dry clothes naturally, taking advantage of their warm weather.

Companies like Whirlpool can learn from disappointing experiences and rethink their strategies. While intent on maintaining its global manufacturing plan, Whirlpool restructured its European operations and laid off almost 8,000 employees. By 1998, total net earnings had doubled those of the previous year. Company officials credited the profit increase to improved European operations.[34]

Because religion plays an important role in every society, businesspeople must cultivate sensitivity to the dominant religions in countries where they operate. Understanding religious cycles and the timing of major holidays can help to prevent embarrassing moments when scheduling meetings, trade shows, conferences, or events such as the dedication of a new manufacturing plant. For example, people doing business in Saudi Arabia must take into account the month-long Ramadan observance, when companies do no work after noon. Friday is the Moslem Sabbath, so the Saudi work week runs from Saturday through Thursday.[35]

Companies can unknowingly offend members of religious groups. Nike's Summer Hoops basketball shoes sported the word "air" written in stylized script with flame-like letters, as shown in Figure 4.9. Moslems complained that the logo looked like the Arabic word for Allah, or God, and the Council on American-Islamic Relations threatened a worldwide boycott. Nike recalled the shoes and discontinued production.[36]

Economic Differences

Business opportunities are flourishing in densely populated countries such as China and India, as local consumers eagerly buy Western products. While such prospects might tempt American firms, managers must first consider the economic factors involved in doing business in these markets. A country's size, per-capita income, and stage of economic development are among the economic factors to consider when evaluating it as a candidate for an international business venture.

In 1998, the popular newsmagazine *Time* launched a Latin American edition. While the Spanish-language edition reported on such global issues as cloning, the decidedly Latin American focus of the new magazine generated sales of over 800,000 copies.

Along with these factors, businesses should also consider a country's infrastructure. **Infrastructure** refers to basic systems of communication (television, radio, print media, telecommunications), transportation (roads and highways, railroads, airports), and energy facilities (power plants, gas and electric utilities). These economic factors are more critical in developing countries. People in Japan enjoy a high standard of living. They live in a society with a well-established infrastructure and a per-capita GDP of about $24,000. Their neighbors in China, where the per-capita GDP is only $3,200, live in much more primitive conditions, and few families have telephone and electric service.

The need for improving national infrastructures is a priority of such global firms as telecommunications giant AT&T, as shown in Figure 4.10. AT&T provides long-distance service to every country and territory in the world—280 total—and has operations and business alliances in over 30 countries, providing satellite, digital, and wireless communication services.

Despite growing similarities in infrastructure, when crossing borders the world over, people encounter basic economic differences: national currencies. Although many countries trade in U.S. dollars, firms may trade in the local currency—for example, the Mexican peso, Chinese yuan, Indonesian rupee, Swiss franc, Japanese yen, and English pound. Foreign currency fluctuations may present added problems for global businesses.

Currency Shifts As explained earlier in the chapter, the values of the world's major currencies fluctuate in relation to each other. The recent financial crisis in Asian markets has shown how exchange rates affect the economic environment for businesses. As exchange rates in many Asian countries dropped, people who owned U.S. dollars were able to buy more than they could have before the changes. This development brought an advantage to U.S. residents who dreamed of relaxing on vacations to Bali as well as to businesses importing clothing made in China and Korea. With the increasing value of the dollar compared to local currencies, tourists pay significantly less for hotel rooms and food than if they were traveling when the value of the dollar had fallen.

Residents, local businesses, and U.S. firms depending on Asian sales found themselves in much less fortunate circumstances. Vans Inc., a shoemaker with substantial Asian export sales, cut its workforce by 30 percent in response to sharply reduced sales there, particularly in Japan. San Diego-based Qualcomm, a company that supplies wireless telecommunications systems to Asia and developing countries, laid off 700 employees following cancellation of orders for circuit components from South Korea.[37]

Political and Legal Differences

Similar to social, cultural, and economic differences, legal and political differences in host countries can pose barriers to international trade. Indonesian laws prohibit foreign firms from creating their own wholesale or retail distribution channels, forcing outside companies to work through local distributors. Brazilian law requires foreign-owned manufacturers to buy most of their supplies from local vendors. Managers involved in international business must be well-versed in legislation that affects their industries if they want to compete in today's world marketplace.

Some countries impose general trade restrictions. Others have established detailed rules that regulate how foreign companies can do business. The one consistency among all countries is the striking lack of consistent laws and regulations governing the conduct of business.

Political Climate An important factor in any international business investment is the stability of the political climate. The political structures of many nations promote stability similar to that in the United States. Other nations, such as Iraq, Congo, and Bosnia, feature quite different—and frequently changing—structures. Host nations often pass laws designed to protect their own interests, often at the expense of foreign businesses. In South Korea, for example, government subsidies benefit domestic consumer electronics producers, and government restrictions limit imports of electronic equipment.

During the past decade, the political structures of Russia, Turkey, the former Yugoslavia, Hong Kong, and

Figure 4.9 **Nike: Discontinuing a Potentially Offensive Shoe Design**

Nike's "Air" logo

The Arabic word for Allah

several eastern European countries (including the Czech Republic and Poland) have seen dramatic changes. Such political changes almost bring changes in the legal environment. Hong Kong is an example of an economy where political developments produced changes in the legal and cultural environments.

Hong Kong Reunited
In 1997, Hong Kong ended its status as a British colony and rejoined the People's Republic of China. As Figure 4.11 suggests, this tiny former seaport colony on the southern edge of China is blessed with a rich culture, one of the world's great ports, and an energetic, entrepreneurial population. Previously considered the freest economy in the world, Hong Kong has entered a period of uncertainty as both local and Western businesses have worried about dealing with the Chinese government with its penchant for tight control.[38]

In the months following the takeover, business as usual continued in Hong Kong, and China seemed more interested in continued business success for the former colony than in promoting any ideological changes. A few changes were implemented, such as switching from English to Chinese as the official language. In addition, some traditional legal premises changed with the extension of Chinese laws to Hong Kong. Chinese law operates on the principle that you cannot do something unless the law says you can. In Hong Kong, residents had previously operated on the principle that they could do anything not prohibited by law.[39]

Figure 4.10 **Telecommunications: Critical Component of a Nation's Infrastructure**

Have you ever studied with a classmate thousands of miles away?

YOU WILL

In the near future you'll share your classroom with students thousands of miles away. Using powerful, two-way sound and video hook-ups. That will let you study with anyone who shares your interests. No matter where they are.
The world-wide classroom.
The company that will bring it to you is AT&T.

AT&T

Legal Environment When conducting business internationally, managers must be familiar with three dimensions of the legal environment: U.S. law, international regulations, and the laws of the countries where they plan to trade. Some laws protect the rights of foreign companies to compete in the United States. Other laws dictate actions allowed for U.S. companies doing business in foreign countries.

For example, the 1978 *Foreign Corrupt Practices Act* forbids U.S. companies from bribing foreign officials, political candidates, or government representatives. This act, passed by Congress in a rush to clean up Watergate-era misdeeds, prescribes fines and jail time for American managers who are aware of illegal payoffs. By contrast, French and German laws not only decline to prohibit payments of bribes to foreign officials, but they allow tax deductions for these expenses.[40]

Still, official corruption is an international problem. Its pervasiveness, combined with U.S. prohibitions, creates a difficult obstacle for Americans who want to do business in many foreign countries. Chinese pay *huilu,* and Russians rely on *vzyatka.* In the Middle East, palms are greased with *baksheesh,* while a bribe in Mexico is called *una mordida*—"a bite." Figure 4.12 compares 53 countries based on surveys of perceived corruption.[41]

The *Helms-Burton Act,* a controversial law enacted in 1996, is another example of a legal barrier to international commerce. The act imposes trade sanctions against Cuba and permits U.S. companies and citizens to sue foreign companies and their executives that use assets expropriated from U.S. owners to do business in Cuba. It also denies U.S. visas to executives of firms facing lawsuits for violating the act.

The growth of e-commerce with the unfolding information age has introduced new elements to the legal climate of international business. Ideas, patents, brand names, trademarks, copyrights, and other intellectual property are difficult to police given the availability of information on the Internet. However, some countries are

| **Figure 4.11** | **Hong Kong's Changing Political Environment** |

adopting laws to protect information obtained by electronic contacts. For example, Malaysia's Computer Crimes Act carries stiff fines and long jail terms for those convicted of illegally accessing computers and using information that passes through them. China also restricts use of the Internet with the stated objective of "protecting national security and social stability."[42] The United States is taking a less restrictive stance on regulating e-commerce, favoring a market-determined approach. This chapter's Solving an Ethical Controversy discusses another element of the legal environment for trade with China.

International Regulations To regulate international commerce, the United States and many other countries have ratified treaties and signed agreements that dictate the conduct of international business and protect some of its activities. The United States has entered into many *friendship, commerce, and navigation (FCN) treaties* with other nations. Such treaties address many aspects of international business relations, including the right to conduct business in the treaty partner's domestic market. Other international business agreements concern product standards, patents, trademarks, reciprocal tax policies, export controls, international air travel, and international communications.

Many types of regulations affect the actions of managers doing business in international markets. Worldwide producers and marketers must not only maintain required minimum quality levels for all the countries in which they operate, but they must also comply with numerous specific, local regulations. For example, the European Union has introduced a standardized system of presenting ecological information on labels for certain products. Other European regulations deal with information and privacy issues. The Data Protection Act in the United Kingdom, for instance, restricts the ways in which direct marketers can use computer-generated lists for promotional campaigns.

Figure 4.12 **Corruption in Business and Government: The Clean and the Sleazy**

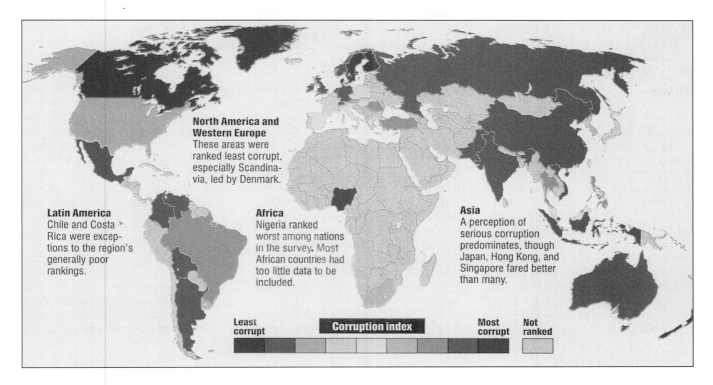

North America and Western Europe
These areas were ranked least corrupt, especially Scandinavia, led by Denmark.

Latin America
Chile and Costa Rica were exceptions to the region's generally poor rankings.

Africa
Nigeria ranked worst among nations in the survey. Most African countries had too little data to be included.

Asia
A perception of serious corruption predominates, though Japan, Hong Kong, and Singapore fared better than many.

Least corrupt — Corruption index — Most corrupt — Not ranked

Host-country laws also influence the international efforts of foreign companies. Borg-Warner, a Chicago-based auto parts manufacturer, was a recent victim of Chinese laws because of an ill-fated venture with a local partner, SATF. The planned joint effort ended when Borg-Warner learned that its supposed partner was actually opening a rival transmission factory. Borg-Warner sued in Chinese courts and lost. SATF's countersuit was successful, resulting in the Chinese firm being awarded all of Borg-Warner's $2.2 million investment in the project. To make matters worse, the U.S. firm was not informed of the result until after the deadline for filing appeals.[43]

To avoid problems resulting from unfamiliarity with local or international laws affecting trade, firms often rely on expertise provided by government agencies and private consultants. Figure 4.13 describes how the international management advisor Arthur Andersen guided a U.S. firm through a maze of foreign business and tax regulations.

Software piracy offers an example of huge problems that can result from the lack of international regulations. Chinese outlaws illegally reproduce U.S. software as well as music and movies, costing American firms billions of dollars in lost revenues. Latin America is another area with rampant piracy: Of every $100 in software sales there, an estimated

$68 goes to pirates. Microsoft manager Alessandro Annoscia estimates that without piracy, the company's Latin American sales would be over $1 billion, rather than $500,000. He is optimistic that the company is making progress, though. Mexico, in particular, has enacted strong antipiracy laws.[44]

Types of Trade Restrictions

Trade restrictions such as tariffs and administrative procedures create additional barriers to international business. They may limit consumer choices while simultaneously increasing the costs of foreign-made products. Trade restrictions are also imposed to protect citizens' security, health, and jobs; for example, a government may limit exports of strategic and defense-related goods to unfriendly countries to protect its security. Bans on imports of insecticide-contaminated farm products protect health. Restrictions on imports protect domestic jobs in the importing country.

Trade restrictions grow out of a country's legal structure, often in response to the political environment. Some restrictions, such as those applied by the U.S. government to deter trade with Iraq and Cuba, are intended to punish or protest countries' political actions. Other restrictions

SOLVING AN ETHICAL CONTROVERSY

Who Favors China the Most?

Every year, questions about trade with China incite predictable drama. Should the U.S. government grant the world's largest country—and the last major communist power—most-favored-nation (MFN) trading status?

With U.S.-China trade totaling $65 billion, it is not surprising that global business giants like Boeing, General Motors, TRW, and United Technologies lobby hard each year to continue China's MFN status. Each has invested hundreds of millions of dollars there, and future deals could be at stake. Last year, Boeing lost a $1.5 billion jet order

to Europe's Airbus Industrie because, in the words of China's premier Li Peng, "They do not attach political strings to cooperation with China."

In reality, most opposition to MFN status for China has nothing to do with trade. Efforts to revoke it have traditionally focused on concerns about human rights, political freedom, and use of prison labor in factories. More recent allegations of wrongdoing involve possible illegal political contributions during the 1996 U.S. presidential elections. Opponents want to deny MFN treatment as a way to punish China or at least force it to improve its human rights record.

But how big a deal is most-favored-nation status? The name implies more

beneficial treatment than a country actually experiences. MFN status qualifies the trading partner for low import taxes and streamlined negotiating processes. However, every nation but seven currently has this designation. Only Afghanistan, Cuba, Laos, Montenegro, North Korea, Serbia, and Vietnam lack MFN status, and the U.S. government currently bans trade with three others—Iran, Iraq, and Libya.

Should China Have MFN Trade Status?

PRO

1. As global powers, China and the United States must be able to trade with each other without erecting

---

Figure 4.13   **Using Consultants to Avoid International Legal Problems**

barriers designed to achieve objectives unrelated to trade.

2. Building business and economic ties—and therefore creating jobs—is one way of improving human rights.

3. Since other countries are already actively pursuing investments in China, denying MFN status would benefit U.S. business competitors, should China retaliate.

4. China's population of 1.25 billion is a potentially huge consumer market. The United States should not risk access to these potential sales by undermining trade relations.

5. With Hong Kong now under Chinese control, failure to renew MFN

status could put valuable, long-term business relationships at risk.

CON

1. The Chinese government has made no move toward halting human-rights violations against its people. Withdrawing MFN status could force changes, if the country's leaders believe their economy might suffer.

2. China is a known dealer of weapons to "rogue states" around the world and should be punished for these sales.

3. The United States runs a huge trade deficit with China, in part because that nation uses unfair trading practices. The U.S. government should end China's MFN status until those practices are discontinued.

SUMMARY

Because China's MFN status is as much a political litmus test as a practical trade matter, annual debates over the issue will continue to pit human-rights protesters against business interests. Human-rights advocates want to use the annual waiver to get China's leaders to improve their record. Big business wants to continue economic ties with the country to generate sales and maintain the flow of profits.

Sources: Donna Smith, "Daley Sees Uphill Battle on China in U.S. Congress," Reuters Limited, April 15, 1999; Paul Magnusso, "China: The Great Brawl," *Business Week*, June 16, 1997, pp. 32-34; Bill Nichols, "This Year, Sharper Edge to Trade Debate," *USA Today*, May 20–21, 1997, p. 7A; and Greg McDonald, "China Trade Status Survives in House," *Houston Chronicle*, June 24, 1997.

are imposed to promote trade with certain countries. Still others protect countries from unfair competition. Table 4.4 summarizes the arguments for and against trade restrictions.

Regardless of the political reasons for trade restrictions, most take the form of tariffs. In addition to tariffs, governments impose a number of nontariff—or administrative—barriers. These include quotas and embargoes.

Tariffs **Tariffs** are taxes, surcharges, or duties on foreign products. Governments assess two types of tariffs—revenue and protective tariffs—both of which make imports more expensive for domestic buyers. Revenue tariffs generate income for the government. For example, upon returning home, U.S. leisure travelers who bring back goods are taxed 10 percent of the amount in excess of $400. This duty goes directly to the U.S. Treasury. The sole purpose of a protective tariff is to raise the retail price of imported products to match or exceed the prices of similar products manufactured in the home country.

Many Americans prefer luxury German and Japanese cars to comparable American cars. If the United States imposed a protective tariff on foreign-made automobiles, the objective would be to boost the financial incentive to buy domestic cars. Current

U.S. tariffs discourage importing such luxury goods as Rolex watches. In other words, protective tariffs seek to level the playing field for local competitors.

Nontariff Barriers Nontariff, or administrative, trade barriers restrict imports in more subtle ways than tariffs. These measures may take such forms as customs barriers, quotas on imports, unnecessarily restrictive standards for imports, and export subsidies. Because many countries have recently substantially reduced tariffs or eliminated them entirely, these nontariff barriers are increasingly used to boost exports and control flows of imported products. For example, pharmaceutical companies wait 4 years on average for approval to import drugs to Japan. During this time, a Japanese drug company gains time to develop a local version of the product.

Customs regulations can also create trade barriers. France tried to protect its manufacturers of videocassette recorders by requiring all imported VCRs to pass through one customs station at Poitiers. Located in the middle of the country, the station was hard to reach, open only a few

Business Directory

tariff tax imposed by the importing country on goods that cross its borders.

Table 4.4 Arguments For and Against Trade Restrictions

For 👍	Against 👎
Protect national defense and citizens' health	Raise prices for consumers
Protect new or weak industries	Restrict consumer choices
Protect against a practice called *dumping,* in which products are sold for less abroad than in the home market, competing unfairly with domestic goods.	
Protect domestic jobs in the face of foreign competition	Result in loss of jobs
Retaliate for another country's trade restrictions	Cause inefficient allocations of international resources

days each week, and staffed by only a few customs officials who insisted on inspecting individual packages. This totally legal system caused major delays in processing VCR imports.[45]

Quotas limit the amounts of particular products that countries can import during specified time periods. Limits may be set as quantities (number of cars or bushels of wheat) or as values (dollars worth of cigarettes). Governments regularly set quotas for agricultural products and sometimes for imported automobiles.

Quotas help to prevent **dumping,** a practice that developed during the 1980s. In one form of dumping, a company sells products abroad at prices below their costs of production. In another, a company exports a large quantity of a product at a lower price than the same product in the home market and drives down the price of the domestic product. Dumping benefits domestic consumers in the importing market, but it hurts domestic producers. It also allows companies to gain quick entry to foreign markets.

While charges of dumping are difficult to prove, countries may establish quotas if they suspect it. In addition to establishing quotas, companies can protect themselves against dumping by requesting that their government impose an antidumping duty, thus offsetting the cost advantage of the foreign good.

More severe than a quota, an **embargo** imposes a total ban on importing a designated product or a total halt to trading with a particular country. In addition to their punitive effects, embargoes can protect citizens' health. Embargo durations can vary. The U.S. government imposed an embargo on trade with Cuba in 1960, 2 years after a successful revolution led by Fidel Castro. Cuban exports such as sugar and cigars were not permitted to enter the United States, and U.S. companies were prohibited from investing in Cuba. The 1991 embargo imposed on Iraq in response to its invasion of Kuwait prohibits imports of Iraqi oil to the United States.

Another form of administrative trade restriction involves **exchange controls.** Imposed through a central bank or government agency, exchange controls affect both exporters and importers. Firms that gain foreign currencies through exporting are required to sell them to the central bank or another agency. Importers must buy foreign currencies to pay for their purchases from the same agency. The exchange control authority can then allocate, expand, or restrict foreign exchange to satisfy national policy goals.

REDUCING BARRIERS TO INTERNATIONAL TRADE

While tariffs and administrative barriers still restrict trade, overall the world is moving toward free trade. Several types of organizations ease barriers to international trade. These include groups that monitor trade policies and practices and institutions that offer monetary assistance. Another type of federation designed to ease trade barriers is the multinational economic community, such as the European Union. This section looks at the roles these organizations play.

Business Directory

World Trade Organization (WTO) institution with 132 members that succeeds TT in monitoring and enforcing trade agreements.

Organizations Promoting International Trade

For the 50 years of its existence, the **General Agree-**

ment on **Tariffs and Trade (GATT),** an international trade accord, sponsored a series of negotiations, called *rounds,* that substantially reduced worldwide tariffs and other barriers. Major industrialized nations founded the multinational organization in 1947 to work toward reducing tariffs and relaxing import quotas. The last set of negotiations (the Uruguay Round) cut average tariffs by one-third, in excess of $700 billion, reduced farm subsidies, and improved protection for copyright and patent holders. In addition, international trading rules now apply to various service industries, with specific details yet to be resolved. Finally, the new agreement established the **World Trade Organization (WTO)** to succeed GATT. This new organization includes representatives from 132 countries.

World Trade Organization Since 1995, the WTO has monitored GATT agreements among the member nations, mediated disputes, and continued the effort to reduce trade barriers throughout the world. Unlike provisions in GATT, the WTO's decisions are binding on parties involved in disputes.

Trade officials continue to debate the direction for WTO. After the years since its founding, the WTO still faces many problems. Telecommunications is a major area of discussion, with developed countries keen to protect their companies' products. Barriers to providing telecommunications services were lifted in 1998 with implementation of the WTO's agreement to liberalize international trade in basic telecommunications services. Over half of WTO members agreed to open their domestic markets to foreign companies. The agreement covers voice and cellular telephony, data transmission, telex, facsimile, fixed and mobile satellite systems, and paging and personal communications systems.[46]

www.wto.org

World Bank Shortly after the end of World War II, industrialized nations formed an organization to lend money to less-developed and developing countries. The **World Bank** primarily funds projects that build or expand nations' infrastructure networks such as transportation, education, and medical systems and facilities. The World Bank and other development banks provide the largest source of advice and assistance to developing nations.

The World Bank received criticism recently for its support of Asian countries suffering from that region's economic crisis. It was chastised, in particular, for lending huge amounts of money to Indonesia in spite of reports of extensive government corruption.[47]

International Monetary Fund Established 1 year after the World Bank, the **International Monetary Fund (IMF)** was created to promote trade through financial cooperation, in the process eliminating barriers. The IMF makes short-term loans to member nations that are unable to meet their budgetary expenses.

It operates as a lender of last resort for troubled nations.[48] In exchange for these emergency loans, IMF lenders frequently extract significant commitments from the borrowing nations to address the problems that led to the crises. These steps may include curtailing imports or even devaluing currency.[49]

Throughout its existence, the IMF has worked to prevent financial crises by warning the international business community when countries encounter problems meeting their financial obligations. Often, the IMF lends to countries to keep them from going into default on prior debts and to prevent economic crises in particular countries from spreading to other nations.

International Economic Communities

International economic communities reduce trade barriers and promote worldwide economic integration. In the simplest approach, countries may establish a *free-trade area* in which they trade freely among themselves without tariffs or trade restrictions. Each maintains its own tariffs for trade outside this area. A *customs union* sets up a free-trade area and specifies a uniform tariff structure for members' trade with nonmember nations. In a *common market,* or economic union, members go beyond a customs union and try to bring all of their government trade rules into agreement. These partnerships succeed in varying degrees.

One example of a free-trade area is the **North American Free Trade Agreement (NAFTA)** enacted by the United States, Canada, and Mexico. Other examples of regional trading blocs include the MERCOSUR customs union (joining Brazil, Argentina, Paraguay, Uruguay, Chile, and Bolivia), and the 10-country ASEAN (Association of South East Asian Nations). To ensure continuing success in meeting its goal of creating peace, stability, and prosperity, ASEAN holds annual meetings where members review developments and give directives for meeting economic and political challenges. Figure 4.14 shows the size of these new economic communities.

They said it

"The next time you see a headline about the IMF lending some country a billion dollars, think about it this way. If you spent $100,000 every day of the week, it would take you more than 27 years to spend a billion dollars."

Anonymous

| Figure 4.14 | **NAFTA, MERCOSUR, and ASEAN Free-Trade Areas** |

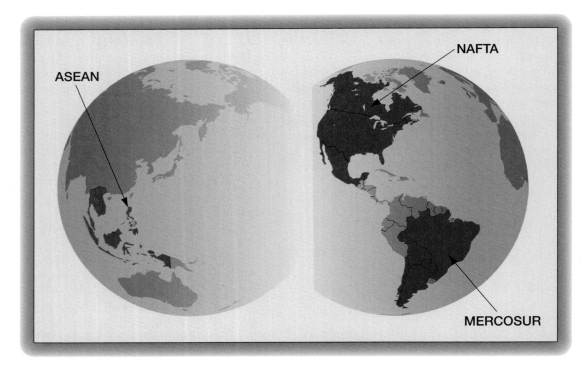

NAFTA

The North American Free Trade Agreement (NAFTA) became effective in 1994, creating the world's largest free-trade zone with the United States, Canada, and Mexico. By eliminating all trade barriers and investment restrictions among the three nations over a 15-year period, NAFTA opens more doors for free trade. The agreement also eases regulations governing trade in services, such as banking, and establishes uniform legal requirements for protection of intellectual property.

The three signatory countries can trade with one another without tariffs or other trade barriers, simplifying shipments of goods across the partners' borders. Standardized customs and uniform labeling regulations create economic efficiencies and smooth import and export procedures.

By eliminating trade barriers, NAFTA expands choices of products and suppliers for consumers. Domestic producers in the United States, Canada, and Mexico have gained free access to a larger market. Many items are produced at lower per-unit costs than before NAFTA, because companies are able to plan for larger volumes of output.

NAFTA's Effect on the United States, Canada, and Mexico Although NAFTA was approved based on prospects of expanding exports, generating new jobs, and ensuring consumers in all three nations of the best quality products at the best prices, it has produced mixed results to date. Trade between the partners has increased steadily (up 44 percent since 1994), and U.S. exports to Mexico have increased 37 percent, despite the 1994 peso devaluation and subsequent recession in that country. Mexican tariffs on U.S. exports were reduced from 10 percent to 2.9 percent, and U.S. firms now supply more than 75 percent of all Mexican imports.[50]

With the Mexican economic problems and almost 10 years remaining before all trade barriers must disappear, no clear picture has yet emerged of the overall effect of NAFTA. Pre-NAFTA tariffs, particularly on Mexican goods, were already low, and many U.S. factories had moved to Mexico and other nations prior to 1995. China continues to lead the world in U.S. imports, and Mexico has replaced Japan as the second-largest market for U.S.-made products.[51]

As noted earlier, NAFTA has brought billions of dollars in direct foreign investment to the U.S.-Mexican border region. Because of the gradual elimination of tariffs on goods made or assembled in North America and traded among the three countries, NAFTA encourages companies to locate in North America while maintaining competitiveness.[52]

NAFTA's Effect on Jobs Another promised NAFTA benefit was job creation and increased wages in all three nations. U.S. jobs supported by exports to Mexico and Canada have grown by 300,000, a net gain of almost 185,000. In addition, new markets on both sides of the border have been opened. Since NAFTA was signed into law, California's exports to Mexico increased almost 50 percent. The state's export trade to Mexico supports an estimated 126,000 California jobs. For example, Mexico now represents the largest foreign market for San Diego companies (42 percent of all exports).[53]

Expanding NAFTA to Other Countries The promised success of NAFTA encouraged the Clinton administration to pursue initiatives expanding the agreement to other countries in the Americas. Chile is the most likely candidate to be added, which would broaden NAFTA's scope to make AFTA, the American Free Trade Agreement. Supporters of this expansion effort believe this growth will lead to a free-trade zone for the entire Western Hemisphere.

European Union

Perhaps the best-known example of an international economic community is the **European Union (EU).** The European Union combines 15 countries, 350 million people, and a total GDP of $5 trillion to form a huge common market. Several eastern European countries and former Soviet republics have also applied for EU membership.

To achieve its goal of a borderless Europe, the EU intends to remove all barriers to free trade among its members. This highly complex process involves standardizing business regulations and requirements, standardizing import duties and taxes, and eliminating customs checks, so that companies can transport goods from England to Italy as easily as from New York City to Boston.

Beginning in 1999, the EU plans to form an Economic and Monetary Union (EMU) and introduce the euro to replace currencies like the French franc and Italian lira. Potential benefits include eliminating the economic costs of exchanging one currency for another and simplifying price comparisons.[54] However, not all of the 15 EU members will be part of the EMU. Britain, Sweden, and Denmark have opted not to join. Their reasons for opposing the euro include histories of successful international commerce and nationalistic feelings.

To take advantage of the EU's move toward trade liberalization, the United States and the European Union are currently involved in negotiations to reduce transatlantic trade barriers. Although transatlantic trade is relatively free already, barriers remain in a number of industries. U.S. policies restrict shipping and textiles, and those in the EU limit agricultural and audiovisual products.[55]

GOING GLOBAL

While expanding into overseas markets offers increased profit potential and marketing opportunities, it also introduces new complexities to a firm's business operations. Before making the decision to go global, a company faces a number of key decisions, including:

▼ Determining which foreign market(s) to enter

They said it

"Don't overlook the importance of worldwide thinking. A company that keeps its eye on Tom, Dick, and Harry is going to miss Pierre, Hans, and Yoshio."

Al Ries (1929–)
American advertising executive

▼ Analyzing the expenditures required to enter a new market

    ▼ Deciding on the best way to organize the overseas operations

These issues vary in importance depending on the level of involvement a company chooses. For example, education and worker training in the host country is much more important for a bank planning to open a foreign branch or an electronics manufacturer building an Asian factory than to a firm that is simply planning to export American-made products.

The choice of which markets to enter usually follows extensive research focusing on local demand for the firm's products, availability of needed resources, and ability of the local workforce to produce world-class quality. Other factors include existing and potential competition, tariff rates, currency stability, investment barriers, and even possible corruption in the customs service.[56]

A variety of government and other sources are available to facilitate this research process. A good starting place is the *CIA World Factbook,* which contains country-by-country information on geography, population, government, economy, and infrastructure.

www. **www.odci.gov/cia/publications**

U.S. Department of Commerce counselors at the agency's 68 district offices offer a full range of international business advice, including computerized market data and names of business and government contacts in over 60 countries. As Table 4.5 shows, the Internet has simplified the process of gathering international trade information.

Levels of Involvement

After the company has completed its research and decided to enter a foreign market, it can choose one or more of the entry strategies shown in Figure 4.15:

▼ Exporting or importing

▼ Entering into contractual agreements like franchising, licensing, and subcontracting deals

▼ Direct investment in the foreign market through acquisitions, joint ventures, or establishing an overseas division.

While the company's risk increases with the level of its involvement, so does its overall control of all aspects of

Table 4.5	International Trade Research Resources on the Internet
Web Site and Address	**General Description**
Asia, Inc. www.asia-inc.com	Covering business news in Asia, this Web site features articles on Asian countries from India to Japan.
Europages www.europages.com	This resource offers a contact tool and directory of Europe's top 150,000 companies from 25 European countries.
Mexico Business www.nafta.net/mexbiz	Leading information source on doing business in and with Mexico, including a guide to key Mexican companies.
Doing Business in Canada www.tpusa.com/naft/nafta-facts/canada/html	This site offers comprehensive information on how to trade with our northern neighbor.
World Trade Organization gatekeeper.unicc.org/wto	This resource provides details on the trade policies of various governments.
STAT-USA www.stat-use.gov	This massive resource lists trade and economic data, information about trends, daily intelligence reports, and background data. Access requires a paid subscription to the service.
U.S. Business Advisor bacchus.fedworld.gov/index2.html	This one-stop resource gives access to a full range of federal government information, services, and transactions.
U.S. State Department Travel Warnings travel.state.gov/travel-warnings.html	The State Dept. lists its latest travel warnings about conditions that may affect safety abroad, supplemented by a list of consulate addresses and country information.

producing and selling its good or service. Companies frequently combine more than one of these strategies in a single country. In Brazil, Wal-Mart owns five retail stores but depends on contract truckers or its suppliers for local delivery of most of the goods it imports to these stores.[57]

Importers and Exporters When a firm brings in goods produced abroad to sell domestically, it is an importer. Likewise, companies are exporters when they produce goods at home and sell them in overseas markets. This strategy provides the lowest level of international involvement, with the least risk and control.

An importer must assess the local demand for a product before importing it from another country. Baltimore-based Sweet-N-Spicy Foods has targeted West Indians living in the Washington, D.C. metropolitan area who are nostalgic for the flavors of their homeland. The company ships in 200 different types of Caribbean fruits and vegetables like callaloo, peppers, thyme, and yams from Jamaica each week. Co-owner Mike Chin estimates that Sweet-N-Spicy spends approximately $1,000 a week on transportation to import the food, and depends on a number of different Jamaican suppliers to fill each order.[58]

Exports are frequently handled by special intermediaries called *export trading companies*. These firms search out competitively priced local merchandise and then resell it abroad at prices high enough to cover expenses and earn profits. When a retail chain like Dallas-based Pier One Imports wants to purchase West African products for its store shelves, it may contact an export trading company operating in a country such as Ghana. The local firm is responsi-

ble for quality assurance, packaging the order for trans-Atlantic shipment, arranging transportation, and handling the customs paperwork and other steps required to move the product from Ghana to the United States.

Firms engage in exporting of two types: indirect and direct exporting. A company engages in *indirect exporting* when it manufactures a product, such as an electronic component, that becomes part of another product that is sold in foreign markets. The second method, *direct exporting*, occurs when a company seeks to sell its product in markets outside its own country. Often the first step for companies entering foreign markets, it is the most common form of international business. Firms that find success in exporting their products may then move on to other entry strategies.

In addition to dealing with export trading companies to reach foreign markets, novice exporters may choose two other alternatives: export management companies and offset agreements. Rather than simply relying on an export trading company to assist in locating foreign products or foreign markets, an exporting firm depends on an *export management company* for advice and expertise. These international specialists help the first-time exporter with paperwork, making contacts with local buyers, and compliance with local laws governing labeling, product safety, and performance testing. At the same time, the exporting firm retains much more control than would be possible with an export trading company.

An *offset agreement* matches a small business with a major international firm. It basically makes the small firm a subcontractor to the larger one. Such an entry strategy helps a new exporter by allowing it to share in the larger company's international expertise. The small firm also benefits in such important areas as international transaction documents and financing.

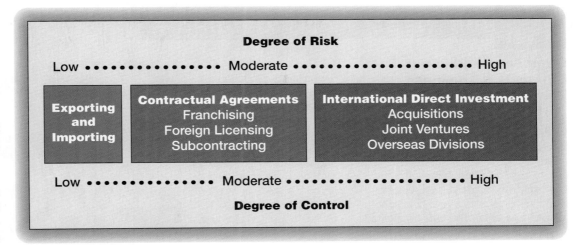

Figure 4.15 Levels of Involvement in International Business

Countertrade An estimated 15 to 30 percent of all international trade involves payments made in the form of local products, not currency. This system of international bartering agreements is called **countertrade.**

A common reason for resorting to international barter is inadequate access to needed foreign currency. To complete an international sales agreement, the seller may agree to accept part of the purchase cost in currency and the remainder in other merchandise. Since the seller may decide to locate a buyer for the bartered goods prior to completing the transaction, a number of international buyers and sellers frequently join together in a single agreement.

Countertrade may often be a firm's only opportunity to enter a particular market. Many developing countries simply cannot obtain enough credit or financial assistance to afford the imports that their people want. Countries with heavy debt burdens also resort to countertrade. Russian buyers, with their country's so-called *soft currency,* may resort to trading local products ranging from crude oil to diamonds to vodka as payments for purchases from foreign companies unwilling to accept Russian rubles. Still other countries, such as China, may restrict imports. Under such circumstances countertrade may be the only practical way to win government approval to import needed products.

Contractual Agreements Once a company, large or small, gains some experience in international sales, it may decide to enter into contractual agreements with local parties. These arrangements can include franchising, foreign licensing, and subcontracting.

Franchising Common among U.S. companies, franchising can work well for companies seeking to expand into international markets, too. A **franchise,** as described in detail in Chapter 5, is a contractual agreement in which a wholesaler or retailer (the franchisee) gains the right to sell the franchisor's products under that company's brand name if

it agrees to the related operating requirements. The franchisee can also receive marketing, management, and business services from the franchisor. While these arrangements are common among leading fast-food brands such as Pizza Hut, McDonald's, and KFC, other kinds of service providers often look to franchising as an international marketplace option.

Coverall North America is one of them. Specializing in commercial janitorial services, Coverall has 3,500 franchises worldwide. Founder Alex Roudi determined to take the concept overseas soon after his company's 1985 launch. He has shown considerable adaptability to make the concept work. Each country presents a different environment, with its own set of labor and tax laws. Differences in cultural constraints include varying attitudes toward entrepreneurs. In the Middle East, people going into business for themselves, including franchisees, must have sponsors.[59]

Foreign Licensing In a **foreign licensing agreement,** one firm allows another to produce or sell its product, or use its trademark, patent, or manufacturing processes in a specific geographic area. In return, the firm gets a royalty or other compensation.

Licensing can be an advantageous choice for a small manufacturer anxious to launch a well-known product overseas. Not only does it get a market-tested product from another market, but it must raise little or no investment to begin operating. The arrangement can also allow entry into a market otherwise closed to imports due to government restrictions.

For many years, Famous Trails, a small San Diego sporting goods manufacturer, had an agreement with Mitsubishi to sell Famous Trails products in Japan. When the company decided to go in a different direction and stopped

BUSINESS HALL OF SHAME

Overseas Child Labor Clouds U.S. Business Ventures

While his Western counterparts find themselves in middle-school classrooms, on local playgrounds, or at the library, the Bangladeshi preteen shown here spends his days in the factory working for a few cents per hour to help support his family. The use of exploited workers, including children, in foreign factories is a touchy issue for many well-known firms. Nike, Minute Maid, Wal-Mart, and Disney are just a few of the companies that find this issue discomforting, complicated by their dependence on subcontractors who may not work under their direct supervision.

Consumers like the No Sweatshop Coalition in New York see a straightforward issue. These women want nothing to do with clothing made by exploited workers, including children. To clearly demonstrate their point, they have organized events like "Let's Go No Sweatshopping," in which they ask selected storekeepers about the conditions under which garments offered for sale were made.

According to International Labor Organization (ILO) standards, the minimum age for employment should not

be less than 15 years old. A minimum age of 14 is allowed in countries with poorly developed economic and edu-

---

manufacturing in the United States, Mitsubishi approached its management with an offer to license various products in Japan under the Famous Trails logo. Mitsubishi now distributes backpacks, sweatshirts, and other popular items to Japanese department stores, and Famous Trails receives a percentage of the licensee's income from sales.[60]

Subcontracting The third type of contractual agreement, **subcontracting,** involves hiring local companies to produce, distribute, or sell goods or services. This move allows the foreign firm to take advantage of the subcontractor's expertise in local culture, contacts, and regulations. Subcontracting works equally well for mail-order companies, which can farm out order fulfillment and customer service functions to local businesses. Manufacturers practice subcontracting hoping to save money on import duties and labor costs, and businesses go this route to market products best sold by locals in a given country.

Ed Anderson invented a doughnut machine that evolved into a business called Lil' Orbits. Originally designed for American fairs, he thought the machines might generate international success. In 1987, after placing a small ad in a U.S. Department of Commerce publication, he received a huge number of responses. Instead of going overseas himself to find customers, Anderson hired foreign distributors to sell what has grown to a line of seven machines, as well as doughnut mix. With 42 people working

on his company's behalf, Lil' Orbits can now be bought in more than 80 countries.[61]

However, companies cannot always control their subcontractors' business practices. The Business Hall of Shame discusses how several major U.S. companies found themselves in an embarrassing position, because subcontractors used child labor to manufacture clothing.

International Direct Investment Investing directly in production and marketing operations in a foreign country is the ultimate level of global involvement. Over time, a firm may develop experience and success in conducting business in other countries through exporting and contractual agreements. Its managers may then decide to establish manufacturing facilities in those countries, open branch offices, or buy ownership interests in local companies in desirable markets.

An *acquisition* allows a company to purchase another existing company in the host country. In 1997, Wal-Mart spent $1.2 billion to buy Cifra, Mexico's largest retailer. Originally, the two companies formed a partnership that included 145 stores and restaurants. Then Wal-Mart bought out Cifra's position and took complete control of the retail operation.[62]

Joint ventures, like Wal-Mart's initial arrangement with Cifra, allow companies to share risks, costs, profits, and management responsibilities with one or more host country nationals. In 1997, NBC joined forces with Tele-

cational facilities. Economic exploitation of children is also a violation of United Nations rules. Yet the ILO places the number of illegal child laborers at between 100 and 200 million, most of them in Asia.

Although the most highly publicized finger-pointing involved Wal-Mart's line of clothing endorsed by TV personality Kathie Lee Gifford, allegedly produced by Honduran children, other U.S. firms have also been under scrutiny. The Gap has been accused of selling clothing made in Salvadoran sweatshops that employ young workers. Levi Strauss is currently investigating reports that its clothing is supplied by an independent contractor employing young girls from Bangladesh.

"The sad fact is that far too many of the products we may buy for loved ones . . . are made by the sweat and toil of children," says Iowa's U.S. Senator Tom Harkin. Harkin recently en-

dorsed a U.S. Labor Department proposal that U.S. retailers should voluntarily launch labeling programs guaranteeing that the goods they sell are not made by children.

Companies relying on foreign production of their products are also banding together to stop child-labor practices. In 1997, Reebok, Nike, and other sporting goods companies announced that they would continue to purchase Pakistani-made soccer balls only if the suppliers provided assurances that they were not made by children.

Confidence in such a belief would require strict monitoring, however, and a commitment to crack down on overseas subcontractors and factories that exploit their workforces. As Reebok CEO Paul Fireman remarked about his industry's efforts, "Unless everyone is playing with a ball that's free of child labor, this thing is a farce."

QUESTIONS FOR CRITICAL THINKING

1. How can individuals learn whether the products they use are made by children? What kind of actions should U.S. companies take to monitor manufacturing practices of their overseas subcontractors?

2. Should trade agreements between countries include provisions to ban child labor? How could they be enforced?

Sources: Margaret Loftus, "A Swoosh under Siege," *U.S. News & World Report*, April 12, 1999, p. 40; Stanley Meisler, "Labor Dept. Recommends 'Child-Labor-Free' Labels," *Los Angeles Times*, December 19, 1997, p. D3; Gran McCool, "Children Question Disney about Working Conditions," *Reuters Business Report*, December 6, 1996; and "Sports Firms United in Child Labor Project," *Los Angeles Times*, February 15, 1997, p. D3.

visa S.A. de C.V. in Mexico City to distribute NBC's two cable networks in Mexico. Under the agreement, Sky Mexico, a satellite direct-broadcast operation, will broadcast MSNBC and CNBC throughout the country.[63]

By setting up an *overseas division,* a company can conduct a significant amount of its business overseas. This strategy differs from that of a multinational company in that a company with overseas divisions remains primarily a domestic organization with international operations. Its focus stays on the domestic market of the home country.

From Multinational Corporation to Global Business

A **multinational corporation (MNC)** is an organization with significant foreign operations. As Table 4.6 shows, firms headquartered in the United States and Japan dominate the list of the world's largest multinationals. Of the top 20 multinational corporations, only Royal Dutch/Shell (with headquarters divided between Britain and the Netherlands) and Germany's Daimler-Benz locate their head offices outside the United States or Japan. The

United States is home to one-third of the top 500 MNCs, followed by Japan with 25 percent, and France and Germany with about 8 percent each. Such well-known U.S.-based firms as IBM, Wal-Mart, General Electric, AT&T, and Mobil are included among the 20 largest MNCs.

Since the 1960s, when the first concerns surfaced about their influence on international business, multinationals have undergone a number of dramatic changes. For one, they are no longer almost exclusively U.S. phenomena. Today's MNC is just as likely to be based in Japan (Sony, Nissan, and Matsushita, for example), Germany (DaimlerChrysler, Bayer, or BASF), or Great Britain (British Petroleum, Cadbury Schweppes, or Glaxo Wellcome). Additionally, multinationals integrate capital, technologies, and even ideas from within their various global operations. These operations no longer function as distant market outposts.

Many U.S. multinationals, including Nike and Wal-Mart, have expanded their overseas operations, because

Business Directory

multinational corporation (MNC) firm with significant operations and marketing activities outside its home country.

Table 4.6	The World's Top Ten Multinationals	
Rank and Company	Corporate Headquarters	Revenues (in billions)
1. General Motors Corp.	United States	$168
2. Ford Motor Co.	United States	147
3. Mitsui	Japan	145
4. Mitsubishi	Japan	140
5. Itochu	Japan	136
6. Royal Dutch/Shell	United Kingdom/ Netherlands	128
7. Marubeni	Japan	124
8. Exxon	United States	119
9. Sumitomo	Japan	119
10. Toyota	Japan	109

they feel that domestic markets are peaking and foreign markets offer greater sales and profit potential. Also multinationals employ large numbers of foreign workers compared to their U.S.-national workforces. While foreign workers provide low-cost labor in some regions, many multinationals are locating high-tech facilities in countries with large numbers of technical-school graduates.

India's wealth of engineering talent has made it a popular country for technology-oriented companies. As Figure 4.16 points out, companies like Motorola are making substantial investments in nations sometimes labeled *developing countries*. "We are in India because that's where a lot of talent is," says Amreesh Modi, head of Motorola's Global Software Division. The communications and computer giant is also in other nations—from Brazil to China.[64]

As multinationals contribute to a global economy, they reap the benefits of the global marketplace. Chinese consumers love Kentucky Fried Chicken. Consumers in countries as geographically and culturally distant as Saudi Arabia and Canada shave with Gillette's razor blades, wash clothes with Procter & Gamble's Tide detergent, and use computers with Intel chips inside. Half of Procter & Gamble's revenues and one-third of its net profits come from global operations. The multinational's Joy dishwashing liquid is a market leader in Japan.

Figure 4.16 Direct Investment by a Communications/Computer Multinational

INTERNATIONAL ORGANIZATION STRUCTURES

The decision to go global must be followed by a series of additional decisions that specify the most appropriate organization structure for the expanded operation. The level of involvement in international business is a key factor in these decisions. While a firm engaged in simple export activities may be best served by an export trading company, another company with extensive overseas sales may establish its own sales force for each country in which it operates. Figure 4.17 lists the alternative international organization structures that global business firms typically adopt.

Independent Agents

One method of entering international markets avoids the need to commit a major investment for developing and maintaining an overseas sales force: Use **independent agents.** These marketing intermediaries serve as independent sales forces in foreign markets, earning commissions on sales they book. They typically make sales calls on prospective customers, collect payments, and ensure customer satisfaction. Most cover limited geographic markets and hold down costs by representing multiple companies that produce related, noncompeting products.

Companies entering new foreign markets frequently rely on independent agents for several reasons:

▼ They understand their target markets, including customs and local environments.

▼ They represent minimal-risk entry alternatives for first-time exporters. If the firm is unhappy with an independent representative, it can terminate the relationship, usually at a low cost.

▼ Since most exporter-independent agent agreements specify compensation based on sales, they limit financial risks.

Exporters considering distributing through independent agents can secure names of local agents in various countries by contacting state export bureaus of the U.S. Department of Commerce. These agencies can also assist in developing sales agreements.

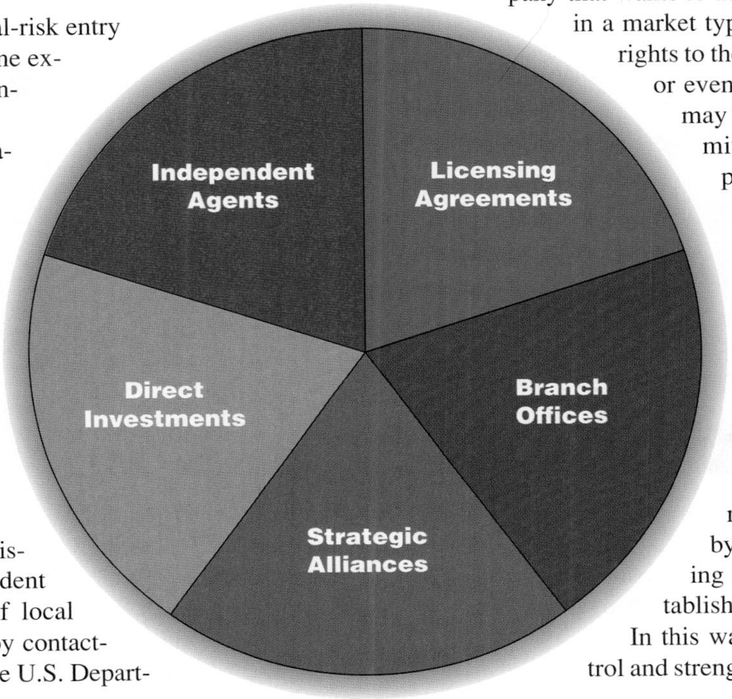

Figure 4.17 **International Organization Structure Alternatives**

depend on sales of the licensed products for their revenues. Because they invest more resources in the product than independent agents would, they often provide more effective representation in foreign markets.

Licensing agreements are relatively inexpensive and easy to create. The license holder is familiar with the target market, and the exporting company can draw on its experience and expertise instead of spending money researching the market and culture.

Licensing agreements bring an important limitation, however: They usually specify long time periods. A company that wants to attract the best license holder in a market typically must grant exclusive rights to the product for a 5-year period or even a longer time. While firms may benefit from such time commitments if license holders provide effective support, these contracts are difficult to terminate if the license holders prove ineffective partners.

Branch Offices

A branch office involves a different kind of commitment to foreign investment by a company. Instead of relying on a third party, the firm establishes its own overseas facility. In this way, it both improves its control and strengthens its presence in the host country.

To maintain a branch office in another country, a firm must develop an understanding of both the local market and its culture. This requirement demands a more extensive investment in time and experience than working with an independent agent or licensee. Many firms choose to combine branch offices and licensing agreements. The two strategies can complement each other, since license holders provide access to the local market, and the branch office can oversee the activities of the license holder.

Licensing Agreements

Some firms try to secure international sales revenues without making significant foreign investments by licensing their products, brand names, or production processes to other firms. The Famous Trails licensing agreement with Japan's Mitsubishi discussed earlier is a good example. This arrangement gives the firm receiving the license exclusive rights to use the production process or manufacture and/or market the product in a specified market. In return, the firm granting the license typically receives an upfront fee plus ongoing royalties based on a percentage of product sales.

Licensing agreements can be advantageous deals for companies seeking to enter foreign markets. License holders are usually relatively large, well-known companies that

Strategic Alliances

Similar to a joint venture, a **strategic alliance** is an international business strategy in which a company finds a partner in the country where it wants to do business. These partnerships can create competitive advantages in new markets by allowing the parties to combine resources and capital into new, jointly owned business ventures. Both the

risks and profits are shared, firms maintain control over their international activities, and they benefit from the local market expertise of their partners.

This kind of partnership has been increasing at an estimated rate of 20 percent a year. This trend is likely to continue since a number of countries, including Mexico and China, have implemented laws that require foreign firms doing business in their countries to work through such alliances.

In the ad shown in Figure 4.18, the Italian telecommunications giant STET/Telecom emphasizes the strengths it brings to the strategic alliances in which it participates. In 1997, for example, it formed an alliance with AT&T to deliver telecommunications services in Latin America. Both parties chose this international organization structure, because it allowed them to build on their complementary strengths to establish a strong presence.[65]

Direct Investment

Unlike strategic alliances, a firm makes a **direct investment** in a foreign market when it buys an existing company or establishes a factory, retail outlets, or other facilities there. Direct investment entails the most complete involvement in foreign trade, but it also brings the most

risk. Companies that invest directly in other countries must consider a number of issues discussed in this chapter, including the cultural environments, political stability, labor markets, and currency stability they will likely encounter.

As Figure 4.19 shows, U.S. companies—the most active in international direct investments—allocated about half of their $90 billion in total direct investment to Europe. The U.S. market is also a popular investment location for foreign firms, which recently invested almost $85 million in projects ranging from a Mercedes-Benz assembly plant to the Seattle Mariners major league baseball team.

Some countries, eager to encourage foreign investment, are not just accepting overseas involvement, they are helping to facilitate it. In China, the Beijing government contracted with partners in Singapore to develop an industrial park in Suzhou, near Shanghai. In business since 1994, the Suzhou Industrial Park has received investment commitments from such major international corporations as RJR Nabisco, Samsung Electronics, Black & Decker, and Eli Lilly.[66]

An interesting twist on international direct investment is Mexico's *maquiladora* plants, mentioned earlier in the chapter. Established in border cities like Tijuana, Juarez, and Nuevo Laredo, these foreign-owned factories hire low-wage Mexican workers to produce products at low cost, mostly for sale across the U.S. border. In Tijuana alone,

560 *maquiladoras* are currently operating. To sweeten incentives for such investments, the Mexican government allows manufacturers to import needed components without paying import duties.

Companies that have taken advantage of this innovation include Japanese multinationals Sony and Sanyo, as well as Korea's Samsung, Hyundai, and LG Electronics. Samsung recently spent $212 million to build a television and computer-monitor plant in a

| Figure 4.19 | Destinations of Direct Investment Dollars |

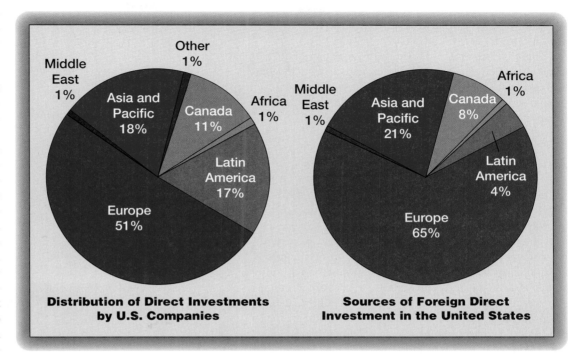

Distribution of Direct Investments by U.S. Companies

Sources of Foreign Direct Investment in the United States

former olive grove. The company plans to spend another $580 million to expand the plant, which will eventually employ 9,300 people.[67]

DEVELOPING A STRATEGY FOR INTERNATIONAL BUSINESS

In developing a framework within which to conduct international business, managers must first evaluate their corporate objectives, organizational strengths and weaknesses, and strategies for product development and marketing. They can choose to combine these elements in either a global strategy or a multidomestic strategy.

Global Business Strategies

A **global business (or *standardization*) strategy** specifies a standardized, worldwide product and marketing strategy. The firm sells the same product in essentially the same manner throughout the world. Many companies simply modify their domestic business strategies by translating promotional brochures and product-use instructions into the languages of the host nations.

Ford Motor Co. created a single development organization when it launched its Ford 2000 global strategy. It merged its regional U.S., European, Asian, and Latin American operations into a single, worldwide company that adopts the best practices from all over the world. Ford management's goal is to create cars in standardized categories to be sold worldwide, reducing the company's costs dramatically by engineering products only once, rather than multiple times for different markets. For example, instead of making two similar four-cylinder engines, one for North America and one for Europe, the company will build one power unit for both markets.

Ford's Ka, a minicar built to compete in price-sensitive markets, was developed in a record time of just over 2 years. To reduce retooling and other start-up costs, the Ka uses the Ford Fiesta chassis and a number of other pre-assembled components. Following early marketplace success, Ford introduced a sister car, the Puma coupe. Spain was selected for the first Ka assembly plant; the second was located in Brazil.

Introduction of the coupe version of the Ka shows that Ford executives will not ignore customer preferences.

Business Directory

global business strategy reliance on a standardized marketing mix that guides marketing decisions with minimal modifications in all of a firm's domestic and foreign markets.

However, by consolidating engine and transmission options and recycling existing platform types, the company intends to move quickly and efficiently into new ventures. At least 50 percent of all Ka components were originally designed for other Ford models.[68]

A global marketing perspective can be appropriate for some goods and services and certain market segments that are common to many nations. The approach works for products with universal appeal, like Coca-Cola, and for luxury items like jewelry.

Multidomestic Business Strategies

Under a **multidomestic business (or** *adaptation***) strategy,** the firm treats each national market in a different way. It develops products and marketing strategies that appeal to the customs, tastes, and buying habits of particular national markets. Software maker Microsoft pursues a multidomestic strategy by adapting its products for specific markets. It must design software to support different languages and writing styles, an especially daunting challenge when languages differ from English even in their alphabets, as do Arabic, Hebrew, Russian, Chinese, and Japanese. Microsoft also hires mostly local managers for its overseas operations, which span 60 countries. "That's key," says CEO Bill Gates. "It sends the wrong message to have a foreigner come in and run things." Microsoft sets up partnerships with small, local companies that know how to sell in their markets, creating a multidomestic strategy that is working. Overseas sales now account for 57 percent of revenues, with sales growth in China, India, and Southeast Asia topping 55 percent a year.[69]

Sources of Export Assistance

Regardless of the global business strategy that a company chooses, it may require export assistance. Companies can tap a variety of resources for this help. For example, the U.S. Department of Commerce maintains a toll-free information hot line (1–800–872–8723) that describes various federal export programs.

www.ita.doc.gov

Companies can also seek advice from trade counselors at the Commerce Department's 68 district offices, who can offer information about exporting, computerized market data, and names of contacts in more than 60 countries. Some of these services are free; others are reasonably priced.

▼ *National Trade Data Bank.* This large database, updated monthly, collects market reports on foreign demand for specific products. It is available at Commerce Department district offices or by subscription.

▼ *Agent/distributor services.* This search service helps companies to locate overseas distributors for their products.

▼ *Commercial News USA.* This monthly export catalog/magazine promotes U.S. goods and services to 100,000 international buyers in over 150 countries. An electronic version now on the Web helps foreign importers to find American companies.

www.cnewsusa.com

▼ *Catalog and video shows.* This service displays companies' catalogs or demonstration videos at shows held at U.S. consulates or embassies. Shows are oriented toward particular industries, such as medical supplies or marine equipment.

▼ *Matchmaker missions.* Sponsored visits help U.S. firms in specific industries to meet potential customers in foreign countries.

▼ *Trade shows.* Commerce Department-sponsored trade shows in other countries create effective forums for obtaining market information and meeting customers.

WHAT'S AHEAD

As this chapter has shown, both large and small businesses are relying on world trade almost as much as are major corporations. Chapter 5 examines the special advantages and challenges that small-business owners encounter. A critical decision facing any new business is the choice of the most appropriate form of business ownership. Chapter 5 examines the major ownership structures—sole proprietorship, partnership, and corporation—and assesses the pros and cons of each one. The chapter closes with a discussion of recent trends affecting business ownership, such as the growing impact of franchising and business consolidations through mergers and acquisitions.

Business Directory

multidomestic business strategy reliance on market segmentation to identify specific foreign markets and tailor the marketing mix to match their specific traits.

SUMMARY OF LEARNING GOALS

1. Explain the importance of international business and the main reasons why nations trade.

The United States is both the largest importer and the largest exporter in the world, although less than 5 percent of the world's population lives within its borders. With the increasing globalization of the world's economies, the international marketplace offers tremendous opportunities to U.S. and foreign businesses to expand into new markets for their goods and services. Doing business globally also provides new sources of materials and labor. Trading with other countries also reduces a company's dependence on economic conditions in its home market. Countries that encourage international trade enjoy higher levels of economic activity, employment, and wages than those that restrict it. The major world markets are North America, western Europe, the Pacific Rim, and Latin America. Emerging markets such as China and Brazil will become increasingly important to U.S. businesses over the next decade.

2. Discuss the relationship of absolute and comparative advantage to international trade.

Countries usually benefit if they specialize in producing certain goods or services. A country has an absolute advantage if it holds a monopoly or produces a good or service at the lowest cost. It has a comparative advantage if it can supply a particular product more efficiently or at a lower cost than it can produce another item.

3. Describe how nations measure international trade and the significance of exchange rates.

Companies measure the level of international trade by calculating trade surpluses or deficits, that is, the balance of trade, which represents the difference between exports and imports. The term *balance of payments* refers to the overall flow of money into or out of a country, including overseas loans and borrowing, international investments, profits from such investments, and foreign aid. An exchange rate is the value of a nation's currency relative to the currency of another nation. Currency values typically fluctuate, or "float," relative to the supply and demand for specific currencies in the world market. When the value of the dollar falls compared to other currencies, the cost of U.S. goods abroad declines, and demand for exports may rise. An increase in the value of the dollar raises the prices of U.S. goods sold abroad, but it reduces the prices of foreign goods sold in the United States.

4. Identify the major barriers that confront global businesses.

Businesses face several types of obstacles in the global marketplace. Companies must be sensitive to social and cultural differences, such as languages, values, and religions, when operating in other countries. Economic differences include standards of living and levels of infrastructure development. Legal and political barriers are among the most difficult to breach. Each country sets its own laws regulating business practices. Trade restrictions like tariffs and administrative barriers also present obstacles to international business.

5. Explain how international trade organizations and economic communities reduce barriers to international trade.

Many international organizations seek to promote international trade by reducing barriers. The list includes the World Trade Organization, World Bank, and International Monetary Fund. Multinational economic communities remove barriers to flows of goods, capital, and people across the borders of member nations. The two major economic communities are the North American Free Trade Association (NAFTA) and the European Union (EU).

6. Compare the different levels of involvement used by businesses when entering global markets.

Exporting and importing, the first level of involvement in international business, entails the lowest degree of both risk and control. Companies may rely on export trading or management companies to assist in distribution of their products. Contractual agreements such as franchising, foreign licensing, and subcontracting offer additional, flexible options. Franchising and licensing are especially appropriate for services. Companies may also choose local subcontractors to produce goods for local sales. International direct investment in production and marketing facilities provides the highest degree of control but also the greatest risk. Firms make direct investments by acquiring foreign companies or facilities, forming joint ventures with local firms, and setting up their own overseas divisions.

7. Describe the types of international organizational structures available to businesses.

Once a company's managers decide on the desired level of international involvement, they must choose the appropriate organization structure for their overseas venture. An independent agent represents an exporter in a foreign market. A license holder makes a larger investment in the product than an independent agent, perhaps motivating better representation for the product. However, licensing arrangements require longer time commitments than working with independent agents. Branch offices are units of an international firm located in foreign countries. Strategic alliances are joint ventures with local companies that combine resources and capital to create competitive advantage.

8. Distinguish between a global business strategy and a multidomestic business strategy.

A company that adopts a global (or standardization) strategy develops a single, standardized product and marketing strategy for implementation throughout the world. The firm sells the same product in essentially the same manner throughout the world. Under a multidomestic (or adaptation) strategy, the firm develops a different treatment for each national market. It develops products and marketing strategies that appeal to the customs, tastes, and buying habits of particular national markets.

TEN BUSINESS TERMS YOU NEED TO KNOW

exports	World Trade Organization (WTO)
imports	multinational corporation (MNC)
balance of trade	
balance of payments	global business strategy
exchange rate	multidomestic business strategy
tariff	

Other Important Business Terms

devaluation	European Union (EU)
infrastructure	countertrade
quota	franchise
dumping	foreign licensing agreement
embargo	subcontracting
exchange control	joint venture
General Agreement on Tariffs and Trade (GATT)	independent agent
	strategic alliance
World Bank	direct investment
International Monetary Fund (IMF)	*maquiladora*
North American Free Trade Agreement (NAFTA)	

REVIEW QUESTIONS

1. Summarize the major reason nations and businesses engage in international trade.
2. Distinguish between the concepts of absolute advantage and comparative advantage. Cite examples of both.
3. Can a nation have a favorable balance of trade and an unfavorable balance of payments? Defend your answer.
4. Explain how exchange rates are established. What factors can affect them?
5. Describe three types of barriers that firms may face in international business. Give an example of each.
6. Explain the difference between a revenue tariff and a protective tariff. What other types of trade restrictions affect international trade?
7. Identify three international organizations or economic communities and explain how they reduce barriers to international trade.
8. Explain the different levels of involvement in international business and give an example of each.

9. Differentiate between various types of international organizational structures that firms can use to go global.
10. How does a firm that follows a multidomestic strategy operate in the global marketplace?

QUESTIONS FOR CRITICAL THINKING

1. Now that the Internet has opened up the opportunity for borderless trade, what impact do you think it will have on how countries set trade standards?
2. In recent years, what countries have proved to be more risky markets for foreign investment? Why? Use examples of cultural, economic, political, and legal factors to explain your choices.
3. China took over Hong Kong in 1997, creating uncertainty in global markets, especially the United States, about the future of trade relations with one of the world's most prosperous and friendly nations. Identify some practices that H. C. Tung, Hong Kong's new leader, might use to minimize the effect of political differences on international business. What can the United States do to maintain strong business relations with Hong Kong?
4. Over the past 50 years, the World Bank and the IMF have helped many developing countries enter and maintain their positions in the world of international business, even when governments of those countries were known to be corrupt. One such country is Indonesia, which now has a significantly more advanced infrastructure and is a major player in international trade. Indonesia, along with its neighbors, has suffered from Southeast Asia's recent economic crisis. Many world leaders do not support efforts of the World Bank and the IMF to shore up the economy.

   Do you think it is important to provide monetary support to such countries even if government corruption exists? Describe some consequences on the world marketplace that might result from lending such support.
5. Although large multinationals receive the lion's share of attention for going global, small business exports are a growing trend. U.S. exercise video company Kresics Inc. recognized that the U.S. market was saturated by competition from superstars like Cindy Crawford and Richard Simmons. After learning that only about 10 commercial exercise videos were available in Japan, company president Krescenthia David pulled most of her products from U.S. store shelves, remade them for the Japanese market, and began exporting them. Now 90 percent of Kresics's sales are to Japan. Discuss the risks and opportunities that Kresics and other small businesses face when they enter overseas markets.

Experiential Exercise

Directions: This exercise helps you assess your global awareness. Answer the following ten questions to test your knowledge.

1. List the six countries that contain one-half the total population of the world:
   1.
   2.
   3.
   4.
   5.
   6.

2. The five most commonly spoken languages are:
   1.
   2.
   3.
   4.
   5.

3. How many of the world's languages have at least 1 million speakers?
   a. 73
   b. 123
   c. 223

4. How many nations were there in 1992?
   a. 288
   b. 188
   c. 88

5. Which nation is home to the largest number of commercial banks?

6. Between 1960 and 1987, the world spent approximately $10 trillion on health care. How much did the world spend on the military?
   a. $7 trillion
   b $10 trillion
   c. $17 trillion
   d. $25 trillion

7. According to the United Nations, what percentage of the world's work (paid and unpaid) is done by women?
   a. 33%
   b. 50%
   c. 67%
   d. 75%

8. According to the United Nations, what percentage of the world's income is earned by women?
   a. 10%
   b. 30%
   c. 50%
   d. 70%

9. The nations of Africa, Asia, Latin America, and the Middle East, often referred to as the Third World, contain about 78 percent of the world's population. What percentage of the world's monetary income do they possess?
   a. 10%
   b. 20%
   c. 30%
   d. 40%

10. Americans make up approximately 5 percent of the world's population. What percentage of the world's resources do Americans consume?
    a. 15%
    b. 25%
    c. 35%
    d. 45%

Answers

1. China (1.1 billion)
   India (882 million)
   United States (256 million)
   Indonesia (185 million)
   Brazil (151 million)
   Russia (149 million)
2. Mandarin
   English
   Hindi
   Spanish
   Russian

3. c. 223
4. b. 188
5. Japan
6. c. $17 trillion
7. c. 67%
8. a. 10%
9. b. 20%
10. c. 35%

Source: Adapted from Jan Drum, Steve Hughes, and George Otere, "State-of-the-World Test," in *Global Winners*. (Yarmouth, ME): Intercultural Press, Inc., 1994.

Nothing but Net

1. **Going Global.** One company that has made its mark on every continent, except Antarctica, is McDonald's, with over 22,000 restaurants in 109 countries. Check out their international Web site at the address listed and record five interesting facts you learned about McDonald's international operations.

   www.mcdonalds.com/surftheworld/index.html

2. **The World Bank.** Visit the World Bank's Web site and locate the section that provides information on the countries and regions the World Bank serves. Select a country that interests you and report on the projects funded by the World Bank there.

   www.worldbank.org

3. **European Union.** Use your search engine to find the latest information related to the new euro currency discussed in this chapter. The Web site listed provides many links to EU information. Select an additional EU topic to explore and summarize your findings in a one-page report.

   www.lib.berkeley.edu/GSSI/eu.html

Note: Internet Web addresses change frequently. If you do not find the exact sites listed, you may need to access the organization's or company's home page and search from there.

VIDEO CASE 4

PIER 1 IMPORTS—PLANNING FOR WORLDWIDE GROWTH

By mid-1996, Pier 1 Imports was on its way to record sales and earnings. An exciting new merchandise mix combined with the company's first television advertising campaign, had dramatically increased store traffic. Shoppers were attracted to retail stores vastly different from the Pier 1 of the early 1980s.

The old Pier 1 struggled with a disappointing merchandise selection and an outdated image. To turn the retail chain around, its board of directors brought in a new CEO, Clark Johnson. The strategic plan he and his management team devised in 1985 centered around an ambitious program to double the number of Pier 1 stores.

Other components of the plan included upgrades and expansion of merchandise offerings and investments of $27 million in new corporate systems aimed at improving efficiency. For example, new inventory systems enabled the company to reduce inventory levels in the stores and distribution centers. Customer service has been greatly enhanced by more sophistcated store checkout equipment that facilitates price checking, credit-card processing, and communications with other stores. But nowhere has the investment in systems had a greater payoff than in the logistics area. Beginning with order entry in foreign countries, through shipment from the company's six massive distribution centers to company stores, merchandise is monitored each step of the way, providing a significant increase in cost-effectiveness.

Has Pier 1's growth been a smooth process? Hardly! In 1990, as the U.S. economy slowed down, so did consumer buying. Like other retailers, Pier 1 focused on controlling costs and increasing the efficiency of its operations. By 1992, however, on Pier 1's 30th anniversary, record earnings were again reported. During the early 1990s, Pier 1 once again invested in an extensive strategic planning process.

What are management's current plans for their organization? In a corporate document entitled *A Strategy for Profitable Worldwide Growth,* management states that "Pier 1 Imports will expand its North American retail operations to 900 stores by the year 2000 and enter new worldwide retail markets through direct investment and partnerships." Other strategic goals for the year 2000 include:

▼ Achieve $1.25 billion in sales and produce $75 million in net income.

▼ Introduce Pier 1 stores internationally with direct investment in selected countries.

▼ Expand the Pier 1 market presence in Southeast Asia, Mexico, and Central and South America through franchise agreements and joint ventures.

▼ Enter new specialty retail markets in North America to be chosen using several specific and consistent criteria.

▼ Establish a major procurement, logistics, and distribution presence in Singapore to reinforce the company's international sourcing capacity.

With goals and a strategic plan in place, Pier 1 Imports' management believes that the company's focus is clear. "When 2000 arrives, our goal is to look back and verify:

▼ We defined a clear strategy and executed it well through the end of the 1990s.

▼ We produced long-term financial results that exceeded expectations.

▼ We identified global opportunities along the way, moved decisively, and increased the intrinsic value of Pier 1 Imports.

▼ We remained sensitive to each market area and adapted readily to customer wants and needs.

▼ We focused clearly on our basic strategy of profitable growth through market expansion, new store openings, maximizing profitability of existing units, motivating our associates, and remaining dedicated to our customers."

Building on their past successes, Pier 1 Imports is committed to achieving these goals.

Questions

1. What barriers to global business is Pier 1 Imports likely to encounter? Explain.

2. Describe Pier 1 Imports' corporate strategy. Give examples of how these goals can be achieved throughout the organization.

3. Distinguish between a global strategy and a multinational strategy. Where does Pier 1 Imports fit?

4. What are the different approaches to doing business abroad? Which of these are being pursued by Pier 1 Imports?

Careers in Business

INTRODUCTION

Included with *Contemporary Business* is a CD-ROM titled "Discovering Your Business Career." After following the installation instructions in the "Read Me" file on the CD-ROM, you will have placed two programs on your computer: *Discovering Your Business Career* and *Career Design*. Both of these programs are placed in the program group called "Career Assistance."

   Discovering Your Business Career helps you learn about and assess your compatibility with a wide range of careers in the business world:

- ▼ Accounting
- ▼ Corporate financial management
- ▼ Information systems
- ▼ Risk management/insurance
- ▼ Retail bank management
- ▼ Sales
- ▼ Store operations

As you explore each career, you will receive broad guidance and practical advice on everything from clarifying the depth of your interest in a particular business career to preparing and implementing an effective job search strategy.

   You will also be able to access complete career profiles about each area. Through videos, multimedia slide shows, and extensive textual content, the profiles present a detailed, up-to-date picture of current compensation levels, job responsibilities, career paths, and skills required to be successful in that career. Exercises related to those careers begin in the "Careers in Business" section for Part 4. The *Internet Business Connection*, an integrated part of the program, links you to relevant Web sites for learning more about each business career, including current job opportunities.

   The *Career Design* program offers a series of exercises based on the work of John Crystal, the major contributor to the best-selling career book of all time, *What Color Is Your Parachute*, by Richard N. Bolles. These exercises help you:

- ▼ Decide on a major.
- ▼ Identify your best skills.

- ▼ Discover what career to pursue.
- ▼ Find out if starting a business may be your appropriate career path.
- ▼ Determine your key preferences for co-workers and working conditions.
- ▼ Create a custom resumé that stands out from others.
- ▼ Develop communication skills by organizing your thoughts in writing.

As the new century proceeds, the pace of change in the business world will continue to accelerate and students who know what careers they want to pursue will enjoy a dramatic advantage. The best way to ensure that you land the right job when you graduate is to start your career preparations now. Begin by learning how to match your individual abilities and interests to specific career alternatives. Based on this knowledge, you will be able to create an academic plan that will result in securing that first job in your career path. Your instructor and the "Business Career Exercises" will help you to accomplish this.

   In the following section, and at the end of every part in *Contemporary Business,* you will find instructions for completing "Business Career Exercises" using the free CD-ROM provided with your text. These exercises show you how to apply what you learn in the course to your career.

BUSINESS CAREER EXERCISES

Career Questionnaire

The first step in your business career exploration is to complete a questionnaire in which you rate a broad range of business-related job activities. For example, you rate from "very appealing" to "very unappealing" the statement, "Making financial forecasts about your company's profits based on the assumptions you have made about how many units will sell, the selling price, and the expenses." You also rate yourself according to ten broad career factors that measure your priorities about your work environment, compensation, and progression in your career.

   In later sections of the book, you'll learn how to connect the results of this questionnaire with the business subjects you're currently studying. For example, when studying marketing, you'll discover what the questionnaire reveals about your interest in marketing careers such as sales.

How to Locate the Exercise Launch *Discovering Your Business Career* from the "Career Assistance" program group. Then select "Questionnaire" in the upper right corner of the main menu.

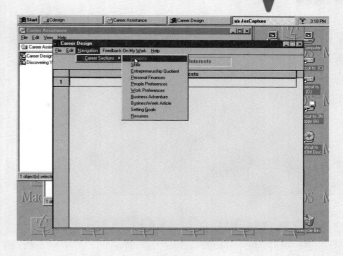

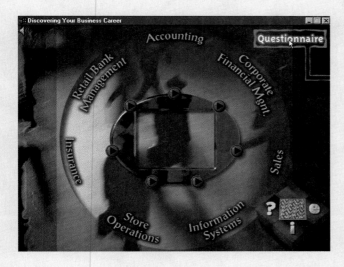

Interests and Fascinations

Anything that interests you can be an important clue about your career direction, and this exercise helps you clarify those interests. When you are asked to list your interests, take the program's advice and type in as many of your interests as you can, regardless of whether you think they are job related. Since your introductory business course provides a unique opportunity to discover what areas of business fascinate you, start this exercise by reviewing the chapters you have completed so far and write down any topics of interest. Then add these to your "Interests and Fascinations" list on the computer.

This exercise will help you to:

▼ Discover and keep track of your interests throughout the course.

▼ Understand that choosing a career that interests you can result in better pay and job satisfaction.

▼ Get a start in finding out what major to choose.

How to Locate the Exercise Launch *Career Design* from the "Career Assistance" program group. Then select "Navigation" from the menu at the top of the screen, followed by "Career Sections" and then "Interests."

Business Adventure

Now that you have completed the "Interests and Fascinations" exercise, here is another one that helps you discover even more about what you want. This exercise stimulates your imagination about the things you would like to do in the field of business. The more you write, the better.

This exercise will help you to:

▼ Discover some of your interests in the business world.

▼ Feel encouraged to actively pursue your dreams.

▼ Clarify your goals and determine what areas of life are important to you.

▼ Stimulate your thinking about what you want to accomplish in your life.

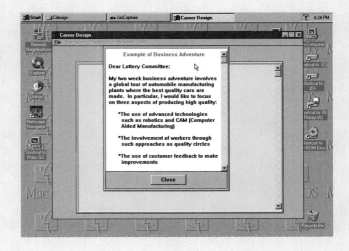

How to Locate the Exercise Launch *Career Design* from the "Career Assistance" program group. Then select "Navigation" from the menu at the top of the screen, followed by "Career Sections" and then "Business Adventure."

moneyhunte

jee

Forward   Home   Reload

p://www.jumbosports.com

PART II | **Starting and Growing Your Business**

ALL BUSINESS ADMINISTRA

WW.SBA.GOV

enterprise

more

w.internatio

razorfish.com

www.razorfish.com

www.razorfish.com

www.razorfish.com

razorfish.com

the razorfi
subnetwork

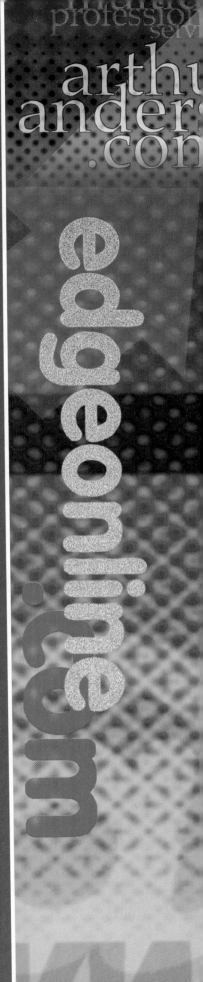

chapter 5

Options for Organizing Small and Large Businesses

America Online Buys More Real Estate in Cyberspace

Ask any real estate specialist the three most important words in that profession and you're most likely to hear "Location, location, location." These factors come into play when buying and selling real estate in town, in the suburbs, or out in the country. They also apply to cyberspace, and giant Internet provider America Online (AOL) knows it. With 16 million subscribers, AOL boasts the largest online population on earth. It has also designed the Web's largest virtual shopping mall, with 400 stores ranging from J. Crew to J & R Computer World. These tenants pay AOL millions (some of them $50 million and more) for their prime location. So what more could AOL want? A lot more.

Whether large or small, most business organizations seek growth as a means of accomplishing their objectives to their owners, customers, and employees. But once you've grown into a huge company, the question becomes one of how to grow even bigger. Rather than spending years of plowing more and more funds into the firm to finance growth, a number of firms decide to expand their operations by acquiring the strengths provided by other companies. In short, they purchase (acquire) another company, or they merge with one or more companies. Successful mergers and acquisitions strengthen all the parties involved. But even proposed combinations that look great on paper involve considerable risk, and a doomed business marriage results in large and lasting costs to everyone.

AOL's management realized that their company had been remarkably successful within the space of a few years. They also knew that their firm needed to widen its lead and expand its areas of operation. Already a success at creating an attractive online experience for new Web surfers (who can barely plug in their PCs), AOL needed to attract an even larger audience willing to spend more shopping money on the Web. Although it occupied the number one advertising spot on rival Microsoft's Channels section of Windows 98, AOL needed an even better location.

www.aol.com
www.netscape.com

Already leasing virtual real estate to tenants and helping them promote their shopping sites, AOL needed to help these tenants build their commerce service with powerful software. But in most cases, the company had neither the resources nor the expertise to satisfy its needs for growth. So how did AOL solve its problem? It bought Netscape—lock, stock, and browser.

Netscape is best known for its Internet browser. The 1994 launch of its Navigator 1.0 marked a major change in the world of e-commerce. With the click of a mouse, the Internet was accessible to people at home as well as at work. Netscape's software was improving people's lives—and with more than just its browser. It also included industrial-strength Web tools and "back-office" e-commerce programs to help companies do business and make sales over the Web. Then there's the Netcenter portal. A *portal* is a full-service Web site, an online launching pad, entertainment network, and shopping mall rolled into one. A first stop for most Web surfers, portals offer search engines, shopping areas, and other services that attract a lot of traffic.

Talk about location! Netcenter is one of the most heavily visited portals on the Web, mainly because it automatically pops up whenever someone clicks to open a Netscape browser. (Even though users can easily change that automatic setting, they either don't know that or don't care.) With 9 million registered users, Netcenter's traffic numbers are mind-boggling.

America Online bought it all—the browser, the software (and the programmers to go with it), and Netcenter (the location of locations)—for $10 billion. The fit looks good. First, with netscape.com, aol.com, and the AOL service itself, the company's audience now numbers in the tens of millions. Second, Netcenter balances AOL's heavy evening and weekend use by the home market with more white-collar traffic, which is the heaviest on weekdays from 9 to 5. Third, AOL now has the option of switching its built-in browser from rival Microsoft's Internet Explorer to Netscape's Navigator. And fourth, but far from the least, AOL now has the software and expertise to plunge into e-commerce, not only with its current tenants but also with the tenants that will be moving into its ever-expanding shopping mall. Consumer advocates criticize the acquisition as further concentration of an already too small Internet software industry. But with forecasts for e-shopping ranging from dramatically huge to overwhelmingly huge (from tens to hundreds of billions of dollars within three or four years), securing the real estate now seems like a good idea.[1]

CHAPTER OVERVIEW

If you have ever thought of operating your own business, you are not alone. In fact, on any given day in the United States, more people are trying to start new businesses than are getting married or having children. However, before entering the world of contemporary business, an entrepreneur needs to understand its framework.

Like America Online, every business owner must choose the type of legal ownership that best meets the company's needs. Several variables affect the choice of the best way to organize your business:

- ▼ How easily can you form this type of organization?

- ▼ How much financial liability can you afford to accept?

- ▼ What financial resources do you have?

- ▼ What strengths and weaknesses do you see in other businesses in the industry?

- ▼ What are your own strengths and weaknesses?

This chapter begins with a focus on small-business ownership, including a discussion of the advantages and disadvantages of small-business ventures and a look at the services provided by the U.S. government's Small Business Administration. The role of women and minorities in small business is discussed in detail as well as global opportunities for small-business owners. The chapter then turns to an overview of the three types of private business ownership—sole proprietorships, partnerships, and corporations. Next, the chapter takes an in-depth view of the structures and operations typical of large corporations. Finally, it reviews the trends in business with a fresh look at mergers, acquisitions, and multinational corporations. The chapter ends with an explanation of public and collective ownership.

MOST BUSINESSES ARE SMALL BUSINESSES

Although many people associate the term *business* with international giants like Exxon,

Figure 5.1 **Women and Minority Ownership of U.S.-Based Small Businesses**

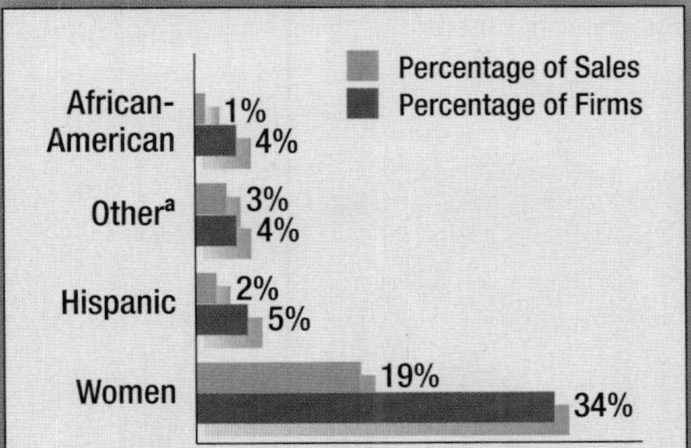

Percentage of Sales
Percentage of Firms

African-American — 1% / 4%
Other[a] — 3% / 4%
Hispanic — 2% / 5%
Women — 19% / 34%

[a] Includes Asian, Pacific Islander, Native American, and Native Alaskan.

Citibank, Wal-Mart, and General Electric, 19 of every 20 businesses in the United States employ fewer than 50 people. Of all the new businesses started last year, 20 percent are one- or two-person operations.

Small business is also the launching pad for entrepreneurs from every sector of the U.S. economy. As Figure 5.1 indicates, one-third of the nation's 17 million small businesses are owned by women. Hispanic-owned businesses account for 5 percent of all U.S. small businesses, and African-Americans own another 4 percent. In total, small businesses generate annual sales of over $3 trillion.

What Is a Small Business?

How do you distinguish a small business from a large one? Is sales the key indicator? What about market share or number of employees? The Small Business Administration (SBA), the federal agency most directly involved with this sector of the economy, considers a **small business** to be a firm that is independently owned and operated and is not dominant in its field.[2] The SBA also considers annual sales and number of employees in some industries to identify small businesses.

- ▼ A manufacturer is considered a small business if it employs fewer than 1,500 workers; a small wholesaler can employ no more than 100 workers.

- ▼ A retailer can generate up to $14.5 million in annual sales and still be considered a small business.

Quantitative standards such as maximum sales, market share, or number of employees frequently determine qualifications for loan programs developed to assist small businesses or procurement programs attempting to encourage proposals from them.

Business Directory

small business firm that is independently owned and operated, not dominant in its field, and meets certain size standards for income or number of employees.

Typical Small Business Ventures

For decades, small businesses have competed against some of the world's largest organizations as well as multitudes of other small companies. Judi Jacobsen, owner of Madison Park Greetings, is motivated by the competition from card giants Hallmark and American Greetings. Jacobsen and her 35 employees have found so much success with a line of 400 boutique greeting cards that she recently was named Small Business Person of the Year by the Small Business Administration. Her motto is, "Try to keep ahead of the trends and find your niche."[3]

For centuries, retailing and service establishments have remained the most common nonfarming small businesses. Take Longfellow's Wayside Inn in Sudbury, Massachusetts. Although only one U.S. business in four has celebrated its 25th anniversary, the Wayside Inn has been serving "man, woman, and beast" since the early 1700s and is probably the oldest home-grown business in the United States.[4] As Figure 5.2 indicates, small businesses dominate four industries: business services, eating and drinking establishments, wholesale trade—durable goods, and special trade contracting.

Retailing is another important industry for today's small businessperson. General merchandising giants like Wal-Mart, Kmart, and Sears may be the best-known retailing firms, but small, privately owned retail stores outnumber them. Small-business retailing includes stores that sell shoes, jewelry, office supplies and stationery, apparel, flowers, drugs, convenience foods, and thousands of other products. In fact, one-fifth of the nation's women-owned small businesses compete in the retail sector. Becky and Mike Busath are a good example. The two business partners turned Becky's love of baking bread into a successful small business by opening the Stone Ground Bread Company in San Antonio, Texas, where they sell whole-grain bread made fresh every day.[5]

Most farming is still the work of small businesses. The family farm is a classic example of a small-business operation; it is independently owned and operated, with relatively few employees, but with substantial reliance on unpaid, family labor. In fact, family-owned businesses are once again a popular form of business ownership, as retiring baby boomers and their Generation X children join forces.

Giant card-makers didn't hinder Judi Jacobsen of Madison Park Greetings.

▼ Julia (JJ) Gonson and her dad, Don, started their own record label, Undercover, with $6,000 in savings from JJ and another $30,000 investment from Don. Their first product, a cover album of David Bowie songs, sold 7,000 copies and recouped its $15,000 cost. Six more CDs were released in 1998.

▼ Barry Levin, a 64-year-old Bostonian, and his son Gregg will generate $1 million in sales this year from what Barry considered a dumb idea: making the brim of a baseball cap curve the right way when worn backward. Gregg educated his father on the number of people who wear caps and showed him a plastic gizmo he had designed that would perfectly bend the cap's visor. Today their company, The Perfect Curve, has 250 accounts at 350 sporting goods and specialty cap stores.[6]

One of every two companies is a **home-based business**—operated from the residence of the business owner. This arrangement is especially popular for fledgling firms; 57 percent of firms with revenues of $25,000 or less are home-based companies, contrasted with only 5 percent of the firms generating sales of $1 million or more.

Home-based businesses are not only widespread, but their number is rapidly growing. Today, more than 14 million people are self-employed, and 15 million Americans earn extra income from part-time work at home.[7] Home-based business owners earn six-figure annual incomes in several industries, including business brokers, business plan writers, desktop video producers, executive searchers, export agents, home inspectors, and management consultants. A major factor in the growth of home-based businesses is the increased availability of personal computers and such communications devices as fax machines, low-cost photocopiers, and electronic mail.

Many new-technology firms, those that design, produce, and market scientific innovations, begin as small businesses. Razorfish, a New York City company devoted to designing elegant Web sites, began small and later merged with another small company, avant garde interactive advertising firm Avalanche Systems. Even today, the successful combination has only a total of 85 employees.[8]

American business history is filled with inspirational stories of great inventors who launched companies in barns, garages, warehouses, and attics. For young visionaries like Apple Computer founders Stephen Jobs and Steve Wozniak, the logical option for transforming their technical idea into a commercial reality was to begin work in a family garage. The Business Tool Kit on page 167 offers tips on operating a home-based business. The impact of today's entrepreneurs, including home-based businesses, is discussed in more depth in Chapter 6.

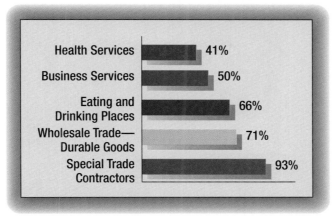

Figure 5.2 **Top Five Industries for Small Business**

Industry	Percent
Health Services	41%
Business Services	50%
Eating and Drinking Places	66%
Wholesale Trade—Durable Goods	71%
Special Trade Contractors	93%

tion levels than do employees of larger firms.[10]

Creating New Industries

Small businesses make tremendous contributions to the U.S. economy and society as a whole. A later section of this chapter will examine in more detail the opportunities that small businesses offer for women and minorities. The small-business sector also gives entrepreneurs an outlet for developing their ideas and perhaps for creating entirely new industries. Many of today's successful high-tech firms—Netscape, Cisco Systems, Yahoo!, and Dell Computer—began as small businesses.

CONTRIBUTIONS OF SMALL BUSINESS TO THE ECONOMY

Small businesses form the core of the U.S. economy, accounting for 52 percent of all sales and half of the private gross domestic product. They account for 99.7 percent of all U.S. employers, with 54 percent of the nation's private workforce.[9]

Even more impressive is the number of new jobs created each year by small businesses. While recent employment data reveal that giant firms employing 500 or more people actually reduced their total staffing, industry sectors dominated by small businesses created almost two-thirds of all new jobs. As Figure 5.3 reveals, tiny firms with one to four employees created 49 percent of the nation's new jobs.

Even if you never plan to start your own business, you will probably work for a small business at some point in your career. If you're looking for your first job, chances are a small business will provide it. Small firms generate two-thirds of all first-time employment opportunities. And once you get hired by a small business, you may just decide to stay for the long haul. Recent research studies report another important finding of interest to new employees: People who work for small businesses report higher job satisfac-

Gregg Levin convinced his father, Barry, to go into business with him selling a plastic ball-cap-bending gizmo called The Perfect Curve.

Another contribution of small business is its ability to provide needed services to the larger corporate community. The movement toward corporate downsizing that began in the early 1990s created a demand for other businesses to perform activities previously handled by company employees. Outsourcing such activities as security, employee benefits management, maintenance, and logistics created opportunities that were often filled by employees of small businesses.

Attracting New Industries Urban planners realize the importance of small businesses to their cities, and successful revitalization programs have improved conditions in depressed areas by attracting new industries. Fort Myers, Florida, more than doubled its population by attracting young professionals and small-business owners. Downtown Houston experienced a revival when Bellaire Boulevard was converted into a line of strip-mall stores to accommodate the increasing number of Asians, Hispanic Americans, and African-Americans who now constitute two-thirds of the city's population.[11]

But how do cities make these areas such attractive locations? Among the most important qualities reported by entrepreneurs deciding to relocate in previously neglected urban areas are available workers, inexpensive facilities, strong markets, availability of government-funded worker-training programs, funding sources, and positive attitudes shown by city officials and local community groups regarding the businesses.

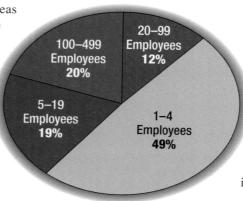

Figure 5.3 Importance of Small Businesses in New-Job Creation

The Small Business Administration (SBA) reports that small firms produce twice as many product innovations per employee as larger firms. In addition, they obtain more patents per sales dollar than larger businesses do, which indicates that small businesses make more discoveries. The airplane, audiotape recorder, double-knit fabric, optical scanner, personal computer, soft contact lens, and the zipper are all important 20th-century innovations that were developed by small businesses.[13]

ADVANTAGES OF A SMALL BUSINESS

Small businesses are not simply smaller versions of large corporations. They differ greatly in forms of organization, market positions, staff capabilities, managerial styles, organizational structures, and financial resources. But these differences usually seem like strengths to small-business owners, who find many advantages in operating small businesses as compared to working within large, powerful, multinational corporations. As Figure 5.4 indicates, the four most important advantages are innovation, superior customer service, lower costs, and opportunities to fill isolated niches.

Innovation

In order to compete effectively with giant corporations backed by massive resources, small firms often have to find new and creative ways of conducting business. The Business Hall of Fame box reports one case of a company that took its public securities offerings to the Internet. Vulcan Breweries offered stocks directly to the public over the Web, where the experiment both succeeded and failed.

Small businesses are often fertile ground in which to plant innovative ideas for new goods and services. After Neil Senturia had difficulty accessing online services when he was traveling, his California-based Atcom/Info developed the Cyberbooth. Travelers can now use Atcom's Internet kiosks to visit the Internet and read their e-mail at 167 airports, convention centers, and hotels.[12]

Superior Customer Service

A small firm can often operate with greater flexibility than can a large corporation, allowing it to tailor its product line and services to the needs of its customers. InterActive Custom Clothes does that—literally—for its customers. Consumers can visit InterActive's Web site, answer a few questions including their body measurements, and have their own custom-tailored jeans made within an hour. InterActive's computer program uses artificial intelligence to transmit the personal specifications to a machine that cuts the 19 pieces of cloth that make up a pair of jeans. Among the options are colored rivets, leather labels, novelty buttons, and a wide selection of fabrics. To get this kind of service a few years ago, says co-founder Peter del Rio, "You would have your clothes made by a master tailor. Now you have your own virtual master tailor."[14]

WWW. **www.ic3d.com**

Low Costs

Small firms can often provide goods and services at prices that large firms cannot match. Small businesses usually minimize overhead costs—costs not directly related to providing specific goods and services—allowing them to earn profits on low prices.

A typical small business sets up a lean organization with a small staff and few support personnel. The limitation on overhead costs made possible by maintaining a small permanent staff can provide a

| Innovation
Example: Start-up business to offer online grocery shopping and delivery | Superior Customer Service
Example: Free alterations on clothing purchases from a small boutique |
| Lower Costs
Example: Small retailer who can prepare sales flyers on a personal computer | Isolated Niches
Example: Retail store that specializes in selling products designed for left-handed consumers |

Figure 5.4 Advantages of Small-Business Ownership

distinct advantage for a small business. Instead of hiring high-income attorneys and accountants as permanent staff members, small-business owner-managers typically hire them when needed for special projects or as outside consultants. This approach typically helps to restrain payroll costs for the small business.[15] The ad in Figure 5.5 highlights the benefits gained by small businesses when they contract as needed with outside professionals.

Another source of cost savings is the quantity and quality of work performed by the business owner. Entrepreneurs typically work long hours with no overtime or holiday pay. In addition, their family members frequently contribute services at little or no pay as bookkeepers, laborers, receptionists, production assistants, and delivery personnel.

Even a small business like InterActive Custom Clothes can provide one-on-one service to its customers using the World Wide Web. At this site, customers can make their selections and place orders for jeans tailored to their measurements.

Low overhead also helps to keep the costs of small business operations at minimal levels. Many such businesses avoid rent and utility expenses by operating out of the owners' homes. In addition, these firms often carry little or no inventory, further reducing total operating costs.

Filling Isolated Market Niches

Large, growth-oriented businesses tend to focus on large segments of the overall market. The growth prospects of small market niches are simply too limited and the expenses involved in serving them too great to justify the required time and effort. Because high overhead costs force large firms to set minimum sizes for their target markets, small, underserved market niches have always attracted small businesses willing and able to serve them.

BUSINESS HALL OF FAME

Vulcan Breweries Seeks Micro-Investors on the Net

Today's beer aficionados increasingly are asking for beers and ales produced by microbreweries. Typically sold in local regions, they offer drinkers an exclusive image and unique taste. Alabamians can quench their thirst with any of the several beers produced by Birmingham's Vulcan Breweries.

Smaller than regular breweries, micros generally produce fewer than 10,000 barrels a year and often sell on the premises. Many are now setting up Web sites to increase product awareness and sales. Vulcan is using its Web site to secure investment funds also.

When Vulcan's management decided to launch two new products, they knew the move would involve new bottling equipment, new labeling, and new marketing efforts—in short, it would involve a lot of money it didn't have. The total price tag was estimated at $5 million.

The typical financing sources were considered: a bank loan, sale of stock to the general public, a merger. Selling stock seemed most promising, but the traditional method of "going public" appeared cost-prohibitive given the typical legal and underwriting fees ranging from $200,000 to $2 million. In addition to the roadblocks these fees represented, the corporate fundraisers knew it would be difficult to find a brokerage firm willing to handle a small $5 million deal. The whole process can be "too much work for too little money," says Vulcan President Lee Busby.

www. **www.vulcanbeer.com**

One benefit of stock offerings under $4 million is that they are exempt from much of the federal regulations controlling larger stock sales. Vulcan's management team chose a novel means: They would sell their stock on the Internet. Approvals were obtained from the federal Securities and Exchange Commission (SEC) and from Alabama's state securities commission.

To attract independent stock buyers, the Vulcan offering price was kept low: 100 shares at $1.85 each. Selling stock at such prices meant that thousands of buyers would have to be at-

---

Figure 5.5 **Reaping the Benefits of Hiring Outside Professionals**

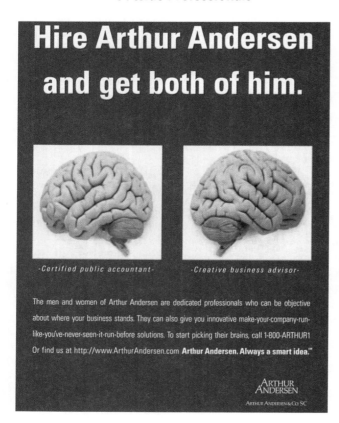

In addition, certain types of businesses favor small organizations. Many service businesses illustrate this point. Finally, economic and organizational factors may dictate that an industry consist primarily of small firms. Upscale restaurants and personal shopping services are typically small business operations.

Former high school teacher Joel McIntosh found an isolated niche when he tried to locate educational materials to use in his classes for gifted children in Waco, Texas. After deciding that available materials were inadequate, he used simple desktop publishing equipment to publish and distribute magazines and books to help other teachers and parents of gifted children. Although still a small business, McIntosh's Prufrock Press has grown to become one of the largest independent education publishers.[16]

www. **www.prufrock.com**

DISADVANTAGES OF A SMALL BUSINESS

Although small businesses bring a number of strengths to the competitive marketplace, they also have a variety of

Vulcan Breweries is only offering two sensational new brews -- Vulcan Beer, a crisp pilsner-style beer, and Vulcan Hefe Weizen, an unfiltered German-style wheat beer --

For additional information not found in this web site, we encourage you to call us at 800-972-8729 or email us.

Also visit Where the Money Goes...

tracted to raise $5 million. It was slow going at first, with only 70,000 shares sold for a grand total of $130,000. Since international stock buyers aren't limited by U.S. laws, Vulcan also enticed buyers from as far away as Russia.

But the unorthodox method of raising money produced unexpected benefits. Hundreds of stockholders are now actively promoting the company. "Those $185-a-whackers are becoming

mini-reps for the company," explains Busby. They are asking their grocers to carry the beer, convincing their friends to buy it, and complaining when it's unavailable. In its home market of Birmingham, Vulcan's products are now outselling Abita—previously the best-selling microbrewery in the South—and beating Jack Daniel's beer for market share.

The Internet may not yet be the

sales channel of choice for most firms seeking to sell stock, but it has been a great start for Vulcan's expansion plans. The little microbrewer is on the leading edge of companies offering stock to micro-investors on the Net.

QUESTIONS FOR CRITICAL THINKING

1. **If banks are reluctant to lend to small businesses, why are investors willing to risk their money on these ventures? Explain your answer.**

2. **Could Vulcan have come closer to their $5 million goal by setting their minimum commitment higher—say $100,000? Explain.**

Sources: Birmingham Brewmasters Web site, accessed at www.bham.net, February 25, 1999; and Verna Gates, "Brewing a Small Cap Marketing Coup," *Business Alabama Monthly*, February 1998, pp. 17–19.

disadvantages in competing with larger, better established firms. A small business may find itself especially vulnerable during an economic downturn, since it may have accumulated fewer resources than its larger competitors to cushion a sales decline.

The primary disadvantages facing today's small businesses include management shortcomings, inadequate financing, and government regulations. These issues—quality and depth of management, availability of financing, and ability to wade through government rules and requirements—are so important that firms with major deficiencies in one or more areas often find themselves in bankruptcy proceedings. As Figure 5.6 shows, almost one new business in four will permanently close its doors within 2 years of opening them, and 62 percent will fail within the first 6 years of operation. While highly motivated and well-trained business owner-

managers can overcome these potential problems, they should analyze all of these issues before starting new companies.

Management Shortcomings

Among the most common discoveries at a post mortem examination of a small-business failure is inadequate management. Business founders often possess great strengths in specific areas such as marketing or interpersonal relations, but they suffer from hopeless deficiencies in others

Figure 5.6 **Business Failures**

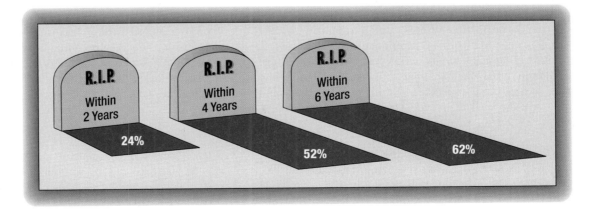

The Five Best Businesses to Start from Your Dorm

Are you anxious to get started in the world of business? Do you want to accumulate some real-world experience, build your resume, or simply make some money? The following suggestions may be just the ticket to making your next school term happier, busier, and richer than this one.

▼ *Web-Site Developing.* Three Boston University roommates began by using their own computers and university scanners to help a local hair salon launch a Web site. Their company, Net One, earned over $80,000 in 1998.

▼ *Resumé Writing.* Armed with a good $1,000 graphics software program such as Quark Xpress or PageMaker and a way with words, you can earn between $10 and $15 per hour.

▼ *Computer Repair.* Almost one-third of the nation's 15 million college students own personal computers. Students who know how to repair these machines when they go on the blink can earn between $10 and $20 per hour.

▼ *Word Processing.* A student with good typing skills, a personal computer, and a printer can earn money charging flat fees for completed projects or a set price per page. Pass out flyers in the community to inform local companies of your business.

▼ *Laundry Pickup and Delivery.* Contact local laundries to obtain a bulk discount, then offer pickup and delivery service to student customers who are charged the same amount they would pay if they brought in the laundry themselves. A 50-customer list can generate $150 per week.

For peer support, business resources, and contacts with other entrepreneurs around the world, contact the Young Entrepreneurs Network in Boston at (617) 867–4690 or visit their Web site:

WWW. www.idye.com

Source: Business suggestions in Frances Huffman, "Most Likely to Succeed," *Business Start-Ups*, March 1998, pp. 54–59.

---

like finance or order fulfillment. Large firms recruit trained specialists to manage individual functions; small businesses frequently rely on small staffs who must be adept at varied skills.

An even worse result frequently occurs when people go into business with little, if any, business training. Some new businesses are begun almost entirely on the basis of what seems like a great idea for a new product. Managers assume that they will acquire needed business expertise on the job. All too often, the result is business bankruptcy.

If you are seriously contemplating starting a new business, heed a word of warning: learn the basics of business *first,* and *second,* recognize your limitations. Although most small-business owners recognize the need to seek out the specialized skills of accountants and attorneys for financial and legal assistance, they often hesitate to turn to consultants and other advisors for assistance in areas where they lack knowledge or experience.

Nouveau Contemporary Goods, a Baltimore retail outlet selling everything from greeting cards to furniture, grew much faster than owners Steve Appel and Lee Whitehead ever anticipated. Since 1996, the store has

doubled its staff as sales have climbed to $1.2 million. Since neither partner brought any retailing experience to the venture, they agreed that they needed help to manage such rapid change. The partners brought in a retail consultant to help them plan future strategies and develop retailing skills of employees and managers.[17]

Founders of new businesses frequently struggle with an ailment that might be called "the rose-colored-glasses" syndrome. Filled with excitement about the potential of newly designed products, they may neglect important details like marketing research intended to determine whether potential customers share their excitement. Someone considering launching a new business should first determine whether the proposed product meets the needs of a large enough market and whether they can convince the public of its superiority over competing offerings.

International Brownie founder Cindy Rice almost talked herself out of implementing her business idea before even starting. The future gourmet brownie entrepreneur started worrying when she noticed a retail store in a nearby shopping mall selling trays of brownies that looked just like the ones she planned to sell. "When I saw products that were similar to mine, I used to be afraid they were going to take away my customers. Then I realized that what it really meant was that there's a market out there for my product." To help distinguish her products, which she sells via the Internet and direct-mail orders, from those of competitors, Rice emphasizes superior product quality and unparalleled customer service.[18]

Inadequate Financing

Another leading cause of small-business problems is inadequate financing. In too many instances, entrepreneurs start new businesses assuming that their firms will generate enough funds from the first month's sales to finance continuing operations. Building a business takes time, though. Employees must be trained, equipment purchased, deposits paid for rent and utilities, and marketing dollars must be spent to inform potential customers about the new firm and its product offerings. Unless the owner has set aside enough funds to cover cash shortfalls during the first several months in which the business is becoming established, the venture may collapse at an early stage.

After surviving the cash crunch that often accompanies the first months of operation, a business must confront another major financial problem: uneven cash flows. For most small and large businesses, cash inflows and outflows do not display even patterns; instead, they fluctuate greatly at different times of the year. Small retail outlets frequently generate much of their annual sales revenues during the December holiday period. Florists make most of their deliveries during three holidays: Valentine's Day, Easter, and Mother's Day. Large firms may build up sufficient cash reserves to weather periods of below-average sales, or they can turn to banks and other lenders for short-term loans; new business start-ups often lack both cash balances and access to sources of additional funds.

With no track record and few assets to pledge as collateral, the owners of a small business usually discover that banks are highly reluctant to make business loans. As Table 5.1 shows, personal savings or personal loans made by owners provide the primary sources of start-up funding.

Irwin Simon took out a second mortgage on his home to raise the money he needed to buy a kosher frozen-food business. But the risky decision paid off. Simon's Hain Food Group eventually grew into a $65-million-a-year business success.[19]

Small-business owners also rely heavily on credit cards as a source of short-term— but high-cost—financing. A recent survey revealed that 39 percent of all small-business owners use their personal credit cards for business purposes. The heaviest users of credit cards for business financing are tiny firms with fewer than 10 employees.[20]

Banks often provide limited funding for small companies that meet stringent criteria. In addition, the high risks and relatively high processing expenses involved in making small loans often cause lenders to charge high interest rates to small-business borrowers. Only one business loan in five made by U.S. commercial banks is for less than $100,000.[21] The five banks ranked highest among small-business borrowers are Wells Fargo, NationsBank, Keybank, Bank One, and First Union National Bank.[22]

Some business pioneers take unusual approaches to scaling obstacles between themselves and new-business financing—and this kind of innovation can lead to handsome payoffs. Henry Gibson is a good example. Gibson is one of 30 owners of the Big Wash, a highly successful

They said it

"Being in your own business is working 80 hours a week so that you can avoid working 40 hours a week for someone else."

Ramona E. F. Arnett
President, Ramona
Enterprises, Inc.

Table 5.1	Sources of Start-Up Funding

Source of Funds	Percentage of Business Owners Obtaining at Least Some of Their Start-up Funds from This Source
Personal savings	72%[a]
Banks	45
Friends and/or relatives	28
Individual investors (not friends or relatives)	10
Government-guaranteed loans	7
Venture capital firms	1

[a] Total exceeds 100 percent due to use of multiple sources of funding by some firms.

Washington, D.C. laundry. Gibson knew it would not be easy to raise the $250,000 needed to set up a coin-operated laundry, so he thought about what a giant business would likely do in his place. Then he settled on his big idea—he would sell shares of stock in the venture at $100 each. Many of the first investors were fellow church members, others were neighbors who knew and believed in Gibson's ability and the need for a convenient laundry. Most of them could afford to buy only one share, but few bought as many as 50. Once Gibson had raised $30,000, he applied for a loan from a local bank and raised $60,000 in grants from seven different foundations. Today, Big Wash is an unquestioned success, having already returned its owners $175 for each share they own. Gibson has also been rewarded for all his efforts. As he puts it, "It's the best thing I've ever done."[23]

Government Regulation

Small-business owners often complain bitterly of excessive government regulation and red tape. Paperwork costs alone account for billions of small-business dollars each year. A large company with a substantial staff can usually cope better with requirements for forms and reports. Many experts within and outside government recognize the need to reduce the paperwork required of small businesses, since they simply lack the capabilities to handle the burden. Small businesses often struggle to absorb the costs of government paperwork because of their slim profit margins. Some small firms close down for this reason alone.

Taxes are another burdensome expense for a small business. In addition to state and federal income taxes, employers must pay taxes covering workers' compensation insurance and unemployment benefits.

INCREASING THE LIKELIHOOD OF BUSINESS SUCCESS

How can a prospective owner gain the numerous advantages of running a small business while also avoiding the disadvantages? Successful entrepreneurs make two critical recommendations:

▼ Develop a business plan.

▼ Use the resources provided by such agencies as the Small Business Administration and local business incubators for information, advice, funding, and networking opportunities.

They said it

"Banks will lend you money if you can prove you don't need it."

Mark Twain (1835–1910)
American author

Creating a Business Plan

Creating a business plan represents perhaps the most important task that an entrepreneur faces. An effective business plan can make the difference between a company that succeeds and one that fails. A **business plan** is a written document that provides an orderly statement of a company's goals, the methods by which it intends to achieve those goals, and the standards by which it will measure achievements.

Plans give a sense of purpose to an organization. They provide guidance, influence, and leadership, as well as communicating ideas about goals and the means of achieving them to associates, employees, and others. In addition, they set standards against which achievements can be measured. Planning usually works best when the entire organization participates in the process. Planning can combine good ideas presented by employees and communicate information while making everyone feel a part of the team.

Although no one format best suits all situations, a good small-business plan will include a detailed time frame for achieving specific goals, projections of money flows (both income received by the business and funds disbursed to pay expenses), and units for measuring achievement. A business plan should also cover the methods by which the firm will achieve specific goals, procedures it will follow, and values that define important standards for conduct. Perhaps most importantly, the plan should always be open to revision.

Before writing a business plan, a business owner should answer some questions:

▼ How would you explain your idea to a friend?

▼ What purpose does your business serve? How does your idea differ from those behind existing businesses?

Business Directory

business plan written document that provides an orderly statement of a company's goals, the methods by which it intends to achieve those goals, and the standards by which it will measure achievements.

▼ What is the state of the industry you are entering? Who will be your customers or clients?

▼ How will you market the firm's goods or services?

▼ How much will you charge?

▼ How will you finance your business?

▼ What characteristics qualify you to run this business?

Give special attention to the name of your proposed business. Does the name reflect the firm's goals? Is it already registered by someone else? Does it convey any hidden meanings to other people? What does it mean phonetically in other languages? Is it offensive to any religious or ethnic groups?

Be sure to do adequate research. Trade journals are excellent sources of industry-related information. The Small Business Development Centers (SBDC) on many college campuses, the Small Business Administration in Washington, D.C., many local Chambers of Commerce, and your local library can also assist in this research. You may gain useful insights by talking to suppliers in the industry and to local licensing authorities. How many similar businesses have succeeded? How many have failed? Why? What risks are specific to your industry? What markups are typical in the industry's pricing structure? What are common levels of expenses and profit percentages?

Components of a business plan typically include:

▼ An executive summary should answer the who, what, why, when, where, and how questions for the business in brief. (Although the summary appears early in the plan, it probably should be the last element written.)

▼ An introduction should give a general statement of the concept, purpose, and objectives of the proposed business, along with an overview of the industry. This element should include a brief description of the owner's education, experience, and training, with references to a resume included later in the plan.

▼ A marketing section should describe the firm's target market, its anticipated competitors, and plans for distri-

bution, advertising, pricing, and locations of facilities. This section should cover the background of the industry and industry trends as well as the potential of the new venture. It should also point out any unique or distinctive features of the business and explain the reasons for choosing a particular start-up date.

▼ The marketing section should also cover equipment rental, leasing, or purchase costs, and the influences of traffic volume, neighboring businesses, demographics, parking, accessibility, and visibility. Further discussion should review labor costs, utility access and rates, police and fire protection, zoning restrictions, and other government rules and regulations.

▼ Another section should detail an operating plan forecast, a plan for obtaining capital, and a description of plans for spending funds.

▼ A section should estimate assets and liabilities and analyze when the firm will reach the break-even point (the level of sales at which revenues equal costs).

▼ A plan written to obtain funding should include resumes of the principals of the business.

A business plan should cover some other topics, as well, including whether the firm will be organized as a sole proprietorship, partnership, or corporation; when it will need to hire employees and what job descriptions will guide their work; the lines of authority in the business; a risk management plan, including detailed information on insurance; a list of suppliers and methods for assessing their reliability and competence; and a policy for extending credit to customers.

Since business plans are essential tools for securing outside funds, the financial section requires particular attention to detail. As Lucien Campolo, co-founder of Miami-based suntan-oil producer South Beach Sun Co., explains, "If you wait until you have enough money to take a shot at starting your own business, you'll be waiting your entire life. You need to put together the plan, put together the idea, and just get started."[24]

If the plan becomes part of a request for financing, the banker will examine the owner's management

At 28, Kelly and Lucien Campolo proved what they've known all along: Sun-care products are hot stuff.

skills and experience, the risk of the enterprise, available collateral, and the ability to repay the loan. Potential outside investors are more likely to evaluate the potential for profits and growth and place less emphasis on downside risks.

If certain assumptions underlie the body of the plan, tie them into the financial section. A plan for two outlets, for example, should provide cash-flow projections that show how the firm will pay their costs. Deal with both significant and insignificant variables. The bankers or investors who analyze a plan may not know whether your firm will spend $250 or $25,000 to install an exotic, high-tech part, but they will know that a telephone system for 50 people will cost more than $250 per month. Carelessness with seemingly insignificant variables can undercut credibility.

Itemize monthly expenses rather than simply projecting annual amounts. A firm with $100,000 in annual costs may not spend exactly $8,333 each month. It must pay some expenses monthly and some once each year. An owner who must cover several large, annual payments at the beginning of the year will be running back to financiers in the first month to explain problems with the cash-flow projection—not a good way to start.

In addition to cash-flow projections, a business plan should project a detailed profit-and-loss statement. It must also state all assumptions it makes about the conditions under which the firm will operate. The Business Hall of Shame discusses how assumptions about a market may prove disastrously wrong.

The assembled plan should include a table of contents so that readers can turn directly to the parts that most interest them. Make sure that the plan is presented in an attractive and professional format.

Small Business Administration

A number of invaluable resources for small businesses are provided by the Small Business Administration (SBA). The SBA is the principal government agency concerned with helping small U.S. firms. It is the advocate for small businesses within the federal government. About 4,000 employees staff the SBA's Washington headquarters and its regional and field offices. Its primary operating functions include providing financial assistance, aiding in

government procurement matters, and providing management training and consulting.

 www.sba.gov

Financial Assistance from the SBA Contrary to popular belief, the SBA seldom provides direct business loans. Its major financing contributions are the guarantees it provides for small-business loans made by private lenders, including banks and other institutions. Direct SBA loans are available in only a few special situations, such as natural disaster recovery and energy conservation or development programs. Even in these special instances, a business applicant must contribute at least 30 percent of the proposed project's total cost in cash, home equity, or stocks in order to qualify.

The SBA also guarantees *microloans* of less than $25,000 to very small firms. These loans are available from more than 100 sources throughout the United States, most of them not-for-profit business development groups. Other sources of microloans include the federal Economic Development Administration, some state governments, and certain private lenders, such as credit unions and community development groups.

Small business loans are also available through an SBA-licensed organization called a **Small Business Investment Company (SBIC).** SBICs can borrow up to four times the amount of their capitalization from the federal government and use the funds to make loans. Last year, they loaned $2.4 billion to small businesses for equity capital and other financial needs. SBICs are also likely to be more flexible than banks in their lending decisions. Well-known companies that used SBIC loans for start-up financing include Apple Computer, Callaway Golf Company, America Online, Federal Express, Intel, and Sun Microsystems.[25]

www.ace-net.sr.unh.edu/

Another financial resource underwritten by the SBA is the Angel Capital Electronic Network (ACE-Net), which matches entrepreneurs looking for start-up capital with potential investors. Entrepreneurs post information about their businesses on ACE-Net's Web site, where potential investors can review it. Interested parties contact the firms. The goal is

They said it

"To open a business is very easy; to keep it open is very difficult."

Chinese proverb

Business Directory

Small Business Administration (SBA) federal agency that assists small businesses by providing management training and consulting, financial advice, and support in securing government contracts.

Table 5.2	Programs and Services of the Small Business Administration

A. BUSINESS COUNSELING AND TRAINING

Small Business Development Center (SBDC)
Over 900 SBDCs provide management and technical assistance to small businesses and would-be entrepreneurs. They are cooperative efforts among the SBA, the academic community, the private sector, and state and local governments.

Service Corps of Retired Executives (SCORE)
Nationwide, 12,400 SCORE volunteers in nearly 400 chapters provide expert advice, based on years of firsthand experience and shared knowledge, on virtually every phase of business.

Business Information Center (BIC)
BICs offer small-business owners access to state-of-the-art computer hardware and software as well as counseling by SCORE volunteers.

Women's Network for Entrepreneurial Training (WNET); Veterans' Entrepreneurial Training (VET); and Office of Native American Affairs (ONAA)
These three programs provide in-depth entrepreneurial training for women, veterans, and Native Americans. Resources include workshops and mentoring programs.

B. LENDING PROGRAMS

Women's and Minority Prequalification Loans
These programs enable the SBA to prequalify a loan guaranty for a woman or minority business owner before approaching a lender. The program focuses on an applicant's character, credit, experience, and reliability rather than collateral.

FA$TRAK
A new loan program, piloted with selected banks nationwide, FA$TRAK provides additional incentive to lenders to make small-business loans.

7(m) MicroLoan
The MicroLoan program provides short-term loans ranging from under $100 to $25,000 for small-scale financing purposes such as inventory, supplies, and working capital.

C. INTERNATIONAL TRADE ASSISTANCE

U.S. Export Assistance Center (USEAC)
USEACs combine in single locations the trade-promotion and export-finance resources of the SBA, the U.S. Department of Commerce, and the Export-Import Bank of the United States.

D. FEDERAL GOVERNMENT PROCUREMENT

Prime Contracting and Subcontracting
This program increases opportunities for small businesses in the federal acquisition process. It initiates small-business set-asides, identifies new small-business sources, and counsels small firms on how to do business with the federal government.

---

to help businesses seeking smaller amounts of capital than those typically handled by venture capital firms.[26]

Other Specialized Assistance Although government purchases represent a sizable market, small companies have difficulty in competing for this business with giant firms, which employ specialists to handle the volumes of paperwork involved in preparing proposals and completing bid applications. Today, many government procurement programs specifically set aside shares for small companies; an additional SBA role involves assisting small firms in securing these contracts.

A **set-aside program** specifies that certain government contracts (or portions of those contracts) are re-

stricted to small businesses. Every federal agency with buying authority must maintain an Office of Small and Disadvantaged Business Utilization to ensure that small businesses receive a reasonable portion of government procurement contracts.

In addition to financial advice and guaranteed loan programs, the SBA provides a variety of other services to small businesses, including toll-free telephone numbers and online resources to answer questions. It offers hundreds of publications at little or no cost, and it sponsors popular conferences and seminars. Table 5.2 summarizes several of the programs that the SBA currently offers to small-business owners.

Pat Creedon turned to the Service Corps of Retired Executives (SCORE) for help when her 5-year-old electrical contracting firm, Creedon Controls, encountered cash flow problems. Customers owed money but were not paying their bills on time; in turn, Creedon was struggling to meet her company's financial obligations. A SCORE counselor helped Creedon to write a business plan that enabled her to double the firm's credit line to $100,000. With the larger credit line, Creedon was better able to ride out periods when accounts didn't pay on time.[27]

Business Incubators

In recent years, local community agencies interested in encouraging business development have implemented a concept called a **business incubator** to provide low-cost, shared business facilities to small, start-up ventures. A typical incubator might section off space in an abandoned plant and rent it to various small firms. Tenants often share secretaries, copiers, and other business services.

About 600 business incubator programs now operate nationwide. Some are operated by industrial development authorities, others by not-for-profit organizations, colleges and universities, or even by private investors. These facilities offer management support services and valuable management advice from in-house mentors.

Some incubator programs specialize in particular industries or types of businesses. The Entergy Arts Business Center in New Orleans offers a place where artists and graphic designers can gain expert advice about running businesses. Jocelyn Burrell, an artist specializing in jewelry, metal, and mixed media, finds that Entergy

| Figure 5.7 | Large Firms Providing Specialized Services for Small Businesses |

gives her a chance to network with others running art businesses and find new markets for her work.[28]

Large Corporations Assisting Small Businesses

Corporate giants often devise special programs aimed at solving small-business problems. In doing so, they are not acting out of humanitarian interests. Instead, they recognize the size of the small-business market, its growth rate and buying power, and the financial rewards for firms that support small businesses. Figure 5.7 provides an example of a large company attempting to meet this challenge. AT&T offers custom-tailored assistance in designing and operating a Web site. First Union Bank also offers small businesses easy-to-use financial services complete with 24-hour loan approvals, account statements faxed daily, and automatic transfers of surplus cash into interest-paying accounts.

Wal-Mart is another international giant familiar with the expression, "One hand washes the other." The world's largest retailer has long supported small businesses. The Wal-Mart Innovation Network (WIN) and the Support American Made Products program have already helped more than 3,000 inventors and entrepreneurs by evaluating their products and prototypes for possible distribution by the chain. To determine Wal-Mart's interest in adding your product to its store offerings, call 1-501-273-4000 and ask the WIN representative to send you an application form. Return the application with detailed company information, a $175 evaluation fee, and a prototype of your product. Within 60 days, WIN evaluators will send you a detailed critique covering issues like product quality, packaging, service capacity, capitalization levels, and a decision on whether your product will be placed on Wal-Mart shelves.

These efforts not only help small businesses; they are also pivotal in Wal-Mart's success. Gerald Udell, ad-

Business Directory

business incubator organization that provides low-cost, shared facilities to small, start-up ventures.

ministrator of both programs, points out, "Wal-Mart doesn't want to end up with empty shelves."[29]

SMALL-BUSINESS OPPORTUNITIES FOR WOMEN AND MINORITIES

The thousands of new business start-ups each year include growing numbers of women-owned firms as well as new businesses launched by African-Americans, Hispanics, and members of other minority groups. These entrepreneurs see small-business ownership and operation as an attractive and lucrative alternative to working for someone else. Figure 5.8 shows the types of businesses commonly owned by women and minorities.

Women-Owned Businesses

In the United States today, nearly 8 million women-owned firms provide jobs for 16 million people—more than are employed by the Fortune 500 industrial firms. Two of the largest women-owned businesses in the United States are packaged-food giant Beatrice Foods and Raley's, a supermarket chain.

Increasing numbers of women are starting their own companies for several reasons. Some may leave large corporations when they feel blocked from opportunities for advancement, that is, when they hit the so-called *glass ceiling*, as discussed in Chapter 9. Other women may want flexible working hours so they can spend time with their families. Still others may have lost their jobs when their employers downsized or left because they became frustrated with the bureaucracies in large companies.

Of all the minority classifications in the United States, minority women-owned firms have far outpaced others in their growth. During the past 20 years, the number of minority-owned firms grew 47 percent. During this same time, women-owned firms almost doubled that rate at 78 percent, while businesses owned by minority women grew at an astounding 153 percent.[30]

Over half of women-owned firms are service businesses, and another 18 percent are retail stores—many of them competing in segments traditionally dominated by men.[31] Louisa Hechavarrias took out a $2,000 loan to open Friendly Auto Glass, a mobile windshield repair company. She runs the firm from her home, keeping her

costs low at the same time she keeps tabs on her three young children.[32]

Along with this strong growth, women have been able to establish a powerful support network in a relatively short time. Many nationwide business assistance programs serve only women. In Boston, the Center for Women & Enterprise offers training and workshops; in Chicago, the Women's Business Development Center instructs female would-be business owners on matters of financing; in San Francisco, the Women's Initiative for Self Employment not only provides bilingual entrepreneurship training, but also offers technical assistance and financing to low-income women.[33]

Hispanic-Owned Businesses

Hispanics are the nation's largest group of minority business owners. During the past decade, the Hispanic population and the number of Hispanic-owned businesses have more than doubled. Many economists foresee even more growth ahead for this sector, especially as trade between the United States and Latin America increases with the implementation of NAFTA.

Despite their progress, Hispanic entrepreneurs, like other minority business owners, still face some obstacles. Minority entrepreneurs tend to start businesses on a smaller scale and have more difficulty finding investors than white entrepreneurs. Some industry analysts believe

| **Figure 5.8** | **Types of Businesses Owned by Minorities and Women** |

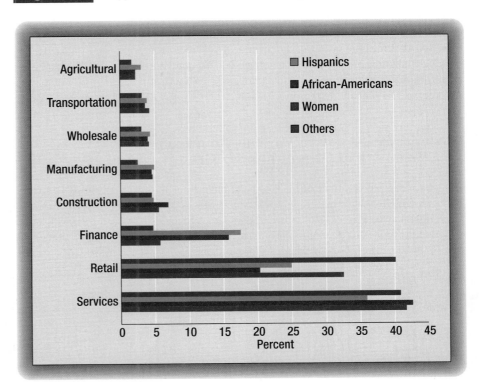

BUSINESS HALL OF SHAME

Closing Day at Centaur Zone Cafe

When W. David Waters opened the Centaur Zone Cafe in Honolulu, he dreamed of growing his new company into an international franchise of coffeehouses. "I thought we'd either be an overnight sensation or we'd flop," he remembers. But when closing day came a short year later, he recalls, "It was nothing romantic. It just sort of opened and just sort of closed."

Waters was full of confidence when he started out and expected to be a success. Failure was not in his vocabulary. With a dual degree in international management and finance, he knew where to start. He began by conducting research.

Waters thought downtown Honolulu would be an excellent location

for a coffeehouse. He saw two types of customers there: the artsy crowd from the Hawaii Theatre located across the street from his proposed location and the wealthy Asian students from Hawaii Pacific University, just around the corner. Tourists were also expected to add to his clientele. After talking with other coffeehouse owners, a representative from SCORE (Service Core of Retired Executives), and the director of a national coffee organization, Waters wrote up his business plan.

Next, he went in search of start-up capital. He combined $10,000 from his own savings and credit cards with $13,000 from a Japanese investor. But his greatest support came from his father, who loaned him $20,000. With the planning and financing taken care of, Waters signed the lease on the downtown location he had chosen for

the Centaur Zone Cafe. He painted and decorated the cafe with used furniture reupholstered in animal prints and purple velvet. While he was fixing up the place, people kept stopping by, eager for the cafe to open. "We thought once the doors opened, people would come in," says Waters.

Finally, the Centaur Zone officially opened. But the first day was slow and depressing. Waters also hoped that many of the people attending a dance performance that night at the Hawaii Theatre would stop in for a cup of coffee after the show. "We passed out fliers, and we bought all these desserts," explains Waters. "The theater closed, and everybody just walked by. Less than 10 people came in. It was so embarrassing."

Eventually, word-of-mouth spread to the university campus, and college students began hanging out at the

that minority entrepreneurs have more trouble buying franchises. Even today, minorities own only 5 percent of U.S. franchise businesses, just one-fourth the amount expected based on their proportion of the total U.S. population. Ask Susan Kezios, president of Women in Franchising, a Chicago-based association that provides services for women and minorities who are interested in franchising opportunities. Minority groups, says Kezios, are "the last markets on franchisors' list of priorities."[34]

Businesses Owned by African-Americans and Members of Other Minority Groups

In recent years, the number of black-owned businesses has almost doubled—twice the growth of U.S. businesses overall. In fact, the 100 largest black-owned companies together generated revenues of over $14 billion last year.[35]

A few years ago, Charles Hardesty became one of the 7

million Americans each year who realize their dream of business ownership. Every Friday night, Hardesty would drive 4 hours to the Atlantic coast, buy 600 pounds of fresh shrimp, and return to spend weekends at a Winston-Salem, North Carolina flea market. When Hardesty learned that one of his customers wanted to sell his seafood restaurant, he decided to change careers. Pooling his life savings and a bank loan, Hardesty came up with $18,000 and the Forsyth Seafood Cafe was born. Since then he has opened a second seafood restaurant and rakes in $700,000 in sales each year.[36]

THE FRANCHISING ALTERNATIVE

The franchising concept has played a major role in the growth of small business. **Franchising** is a contractual business arrangement between a manufacturer or another supplier and a dealer. The contract specifies the methods by which the dealer markets the good or service of the supplier. Franchises can involve both goods and services; some of the best known are Domino's, McDonald's, and Subway.

Starting a small, independent company can be a

Business Directory

franchising contractual agreement that specifies the methods by which a dealer can produce and market a supplier's good or service.

cafe. After three weeks, the business broke even. "We were making enough money to pay the rent and electricity," says Waters, "but not enough for me to pay my own bills." But when summer came, the students went home, and business dropped again. He got an extension on his rent until fall, but by that time, Hawaii's economic downturn was taking its toll. Then the financial crisis hit Asia, and tourism slowed. The cafe was hit hard. After only a year, the Centaur Zone Cafe closed its doors. "Until the end," explains Waters, "we thought something miraculous would happen."

So what happened to Waters's business plan? Business consultant Sam Slom thinks that Waters's basic assumptions weren't realistic. For one thing, unlike malls, "downtown areas are more transient," explains Slom. In addition, Slom points out that the costs of doing business in Hawaii are high as a result of such mandatory employee benefits as medical, workers' compensation, unemployment insur-

ance, and liability costs, which can add 50 percent to payroll costs. But Waters's biggest mistake, according to Slom, was "underestimating the consequences of Hawaii's worst-in-the-nation business and tax climate, "which had crushed big and small businesses alike and broken many able entrepreneurs during the past decade.

Would Waters someday consider starting another business? He says yes. After all, someone once described a successful entrepreneur as a person who has already experienced at least three business failures.

QUESTIONS FOR CRITICAL THINKING

1. When asked about his experience with the Centaur Zone Cafe, Waters says, "I never dreamed we would just drag along, hanging on to tidbits of hope here and there. It was emotionally and psychologically trying." The times were tough, he says, "part of me kept

wanting to go on. Closing wasn't my choice." Why do you think he was unable to see the writing on the wall? Explain your answer.

2. How could Waters have more fully investigated the likelihood of getting customers in the Centaur Zone? Would more research have helped? What about surveys or personal interviews?

Sources: Cheryl McManus, "Uh-Oh: Business Failures Up," *Inc.*, January 1999, p. 79; and Janean Chun, "Out of Business," *Entrepreneur*, August 1998, pp. 12–13.

risky, time-consuming endeavor, but franchising can reduce the amount of time and effort needed to expand. For instance, Ken Rosenthal knew he wanted to start a bakery, but he also knew he wanted to avoid the long hours that this service-oriented business frequently requires. "I'll never forget one story," he recalls. "This guy was working around the clock. He'd come home, get in the shower, turn on the water, and sit on the floor to rest. And when the hot water ran out and the shower ran cold, it was time to go back to work." When Rosenthal opened a bakery/cafe called the Saint Louis Bread Company, he planned from the beginning to franchise his concept. With a franchise, comments the company's CEO David Hutkin, "You give away a big percentage, and you don't make as much money, but it's a cheaper way to grow."

Thanks to franchising, in just 10 years, the Saint Louis Bread Company has grown from one cafe to more than 17 today. Rosenthal keeps two large notebooks filled with inquiries from 400 potential franchisees. Notes Myron Klevens, one of Rosenthal's partners. "We'd like to be kind of the itsy-bitsy spider—here's St. Louis, and here's someplace else, here's someplace else, and sort of link them all up."[37]

The Franchising Sector

Franchising started just after the Civil War, when the Singer Company began to franchise sewing-machine outlets. The concept became increasingly popular after 1900 within the

With a new restaurant to go with their seafood market and takeout grill, Charles A. Hardesty and his wife, Virginia, are satisfying their appetite for business growth.

| Figure 5.9 | **Franchises in the Service Sector** |

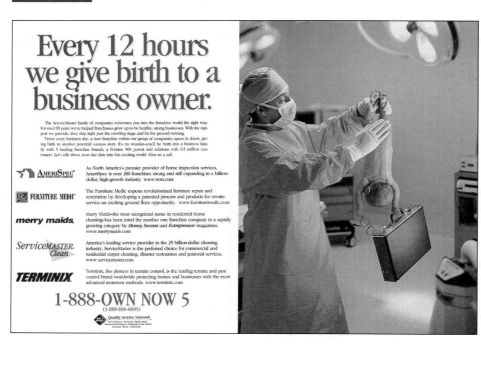

automobile industry. Automobile travel led to demands for gasoline, oil, and tires; makers of all of these commodities franchised dealers to distribute them. Soft-drink and lodging firms offered additional popular franchises.

Quality Service Network is one of the largest franchisors of consumer and business services. Included in its portfolio of franchise alternatives are a termite and pest control firm (Terminix), a home inspection company (AmeriSpec), a furniture repair and restoration business (Furniture Medic), Merry Maids residential home cleaning, and commercial and residential carpet-cleaning specialist Servicemaster Clean. As Figure 5.9 points out, the company is growing at the rate of one new business every 12 hours.

The franchising concept continues its rapid growth. Total U.S. sales from franchising are expected to top $1 trillion by 2000. Franchising is also popular overseas. In Australia, for example, franchise sales topped $60 billion in 2000.

Franchising Agreements

The two principals in a franchising agreement are the franchisee and the franchisor. The dealer is the *franchisee,* a small-business owner who contracts to sell the good or service of the supplier—the *franchisor*—in exchange for some payment (usually a flat fee plus future royalties or commissions). The franchisor typically provides building plans, site selection help, managerial and accounting systems, and other services to assist the franchisee. The franchisor also provides name recognition for the small-business owner who becomes a franchisee. This public image is created by advertising cam-

paigns, and the franchisee typically contributes to cover such costs.

The franchisee purchases both tangible and intangible assets from the franchisor. A franchisor may charge a management fee in addition to its initial franchise fee and a percentage of sales or profits. Another may require contributions to a promotional fund. Total costs can vary over a wide range. Start-up costs for a Wendy's fast-food restaurant can run anywhere from $805,000 to $1.3 million. By contrast, start-up costs for a coverall cleaning service franchise average $2,500.

Many franchisors provide some type of training for new franchisees and their employees. The Saint Louis Bread Company, for example, offers 56 training modules on topics such as "Espresso Standards" and "Product Packaging"; workers who hold different positions within a franchise must complete different combinations of modules.

Benefits and Problems of Franchising

As for any other business property, the buyer of a franchise bears the responsibility for researching what he or she is buying. Poorly financed or poorly managed franchise systems offer opportunities no better than those in poorly financed or poorly managed independent businesses. Thousands of franchise businesses close each year, and estimates of franchise failure rates range from 30 percent to 50 percent. The franchising concept does not eliminate the risks of a potential small-business investment; it merely adds alternatives.

Advantages of franchises include a prior performance record, a recognizable company name, a tested management program, and business training. An existing franchise has posted a performance record on which the prospective buyer can base comparisons and judgments. Earlier results can indicate the likelihood of success in a proposed venture. In addition, a widely recognized name gives the franchisee a tremendous advantage; car dealers, for instance, know that their brand-name products will attract particular segments of the market. A tested management program usually allows the prospective franchisee to avoid worrying about setting up an accounting system, establishing quality control standards, or designing employment application forms. In addition, some franchisors offer valuable business training. McDonald's, for instance, teaches the basics of operating a franchise at its Hamburger University in Oak Brook, Illinois.

On the negative side, franchise fees and future payments can be a very expensive cost category. International fast-food giant McDonald's continues to add new franchisees, both in the United States and abroad. The fast-food pioneer has made successful efforts to achieve diversity in franchise ownership. Today, one McDonald's franchise in eight is black-owned. These restaurants employ 65,000 workers and generate annual revenues of $1.1 billion.[38] Messages such as the one shown in Figure 5.10 to potential McDonald's owners demonstrate the firm's commitment to attracting additional women and minority owners.

As a general rule, however, the typical owner of a franchise with the tested management system, proven performance record, and globally recognized brand name of a McDonald's will spend between $400,000 and $600,000, depending on the location, in start-up costs. Among people able to pass this obstacle, less than one applicant in ten will be awarded a franchise.

For another potential drawback, the franchisee is judged by the actions of his or her peers. A successful franchise unit can lose customers if other units of the same franchise fail. A strong, effective program of managerial control is essential to offset any bad impressions created by unsuccessful franchises.

Finally, someone who is considering buying a franchise must think first about whether he or she has the right personality for the endeavor. Chapter 6 features an in-depth discussion of the basic characteristics that entrepreneurs should bring to their new endeavors.

SMALL BUSINESS GOES GLOBAL

Traditionally, a very small percentage of U.S. businesses were involved in importing and exporting. International businesses confronted high costs and many other challenges, including cultural, legal, and economic barriers.

Figure 5.10 **High Franchise Fees and Stringent Management Requirements: Significant Hurdles for People Who Want to Own Well-Known Franchises**

But this situation is quickly changing as global involvement in contemporary business is fast becoming synonymous with electronic commerce and the Internet. A small business can enter new markets today as easily as getting a Web address and setting up a home page.

A recent survey of more than 700 U.S. small businesses revealed that they tend to target markets that conduct business in English; also, they prefer one-on-one relationships and work under favorable trade agreements. Canada is the most favored nation to receive goods and services from U.S. small-business exporters.[39]

Role of the Internet in International Expansion

Some small businesses generate much of their annual revenue from overseas sales. Suzanne Southard, for example, started Texas Trading to export clothes, accessories, sports equipment, and snack food to Swedish consumers. Last year, she shipped more than $30,000 worth of goods to Sweden from her home-based office in Dallas.

Kris Olson's ski clothing firm, Beater Wear, uses its Web site as a promotional tool for extending the selling season from 5 months to year-round. Via the Internet, Olson can expose his small business to consumers in the Southern Hemisphere, where the seasons are reversed from those in the Northern Hemisphere. The Beater Wear Web site now receives 2,700 visits a day and has dramatically increased its position in its industry. Ski magazines now promote Beater Wear in exchange for commissions on resulting product sales.[40]

www. www.beater.com

Even if they don't maintain Web sites, the Internet can be an important information resource for companies hoping to sell their goods and services in other countries.

By surfing the WWW, small-business owners can find leads on potential customers, gather information about overseas markets, and pinpoint government restrictions. Table 5.3 lists some of the many trade and exporting resources available on the Internet.

Licensing as a Growth Strategy

As the previous chapter discussed, licensing is a relatively simple way to enter a foreign market. Under a *licensing agreement,* one firm allows another to use its intellectual property in exchange for compensation in the form of royalties. Examples of intellectual property include trademarks, patents, copyrights, and technical know-how. For instance, a firm that has developed a new type of packaging might license the process to foreign companies.

Licensing can be a very lucrative opportunity for a small business that targets collector products. Nearly 14 million American households are collector households, and half of those include children. Top collector items for young girls are dolls and stuffed animals, while boys prefer sports cards and miniature cars. Kristin Edstrom, licensing manager for Ty Inc., marketer of the popular Beanie Babies, has taken licensing to the limit. Ty is developing a licensed fan club program and newsletter and discussing publishing, TV, and film deals with potential licensees.[41]

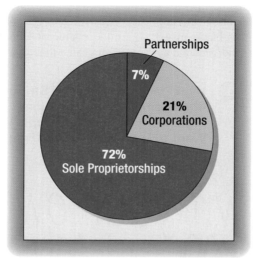

Figure 5.11 **Forms of Business Ownership**

Exporting through Intermediaries

Sometimes a small firm can achieve exporting success by teaming up with another firm that can provide services it cannot afford on its own. An *export management company* is a domestic firm that specializes in performing international marketing services as a commissioned representative or distributor for other companies. Another option for a small firm is to purchase needed goods and sell its products internationally through an *export trading company,* a general trading firm that plays varied roles in world commerce, in turn importing, exporting, countertrading, investing, and manufacturing.

ALTERNATIVES FOR ORGANIZING A BUSINESS

Every business fits one of three categories of legal ownership: sole proprietorships, partnerships, and corporations. As Figure 5.11 shows, sole proprietorships are the most common form of business ownership. However, the simple *number* of firms organized according to each model may overstate the importance of sole proprietorships and understate the role of corporations in generating revenues, producing and marketing goods and services, creating jobs, and paying taxes. After all, General Motors is only one of the corporations represented in Figure 5.11,

---

Table 5.3	Small-Business Online Exporting Resources

U.S. Department of Commerce International Trade Administration
This agency offers answers to the most frequently asked questions about international trade and provides information about markets around the world.

www.ita.doc.gov.

Export-Import Bank of the United States
The Eximbank offers information about obtaining working capital, direct loans, and export insurance.

www.exim.gov.

U.S. Small Business Administration
The SBA offers information on funding sources for exporting firms.

www.sba.gov.

Bureau of Export Administration
This agency provides data about the licenses required to export technology products.

Table 5.4 Comparing the Three Major Forms of Private Ownership

Form of Ownership	Number of Owners	Liability	Advantages	Disadvantages
Sole proprietorship	One owner	Unlimited personal liability for business debts	1. Owner retains all profits 2. Easy to form and dissolve 3. Owner has flexibility	1. Unlimited financial liability 2. Financing limitations 3. Management deficiencies 4. Lack of continuity
Partnership	Two or more owners	Personal assets of any operating partner at risk from business creditors	1. Easy to form 2. Can benefit from complementary management skills 3. Expanded financial capacity	1. Unlimited financial liability 2. Interpersonal conflicts 3. Lack of continuity 4. Difficult to dissolve
Corporation	Unlimited number of shareholders; up to 75 shareholders for S corporations	Limited	1. Limited financial liability 2. Specialized management skills 3. Expanded financial capacity 4. Economies of large-scale operations	1. Difficult and costly to form and dissolve 2. Tax disadvantages 3. Legal restrictions

but its impact on the nation's economy exceeds the collective effect of thousands of small businesses organized as proprietorships.

Each form offers unique advantages and disadvantages, as outlined in Table 5.4. As actor Burt Reynolds discovered a few years ago, these characteristics must be considered very carefully before launching any new business. Reynolds did not organize a restaurant venture as a corporation, leaving him personally liable for $28 million committed for leases and equipment. This section will also briefly examine S corporations, limited-liability partnerships, and limited-liability companies—three specialized organizational forms designed to overcome certain limitations of the traditional ownership structures.[42]

Sole Proprietorships

The most common form of business ownership, the **sole proprietorship** is also the oldest and the simplest, because no legal distinction separates the sole proprietor's status as an individual from his or her status as a business owner. Although sole proprietorships are common in a variety of industries, they are concentrated primarily among small businesses such as repair shops, small retail outlets, and service organizations, like painters, plumbers, and lawn-care specialists.

Sole proprietorships offer advantages that other business entities cannot. For one, they are easy to form and dissolve. (Partnerships are also easy to form, but difficult to dissolve.) A sole proprietorship gives the owner management flexibility and the right to retain all profits, except what goes to the government for personal income taxes. Retention of all profits and responsibility for all losses give sole proprietors the incentive to maximize efficiency in their operations.

Minimal legal requirements simplify entering and exiting a sole proprietorship. Usually the owner must meet only a few legal requirements for starting one, including registering the business or trade name at the county courthouse (to guarantee that two firms do not use the same name) and taking out any necessary licenses. (Local governments require certain kinds of licenses of restaurants, motels, retail stores, and many repair shops.) Some occupational licenses require firms to carry specific types of insurance, such as liability coverage.

Business Directory

sole proprietorship form of business ownership in which the company is owned and operated by a single person.

The ease of dissolving a business set up as a sole proprietorship is an attractive feature for certain types of enterprises. This is a particularly important benefit for temporary businesses set up to handle just a few transactions. For example, someone could create a business to organize a single concert at a local arena.

Ownership flexibility is another advantage of a sole proprietorship. The owner can make management decisions without consulting others, take prompt action when needed, and keep trade secrets where appropriate. You've probably heard people say, "I like being my own boss." This flexibility leads many business owners to prefer the sole proprietorship organization form.

A disadvantage of the sole proprietorship form comes from the owner's financial liability for all debts of the business. Also, the business must operate with financial resources limited to the owner's personal funds and money that he or she can borrow. Such financing limitations can keep the business from expanding. For another disadvantage, the owner must handle a wide range of management and operational tasks; as the firm grows, the owner may not perform all duties with equal effectiveness. Finally, a sole proprietorship lacks long-term continuity, since death, bankruptcy, retirement, or a change in personal interests can terminate it.

Partnerships

Another option for organizing a business is forming a partnership. The Uniform Partnership Act, which regulates this ownership form in most states, defines a **partnership** as an association of two or more persons who operate a business as co-owners by voluntary legal agreement. The partnership has been a traditional form of ownership for professionals offering services, such as physicians, lawyers, and dentists.

Partnerships are easy to form; as with sole proprietorships, the legal requirements involve registering the business

| Figure 5.12 | **Using Life Insurance on Partners to Achieve Business Continuity** |

name and taking out the necessary licenses. Partnerships also offer expanded financial capabilities when each partner invests money. They also usually increase access to borrowed funds as compared to sole proprietorships.

Another advantage is the opportunity for professionals to combine complementary skills and knowledge. Larry Meltzer and Robert Martin, for example, are co-owners of Meltzer & Martin Public Relations in Dallas. "Larry is more creative and I'm more strategic," explains Martin. So Martin focuses on management issues like accounting and human resource management, while Meltzer spends most of his time working with clients to develop effective public relations campaigns. Sharing responsibilities in this way helps them to play off each other's strengths to boost the success of their business.[43]

Like sole proprietorships, most partnerships have the disadvantage of unlimited financial liability. Each partner bears full responsibility for the debts of the firm, and each is legally liable for the actions of the other partners. Partners must pay the partnership's debts from their personal funds if its debts exceed its assets. Breaking up a partnership is also a much harder undertaking than dissolving a sole proprietorship. Rather than simply withdrawing funds from the bank, the partner who wants out must find someone to buy his or her interest in the firm.

In many states, partners can minimize some of these risks by organizing as a *limited liability partnership*. In many respects, such a partnership resembles a general partnership, but laws limit the liability of the partners to the value of their investments in the company.

The death of a partner also threatens the survival of a partnership. A new partnership must be formed, and the estate of the deceased is entitled to a share of the firm's value. To ease the financial strains of such events, business planners recommend life insurance coverage for each partner combined with a buy-sell agreement. As Figure 5.12 points out, the insurance proceeds can repay the deceased partner's heirs and allow the surviving partner to retain control of the business.

Partnerships are also vulnerable to personal conflicts.

Personal disagreements may quickly escalate into business battles. Good communication is the key to resolving conflicts before they damage a partnership's chances for success or even destroy it. Tim Wagner and his partner learned this lesson when they joined forces to buy Webster's, a Milwaukee bookstore-cafe combination. Although the two had been close friends for years, the pressures of running a business together led to unexpected conflicts. "He felt if he was working, I should be working," recalls Wagner. "But what he failed to realize is that I'd work through the night doing the books after he left for the day." Eventually, the two started avoiding each other, the business failed, and for several years, the partners were unable to resume their friendship.[44]

Corporations

A **corporation** is a legal organization with assets and liabilities separate from those of its owner(s). (Regular corporations are sometimes referred to as *C corporations* to distinguish them from other types.) Although even the smallest business can choose the corporate form of organization, most people think of large companies when they hear the term *corporation*. In truth, many corporations are extremely large businesses. Some of the products made by General Motors, the nation's largest corporation, are shown in Figure 5.13.

GM is joined on the list of the nation's largest firms by its U.S.-based auto rival Ford Motor Co. In addition, the list contains two oil companies (Exxon and Mobil), retail giant Wal-Mart, General Electric, IBM, AT&T, and tobacco and food-products producer Philip Morris. Each of the ten companies produces annual revenues over $50 billion. GM generates sales of $1 billion *every two days!*[45]

The corporate ownership form offers considerable ad-

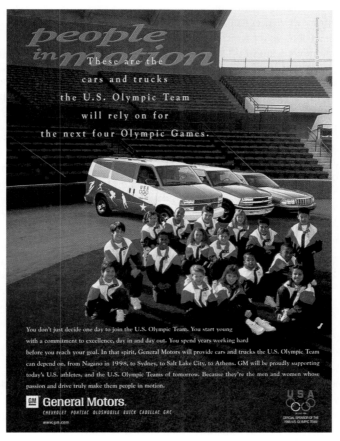

Figure 5.13 **General Motors: America's Largest Corporation**

vantages. First, because a corporation acquires the status of a separate legal entity, the stockholders take only limited financial risk; if the firm fails, they lose only the amounts they have invested. The limited risk of corporate ownership is clearly reflected in corporate names throughout the world. While many U.S. and Canadian corporations include the *Inc.* designation in their names, British firms favor the *Ltd.* abbreviation to publicize their *limited* liability. In Australia, the abbreviation for *Proprietary Limited—Pty. Ltd.*—is frequently included in corporate names.

Corporations offer other advantages. They can draw on the specialized skills of many employees, unlike sole proprietorships and partnerships, for which managerial skills are usually confined to the abilities of the owners. They gain expanded financial capabilities from opportunities to offer direct outside investments such as stock sales.

The large-scale operation permitted by corporate ownership also brings several advantages. Employees can specialize in their most effective tasks. A large firm can generate internal financing for many projects by transferring money from one part of the corporation to another. Long manufacturing runs usually promote efficient production and allow the firm to charge low prices that attract customers.

One disadvantage for a corporation is the potential for double taxation of corporate earnings. After a corporation pays federal, state, and local income taxes on its profits, its owners (stockholders) also pay personal taxes on any distributions of those profits they receive from the corporation in the form of stock dividends. Figure 5.14 shows how this process works.

Corporate ownership also involves some legal issues that sole proprietorships and partnerships do not encounter. The number of laws and regulations that affect corporations has increased dramatically in recent years.

A number of firms have implemented modified forms of the traditional corporate and partnership structures to avoid double taxation of business income while achieving (or retaining) limited financial liability for their owners. Businesses that meet certain size requirements (including ownership by no more than 75 shareholders) may decide to organize as *S corporations* (or *subchapter S corporations*). These firms can elect to pay federal income taxes as partnerships while retaining the liability limitations typical of corporations.

Laws in 47 states allow business owners to form **limited liability companies (LLCs)** to secure the corporate advantage of limited liability while avoiding the double taxation characteristic of corporations. An LLC is governed by an operating agreement that resembles a partnership agreement, except that it reduces each partner's liability for the actions of the other owners.

Changing Legal Structures to Meet Changing Needs

Someone planning to launch a new business must consider dozens of factors before deciding on an appropriate legal form. These include:

▼ Personal financial situations and the need for additional funds for the business start-up and continued operation

▼ Management skills and limitations

▼ Management styles and capabilities for working with partners and other members of top management

▼ Concerns about personal liability exposure

Although the legal form of organization is a major decision facing new business owners, they need not treat it as a permanent decision. Over time, changing conditions such as business growth may prompt the owner of a sole proprietorship or group of partners to switch to a more appropriate form. That's what Deborah Williams did.

Williams launched Black Cat Computer Wholesale as a sole proprietorship, but when the firm started to grow by leaps and bounds, she recognized the need for a change. "The main thing I was worried about was limiting my personal liability," she says, so she switched to an S corporation. It wasn't long, however, before Black Cat's growth caused other concerns. Williams needed financing to fund the firm's rapid expansion. After weighing the advantages and disadvantages, she decided to change once again to a C corporation. "My real goal was to create a broader base of financing for the company."[46]

Figure 5.14 **Double Taxation: A Disadvantage of the Corporate Form of Organization**

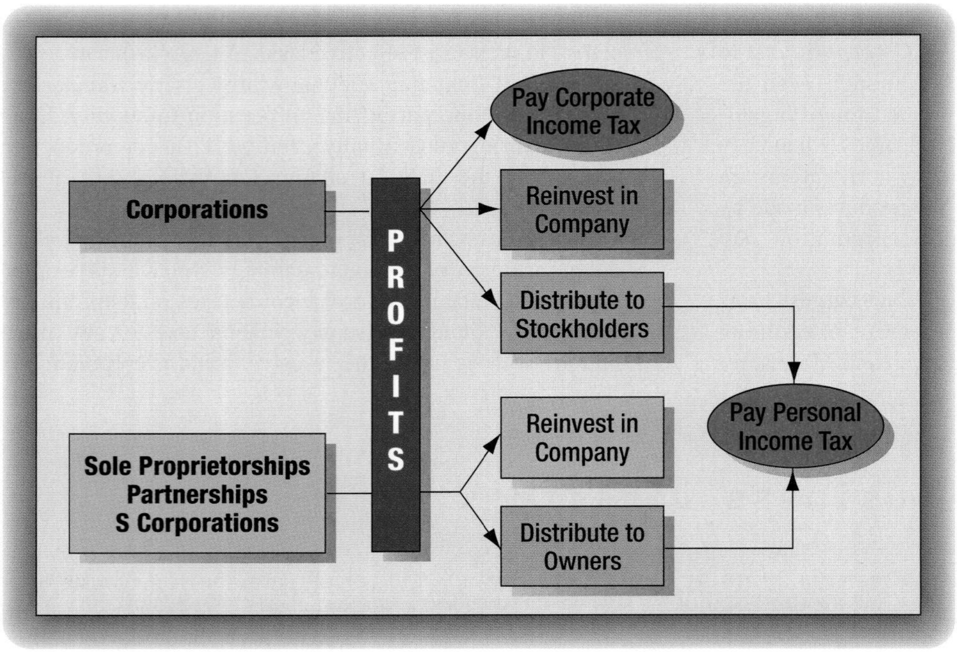

ORGANIZING AND OPERATING A CORPORATION

One of the first decisions in forming a corporation is determining where to locate its headquarters and where it will do business. This section describes the various types of corporations and considers the options and procedures involved in incorporating a business.

Types of Corporations

Corporations fall into three categories: domestic, foreign, or alien corporations. A firm is considered a **domestic corporation** in the state where it is incorporated. When a firm does business in states other than the one where it has filed incorporation papers, it is registered as a **foreign corporation** in each of those states. A firm incorporated in one nation that operates in another is known as an **alien corporation** where it operates. Some firms operate under all three forms of incorporation.

Johnson Products Inc., a maker of personal-care products for African-Americans, operates as a domestic, foreign, and alien corporation. The company is incorporated in Delaware, where it is a domestic corporation, but its headquarters are in Chicago, where it operates a large plant as a foreign corporation. The firm also operates overseas as an alien corporation, with sales and distribution centers in Great Britain and other European countries.

A fourth category of corporations was discussed in the previous chapter. *Multinational corporations* are firms with significant operations and marketing activities outside their home countries. Examples include General Electric, Siemens, and Mitsubishi in heavy electrical equipment and Timex, Seiko, and Citizen in watches.

The Incorporation Process

Suppose that you decide to start a business, and you believe that the corporate form offers the best way to organize it. Where should you set up shop? How do you establish a corporate charter? The following paragraphs discuss the procedures for creating a new corporation.

Where to Incorporate Location is one of the most important considerations for any small-business owner. While most small and medium-sized businesses are incorporated in the states where they do most of their business, a U.S. firm can actually incorporate in any state it chooses. The founders of large corporations, or of those that will do business nationwide, often compare the benefits provided in various states' laws to corporations in various industries. The favorable legal climate in Delaware has prompted a large number of major corporations to incorporate there.

| Figure 5.15 | **States Considered Best—and Worst—for Incorporating a Manufacturing Firm** |

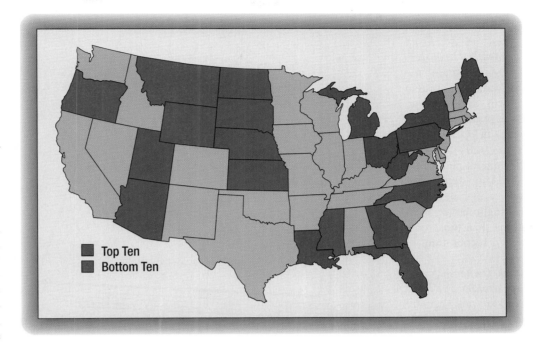

Figure 5.15 shows the ten states considered to be the best choices for incorporating a manufacturing firm as well as the ten states at the bottom of the list.

The Corporate Charter Each state mandates a specific procedure for incorporating a business. Most states require at least three *incorporators*—the individuals who create the corporation—which opens incorporation possibilities to small businesses. Another requirement demands that a new corporation adopt a name dissimilar from those of other businesses; most states require that the name must end with the words *Company, Corporation, Incorporated,* or *Limited* to show that the owners have limited liability. Figure 5.16 lists ten elements of the articles of incorporation that are requirements in most states for chartering a corporation.

The information provided in the articles of incorporation form the basis on which a state grants a **corporate charter,** a legal document that formally establishes a corporation. After securing the charter, the owners articulate the company's bylaws, which describe the rules and procedures for its operation.

Corporate Management

Figure 5.17 illustrates the levels of management in a corporation. **Stockholders** are owners; they acquire shares of stock in the corporation and, therefore, become part owners of it. Some companies, such as family businesses, are owned by relatively few stockholders, and the stock is generally unavailable to outsiders. In such a firm, known as a *closed corporation* or *closely held corporation,* the stockholders also control and manage all activities. In contrast, an *open corporation* sells stock to the general public, establishing diversified ownership, and often leading to larger operations than those of a closed corporation.

Stock Ownership and Stockholder Rights Corporations usually hold annual stockholders' meetings during which managers report on corporate activities and stockholders vote on any decisions that require their approval, including elections of officers.

Shares are usually classified as common or preferred stock. Although owners of *preferred stock* have limited voting rights, they are entitled to receive dividends before common-stock holders and, in the event of a corporate dissolution

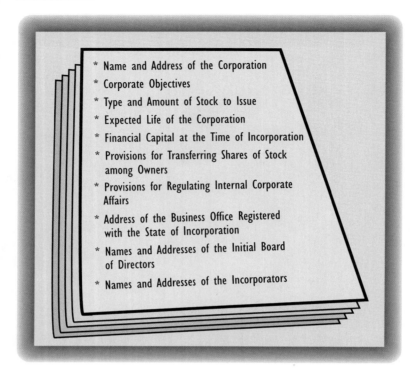

Figure 5.16 **Articles of Incorporation**

* Name and Address of the Corporation
* Corporate Objectives
* Type and Amount of Stock to Issue
* Expected Life of the Corporation
* Financial Capital at the Time of Incorporation
* Provisions for Transferring Shares of Stock among Owners
* Provisions for Regulating Internal Corporate Affairs
* Address of the Business Office Registered with the State of Incorporation
* Names and Addresses of the Initial Board of Directors
* Names and Addresses of the Incorporators

would have first claims on assets once debtors are repaid. Owners of *common stock* have voting rights but only residual claims on the firm's assets; that is, they are last to receive any income distributions (dividends). Since one share is worth only one vote, small stockholders generally have little influence on corporate management actions. The various types of common and preferred stock are described in detail in Chapter 21.

Board of Directors Stockholders elect a **board of directors**—the governing body of a corporation. The board sets overall policy, authorizes major transactions involving the corporation, and hires the chief executive officer (CEO). Most boards include both inside directors (corporate executives) and outside directors, people who are not employed by the organization. Sometimes, the corporation's top executive also chairs the board. Generally, outside directors are also stockholders.

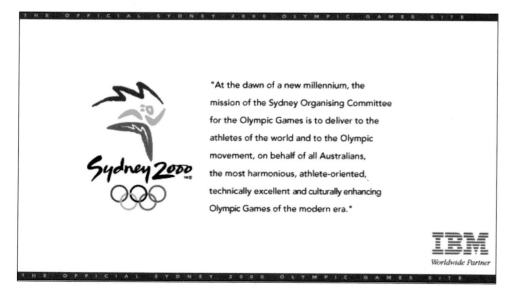

"At the dawn of a new millennium, the mission of the Sydney Organising Committee for the Olympic Games is to deliver to the athletes of the world and to the Olympic movement, on behalf of all Australians, the most harmonious, athlete-oriented, technically excellent and culturally enhancing Olympic Games of the modern era."

For the second time in the past 50 years, the Summer Olympics return to the Land Down Under. In 1956, Melbourne hosted the games; now the torch has passed to Australia's largest city.

Corporate Officers The CEO and other members of top management, such as the chief operating officer (COO), chief information officer (CIO), and chief financial officer (CFO), make most major corporate decisions. Managers at the next level down the hierarchy, middle management, handle the ongoing operational functions of the company. At the bottom tier of management, supervisory personnel coordinate day-to-day operations, assign specific tasks to employees, and often evaluate workers' job performance. The activities and responsibilities of managers at various levels in the organization are described in detail in Chapter 8.

Employee-Owned Corporations

Another alternative in creating a corporation is *employee ownership,* in which workers buy shares of stock in the company that employs them. The corporate organization stays the same, but most stockholders are also employees.

Science Applications International Corp. (SAIC) has achieved dramatic success under this form of corporate organization. SAIC's 25,000 employees own 90 percent of the San Diego firm, and the other 10 percent is owned by former employees. Says one owner-manager, "When I'm making a decision, I don't just make it as a manager, I make it as an owner."[47]

Although the popularity of this form of corporation is growing, almost one-quarter of all employee-owned firms fail. Employee ownership doesn't solve every problem. The employees of United Airlines, for example, engineered a stock buyout in 1994. Since the buyout, sales and profits have risen, but United's top management continues to experience labor disagreements with employee-owners.[48] Employee-owned firms are discussed in more detail in Chapter 11.

Not-for-Profit Corporations

The same business concepts that apply to firms whose objectives include earning profits also apply to *not-for-profit corporations*—which pursue primary objectives other than returning profits to owners.

Over 1 million not-for-profits operate in the United States, employing well over 10 million people and generating an estimated $300 billion in revenues each year. Most states' laws set out separate provisions dealing with the organization structures and operations of not-for-profit corporations. These organizations do not issue

Figure 5.17 **Levels of Management in a Corporation**

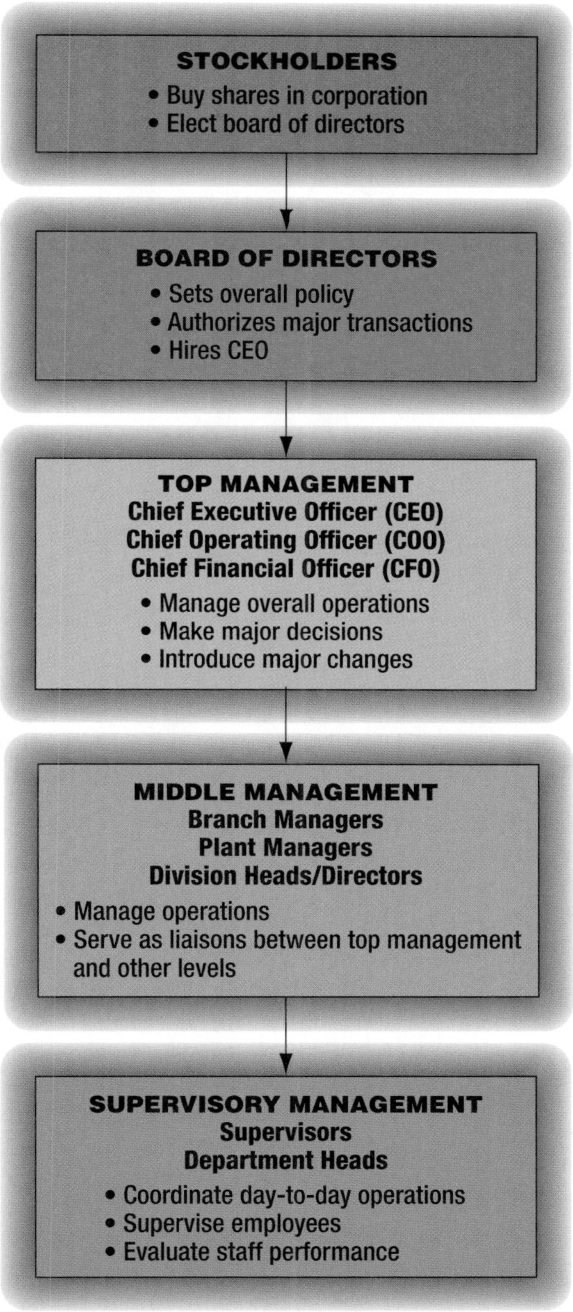

stock certificates, since they pay no dividends to owners, and ownership rarely changes. They are also exempt from paying income taxes. This sector includes museums, libraries, religious and human-service organizations, private secondary schools, health-care facilities, symphony orchestras, zoos, and thousands of other groups such as government agencies, political parties, and labor unions.

Perhaps the best known international not-for-profit runs the Olympic games. Several industry-leading international companies, including Kodak, IBM, Coca-Cola, McDonald's, Xerox, Visa, and UPS, donate expertise, technology, resources, and revenue. The average price for a multinational Olympic sponsorship is $50 million in cash, equipment, and services. Between 1997 and 2000, more than $3.5 billion will be generated through sales of broadcast rights fees, sponsorships, and other marketing programs. The International Olympic Committee redistributes these funds to support athletic training and competition. Around $300 million goes to National Olympic Committees for administrative expenses, sports development, and travel to the games. More than $130 million goes to the seven Winter Sports Federations and 28 Summer Federations to promote their sports. The Olympic cities also help to support the games. The 2000 Sydney Summer Olympics and the 2002 Winter Olympics in Salt Lake City, Utah, will donate more than $23 million worth of accommodations to Olympic athletes and officials.[49]

WHEN BUSINESSES JOIN FORCES

Today's corporate world features many complex unions of companies, not always in the same industry or even in the

| Figure 5.18 | **Billions of Dollars in U.S. Mergers and Acquisitions** |

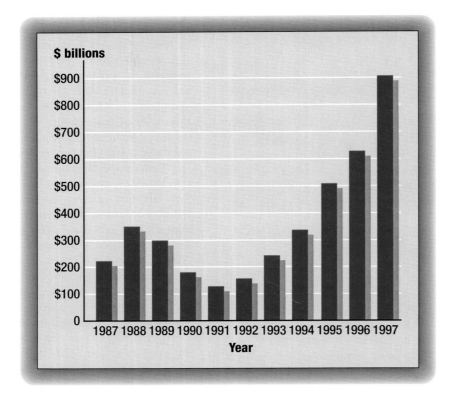

same country. Many well-known firms have changed owners, become parts of other corporations, or split into smaller units. Current trends in corporate ownership include mergers and acquisitions and joint ventures.

Mergers and Acquisitions

Merger mania hit U.S. corporations in the 1980s, and it continues today, setting new records for the number of mergers and acquisitions. The 11,000 mergers during the past year involved companies considered household names with price tags in the billions. Consider just a few:

▼ Mobil and Exxon; $74 billion

▼ Citicorp and Travelers Insurance: $73 billion

▼ Ameritech and SBC Communications: $72 billion

▼ GTE and Bell Atlantic: $71 billion

Says one industry analyst, "Business is almost scary in its intensity."[50] Figure 5.18 shows the recent, dramatic rise in mergers and acquisitions.

The terms *merger* and *acquisition* are often used interchangeably, but their meanings differ. In a **merger,** two or more firms combine to form one company; in an **acquisition,** one firm purchases the property and assumes the obligations of another. Acquisitions also occur when one firm buys a division or subsidiary from another firm. Many mergers and acquisitions cross national borders, as managers attempt to enter new markets and improve global competitiveness for their companies.

Mergers can be classified as vertical, horizontal, or conglomerate mergers. A **vertical merger** combines firms operating at different levels in the production and marketing process. A vertical merger pursues one of two primary goals: (a) to assure adequate flows of raw materials and supplies needed for a firm's products, or (b) to increase distribution. Software giant Microsoft Corp. is well-known for merging with small firms that have developed products with strong market potential. Large petroleum companies often try to reduce the uncertainty of their future petroleum supplies by acquiring successful oil and gas exploration firms. To enhance distribution opportunities, Disney's merger with the ABC television network provided Disney with an additional outlet for its film and television productions.

A **horizontal merger** joins firms in the same industry that wish to diversify, increase their customer bases, cut costs, or offer expanded product lines. When Chemical Bank and Chase Manhattan merged in 1996, the two companies had a total of 75,000 employees and 600 branches. By eliminating overlapping branches and divisions, the new company plans to operate with just 500 branches and reduce its workforce by 12,000 employees.[51]

Business Directory

merger combination of two or more firms to form one company.

acquisition procedure in which one firm acquires the property and assumes the obligations of another.

A **conglomerate merger** combines unrelated firms. The most common reasons for a conglomerate merger are to diversify, to spur sales growth, or to spend a cash surplus that might otherwise make a firm a tempting target for a takeover effort. Conglomerate mergers may join firms in totally unrelated industries. Consider Metromedia International Group Inc., a venture that combines movie-maker Orion Pictures, several eastern European telecommunications companies, and Actava Group, the maker of Snapper lawn mowers. Even apparently related companies may not fit well together after a merger or acquisition, however. Solving an Ethical Controversy discusses the pros and cons of the recent increased merger activity.

Joint Ventures—Specialized Partnerships

A **joint venture** is a partnership between companies formed for a specific undertaking. Sometimes, a company enters into a joint venture with a local firm or government, sharing the operation's costs, risks, management, and profits with its local partner. As discussed in the previous chapter, joint ventures offer particularly attractive ways for small firms to conduct international business, since they bring substantial benefits from partners already operating inside the host countries.

PUBLIC AND COLLECTIVE OWNERSHIP

While most business organizations are owned privately by individuals or groups of people, municipal, state, or national governments own some firms. Also, groups of people collectively own some companies. Public ownership is common in many industries, both in the United States and abroad.

Public Ownership

One alternative to private ownership is some form of **public ownership,** in which a unit or agency of government owns and operates an organization. In the United States, local governments often own parking structures and water systems. The Pennsylvania Turnpike Authority operates a vital highway link across the Keystone state. The federal government operates Hoover Dam in Nevada to provide electricity over a large region.

Government-Owned Corporations

Sometimes, public ownership results when private investors are unwilling to invest, fearing a high probability

failure. This situation occurred with the rural electrification program of the 1930s, which significantly expanded utility lines in sparsely populated areas. At other times, public ownership has replaced private ownership of failed organizations. Certain functions, such as municipal water systems, are considered so important to the public welfare that governments implement public ownership to protect citizens from problems. Finally, some nations have used public business ownership to foster competition by operating public companies as competitive business enterprises. In Bogota, Colombia, the government runs a TV and radio network, Instituto Nacional de Radio & Television, that broadcasts both educational and commercial programs. Public ownership remains common abroad, despite a general trend toward privatization.

Customer-Owned Businesses: Cooperatives

Another alternative to traditional, private business ownership is collective ownership of a production, storage, transportation, and/or marketing organization. Such collective ownership establishes an organization referred to as a **cooperative** (or co-op) whose owners join forces to collectively operate all or part of the functions in their industry.

Cooperatives allow small businesses to obtain quantity purchase discounts, reducing costs and enabling the co-op to pass on the savings to its members. Marketing and advertising expenses are shared among members, and the co-op's facilities can also serve as a distribution center.

Cooperatives are frequently found in small farming communities, but they also serve the needs of large growers of specific crops. For instance, Blue Diamond Growers is a cooperative that represents California almond growers. Retailers have also established co-ops. Ace Hardware is a cooperative of independent hardware store owners. Financial co-ops, such as credit unions, offer members higher interest rates on deposits and lower interest rates on loans than other institutions could provide.

WHAT'S AHEAD

The next chapter shifts the book's focus to the driving forces behind new-business formation: entrepreneurs. It examines the differences between a small-business owner and an entrepreneur and identifies certain personality traits typical of entrepreneurs. The chapter also details the process of launching a new venture, including identifying opportunities, locating needed financing, and turning good ideas into successful businesses. Finally, the chapter explores a method for infusing the entrepreneurial spirit into established businesses—intrapreneurship.

SOLVING AN ETHICAL CONTROVERSY

Are Big Oil Companies Merging into Dangerous Giants?

Every student of U.S. history is familiar with the great monopolies of the late 1800s. John D. Rockefeller and J. Paul Getty are remembered as the oil barons who became two of the most powerful men in America. With the Sherman Antitrust Act, however, monopolies were broken up and competition was restored. Yet, over the past century, as business became more globalized, the industry again found itself in the hands of another oil-production monopoly: the Organization of Petroleum Exporting Countries (OPEC). One way U.S. oil companies staved off OPEC's stranglehold was to merge. Some experts are now questioning whether merger is merely another term for monopoly.

Facing fierce competition on one side and low prices on the other, oil companies are pumping themselves up, growing stronger and bigger. French oil giant Tatal has purchased Belgium's Petrofina for $11.6 billion, creating the world's sixth largest publicly traded oil group. British Petroleum has joined with Amoco in a $55 billion union. U.S. oil firms created the largest oil company in the world when Exxon acquired Mobil for $73.7 billion.

To understand the reason behind the increase in mergers and acquisitions requires a view of the environment surrounding the oil industry. By the turn of the century, crude oil prices had reached a 12-year low as a result of an enormous surplus. The troubled economy in Asia caused oil consumption to drop by 750,000 barrels a day, but oil companies continued producing a million barrels a day more than were being sold. Just finding places to store all the surplus has become a problem. OPEC has made several attempts to cut production, but cheating among its members kept production up and prices down. The market is so saturated that even OPEC has been unable to boost prices.

For U.S. companies, cutting produc-

tion would mean financial disaster. Instead, they are merging to cut overhead costs and squeeze out more profits. That is what Exxon and Mobil are attempting by pooling resources to cover increasingly high costs of exploration in areas such as West Africa and the Caspian Sea, both geographically remote and politically risky. In addition, the combined companies will be able to compete on the world market with other megacompanies.

But critics of the merger wonder whether such a large company will be too powerful, control the market, and thus destroy competition. After all, both Exxon and Mobil are the offspring of Rockefeller's much-feared Standard Oil monopoly (broken up by the U.S. government in 1911). Experts question whether Exxon–Mobil will again be the monopoly its parent was. Supporters claim that the world has changed since Rockefeller's time, that these companies would have trouble surviving without the merger, and that competition can only be served by such consolidation.

? *Should Oil Giants Such as Exxon and Mobil Be Allowed to Merge?*

PRO

1. Mergers are good for U.S. business since larger companies can compete better in foreign markets.

2. Oil mergers reduce the number of players in an industry where too many firms are already fighting for an ever-shrinking prize.

3. Frequently, mergers result in healthier companies that can run more efficiently and thus pass cost savings along to customers.

4. Such mergers are necessary attempts to survive the dwindling roles played by oil firms in the U.S. and global markets.

CON

1. Megamergers destroy healthy competition because fewer players

have more say in controlling production and setting prices.

2. Consumers eventually pay for such mergers with higher prices.

3. As other oil companies compete with the newly merged giants, they will have to consolidate further, leaving even fewer players.

4. Such mergers often force retail service stations to go out of business.

5. Such mergers result in job loss, mostly white-collar. Even the unions agree: "These deals are seldom good for workers."

SUMMARY

During the 1970s, when gas prices soared, the Exxon–Mobil merger would never have survived the regulatory obstacles. But the Federal Trade Commission thinks differently today. Big isn't so bad any more. Many observers believe that you can still have healthy competition with only a few companies.

Moreover, oil is an industry in decline. In Rockefeller's time, petroleum was a cutting-edge energy source and the Standard Oil monopoly controlled 84 percent of the U.S. petroleum market. Today, as the largest oil company in the world, Exxon–Mobil controls some 22 percent of U.S. gasoline sales.

Finally, globalization has changed the structure of industries. Companies can no longer succeed by looking at national markets. Oil companies no longer compete with one another; they compete with all industries, across all borders. American firms like Exxon and Mobil need the flexibility of mergers to compete overseas.

Sources: "Van Miert Says BP/Mobil Problem in Exxon Merger," Reuters Limited, February 24, 1999; Phillip J. Longman and Jack Egan, "Why Big Oil Is Getting a Lot Bigger: Exxon, Mobil, and Rockefeller's Legacy," *U.S. News & World Report*, December 14, 1998, pp. 26–28; Elliot Blair Smith, "Reinventing Monopolies?" *USA Today*, December 3, 1998, pp. 1B–2B; and Thor Valdmanis and Tom Lowry, "$74B Deal Largest Ever," *USA Today*, December 2, 1998, pp. 1B–2B.

SUMMARY OF LEARNING GOALS

1. Define *small business* and identify the industries in which most small firms are established.

A small business can adopt many profiles, from a part-time, home-based business to a company with several hundred employees. A small business is a firm that is independently owned and operated, is not dominant in its field, and meets industry-specific size standards for income or number of employees. Small businesses operate in every industry, but retailing, services, and construction feature the highest proportions of small enterprises.

2. Explain the economic and social contributions of small business.

Small businesses create most of the new jobs in the U.S. economy and employ the majority of U.S. workers. They provide valuable outlets for entrepreneurial activity and often contribute to creation of new industries or development of new business processes. Women and minorities find small-business ownership to be an attractive alternative to the sometimes limited opportunities available to them in large firms. Small firms may also offer enhanced lifestyle flexibility and opportunities to gain personal satisfaction.

3. Compare the advantages and disadvantages of small business.

Small firms can often operate with greater flexibility than larger corporations can achieve. This flexibility allows smaller businesses to provide superior customer service, develop innovative products, and fill small market niches ignored by large firms. However, small businesses also must operate with fewer resources than large corporations can apply. As a result, they may suffer from financial limitations and management inadequacies. Taxes and government regulation can also impose excessive burdens on small businesses.

4. Describe how the Small Business Administration assists small-business owners.

The U.S. Small Business Administration helps small-business owners to obtain financing through a variety of programs that guarantee repayment of their bank loans. The SBA also assists women and minority business owners in obtaining government purchasing contracts. It offers training and information resources, so business owners can improve their odds of success. Finally, the SBA advocates small-business interests within the federal government.

5. Explain how franchising can provide opportunities for both franchisors and franchisees.

A franchisor is a company that sells the rights to use its brand name, operating procedures, and other intellectual property to franchisees. Franchising helps business owners to expand their companies' operations with limited financial investments. Franchisees, the individuals who buy the right to operate a business using the franchisor's intellectual property, gain a proven business system, brand recognition, and training and other support from the franchisor.

6. Identify and explain the three basic forms of business ownership and the advantages and disadvantages of each form.

A single person owns and operates a sole proprietorship. While sole proprietorships are easy to set up and offer great operating flexibility, the owner remains personally liable for all of the firm's debts and legal settlements. In a partnership, two or more individuals agree to share responsibility for owning and running the business. Partnerships are relatively easy to set up, but they do not offer protection from liability. Additionally, partnerships often experience problems when partners fail to communicate or forge effective working relationships. When a business is set up as a corporation, it becomes a separate legal entity. Individual owners receive shares of stock in the firm. Corporations protect owners from legal and financial liability, but double taxation reduces their revenues.

7. Identify the levels of corporate management.

Stockholders, or shareholders, own a corporation. In return for their financial investments, they receive shares of stock in the company. The number of stockholders in a firm can vary widely, depending on whether the firm is privately owned or makes its stock available to the public. Shareholders elect the firm's board of directors, the individuals responsible for overall corporate management. The board has legal authority over the firm's policies. A company's officers are the top managers who oversee its operating decisions.

8. Describe recent trends in mergers and acquisitions.

After a decline in the early 1990s, U.S. corporations are now spending record amounts on mergers and acquisitions. These business combinations occur worldwide, and companies often merge with or acquire other companies to aid their operations across national boundaries. Vertical mergers help a firm to ensure access to adequate raw materials and supplies for production or to improve its distribution outlets. Horizontal mergers occur when firms in the same industry join in an attempt to diversify or offer expanded product lines. Conglomerate mergers combine unrelated firms, often as part of plans to spend cash surpluses that might otherwise make a firm a takeover target.

9. Differentiate among private ownership, public ownership, and collective ownership (cooperatives).

Managers or a group of major stockholders sometimes buy all of a firm's stock. The firm then becomes a privately owned company, and its stock is no longer publicly traded. Some firms allow workers to buy large blocks of stock, so the employees gain ownership stakes. Municipal, state, and national governments also own and operate some businesses. This public business ownership has declined, however, through a recent trend toward privatization of publicly run organizations. In a cooperative, individuals or companies band together to collectively operate all or part of an industry's functions. The cooperative's owners control its activities by electing a board of directors from their members. Cooperatives are usually set up to provide for collective ownership of a production, storage, transportation, or marketing organization that is important to an industry.

TEN BUSINESS TERMS YOU NEED TO KNOW

small business	sole proprietorship
business plan	partnership
Small Business Administration (SBA)	corporation
	merger
business incubator	acquisition
franchising	

Other Important Business Terms

home-based business	stockholder
Small Business Investment Company (SBIC)	board of directors
set-aside program	vertical merger
limited liability company (LLC)	horizontal merger
	conglomerate merger
domestic corporation	joint venture
foreign corporation	public ownership
alien corporation	cooperative
corporate charter	

REVIEW QUESTIONS

1. Explain the meaning of the term *small business.* Discuss the differences between a small business and a large business. What advantages does each offer? What challenges does each type face?
2. How does small business contribute to a nation's economy?
3. The chapter notes that a written business plan can make the difference between success and failure in a new business venture. Develop a brief outline of a business plan, including the major components described in this chapter. Refer to your outline to explain the relationship between an effective plan and business success.
4. What is a franchise? What benefits does franchising provide to a franchisor? Why is franchising attractive to franchisees? Suggest ways in which franchisors and franchisees can improve the effectiveness of franchising for both parties.
5. What is a sole proprietorship? Why is this form of business ownership the most popular one? Discuss the advantages and disadvantages of sole proprietorships.
6. What is a partnership? What advantages and disadvantages characterize this form of business ownership, and how can partners minimize the disadvantages?
7. What is the primary advantage of the corporate form of business ownership? Discuss the differences among a C corporation, an S corporation, and a partnership organized as a limited liability company.
8. How does a corporation operate? What roles do shareholders, the board of directors, top management, middle management, and supervisory management play?
9. Discuss the different types of mergers. List reasons why a firm's management might decide to merge with another company.
10. What is a cooperative? How does it differ from other business entities?

QUESTIONS FOR CRITICAL THINKING

1. You are considering buying a small Oregon partnership that manufactures high-pressure laminated particleboard used to make office cubicles. The firm enjoys an excellent reputation for high-quality products and provides superior customer service and quick turnaround on orders. The firm's two partners currently handle most marketing and sales contacts. Since they have to devote most of their time to running the company, they rely primarily on word-of-mouth recommendations to generate orders. Consequently, the company is currently running at 30 percent of its plant capacity. Production facilities are under long-term leases, and the firm's 35 employees have pledged to stay on after the sale is completed. Last year, the firm earned $522,000 in profits on $2 million in sales. The owners are asking $3.4 million for the company, including $1 million worth of finished inventory.

    What additional information would you need in order to make a purchase decision? What are some sources of financing that you could realistically tap to buy the company? What major challenges would you expect to encounter in running this firm? Suggest how you would overcome these challenges.
2. Choose a small-business owner in your area and interview him or her about the experience of owning one's own business. What advice would this person give about starting a business? What mistakes do new business owners commonly make? Share your findings with the class.
3. Although a rising number of small firms export products to other countries, more than half of small businesses still are not participating in the global marketplace. Why don't more small U.S. firms export their products? What changes would encourage them to do so, in your opinion? Is going global really an option for every small business?
4. Assume that you are involved in establishing the businesses listed here. What form of ownership would you propose for each? Explain your reasoning for each choice by discussing the advantages and disadvantages of each form of ownership.
    a. dry cleaning franchise in New Orleans
    b. Toledo Mud Hens minor league baseball team
    c. Miami-based management consulting firm
    d. Small foundry outside Pittsburgh, Pennsylvania
5. What steps are necessary to set up a corporation in your state or locality? Do these procedures differ from requirements elsewhere? If so, how?

Experiential Exercise

DIRECTIONS: Using this chapter's Business Tool Kits, answer the following questions:

1. From "The Five Best Businesses to Start from Your Dorm" on page 170, select the business idea that you believe you could successfully implement. If none of these ideas is suited to your interests or abilities, select one with which you are confident.
2. Turn to "Ten Keys to Succeeding in a Home-Based Business" on page 167 and circle the tips that are relevant to the business idea you chose in Step 1
3. Turn to the chapter section titled "Creating a Business Plan," beginning on page 172, and think through the answers to the questions included in this section. Outline the components that your business plan should include.

Nothing but Net

1. **Home-Based Businesses.** Assume you are looking for information about starting a home-based business. Find a Web site, such as the one listed, which provides information about home-based business opportunities. Select a home-based business opportunity suited to your interests, skills, and aptitudes that you believe would be a good money-making opportunity. In addition, identify the business tools available at the Web site that could help you get started and prepare a three- to five-minute oral report to be given either in a small-group discussion or to the entire class.

   www.getbuzy.com/

2. **Minority- and Women-Owned Businesses.** The U.S. Small Business Administration provides information and support services for minority- and women-owned businesses. Visit the two Web sites listed and find out what is available through these offices. Compare each mission statement and summarize in one sentence the common purpose between these two agencies of the federal government.
   Office of Women's Business Ownership:

   www.sba.gov/womeninbusiness/

   Office of Minority Enterprise Development:

   www.sba.gov/MED/

3. **Incorporating.** Use a search engine to find information about incorporating in your home state or any other state that interests you. Sites such as the one listed provide information and fee-based services for incorporating your business online. Answer at least one of the following questions:
   (a) What are three uses of a corporation's employer tax ID number?
   (b) What is the filing fee for incorporating in the state you chose?
   (c) Which states have the highest filing fees?
   (d) Which states have the lowest filing fees?

   incorporate-usa.com/index.html

Note: Internet Web addresses change frequently. If you do not find the exact sites listed, you may need to access the organization's or company's home page and search from there.

LOST ARTS—
FINDING SUCCESS THROUGH RESTORATION

Five years ago, while working on furnishing a multimillion dollar house, Gary, deLarios needed a place to do the work and manage the creative art of many artisans. Lost Arts was created. The founder and owner, Gary deLarios says, "the idea behind Lost Arts was to have control over large-scale projects and have many craftsmen under one roof learning from each other. There are few people in the world who do this type of work. We actually have to get the books, do the research, and get out and try to understand and work the medium and the material." The craftsmen at Lost Arts combine today's technology with ancient techniques to speed the creative process of creating "functional art."

Today, Lost Arts operates in the Dallas/Fort Worth area, specializing in design, fabrication, and installation of custom architectural and decorative accessories. The company was founded by Gary deLarios as a sole proprietorship working for one primary client for whom quality, not cost, was the main concern. Moving from one client to several now, "the company must be commercially viable and find a balance between cost and quality in this functional art business," says deLarios.

Other products and services provided by Lost Arts include design consultation and drafting; hand-forged custom architectural hardware; custom interior and exterior light fixture fabrication; glasswork; custom wood-working, including expert wood carving; decorative ironwork; railings; balustrade and metal casting. Lost Arts works on a number of one-of-a-kind projects such as the Historical City Park in Dallas, Texas where craftsmen recreated the entire city, providing a hands-on exhibit of the parks.

For Gary and his brother Patrick, control over projects and having a reputation for providing quality products are important factors in running their small business. With only 10 expert employees, motivation becomes a constant battle. Says deLarios, "two foremost challenges in this business are: organization, that is, having 50 to 70 projects going at one time and having the manpower and materials to make each an artistic creation and, two, cost effectiveness in production, that is, balancing the cost and the quality and keeping the employees happy."

Gary deLarios has a hands-on management philosophy and believes that one must have patience and persistence to succeed. Above all, people must love what they do for a living. "Do work that you believe in, not purely for money," says Gary, "You have to love it to excel." The company has relied on word-of-mouth and has never advertised, yet has more business than it can handle. With gross sales under a million and climbing, and an expanding client base, Lost Arts is looking to modify its form of ownership.

Questions

1. What are the advantages and disadvantages of Lost Arts' current form of ownership?

2. As the company grows, which ownership form would you recommend? Why?

3. What are the advantages and challenges for Gary deLarios in his small business?

chapter 6

Starting Your Own Business: The Entre- preneurship Alternative

Amazon.com: Building the Best Buying Experience on the Web

"We're trying to build the most customer-centric company in the world," says Jeff Bezos, founder and CEO of Amazon.com. Back in 1994, Bezos was working on Wall Street and discovered that Web usage was growing 2300 percent a year. He knew the Internet would soon be everywhere, and he wanted to be part of it. Since then he has been passionately building the kind of company he envisioned—not by *aspiring* to be a corporate model but by *creating* that model. Indeed, the Amazon.com corporate philosophy is simple: "If it's good for our customers, it's worth doing." Bezos wants people to come to Amazon.com, find what they want, discover things they didn't know they wanted, and leave feeling they have a favorite place to shop. In short, Bezos wants Amazon.com to be the best buying experience on the Web.

He started by selling books because he determined that they are the number-one product to sell on the Internet. In 1995 Amazon.com sold books out of a garage to a handful of customers. Today, the company offers millions of books and other items: music CDs, videos, and gifts—not to mention secure credit card payment, personalized recommendations, and streamlined ordering. Even though the company has yet to turn a profit, Amazon.com has become one of the "blue-chip" Internet stocks.

But as successful as his company has become, Bezos is not standing still. "Our customers are loyal right up to the moment someone offers them better service," says Bezos. So he continues to build and expand the company. "What we're trying to do is invent the future of e-commerce," says Bezos, revealing his goal to build not just a better bookstore but a global online retailing operation. And before you can say "innovation," he's on his way.

Amazon.com has already expanded in myriad directions: It operates Planet All (www.planetall.com), a Web-based address book, calendar, and reminder service. And it operates the

Internet Movie Database (www.imdb.com), a comprehensive source of information on more than 150,000 movies and entertainment programs and 500,000 cast and crew members dating from 1892 to the present. In addition, the company has accepted into its "Associates" program Sun Entertainment Holding Corporation (www.sunrecords.com). Based in Nashville, Sun has the exclusive worldwide rights to some 7,000 master recordings by artists including Johnny Cash, Jerry Lee Lewis, and Elvis Presley. Sun's customers are able to purchase music and merchandise from Sun's own extensive library or access

WWW.

www.amazon.com/exec/obidos/subst/home/home.html

Amazon's vast selection. In addition, Sun earns a commission on Amazon.com purchases from anyone who goes there from Sun's Web site.

Nor has the company neglected the *global* part of Bezos's goal. Amazon.com has launched operations in both England and Germany, going head-to-head with rival Barnes & Noble and its partner, German media giant Bertelsmann AG. The Amazon.uk site is based in Slough, England, and carries a catalog of 1.2 million U.K. titles. The Amazon.com.de site is based in Regensburg, Germany, and features 335,000 German titles.

Closer to home, the company invested $5 million to buy a 7 percent stake in Geoworks, which delivers Internet-based content over wireless devices. In the deal, Amazon.com acquired the services and know-how of the 19 software engineers based in Geoworks' Seattle office. The company also has a 46 percent stake in Drugstore.com, which offers a lineup of prescription and nonprescription drugs, cosmetics, and personal-care products. Drugstore.com is promoted on the Amazon.com site.

The company has become an entrepreneurial model for Net wannabes. Just some of the startups copying Amazon.com include Netgrocer.com (groceries), Cooking.com (cookware and specialty foods), Sportscape.com (sporting goods), and FreshFlowerSource (fresh flowers). Of course, that doesn't count out the giant book retailers establishing their own cyber-shopping sites. Bezos is the consummate entrepreneur, working hard to lengthen his lead. Without question, Amazon.com is the benchmark for buying on the Web.[1]

CHAPTER OVERVIEW

Like millions of people, you'd probably love to start and run your own company. Perhaps you've spent time trying to come up with an idea for a business you could launch. If you've been bitten by the entrepreneurial bug, you're not alone. More than ever, people like Amazon.com's Jeff Bezos are choosing the path of entrepreneurship for their careers.

How do you become an entrepreneur? Experts advise that aspiring entrepreneurs should learn as much as possible about the pleasures and pitfalls of entrepreneurship before striking out on their own. By reading newspaper and magazine articles and biographies of successful entrepreneurs, you'll learn how they handled the challenges of starting up their businesses. Advice you need to launch and grow a new venture abounds. Some resources are listed in the Business Toolkit box.

Resources for Aspiring Entrepreneurs

Effective entrepreneurs know where to get information and advice. "If I had to name the single characteristic shared by all the truly successful people I have met over a lifetime, I would say it is the ability to create and nurture a network of contacts," says Harvey Mackay, best-selling author and founder of Mackay Envelope Corp. His advice to aspiring entrepreneurs: "Don't suffer from 'call reluctance.' Pick up the phone or your pen, and ask for the advice you need."

A first step in becoming part of the entrepreneurial network is gathering information. Here are some ideas to get you started:

Subscribe to Magazines

Publications such as *Entrepreneur, Success, Inc., Nation's Business,* and *Black Enterprise* are loaded with articles about entrepreneurs and their experiences and insights on launching new ventures.

Read Books

Your local library and bookstore offer titles such as *How to Start Your Own Business without Losing Your Shirt, The Entrepreneurial Family, The Student Entrepreneur's Guide, The Home-Based Entrepreneur, The Woman Entrepreneur,* and *For Entrepreneurs Only.* Many successful entrepreneurs have written books explaining how they built their businesses, what unexpected obstacles they encountered, and how they dealt with those problems.

Use the Internet

For a catalog of books on entrepreneurship and a review of each title, visit The Entrepreneur's Wave (http://www.en-wave.com). The Entrepreneur's Mind (http://www.benlore.com/index.html) and Entrepreneurial Edge Online (http://www.edgeonline.com) are online magazines that give real-life stories from successful entrepreneurs and advice from business experts. The EntreWorld Web site (http://www.entreworld.org) provides information you need to start, run, and grow a business. Black Enterprise Online (http://www.blackenterprise.com) includes career-oriented content for college students. Each month, the First American Group Purchasing Association site (http://www.firstgpa.com) lists its choices of the ten most valuable sites for entrepreneurs.

www.en-wave.com
www.benlore.com/index.html
www.edgeonline.com
www.entreworld.org
www.blackenterprise.com
www.firstgpa.com

Contact Trade Associations

For information on specific businesses or industries that interest you—for example, retailing—look in *The Encyclopedia of Associations.* Your library has a copy of this reference book, which covers some 20,000 industries. It includes organizations for entrepreneurs, such as:

▼ Association of Collegiate Entrepreneurs, Wichita State University, Center for Entrepreneurship, 1845 Fairmount, Wichita, Kansas, 67260–0147. Phone: 316–689–3000.

▼ The Entrepreneurship Institute, 3592 Corporate Drive, Suite 101, Columbus, Ohio, 43231. Phone: 614–895–1153.

▼ Association of African-American Women Business Owners, P.O. Box 13858, Silver Spring, Maryland, 20911–3858. Phone: 301–585–8051.

▼ Young Entrepreneurs' Organization, 1010 North Glebe Road, Suite 600, Arlington, Virginia, 22201. Phone: 703–527–4500.

▼ International Directory of Young Entrepreneurs, Boston, Massachusetts. Phone: 617–562–8616.

Source: Harvey Mackay quote from Robert McGarvey, "Words from the Wise," *Entrepreneur,* May 1997, pp. 152, 154.

This chapter focuses on pathways for entering the world of entrepreneurship, describing the increasingly important role that entrepreneurs play in the economy and explains why a growing number of people choose this area of business. It discusses the characteristics that help entrepreneurs to succeed and the ways they start new ventures and ends with a discussion of methods by which large companies try to incorporate the entrepreneurial spirit within their organizations.

WHAT IS AN ENTREPRENEUR?

You learned in Chapter 1 that an **entrepreneur** is a risk taker in the private enterprise system, a person who seeks a profitable opportunity and takes the necessary risks to set up and operate a business. Many entrepreneurs start their businesses from scratch, but you don't have to launch your own company to be considered an entrepreneur. Consider Ray Kroc, founder of McDonald's. He started by buying a small hamburger shop and grew this small venture into a multibillion-dollar global business.

Entrepreneurs differ from small-business owners. Rieva Lesonsky, editor of *Entrepreneur* magazine, says,

> Merely owning a business does not make you an entrepreneur, it makes you a small-business owner. . . . Entrepreneurs don't only own their businesses, they run them. Entrepreneurship is not a theoretical mind game but a hands-on, up-to-the-elbows, down-in-the-dirt experience. You cannot be an absentee entrepreneur. . . . [2]

William Wetzel, a University of New Hampshire professor, confirms the difference. "It's totally inappropriate to equate small-business founders and entrepreneurs. One's looking for an income. The other has the intention of building a significant company that can create wealth for the entrepreneur and investors."[3]

Entrepreneurs also differ from managers. Managers are employees who direct the efforts of others to achieve an organization's goals. They use the resources of their organizations—employees, money, equipment, and facilities—to accomplish their work. In contrast, entrepreneurs pursue their own goals and take the initiative to find and organize the resources they need to start their ventures. For example, raising money to back a new venture is one of the entrepreneur's greatest challenges.

Studies of entrepreneurs have identified certain personality traits and behaviors common to them that differ from those required for managerial success. One of these traits is the willingness to assume the risks involved in starting a new venture. Some managers leave jobs with other firms to start their own companies and become successful entrepreneurs. Other managers find that they lack the characteristics required to start and grow a business. Entrepreneurial characteristics are examined in detail in a later section of this chapter.

CATEGORIES OF ENTREPRENEURS

A set of distinct categories comes from the Center for Entrepreneurial Leadership at the State University of New York at Buffalo: classic entrepreneurs, intrapreneurs, and change agents.[4]

Classic entrepreneurs identify business opportunities and allocate available resources to tap those markets. The story of David Marcheschi exemplifies the actions of a classic entrepreneur. Deciding as a college student to market a caffeinated bottled water drink, he graduated and began looking for a chemist to produce a formula for his product, Water Joe. Marcheschi formed a partnership with a bottling company that agreed to distribute the drink, and after only a year of production, sales had reached $12 million. The innovation is a hit not only with college students, but also with truck drivers, athletes, and band members. Marcheschi says that some customers buy Water Joe to make lemonade and orange juice. Some even use it to brew their coffee.[5]

Intrapreneurs are entrepreneurially oriented people who seek to develop new products, ideas, and commercial ventures within large organizations. For example, 3M Company continues to develop innovative products by encouraging intrapreneurship among its personnel. Some of 3M's most successful products began as inspirations of intrapreneurs. Art Frey invented the Post-It Note, and intrapreneurs Connie Hubbard and Raymond Heyer invented the Scotch-Brite Never Rust soap pad. Intrapreneurship will be discussed later in this chapter.

Change agents, also called *turnaround entrepre-*

neurs, are managers who seek to revitalize established firms in order to keep them competitive in the modern marketplace. Joanna Lau is a change agent who turned around Bowmar/ALI, a manufacturer of electronic systems for the defense industry and a firm in bad shape. "We were dying on the vine," said one employee. Close to losing its remaining three customers due to poor product quality and delivery performance and operating at a loss of $1.5 million, Bowmar charted a new course when Lau and a group of employees bought the company and renamed it Lau Technologies. As the company's new owner, Lau visited customers, promising them improved product quality and timely delivery. She followed through on her promise by establishing a total quality management program and financial controls to improve cash flow and reduce company debt. Lau broadened the company's product and customer base by entering the nondefense business of digital imaging. Within 5 years, she transformed the company into a profitable venture with $60 million in sales.[6]

REASONS TO CHOOSE ENTREPRENEURSHIP AS A CAREER PATH

If you had to choose between getting a job or starting your own company, which option would be more appealing to you? According to the Small Business Administration (SBA), about 30 percent of the U.S. population is "always thinking about starting a business," and 4 percent of all working-age adults—7 million people—are actively involved in starting new ventures at any one time.[7] Since the early 1980s, some have observed a heightened interest in entrepreneurial careers, spurred in part by publicity cele-

brating the successes of entrepreneurs like Sam Walton, Martha Stewart, Bill Gates, and Steve Jobs.

The popularity of entrepreneurship is likely to continue. Today's teenagers and preteens say they would rather start their own companies than work for others. Business educators are calling this young group *Generation E,* emphasizing their prospects as future entrepreneurs. A 1996 Gallup poll conducted for the Center for Entrepreneurial Leadership found that 7 of 10 high school students want to start and run their own businesses. "The kids believe their only chance in life is to make a job, not take a job," says Dr. Marilyn Kourilsky, the center's vice president. "They see job security as an issue with their parents . . . [and] they want to be their own boss."[8] People choose to become entrepreneurs for many different reasons. Some are motivated by dissatisfaction with the organizational world, citing desires to escape unreasonable bosses or insufficient rewards and recognition as motives to start their own firms. Other people, like David Marcheschi, start businesses because they believe their ideas represent opportunities to fulfill customer needs. The following motives are often cited as major reasons why people become entrepreneurs.

Typifying a classic entrepreneur, David Marcheschi identified a business opportunity and launched a company to market Water Joe, an innovation that satisfies the desire of people who want the stimulative effect of caffeine without its flavor.

Desire to Be One's Own Boss

Self-management is the motivation that drives many entrepreneurs. In *Inc.* magazine's annual survey of America's top 500 fastest-growing companies, 41 percent of the CEOs cited the same main reason for starting companies: "to be my own boss or to control my own life."[9] The CEOs' top reasons for becoming entrepreneurs are listed in Table 6.1.

Table 6.1	Five Most Common Reasons for Starting a New Firm	
To be my own boss or to control my own life		41%
To make money		16
To create something new		12
To prove I could do it		9
Because I was not rewarded at my old job		6

T. J. Rodgers, CEO of Cypress Semiconductor, knew he'd be his own boss one day. His entrepreneurial urge resulted from the mismanagement he saw at the construction companies where he worked during his high school years. "I've never liked taking orders from morons," says Rodgers. After graduating from college, Rodgers resolved that he'd be CEO of his own firm by the time he was 35. He achieved his personal goal, launching his microchip manufacturing firm as its only employee and growing it into a $600 million company.[10]

Financial Success

Entrepreneurs are wealth creators. Many start their ventures with the specific goal of creating a profitable business and reaping its financial rewards. They believe they won't get rich by working for someone else. "We were brought up to believe that it's better to make 50 cents for yourself than a buck for someone else," says Staci Munic Mintz. While both in their mid-20s, Mintz and her brother started Little Miss Muffin, a company that sells low-fat, low-cholesterol muffins and other bakery items to coffee houses and espresso bars. After a year in business, Little Miss Muffin had 400 customers and earned revenues of $1.5 million.[11]

Although entrepreneurs often mention financial rewards as a motive for starting their businesses, experts advise that a desire to make a pot of gold shouldn't be the entrepreneur's primary motivation. Venture capitalist Barry Weinman says, "We won't work with people who just talk about getting rich. If you're just looking for a windfall, go play the lottery."[12] Professor Jon Goodman, who directs the entrepreneurial program at the University of Southern California, agrees. "I've worked with hundreds of entrepreneurs, and I've never met one who said, 'I want to get rich,' who did," says Goodman. "The successful ones say, 'I want to find a way to do animation faster,' or 'I'm really interested in adhesion.'"[13]

> **They said it**
>
> "The most exhilarating, exciting, and empowering business experience you can have is being an entrepreneur, even though it is as tough and risky a task as you can undertake."
>
> Earl G. Graves, founder and publisher of *Black Enterprise* magazine

Job Security

The millions of people who have lost their jobs due to downsizing give another reason that workers, especially those of the younger generation, are attracted to entrepreneurship. From 1990 to 1995, for example, companies dismissed some 17.1 million employees, and the downsizing trend is expected to continue.[14] In the wake of that trend, people are opting to create their own job security.

Sidney Warren explains, "With all the downsizing going on, there isn't even the appearance of security in corporate America."[15] The 32-year-old left a full-time job to buy a TCBY Treat/Mrs. Fields Cookies cofranchise with two of his friends. A recent survey indicated that most new businesses are started by young people in the 25-to-34 age group.[16] Figure 6.1 shows the percentages of new ventures started by people in different age groups.

Although many prospective employees see little job security in working for others, lack of security is also an issue for entrepreneurs. Clearly, many new ventures fail, but studies on the failure rate for startups have produced different results. Those done by the SBA indicate that 24 percent of new ventures dissolve within 2 years, and 52 percent fold within 4 years. After tracking 3,000 startups over a 3-year period, another study recently found that 77 percent of the firms were still in business, 19 percent had folded, and 4 percent had been sold.[17]

Quality of Life

Entrepreneurship is an attractive career option for people seeking to improve their quality of life. Susan Lammers, a mother of two young children, left her management job at Microsoft to start her own educational software company, Headbone Interactive. "I felt constrained by the system," says Lammers. "They wanted work and family separated, but I wanted them integrated—like the family farm of the agricultural age." Lammers located Headbone's office 5 minutes away from her kids' school so she can participate in their class parties and activities. She's made Headbone a family-friendly workplace, allowing her employees to work flexible hours and to bring their kids to the office.[18]

THE ENVIRONMENT FOR ENTREPRENEURS

If you feel motivated to start your own company, conditions have never suited entrepreneurship better than they do today. For one improvement, society now accepts entrepreneurship as a respectable career choice. "The public's perception of people who start their own companies has dramatically improved," says Bill Sahlman, professor of business administration at Harvard Business School. "They're not outcasts anymore. They're in the mainstream."[19] Jim McCann, founder of 1-800-FLOWERS, explains the change in society's attitude between when he started his company in the late 1970s and today:

> As a person who grew up in a mostly blue collar community, where my parents were products of the postwar era, all I heard at the time was "Get a job with a big company, a secure company. Even get a civil service job." Being an entrepreneur is much more culturally acceptable now than it was. It's a worthwhile, laudable, realistic career alternative for so many people. Today people say, "I want to work in an entrepreneurial environment." Twenty years ago, believe me, you didn't have many people saying that.[20]

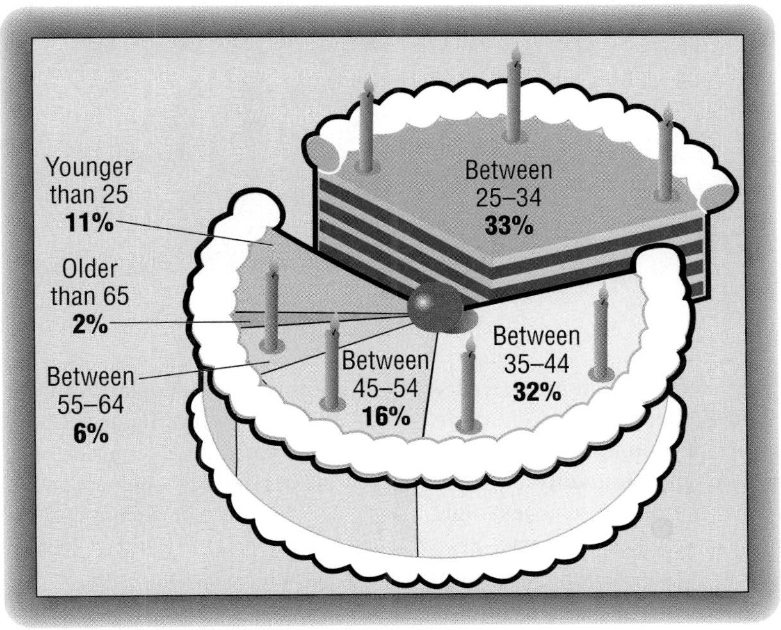

The movement of entrepreneurship toward the business mainstream began in the early 1980s after Steve Jobs of Apple Computer and other high-tech entrepreneurs gained national attention by going public—that is, selling stock in their companies. Today's entrepreneurs are reaping the benefits from growing interest among investors, as discussed later in the chapter. Investors now eagerly back new ventures, making more money more available than before, helping entrepreneurs to find funds to back their startups. In addition to changing public attitudes towards entrepreneurs and the growth in financing options, other factors that support and expand opportunities for entrepreneurs include globalization, education, information technology, and demographic and economic trends.

Globalization

The globalization of business described in the first four chapters of this book has created many opportunities for entrepreneurs. Entrepreneurs are marketing their products abroad and hiring international talent. For example, Jonathan Strum uses the Web-design services of another entrepreneur in Caracas, Venezuela. Strum's startup, Interactive Marketing Partners, is an Internet marketing, design, and development company based in Los Angeles. "Not long ago I would have thought depending on a firm in Caracas for the services we need for our business was outlandish," Strum says. "Now I am importing all my graphic design and most of my programming from overseas."[21]

Entrepreneurs are also forming business partnerships with others like themselves to expand their businesses around the globe. When Ingenico, a French firm that markets smart-card readers, wanted to expand into Australia, China, Singapore, Germany, Russia, and the United States, the company formed strategic alliances with local entrepreneurs in these countries to set up subsidiaries. Gerard Compain, Ingenico's managing director, says, "I wasn't interested in hiring managers. Since we're a relatively small company, I can't bring these people to Paris every month to take their orders." With entrepreneurs, says Compain, "we say, 'Let's go.' Entrepreneurs do things in a way that's smarter, quicker, and simpler. These people know their countries better than we do. And they know how to design and sell products for those markets." Compain's strategy of teaming up with global entrepreneurs helped Ingenico to double its sales within 2 years.[22]

Figure 6.1 **Percentage of Startups by Age Group**

Younger than 25 **11%**

Older than 65 **2%**

Between 55–64 **6%**

Between 45–54 **16%**

Between 25–34 **33%**

Between 35–44 **32%**

Education

The past two decades have brought tremendous growth in the number of educational opportunities for would-be entrepreneurs. Today, some 400 U.S. colleges offer classes in starting and running a business, up from 16 in 1970, and about 125 schools have organized entrepreneurship curricula.[23] Some college programs invite students to apply the practices they learn in the classroom in real-life business settings. For example, at Babson College in Wellesley, Massachusetts, students work with mentors in Boston-area startups.

BUSINESS HALL OF FAME

Selling Cars the High-Tech Way

Pete Ellis followed in the footsteps of his father, who owned a car dealership. At 16, Ellis sold his first car; at 24, he owned his first car dealership. He grew his business into a network of 16 dealerships and related businesses in Arizona and California. Car sales started declining in the early 1990s, however, forcing Ellis to sell or simply to close all of his dealerships. In 1994, he filed for Chapter 7 bankruptcy, losing two houses and $15 million.

Out of a job at 48, Ellis started playing on the Internet using his home computer when he got the idea of selling cars online. In March 1995, he launched Auto-By-Tel (ABT), a car-buying service, online with Prodigy. He hoped the service would generate 50 buyer requests a day. "But on the fourth day, we got 1,348 requests for cars," says Ellis. "That's when we realized this is the way mainstream America wants to buy cars."

Ellis says he started ABT because he never liked the way the car-selling industry worked. "I've always thought the model was wrong—too many unpleasant practices for customers," says Ellis. "I hated my dealerships. I hated the way there would be 20 salesmen waiting to jump on the next customer who walked in the door."

With ABT, Ellis is challenging the auto industry's traditional way of selling cars. He cites information technology as the key factor in changing the balance of power in car buying from the manufacturers and dealers to consumers. "I see the Internet as destroying the old structure," says Ellis. With the Internet, consumers have access to the true costs of cars.

ABT targets serious car buyers who want specific car models. It invites

Many organizations have sprouted up in recent years to teach entrepreneurship to young people. The Center for Entrepreneurial Leadership offers training programs for learners from kindergarten through community college. The center's Entreprep summer program teaches high school juniors how to start and manage a company. Students in Free Enterprise (SIFE) is a national not-for-profit organization in which college students, working with faculty advisors, teach grade school and high school students and other community members the value of free enterprise and entrepreneurship. The San Francisco Renaissance Entrepreneurship Center is a not-for-profit organization offering entrepreneurship training—from introductory to advanced—to disadvantaged students. The Renaissance program supports its entrepreneurs with a business incubator and a financial resource center that links startups with banks and other funding sources.

Information Technology

The explosion in information technology has been one of the biggest boosts for entrepreneurs. As computer and communications technologies have merged, accompanied by dramatically falling costs, entrepreneurs have gained tools that help them to compete with large companies. The Business Hall of Fame box describes how an entrepreneur has created an Internet-based business that is challenging one of America's biggest and most traditional industries.

Information technology helps entrepreneurs to work quickly and efficiently, provide attentive customer service, increase sales, and project professional images. Merchant of Vino Corp., a retailer of fine wine, food, and gift baskets, attributes increases in its customer satisfaction rating to a new bar-coding system and customized software that captures detailed buyer information. Information technology, says Merchant President Marc Jonna, "has increased our customer service tremendously because we don't run out of stock as often. Our customers are delighted because we're more in tune with their buying habits."[24]

Demographic and Economic Trends

Demographic trends, such as the aging of the U.S. population and the growth of dual-income families, create opportunities for entrepreneurs to market new goods and services. Gail Sharp and Nancy Bible left their jobs to launch a day spa, riding the wave of a growing industry built on relieving working women's rising stress levels and tighter

these savvy car shoppers to research vehicles on the Internet and, when they find the cars they want, to fill out purchase requests. ABT sends the requests to the nearest of its nationwide network of some 2,400 dealers. Within 24 to 48 hours after receiving the request, dealers must give buyers a low, haggle-free price quote on new cars, used cars, and leases over the phone. Buyers then pick up their cars at their convenience. By forming strategic alliances with Chase Manhattan Bank, Key Corp., Triad Financial, GE Capital, and American International Group, ABT also offers its customers auto insurance, leasing, and financing.

Auto-By-Tel makes money by charging dealers annual and monthly fees. In return, dealers electronically receive customer purchase requests in their exclusive territories. According to Ellis, ABT can reduce dealers' costs in selling a car by 80 percent. For each new car they sell, dealers typically spend $225 on marketing and $820 in personnel costs. Dealers also benefit

with increased sales. Atamian Honda Volkswagen in Tewksbury, Massachusetts, claims that its link with ABT has boosted unit sales by 40 percent each month and that the ABT sales cost 70 percent less than its traditional sales. "These people who come through ABT represent found business for us," says Sherry Atamian, director of operations. "It's delusional to think we'd get it otherwise." Atamian says dealers have to embrace the ABT program "because the auto industry is changing to being customer driven."

According to Ellis, ABT's mission is "to put ourselves in a consumer-advocacy position" and "to give our dealers a total survival package to keep them in business and profitable for years to come." ABT's rapid growth since it started in 1995 indicates that the company is achieving its mission. Sales of $274,000 in 1995 have grown to more than $15 million. ABT is certainly a hit with consumers. It gets some 4 million hits each month on its Web site (http://www.autobytel.com),

along with more than 85,000 purchase requests per month.

 www.autobytel.com

QUESTIONS FOR CRITICAL THINKING

1. Do you agree with Pete Ellis's statement that the Internet is destroying the traditional way dealers sell cars? Why or why not?

2. Would you buy a car on the Internet? As a car buyer, what would you like and dislike about ABT's Internet service?

Sources: Joanna Glasner, "Autobytel Shares Race Upward," Wired News, March 26, 1999, accessed at www.wired.com; Edward O. Welles, "Burning Down the House," *Inc.*, August 1997, pp. 66–73; and Lynn Beresford, "Full Speed Ahead," *Entrepreneur*, June 1997, pp. 112–113.

time constraints. "People don't have time to get away for a weekend," says Sharp, "but a few hours—that's doable." Sharp and Bible teamed up with Aveda, a cosmetics and body-care company, to open the TallGrass Aveda Day Spa in Evergreen, Colorado, generating terrific customer response. Within 2 years of launching the day spa, the company earns a profit on revenues of $1 million.[25]

David Birch, founder of the economic research firm Cognetics Inc., sees a shift from an industrial economy to a knowledge-based economy. Birch believes that entrepreneurial firms can compete effectively in an economy based on knowledge "because the cost of producing knowledge is very low."[26]

Consider the rapid growth of The Princeton Review, a service that offers classes to prepare high school students for the Scholastic Aptitude Test, a college entrance exam. Entrepreneur John Katzman started this business at the age of 21 and quickly began franchising it. The classes are now offered at 600 locations throughout the United States. With revenues of $70 million, The Princeton Review has complemented its classes with books and software designed to help students make the transition from high school to college. Brisk demand for the firm's offerings has convinced Katzman to redefine his business as "a cross-media education company." He plans to add other courses geared to students

taking licensing tests, such as medical boards, and classes for professionals who want to change their careers.[27]

Entrepreneurship around the World

The growth in entrepreneurship is a worldwide phenomenon. The motto of the 1997 World Economic Forum was "Entrepreneurship in the global public interest." At the conference, the world's most influential business and political leaders discussed how their countries could support entrepreneurial activity. The role of entrepreneurs is growing in most industrialized and newly industrialized nations and in the emerging free-market countries in eastern Europe. In France, for example, 52 percent of new jobs are attributed to startups.[28] In Poland, some 2 million entrepreneurs have started companies since 1989.[29]

Most nations look to the United States as a model for a climate that encourages entrepreneurship. "What we need is a few Bill Gateses in Europe," says David de Pury, who resigned as co-chairman of ABB, one of Europe's largest industrial firms, to start his own financial services company. "The European dream is still to get a cozy job in a big company. We need to change that dream."[30] Until very recently, landing a safe job in a big company was also the dream of Japanese students entering the workforce. But slowing economic growth in Japan and European countries has sparked interest in entrepreneurship as a way to stimulate economic renewal.

Entrepreneurs abroad struggle harder to start businesses than do their U.S. counterparts. Matthias Zahn, a German entrepreneur, says that European startups lack the "food chain" needed to launch new ventures—the educational, financial, and information technology support available in the United States.[31] Other obstacles include government regulations, high taxes, and political attitudes that favor big business. "Owners of startups have virtually no access to bank loans," says Peter Kramer, a German entrepreneur. As president of Europe's 500, a group of the European Union's fastest-growing small businesses, Kramer is leading an effort to establish an environment in which entrepreneurs can flourish.[32]

Among women, entrepreneurship is on the rise throughout the world, according to the Women's Entrepreneurism Worldwide Survey. The survey covered new-venture activity over a 5-year period for 16 countries in the Americas, Europe, Africa, and the Asia-Pacific region. Survey results indicate several major reasons why women start their own firms: economic necessity, high unemployment rates, and the lack of well-paying jobs. Women entrepreneurs in the United States, however, cited greater freedom and flexibility over their careers and few advancement opportunities to top positions in the organizational world as reasons for becoming entrepreneurs.[33]

THE INFLUENCE OF ENTREPRENEURS ON THE ECONOMY

From Thomas Edison's development of the phonograph to the birth of the Apple microcomputer in Steve Jobs's garage, American entrepreneurs have given the world goods and services that have changed the way people live, work, and play. The list includes ball-point pens, Netscape Navigator software, fiberglass skis, Velcro fasteners, the Yahoo! Internet directory, FedEx delivery service, and Big Mac hamburgers. In addition to creating major innovations, entrepreneurs play a significant role in the economy by creating jobs and providing opportunities for women and minorities.

Innovation

Entrepreneurs create new products, build new industries, and bring new life to old industries. Innovators David Filo and Jerry Yang invented a new industry when they launched Yahoo!, a service that helps people locate Web sites that interest them. "This company isn't really about technology," says Yang. "It's about solving people's basic needs for efficiency, effectiveness, and simplicity." Yahoo! was an instant hit with Web surfers, and competitors like Lycos and Excite quickly entered the search engine industry.[34]

Some innovators take an old industry and reshape it. Almost 30 years ago, entrepreneurs Herb Kelleher, a lawyer, and Rollin King, a pilot, founded a new airline based on their vision "that people could fly affordably and have fun along the way." Their innovations include serving passengers peanuts rather than meals, eliminating assigned seating, and encouraging employees to have fun while they work and to entertain passengers. A study by the U.S. Department of Transportation credits Southwest Airlines as the "principal driving force for changes occurring in the airline industry."[35]

> ### DID YOU KNOW?
>
> The Department of Commerce considers these ten countries the most attractive for global business in the twenty-first century: China, Brazil, South Africa, India, Mexico, Indonesia, South Korea, Thailand, Argentina, and Poland.

Job Generation

Entrepreneurs are a vital source of new jobs. Since launching Yahoo! in 1995, Filo and Yang have hired 225 employees. Today, Southwest Airlines has a staff of more than 25,000 employees. As large firms continue to downsize, more new jobs are being generated by entrepreneurships in the United States. Research on job generation and entrepreneurial activity has found that fast-growing startups—about 3 percent of all small firms—have become the principal job creators in the United States. These companies, called *gazelles,* created about 97 percent of the new jobs in the United States between 1991 and 1995. Rapid growth by startups will continue to be a significant source of job creation in the future.[36]

Diversity

Entrepreneurship offers economic opportunities for women and minorities, who often find themselves excluded from well-paying jobs with career advancement opportunities in the corporate world. Discontented with her career prospects, Lolita Sweet, an African-American woman, decided to start a San Francisco limousine service called BAYE Limousines (*BAYE* stands for Bay Area Young Entrepreneurs). For Sweet, building a successful company means developing a diverse workforce. "Our staff is like the United Nations," says Sweet. As a member of the National Foundation for Teaching Entrepreneurship,

Sweet spends two days each week teaching minority students how to start and run a business.[37]

The number of women- and minority-owned startups has grown tremendously in recent years. Hispanic-owned businesses have grown from 100,000 to more than 1 million during the past 18 years.[38] According to U.S. Census Bureau statistics, African-Americans created more than 200,000 new enterprises between 1987 and 1995, a 46 percent increase. Of the 1.3 million new business startups in a recent year, women owned 32 percent.[39]

Realizing the value of both women- and minority-owned startups in creating jobs and promoting diversity, many large companies have developed diversity programs that help these entrepreneurs get startup capital, subcontracts, and other assistance. Eastman Kodak, General Motors, Arthur Andersen, JCPenney, Toyota, and Pacific Gas & Electric are large firms that offer supplier diversity programs. The United Airlines ad in Figure 6.2 illustrates the importance of minority suppliers to the airline's global success. Large companies frequently advertise in magazines like *Black Enterprise* and *Hispanic,* encouraging readers to contact their directors of supplier diversity for information about their diversity programs.

Figure 6.2	United Airlines: A Supporter of Minority Suppliers

mon characteristics. In addition to having similar motivations entrepreneurs share family backgrounds and personality traits.

A recent study revealed that parents' occupations directly influence the likelihood that their children will become entrepreneurs. According to the study, 32 percent of sons with entrepreneurial fathers started their own businesses compared to only 12 percent of sons whose dads were not entrepreneurs. Similarly, 24 percent of daughters with entrepreneurial mothers became entrepreneurs compared to 13 percent of daughters whose mothers weren't entrepreneurs. The study found that most children of entrepreneurial parents started businesses in industries different from those of their parents. It also revealed that while parents' financial support affected their children's decisions to become entrepreneurs, children were most influenced by their parents' attitudes and values, such as the desire to be one's own boss.[40]

"I just always knew that I was going to have my own company or be my own boss someday," says Theodore Waitt, founder of Gateway 2000, a personal computer manufacturer. Waitt's father was an entrepreneurial role model. He discouraged his son from joining the family cattle feedlot business because opportunities there were diminishing due to changes in the industry. But he infused his son with his entrepreneurial spirit. "My father probably could have made more money working for somebody else, but he refused to do that," says Waitt, who started his business at 22 in the family barn.[41]

Researchers have associated many personality traits with successful entrepreneurship. They say entrepreneurs are inquisitive, passionate, self-motivated, honest, courageous, flexible, intelligent, and reliable people. The eight

CHARACTERISTICS OF ENTREPRENEURS

From the examples of entrepreneurship you've read so far, you're probably beginning to think that people who strike out on their own are a different breed. However, researchers found that successful entrepreneurs share com-

Figure 6.3 **Characteristics of Entrepreneurs**

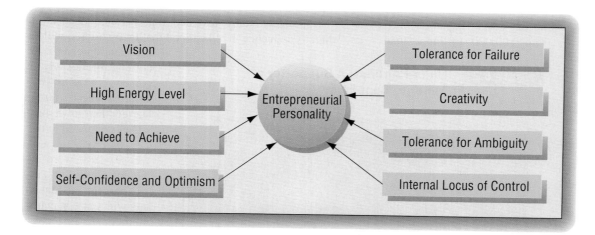

traits summarized in Figure 6.3 are especially important for people who want to succeed as entrepreneurs.[42]

Vision

Entrepreneurs begin with visions or overall ideas for their businesses, and then they passionately pursue these visions. For example, Bill Gates and Paul Allen launched Microsoft with the vision of a computer on every desk and in every home, all running Microsoft software. Their vision has helped Microsoft to become the world's largest marketer of computer software. It has guided the company and provided clear direction for employees as Microsoft has grown, adapted, and prospered in an industry characterized by tremendous technological change. Since the company's founding in 1975, it has grown from a two-person startup to a global industry leader with more than 21,000 employees and $10 billion in revenues. When people ask him about the secret to Microsoft's success, Gates says, "I think the most important element was our original vision."[43]

High Energy Level

Entrepreneurs willingly work hard to realize their visions. Starting and building a company requires an enormous amount of hard work and long hours. Some entrepreneurs work full-time at their regular day jobs and spend weeknights and weekends in launching their startups. Many commonly devote 14-hour days 7 days a week to their new ventures. Patricia Gallup, cofounder and CEO of PC Connection, a mail-order vendor of PCs and peripherals, offers this advice to budding entrepreneurs: "Work all the time. Dream about work."[44]

Sue Szymczak, founder and CEO of Safeway Sling USA, attributes the success of her company to the sweat equity she invested in it. Safeway manufactures nylon and polyester slings for construction cranes, an industry dominated by males. Through hard work and by making top-quality products, Szymczak built one of the most successful firms in her industry. She says, "You can take people like myself who came from a very poor background, with only a high school education, and if you're willing to work yourself nearly to death and risk everything you have, you can succeed."[45]

Need to Achieve

Entrepreneurs work hard because they want to excel. Their strong competitive drives help them to enjoy the challenge of reaching difficult goals and promotes dedication to personal success. Deborah Dolman's need to achieve led her from a job as a court reporter to an entrepreneur running her own court-reporting service. When she noticed increased interest in videotaped court reporting, she hired a sound engineer to develop a videotape system and launched a new company, Dolman & Associates, to market the patented, voice-activated product. "I was extremely undercapitalized from the beginning," Dolman says, "but I told myself, 'I'm going to take my last penny if necessary to get this thing developed.' . . . I never thought of giving up." Not only is Dolman's new venture a success, but she won the Michigan Outstanding Minority Entrepreneur Award and the top prize in Michigan's annual New Product Award competition for her technical innovation.[46]

Self-Confidence and Optimism

Entrepreneurs believe in their ability to succeed, and they instill their optimism in others. Consider Shirley Halperin, publisher of the alternative music magazine *Smug*. "I'm very good at knowing what music people are listening to and what people want to read about," says Halperin. "I know that one day I will be a big publishing person of some kind. I have the ideas and the will to keep going." Halperin's self-confidence and optimism sustain her loyal group of 30 writers, photographers, editors, and designers who work with no pay. One photographer says, "It's so obvious to me that she's going to make it. When she does get big, I want to be right alongside her."[47]

Tolerance for Failure

Entrepreneurs view setbacks and failures as learning experiences. They're not easily discouraged or disappointed when things don't go as planned. "I call my failure my M.B.A.," says Mark Kvamme. With a partner, he started International Solutions with a vision of selling non-English keyboards to foreign computer users in the United States and distributing Macintosh software to international customers. Kvamme had a great idea, and sales climbed quickly to $3 million, but performance quickly turned sour on him. Two of the company's largest customers went bankrupt, and Macintosh sales started to decline. Worse yet, the company never developed adequate control of finances, leaving it with poor systems for keeping track of money made and spent. Kvamme, then 24, dissolved the business and paid back his creditors and vendors by selling his office furniture and running product promotions. "I learned so much more about business when my company was going down than when it was thriving," says Kvamme. As one lesson, he warns entrepreneurs not to rely on one product line or customer and to recognize the importance of controlling costs.

Kvamme and two friends started a new company, CKS Group, a successful ad agency with $130 million in sales that's earned a reputation as the most innovative firm in the business. Kvamme attributes the success of his second venture to his first failure: "A big reason this company came together was that I failed and learned from it," he says.[48]

Creativity

Entrepreneurs typically conceive new ideas for goods and services, and they devise innovative ways to overcome difficult problems and situations. Working as a computer consultant in Columbus, Ohio, Tony Wells always heard questions from customers about where they could get training on new software. Wells asked national software makers the same questions and got this answer: The city was too small to support a training center. He solved the problem by launching Knowledge Development Center, a facility that software firms can rent to provide training classes for their products. Four banks refused to loan Wells the money to start his company, so he mortgaged his house, maxed out his credit cards, and depleted his savings. With money in short supply, Wells devised creative solutions to keep his company operating. One of them was bartering for services he needed but couldn't afford. For example, he traded muffins baked by his brother-in-law, a chef, with another office in his building in return for use of its photocopying machine. Bartering helped Wells to limit his expenses while he built his business.[49]

Tolerance for Ambiguity

Entrepreneurs take in stride the uncertainties associated with launching a venture. Lillian Vernon, founder and CEO of the mail-order company named after her, says, "The biggest lesson every entrepreneur has to understand: Always expect the unexpected—and be prepared to deal with whatever surprises come your way."[50]

Dealing with unexpected events is the norm for most entrepreneurs. Take Kay Meurer. She started her business, Discount Office Interiors, and filled her building with surplus furniture. One day she banked the check for a huge $50,000 sale while "dancing on Cloud Nine." The next day, her building burned to the ground. She lost all her inventory, including the furniture for her big sale, and had to tell the customer to stop payment on his check. Then she learned, with horror, that she was suspected of causing the fire. The police investigating the fire found a gas can next to a huge pile of cardboard boxes on Meurer's loading dock. "My insurance agent wouldn't even talk to me," says Meurer. She wondered how she would prove that she didn't set the fire. A week later the police found the real arsonist, and later Meurer found a new site and reopened her store, which is thriving with $2 million in sales. "No matter what happens," says Meurer, "you've got to do what has to be done."[51]

Internal Locus of Control

Entrepreneurs believe that they control their own fates, so they are said to have an internal locus of control. You won't find an entrepreneur gazing into a crystal ball or looking for a four-leaf clover—they take personal responsibility for the success or failure of their actions rather than believing in luck or fate. They don't make excuses for their shortcomings, nor do they blame others for setbacks and failures. "As entrepreneurs, we are our own biggest obstacle," says Giselle Briden. "The only limits to our success are the ones we put in our own head." After Briden's first business

> **They said it**
>
> "Smart entrepreneurs . . . give their employees the freedom to make decisions so the workers can experience the thrill of being a part of a winning team."
>
> Richard J. Egan,
> CEO of EMC Corp.

BUSINESS HALL OF SHAME

Failure Is Forgiven, Fraud Isn't

Entrepreneurs should feel no shame about failing. Failure may bruise egos, but the damage often is not bad enough to prevent them from trying again and doing better work the second time. Nowhere is failure more acceptable than in the high-tech industry. Investors who finance high-tech startups aren't bothered by failure, either. "Investors here always look at the cup as half full, not half empty," says Ann

Winblad, a software venture capitalist. "They are willing to take chances on entrepreneurs who've made mistakes."

Some investors even prefer to finance failed entrepreneurs. Venture financier Mike Child explains why: "A lot of investors don't like to back guys out of big companies who haven't failed. They haven't learned the issues of meeting payroll, raising money, budgeting for R&D. They just don't know how to run a startup. People who have failed are hungrier and have a keener understanding of the product-market timing interface."

The only way to truly fail as a high-tech entrepreneur is to commit fraud. Writer Geoff Baum says, "Don't bother looking for more VC backing if you cook the books. The industry never rewards entrepreneurs and executives who are caught lying, stealing, or cheating. Ever."

Consider the founder of Platinum Software, which makes accounting software for business customers. The founder and five Platinum executives, including the chief financial officer, were caught committing fraud and found liable for illegally manipulating

---

flopped, she and a partner founded The Magellan Group, a promotion firm that arranges appearances for Anthony Robbins, Deepak Chopra, and other celebrity speakers.[52]

After reading this summary of typical personality traits, maybe you're wondering if you have what it takes to become an entrepreneur. Take the test in the Business Toolkit box later in this chapter to find out. Your results may help you to determine whether you would be successful in starting your own company.

STARTING A NEW VENTURE

The examples of entrepreneurs presented so far have introduced many ways to start a business. This section discusses the process of choosing an idea for a new venture and transforming the idea into a working business.

Selecting a Business Idea

The two most important considerations in choosing an idea for your business are (1) finding something you love to do and are good at doing and (2) determining whether your idea can satisfy a need in the marketplace. You'll willingly work hard doing something you love, and the experience will bring you personal fulfillment. The old adages "Do what makes you happy" and "To thine own self be true" are the best guidelines for deciding on a business idea. Success also depends on customers, though, so ensure that your idea has merit in the marketplace.

Jackie Bazan launched her business, Bazan Entertain-

ment Marketing, by combining what she loves to do with a marketplace need. First she focused on what she enjoyed doing. For Bazan, that meant "not only working in the film industry but also limiting my business to marketing and publicity for African-American and other minority-made and -oriented films." Bazan found a small market niche that needed her services. Her company has handled the marketing and publicity for Spike Lee's films *Get on the Bus* and *4 Little Girls* and for the Oscar-winning boxing documentary *When We Were Kings*.[53]

The following guidelines may help you to select an idea that represents a good entrepreneurial opportunity for you:[54]

- ▼ List your interests and abilities. Include your values and beliefs, your goals and dreams, things you like and dislike doing, and your job experiences.

- ▼ Make another list of the types of businesses that match your interests and abilities.

- ▼ Read newspapers and business and consumer magazines to learn about demographic and economic trends that project needs for products that no one yet offers.

- ▼ Carefully evaluate existing goods and services looking for ways you can improve on them.

- ▼ Decide on a business that matches what you want and offers profit potential.

- ▼ Conduct marketing research to determine whether your business idea will attract enough customers to earn a profit.

required reports of financial information, according to the Securities and Exchange Commission. The executives cooked Platinum's books by declaring revenues for products the company hadn't yet shipped. For example, an independent auditor found that Platinum claimed revenues for one accounting period of $9.3 million, when its real revenues reached only $6.8 million. The company not only falsified its financial statements, but used the inflated revenues to influence stock trades.

The financial misconduct had devastating effects. Investors lost millions of dollars, Platinum's stock price plummeted, some 100 company employees lost their jobs, the firm posted seven straight quarterly losses in revenues, and it limped into the future with a tarnished reputation.

Under the leadership of a new CEO, Platinum is trying to rebuild its image and its sales after settling a $17 million class-action suit. As for the company's founder, the SEC banned him from holding an office in a public company for 10 years. He was fined $100,000 and ordered to pay $1.25 million to settle shareholder lawsuits.

QUESTIONS FOR CRITICAL THINKING

1. **Do you think Platinum's CEO got off too easily by just paying fines and being barred from holding an officer position? Do other students agree with your position?**

2. **Tolerance for failure is one of the entrepreneur's defining characteristics, but the need to achieve is another. How do you think an entrepreneur balances these two characteristics? Where did the balance tip in Platinum's case?**

Sources: "Platinum Software Corporation Named among the Fastest-Growing Windows ISVs," PR Newswire, April 19, 1999; Geoff Baum, "Bouncing Back," *Forbes ASAP*, June 2, 1997, pp. 49–52; Geoff Baum, "When Losers Really Are Losers," *Forbes ASAP*, June 2, 1997, p. 52; Rochelle Garner, "In Need of a Shine," *PC Week*, January 22, 1996, p. A9; and Sam Whitmore, "Platinum Problems Should Spur Wall Street Reforms," *PC Week*, June 6, 1994, p. A13.

▼ Learn as much as you can about the industry in which your new venture will operate, your merchandise or service, and your competitors. Read surveys that project growth in various industries.

Most new ventures are formed to solve problems that people have experienced either at work or in their personal lives. For example, Kristin Roach, an avid snowboarder, started her business because she was frustrated with the choice of unisex outfits then available for snowboarders. The apparel was ill-fitting and uncomfortable because it wasn't designed for women's bodies. Roach dropped out of college to launch Kurvz Extremewear, selling comfortable, stylish, and colorful outfits for women snowboarders.[55]

An entrepreneur's need for marketing research varies depending on the business idea, industry, and competitive conditions. An innovative idea with an unproven potential customer base may require more research than a proposal to improve an existing product. Jens Molbak conducted research to determine if a large enough customer base would welcome his novel idea of marketing a coin-sorting machine. Molbak's research consisted of asking people at grocery stores what they did with their change. "We talked to 1,500 people, and it turned out that three out of four had coins at home, with an average of about $30 at any one time," says Molbak. From this research, Molbak estimated that Americans nationwide stored about $8 billion of coins at home. These results convinced him to proceed with development of his Coinstar machine, which would accept coins in a hopper and return a voucher redeemable for cash at participating grocery stores. Molbak earns a profit on each transaction because the machine keeps 7.5 cents of each dollar it processes. Molbak has installed Coinstar machines in more than 2,000 stores, and the average customer, as his research predicted, deposits $30 worth of coins to be sorted.[56]

Customers love Jens Molbak's innovation, which sorts their stashes of coins and gives them vouchers redeemable for cash.

BUSINESS TOOL KIT

Think You Might Be a Good Entrepreneur?

Answer *yes* or *no* to the following questions:

Yes No

☐ ☐ 1. Are you a first-generation American?

☐ ☐ 2. Were you an honor student?

☐ ☐ 3. Did you enjoy group functions in school—clubs, team sports, even double dates?

☐ ☐ 4. As a youngster, did you frequently prefer to spend time alone?

☐ ☐ 5. As a child, did you have a paper route, a lemonade stand, or some other small enterprise?

☐ ☐ 6. Were you a stubborn child?

☐ ☐ 7. Were you a cautious youngster, the last in the neighborhood to try diving off the high board?

☐ ☐ 8. Do you worry about what others think of you?

☐ ☐ 9. Are you in a rut, tired of the same routine every day?

☐ ☐ 10. Would you be willing to invest your savings—and risk losing all you invested—to go it alone?

☐ ☐ 11. If your new business should fail, would you get to work immediately on another?

☐ ☐ 12. Are you an optimist?

Answers

1. Yes = 1, No = minus 1
2. Yes = minus 4, No = 4
3. Yes = minus 1, No = 1
4. Yes = 1, No = minus 1
5. Yes = 2, No = minus 2
6. Yes = 1, No = minus 1

7. Yes = minus 4, No = 4. (If you were a very daring child, add another 4 points.)
8. Yes = minus 1, No = 1
9. Yes = 2, No = minus 2
10. Yes = 2, No = minus 2
11. Yes = 4, No = minus 4
12. Yes = 2, No = minus 2

Add up your total score. A score of 20 or more points indicates strong entrepreneurial tendencies. A score between 0 and 19 points suggests some possibility for success as an entrepreneur. A score between 0 and minus 10 indicates little chance of successful entrepreneurship. A score below minus 11 indicates someone who's not the entrepreneurial type.

Source: This test was designed by John R. Braun, now a psychologist with CHE Senior Psychological Services, and the Northwestern Mutual Life Insurance Company.

If you're an inventor-entrepreneur like Molbak, you'll need to secure a patent for your product. The Web site, Obtaining a Patent and Invention Development, http://www.bosbbb.org/lit/0022.html presents basic information about applying for a patent and commercializing your invention. It also lists names and addresses of organizations and other resources that can help you to turn an idea into a business.

 www.bosbbb.org/lit/0022.html

In addition to starting a new business from scratch, aspiring entrepreneurs can choose two more popular options: buying existing businesses and buying franchises.

Buying an Existing Business Some entrepreneurs prefer to buy established businesses rather than assuming the risks of starting new ones. Buying an existing business brings many advantages: Employees already in place serve established customers and deal with familiar suppliers, the good or service is known in the marketplace, and the necessary permits and licenses are already secured. It's also much easier to get financing for an existing business. Some sellers may even help the buyers by providing financing and offering to serve as consultants.[57]

To find businesses for sale, contact your local Chamber of Commerce as well as professionals such as lawyers, accountants, and insurance agents. Most people want to buy healthy businesses, while turnaround entrepreneurs enjoy the challenge of buying unprofitable firms and making them generate profits, as mentioned earlier in the chapter.

Buying a Franchise Like buying an established business, a franchise offers a less risky way to begin a business than starting your own firm. But franchising still involves risks of its own. You must do your homework, carefully analyzing the franchisor's terms and capabilities for delivering the support it promises. Energetic preparation helps to ensure that your business will earn a profit and grow.

Although a franchisee must agree to follow the procedures mandated by the franchisor, entrepreneurs can still find ways to inject their creativity into their franchises and make them grow. Consider LaVan Hawkins, who runs 14 Burger King outlets; in partnership with Black Entertainment Television, he plans to operate 475 by 2000. Hawkins learned the fast-food business starting from the bottom by scrubbing toilets and worked his way up to become manager of a Burger King outlet. Since acquiring a franchise of his own, he's made millions of dollars by tailoring the product formulas to the tastes of his customers—inner-city African-Americans. He serves banana shakes and Cajun fries in restaurants lit up with Klieg lights and neon. Customers listen to hip-hop and R&B music. Hawkins wants his restaurants to represent a symbol of hope for inner-city kids. He offers his employees stock options and helps them along career paths to become owner-operators. Although Hawkins's restaurants seem quite different from typical Burger King outlets, they bring in twice the revenue of an average unit.[58]

Creating a Business Plan

In the past, most entrepreneurs launched their ventures without creating formal business plans. While planning is an integral part of managing in the corporate world, entrepreneurs traditionally have favored seat-of-the-pants management. As Amar Bhide, who teaches entrepreneurship at the Harvard Business School, explains:

[A] comprehensive analytical approach to planning doesn't suit most startups. Entrepreneurs typically lack the time and money to interview a representative cross section of potential customers, let alone analyze substitutes, reconstruct competitors' cost structures, or project alternative technology scenarios. In fact, too much analysis can be harmful; by the time an opportunity is investigated fully, it may no longer exist. A city map and restaurant guide on a CD may be a winner in January but worthless if delayed until December.[59]

Jennifer Barclay built a thriving business quickly and without a plan in order to take advantage of an unexpected opportunity.

Jennifer Barclay's experience confirms Professor Bhide's observation. Working in her dad's garage, Barclay crafted handmade T-shirts and sold them at local art fairs. While attending a wholesale fashion show, she unexpectedly received orders for 6,000 pieces of clothing. Then 18 years old, Barclay moved quickly to seize the opportunity of filling the orders, launching Blue Fish Clothing Inc. as a producer of apparel from natural fibers. In the process, she raised capital to buy materials and equipment, found a manufacturing site, and hired employees to make the clothing. Barclay had no time to write a business plan. "If you overanalyze everything, you see how difficult it could be," she says. "It holds people back from [acting on] the wonderful ideas within them." With a strong belief in her one-of-a-kind clothing, Barclay has increased company revenues each year by 35 percent. Blue Fish Clothing is now sold at more than 600 retail stores and boutiques, including Nordstrom and Neiman Marcus.[60]

Although the planning process for entrepreneurs differs from a major company's planning function, today's entrepreneurs are advised to construct business plans following the guidelines presented in Chapter 7. Entrepreneurial business plans vary depending on the type of startup, but the basic elements of such a plan—stating company goals, outlining sales and marketing strategies, and determining financial needs—apply to all types of ventures.

For information about writing a business plan, visit the EntreWorld Web site (http://www.entreworld.org) and click on The Business Plan: Your Blueprint for the Future. The information there covers researching and writing your plan, as well as presenting it to financing sources. To see a sample business plan, visit the page labeled *A Sample Business Plan* at http://www.morebusiness.com/bplan. For an online tutorial in creating a plan, visit http://www.americanexpress.com/smallbusiness/resources/starting/biz_plan/index.html. This site includes an interactive Try It Yourself section that lets you create a plan for a startup and then gives feedback.

Finding Financing

How much money will you need to start your business and where will you get it? Requirements for **seed capital,** funds to launch a company, depend on the nature of your business and the type of facilities and equipment you need. A survey of successful entrepreneurs revealed that they raised an average of $25,000 to start their businesses.[61]

The vast majority of entrepreneurs rely on personal savings, advances on credit cards, and funds from partners, family members, and friends to fund their startups. New ventures secure funds in two forms: debt financing and equity financing.

Debt Financing When entrepreneurs use **debt financing,** they borrow money that they must repay. Loans from banks, finance companies, credit card companies, and family and friends are sources of debt financing. While many entrepreneurs charge business expenses to personal credit cards because it's an easy way to pay, high interest rates make this source of funding an expensive choice. For example, annual interest charges on a credit card can run as high as 20 percent, while a home equity loan (borrowing against the value of a home) currently charges a more reasonable 8½ percent.

www. www.americanexpress.com/smallbusiness/resources/starting/biz_plan/index.html

Still, credit card financing is a viable option for entrepreneurs who expect to grow quickly and know that they can pay off their debt in a short time. Brothers Thomas and Kevin Lane chose this option. They got their idea to produce custom-made baseball bats when Kevin, a pitcher for a minor league affiliate, heard his teammates complain about the poor quality of their bats. The brothers asked their father, a skilled carpenter, to craft several bats for the players to try out.

The players loved the custom bats, but the Lanes waited for approval of their use in the major leagues before taking a $20,000 cash advance on their credit cards to buy the equipment they needed to launch Carolina Clubs. As they expected, "We can't keep up with demand," says Thomas.[62]

Many banks turn down requests for loans to fund startups, fearful of the high risk such ventures entail. Only a small percentage of startups raise seed capital through bank loans, although some new firms can get the SBA-backed loans, as discussed in Chapter 5. While friends, family members, and credit card companies probably won't ask to see a business plan, bank loan officers will. They will also evaluate your credit history.

DID YOU KNOW?

Spike Lee financed his first film using his credit card.

Since a startup has not yet established a business credit history, banks often base lending decisions on evaluations of entrepreneurs' personal credit histories. Banks are more willing to make loans to entrepreneurs who've been in business for a while, show a profit on rising revenues, and need funds to finance expansion. Even then, as the Solving an Ethical Controversy box illustrates, entrepreneurs face serious challenges obtaining bank loans.

Equity Financing When entrepreneurs secure **equity financing,** they invest their own money along with funds

Business Directory

supplied by people and firms that become co-owners of the startups. An entrepreneur does not have to repay equity funds. In exchange for their financial investments, equity investors receive part ownership in the business. Sources of equity financing include family and friends, business partners, venture capital firms, and private investors.

Teaming up with a partner who has funds to invest may benefit an entrepreneur with a good idea and skills but no money. When designer Tommy Hilfiger needed financing for his clothing business, he formed a partnership with Silas Chou, owner of Hong Kong's oldest textile firm, who invested funds and supplied manufacturing expertise. Hilfiger and Chou shared the goal of rapidly growing the business. During the first year of their partnership, they generated sales of $25 million.

Venture capitalists are business organizations or groups of private individuals that invest in new and growing firms. Venture capital supports only a very limited number of startups, because these investors expect very high rates of return, from 28 percent to 40 percent, in short time periods, typically 5 years. Consequently, they invest in firms in fast-growing industries such as technology and communications. One venture capitalist says, "If there's no possibility you're going to hit the $25 million benchmark within 5 years, it's simply a waste of time to pursue institutional venture capital."[63]

A larger group of entrepreneurs consists of angel investors. **Angel investors** are wealthy individuals willing to invest money directly in new ventures for equity stakes. They invest more capital in startups than do venture capitalists. From 90 percent to 100 percent of angel capital is invested in new ventures, compared to just 10 percent of that distributed by venture capitalists. Many angel investors are themselves successful entrepreneurs who want to help aspiring business owners by providing funding that would have helped them when they were launching their businesses. Angel investors back a wide variety of new ventures. Some invest only in certain industries, some invest only in startups with socially responsible missions, and some prefer to back only women entrepreneurs.

Because entrepreneurs have trouble finding wealthy private investors, angel networks form to match business angels with startups in need of capital. One angel network, Investors' Circle, holds conferences twice a year to consider presentations made by entrepreneurs. Investors' Circle provided the financing that saved Kermit Heartstrong's new business, Word Origin Inc., which makes educational board games and puzzles for children. Loans and other capital from Heartstrong's friends and family weren't enough to finance his production for the holiday season. After giving a presentation about his company and his need for cash at an Investors' Circle conference, Heartstrong received a total of $1.5 million in investment capital from 12 different business angels.[64]

As entrepreneurs start their businesses, they spend much of their time seeking and securing financing. Most company founders perform all the activities needed to operate their businesses because they don't have enough money to hire employees. Most entrepreneurs begin as sole proprietors working from their homes. After their initial startup periods, however, entrepreneurs must make many management decisions as their companies begin to grow. They must establish legal entities, buy equipment and choose facilities and locations, assemble teams of employees, and ensure compliance with a host of government regulations. These challenges will be discussed in other chapters throughout this book.

INTRAPRENEURSHIP

Large, established companies try to retain the entrepreneurial spirit by encouraging **intrapreneurship,** the process of promoting innovation within their organizational structures. Today's fast-changing business climate compels large firms to continually innovate in order to maintain their competitive advantages. Entrepreneurial environments created within companies such as 3M, Thermo Electron, Xerox, and Intuit can help these larger firms retain valuable employees who might otherwise leave their jobs to start their own businesses.

Large companies support entrepreneurial activity in varied ways. One leader in this area, 3M Corp., has established companywide policies and procedures that give employees personal freedom to explore new products and technologies. For example, 3M allows its 8,000 researchers to spend 15 percent of their time working on their own ideas without approval from management. Even 3M's hiring process is designed to select innovative people as employees. The company has developed a personality profile of characteristics shared by its top creative scientists. Based on the profile, 3M

Business Directory

venture capitalists a business firm or group of individuals that invests in new and growing firms

angel investors wealthy individuals who invest directly in a new venture in exchange for an equity stake

intrapreneurship the process of promoting innovation within an organization's structure

SOLVING AN ETHICAL CONTROVERSY

Should Banks Lend to Firms with Dual Bottom Lines?

Bagel Works of Keene, New Hampshire, makes bagels and sells them through its own chain of cafes. In business for 9 years, the company proudly defines itself as a socially responsible firm. It recognizes dual bottom lines: It measures success according to the profits it earns and the benefits it brings to employees, the community, and the environment.

Each year, Bagel Works donates about $10,000 worth of bagels to community organizations. It uses environmentally safe—though often expensive—organically grown ingredients to make its bagels. The company treats its employees well by providing them with programs such as gainsharing, in which they receive financial rewards when they meet performance targets.

Bagel Works wanted to expand its headquarters facility and open a cafe in another city. It planned for the expansion by setting aside some cash reserves and raising $500,000 in equity funding, but the company still needed more funds to finance the expansion. Jennifer Pearl, a founder and managing partner, and Richard French, the

company's president, asked their bank for a loan. Unfortunately, Bagel Works didn't show the kind of bottom line that the bank wanted to see. On sales of $3.5 million, the company was showing operating losses.

"The bank loan officer really struggled with the fact that we were incurring these extra expenses [for socially responsible practices] while we weren't making money as a company," says Pearl. The banker wanted Pearl and French to change their principles, but they refused to compromise their social goals just to show a profit.

? Should Banks Give Loans to Firms that Emphasize Social as Well as Profit Goals?

PRO

1. In the long term, socially responsible firms are stronger and ultimately more profitable than more self-oriented companies. Financial incentives like gainsharing decrease employee turnover and reduce the costs of recruiting and training new employees. Product donations to community groups benefit financial performance by increasing customer loyalty and enabling potential customers to sample the products.

2. Expansion periods are tough times for all businesses. Entrepreneurs incur as much risk during growth spurts as at their initial startups. Companies commonly show losses when they are trying to grow. Lenders should be more concerned about strong sales revenues, which indicate that a firm is satisfying its customers, rather than about profits or losses.

CON

1. A firm should strive to treat its employees and community well, but not at the expense of earning a profit. When socially responsible practices hurt a company's net profits, the company should shift its focus to earning money rather than doing good. After all, banks are in business to earn a profit by lending money and charging interest to other profitable firms.

2. While entrepreneurs are prone to take calculated risks, bankers are much more conservative risk takers. They properly avoid the risk of lending money to companies with operating losses. If the company can't repay the loan, the bank loses money.

has crafted questions and scenarios that help company interviewers to gauge the creative skills of job candidates.

In addition to its traditional product development approach, in which managers and researchers work together to develop products, 3M implements two intrapreneurial approaches: skunkworks and pacing programs. One skunkworks project produced 3M's Post-It Notes. Such a project is initiated by an employee who conceives an idea and then recruits resources from within 3M to turn it into a commercial product. Pacing programs are company-initiated projects that focus on a few products and technologies in which 3M sees potential for rapid marketplace winners. The company provides financing, equipment, and people to support such pacing projects. The Scotch-Brite Never Rust wool soap pad was a successful 1990s pacing

project. Within 2 years of its introduction, the pad captured a market share above 17 percent.[65]

A large company that wants to nurture intrapreneurs faces a difficult challenge in dealing with the differences between managers and entrepreneurs. William F. O'Brien, president of Starlight Telecommunications, explains:

There is a natural tension between the way corporate managers think and the way entrepreneurs think. Many executives at large companies work long and hard to achieve reliability and stability within their organization, and may seem overly cautious to the entrepreneur. The entrepreneur's calls for rapid change and willingness to accept risk, on the other hand, can be threatening to the executive.[66]

SUMMARY

Jennifer Pearl and Richard French are members of the new generation of entrepreneurs who care about their employees, their communities, and the environment. These young entrepreneurs "run their businesses like they would run a family. Money is not your No. 1 focus," says Jennifer Kushell, president of the Young Entrepreneurs Network.

Bagel Works eventually found a bank that believed in its dual bottom lines and was willing to lend the company $681,000 to finance its expansion plans. Pearl and French met David Berge, a vice president of Vermont National Bank, at a community event.

David Berge (center), vice president of Vermont National Bank, loaned money to Richard French and Jennifer Pearl's company, helping them to maintain their dual bottom lines.

They persuaded Berge to take a risk on their company, even though it was losing money.

Berge viewed Bagel Works's social programs differently from the firm's first banker. "A company that treats its workers right is probably going to treat its lender right," says Berge. He adds, "Committed workers tend to make a higher-quality product. High quality means a better reputation in the community." The banker was also impressed with the way Bagel Works planned ahead for its expansion by saving cash and raising equity, citing those precautions as signs of responsible management. Finally, talking with Pearl and French about the importance to them of their social programs convinced Berge that he could build a relationship of trust with them.

The funding for the Bagel Works loan came from Vermont National's Socially Responsible Banking (SRB) Fund. Deposits in the SRB Fund are made by people throughout the United States and 16 countries who want their money

to support businesses with social as well as profit goals. According to Berge, who is a director of the fund at Vermont National, the quality of SRB loans is better than that of the bank's other loans. SRB loan customers have a 0 percent delinquency rate on commercial loans of more than 90 days.

Pearl credits Vermont National Bank with helping Bagel Works "get over some of the financial obstacles that we were facing at the time." Company sales continue to climb, and today Bagel Works is turning a profit.

QUESTIONS FOR CRITICAL THINKING

1. Suppose you are a bank loan officer and Jennifer Pearl and Richard French visit your office and ask you for a loan. How much weight would social responsibility goals hold in your decision to grant or deny their request?

2. Would you deposit money in a savings account like the SRB Fund? Why or why not?

Sources: Sam Barry, "Of Bagels, Business, and Bottom Lines," Co-op America Web site, accessed at www.coopamerica.org, April 20, 1999; Rieva Lesonsky, "The Right Path?" *Entrepreneur*, March 1997, p. 6; Sharon Nelton, "Loans with Interest—and Principle," *Nation's Business*, January 1997, pp. 22, 24; and "Talking about Her Generation," *U.S. News & World Report*, September 23, 1996, p. 67.

O'Brien's insight is based on a personal experience. Before launching Starlight, he worked for GTE, the giant telecommunications firm. In charge of GTE's African sales, O'Brien and a colleague, Pete Nielsen, wanted to set up a new venture within the company to compete with the small, locally based telephone companies in Africa that were taking market share from large firms. Encouraged by a sponsor within the firm to develop a business plan for their idea, O'Brien and Nielsen performed their regular jobs and worked nights and weekends on their plan, completing it in 6 months and receiving approval for funding from GTE's new venture group. Then they waited 18 months as their plan moved through the final approval process. During that time, the main

sponsor for their idea retired, and the successor didn't like the idea, nor did he want to lose O'Brien and Nielsen as employees to a new venture. Ultimately, GTE pulled the plug on their idea. O'Brien and Nielsen resigned to form Starlight, which offers telephone service in Somalia and Uganda and plans to expand service in other African countries.

From the perspective of a disappointed intrapreneur, O'Brien has developed the following guidelines for large firms that want to encourage employee intrapreneurship:

1. Identify and disseminate companywide goals relating to new ventures, and encourage managers to support spin-offs that advance those goals.

2. Protect and reward employees who identify new business ideas.

3. Quickly move proposals for new ventures through the approval process.[67]

Recognizing that entrepreneurial employees often leave to form their own startups, some companies actually encourage employees to take the plunge. Several divisions of Lockheed-Martin, the $26 billion defense contractor, offer an Entrepreneurial Leave of Absence Program. The program allows an employee with a new venture idea to take a 2-year, unpaid leave to start the business. After the 2-year period, the employee can leave permanently or hire managers to run the new company and return to work to invent something else. For about a 10 percent stake in the startup, Lockheed-Martin invests about $250,000 in financing the new venture and the company also provides incubator space, management advice, and leads to help identify potential investors. Tim Scott, the first employee to try the leave program, launched Genase LLC, a firm that creates and sells an enzyme for stonewashing denim fabric. Scott decided not to return to Lockheed-Martin. Speaking as a true entrepreneur, Scott said, "I decided that working on my own is what I really want to do."[68]

SUMMARY OF LEARNING GOALS

1. Define the term "entrepreneur," and distinguish among an entrepreneur, a small-business owner, and a manager.

Unlike small-business owners, entrepreneurs own and run their businesses with the goal of building significant firms that create wealth and add jobs. Entrepreneurs are visionaries. They identify opportunities and take the initiative to quickly gather the resources they need to start their businesses. Managers use the resources of their companies to achieve the goals of those organizations.

2. Identify three different types of entrepreneurs.

The three categories are classic entrepreneurs, intrapreneurs, and change agents. A classic entrepreneur identifies a business opportunity and allocates available resources to tap that market. An intrapreneur is an employee who develops a new idea or product within the context of an organizational position. A change agent is a manager who tries to revitalize an existing firm to make it a competitive success.

3. Explain why people choose to become entrepreneurs.

People choose this kind of career for many different reasons. Reasons most frequently cited include desires to be one's own boss, to achieve financial success, to gain job security, and to improve quality of life.

4. Discuss conditions that encourage opportunities for entrepreneurs.

A favorable public perception, availability of financing, the falling cost and widespread availability of information technology, globalization, entrepreneurship education, and changing demographic and economic trends all contribute to a fertile environment for people to start new ventures.

5. Describe the role of entrepreneurs in the economy.

Entrepreneurs play a significant role in the economy as a major source of innovation and job creation. Entrepreneurship also provides many opportunities for women and minorities, who may encounter limits to their progress in established businesses.

6. Identify personality traits that typically characterize successful entrepreneurs.

Successful entrepreneurs share several typical traits, including vision, high energy level, need to achieve, self-confidence and optimism, tolerance for failure, creativity, tolerance for ambiguity, and internal locus of control.

7. Discuss the process of starting a new venture.

Entrepreneurs must select an idea for their business, develop a business plan, obtain financing, and organize the resources they need to operate their startups.

8. Explain how organizations promote intrapreneurship.

Organizations encourage entrepreneurial activity in a variety of ways. Hiring practices, dedicated programs such as skunkworks, and entrepreneurial leaves of absence encourage innovation within large firms.

TEN BUSINESS TERMS YOU NEED TO KNOW

entrepreneur	debt financing
classic entrepreneur	equity financing
intrapreneur	venture capitalist
change agent	angel investor
seed capital	intrapreneurship

REVIEW QUESTIONS

1. Distinguish between entrepreneurs, small-business owners, and managers. Which of these three would you choose as a career? Give a reason for your choice.
2. What are the three categories of entrepreneurs? How do they differ?
3. List some reasons why people become entrepreneurs. If you chose to start up your own company, what would be your primary motive for doing so?
4. Name six conditions that benefit people who want to start new ventures today.
5. Why can Americans launch new firms more easily than Europeans can?
6. What benefits do entrepreneurs bring to the economy?
7. Describe eight characteristics attributed to successful entrepreneurs. In your opinion, which trait is the most important determinant of success?
8. What two factors are most important in selecting an idea on which to base a startup?
9. Explain the differences between debt financing and equity financing. Give an example of each type of financing.
10. What is intrapreneurship? How do entrepreneurs and intrapreneurs differ?

QUESTIONS FOR CRITICAL THINKING

1. People thought that Mark Scatterday was crazy when he told them about his new-venture idea of putting birdseed into a balloon and selling the product for $10. But Scatterday forged ahead anyway, launching Pro-Innovative Concepts to make and market The Gripp, a patented squeeze ball that's bringing in revenues of more than $5 million. What characteristics of entrepreneurs do you think helped Scatterday to succeed in his new venture?

2. Many entrepreneurs choose to start their own businesses because they prefer to be their own bosses. Would you rather work for someone else or be your own boss? What are some advantages and disadvantages of each option?

3. Suppose that the principal of the high school from which you graduated called to ask if you would give a talk on entrepreneurship as a career option during the school's annual career day. The principal worries that many high school students say they want to be entrepreneurs but few realize what this choice involves. What advice would you give to these students?

4. Think of something you love to do—a personal interest or a hobby—that has the potential of being turned into a business. How would you go about determining whether your idea would satisfy enough customers to make it a profitable business?

5. You have just announced to your family members that you're going to start your own business. Your family members are delighted with your decision, as you'll be the first entrepreneur in the family. They have all read stories in newspapers and magazines about the overnight successes of entrepreneurs and are excited about the prospect of having a millionaire in the family. Before you even ask, they offer you money to start your company. No one in your family has ever invested in a business before, so you have to explain to them the difference between debt financing and equity financing. As an entrepreneur, you are optimistic that your business will succeed. But you are also realistic and know that your first venture brings many risks. You are concerned that if your business fails, it will cause family problems because you may not be able to pay back debt financing and family members will lose money they invest as equity financing. How would you resolve this issue?

Experiential Exercise

Directions: To learn more about the entrepreneurial experience, interview a successful entrepreneur either by telephone or in person. The person you interview should have a minimum of three years' entrepreneurial experience. Report your findings in a format requested by your instructor. Possibilities include (1) give a 3- to 5-minute oral report in class, (2) write a 2- to 3-page paper, or (3) compare your findings during a small group discussion with others in your class who have also completed this assignment.

Following are some questions you may use for your interview. Feel free to add to or delete from this list or to prepare another list with questions of your own. Your goal in this exercise is to get firsthand information about the entrepreneurial experience to help you determine whether entrepreneurship might be a career path for you.

1. Entrepreneurs begin with visions, or overall ideas for their businesses, and then they passionately pursue those visions. Describe the vision you had for your organization.
2. Did you start a business with your own idea, buy an established business, or buy a franchise? If you started a business based on your own idea, answer this question: In selecting your business idea, were you able to find something you love to do and are good at doing? How did you determine that your idea would fill a need in the marketplace?
3. Researchers have associated many personality traits with successful entrepreneurship. Which of these describe you? Which trait do you think contributed most to achieving your success? Explain why the trait you selected contributed so much to your success.

   ▼ Vision

   ▼ High energy level

   ▼ Need to achieve

   ▼ Self-confidence and optimism

   ▼ Tolerance for failure

   ▼ Creativity

   ▼ Tolerance for ambiguity

   ▼ Internal locus of control

4. Describe your typical workweek schedule, indicating what time your workday begins and ends and how many days per week you typically work.
5. Describe a setback or failure and how you responded to it.
6. Did you ever take a class or enroll in a program that taught you how to start and run a business?
7. Did you have a documented "Business Plan"? If yes, approximately how many hours did it take you to prepare it? Did you use it to explain and sell your business idea? Was it necessary to get the financing you needed?
8. Did you budget enough for your start-up costs? If not, what expenses did you not plan for that created a cash-flow problem?
9. Explain the procedure you followed to find financing for your new business. Did the process take more or less time than you anticipated? Was finding financing easier or harder than you expected? What's the best advice you can give a person who is seeking financing for starting a new business?
10. What's the most important entrepreneurial idea or advice that you would want to convey to college students contemplating going into business for themselves?

Nothing but Net

1. **Venture capitalists.** Assume you are seeking financing for an entrepreneurial venture and need to check the availability of possible funding. Visit the Web site called America's Business Funding Directory at

   www.businessfinance.com.

   According to the information applicants provide for the search, list the criteria venture capitalists consider when evaluating your capital request. After reviewing the procedure for using this Web site to locate funding sources, examine the tools, references, and resources also available at this site that can help you grow and keep your business strong.

2. **Creativity.** One of the characteristics of entrepreneurs is creativity. Use your search engine to find Web sites related to creativity or visit "Mind-Brain Links" at

   www.tiac.net/users/seeker/brainlinks.html.

   Present a 3- to 5-minute report to your classmates summarizing the most useful and interesting ideas you found that relate to entrepreneurs and creativity.

3. **Franchise opportunities**. On the Internet, you will be able to find a great deal of information about franchising opportunities available for entrepreneurs. Use your Internet search engine to locate a site such as "The Franchise Handbook: On-Line" at

   www.franchise1.com/franchise.html

   or "Business Opportunities Handbook: On-Line" at

   www.ezines.com.

   Select three franchise opportunities that are interesting to you and prepare a table where you can compare information related to each franchise. Across the top of the page list the franchises you've selected; down the left column list information categories provided below (or create your own categories of information); then fill in the columns with the information related to each franchise.

   ▼ Franchising since

   ▼ Number of franchised units

   ▼ Number of company-owned units

   ▼ Franchise fee

   ▼ Capital requirements

   ▼ Training and support provided

Note: Internet Web addresses change frequently. If you do not find the exact sites listed, you may need to access the organization's or company's home page and search there.

TWO ARTISTS OR TWO EXECUTIVES?
THE STORY OF TWO WOMEN BOXING

In 1983, a new venture was born when artist Linda Finnell was commissioned by a non-profit photography gallery to make boxes to be used as artists' portfolios. With her best friend and fellow artist, Julie Cohn, these two women handmade each box while sitting in the middle of Linda's living room. For three more years, the two friends worked together making and selling boxes, cards, and small books before deciding to hire a small number of employees and expand into a retail business. However, hiring employees was a big step. As Julie remarked, "We never thought it would be the way it is right now. I think we really thought it would be the Julie and Linda club forever."

As artists, both women had experienced the challenges, frustrations, and rewards of creating art and then negotiating with galleries for its display and sale. In the mid-80s, Julie and Linda decided that by focusing their joint energy on a business, they could create the life they wanted. They would be the design force behind the art products made by their company, and from the business, they would attain stable, and later, growing incomes. Starting with a capital infusion of only $400, by the early 1990s, the company was grossing nearly half a million dollars.

The early years meant a lot of hard selling as well as finding contract sales representatives to handle additional geographic regions and trade shows at which their company's work was displayed. Once a part-time office manager was hired along with more women in production, Julie and Linda increased the amount of time they spent on designing new products. Still, the day-to-day business details demanded their attention.

Because of the small, family-like nature of Two Women Boxing, policies regarding employees tended to be set with the employees' needs in mind. The women on the production line have always worked at their own pace and set their own schedules. This, in part, fits well with the nature of one-of-a-kind handicrafts. On the other hand, as the demand for higher volume and rapid delivery has increased, this type of flexibility is more costly to the business. A new piece rate pay system provides an incentive for helping to meet the production schedule. Currently, the production manager is working to create production jobs with more autonomy. This means that the employees are beginning to handle the ordering of materials, shipping, and some design elements. This new system clearly demands a fairly high level of cross-training, something that has always been part of this small firm. But it also demands more of the employees. As Julie noted, "The people who will work out well are the self-starters."

The pull between a completely employee-centered work environment and the needs of the business has at times created tension for the owners. "That's been one of the hardest things in the business—to be an employer and to try to play out both sides of what it must be like to be the person who's trying not to hand down rules, but to create a working structure," according to Julie.

By 1996, Two Women Boxing and its founders had hired a small staff of professional managers: two full-time office managers and a production manager. Still, as long as the company maintained a production orientation, Julie and Linda were called upon to handle management, marketing, supplier, and financial concerns. And that's not what they want any longer. These two entrepreneurs "started the business to support their art," and that's what they are working to get back to. Julie and Linda are consciously moving the business away from manufacturing and toward the design side. They are licensing their designs to companies, like Fitz and Floyd of Dallas and Sylvestrie, that make china, giftware, and other "tabletop" items. Although they are proud of their company's work in manufacturing—the competition and costs make it less fun—the design side is their joy. Julie and Linda have been forward thinking over the years and have continuously analyzed the direction of their business. They are therefore well-prepared to move forward on this repositioning of their business.

Questions

1. What are the advantages and disadvantages of owning a small business? Apply these to Two Women Boxing and explain your decisions.

2. What are some of the characteristics of an entrepreneur? Give examples of how these characteristics apply to Two Women Boxing.

3. As the company grows, where could Two Women Boxing find the financing?

4. How would you go about starting your own business? How would it differ from Two Women Boxing?

chapter 7

Strategies for Business Success in the Relationship Era

LEARNING GOALS

1. Explain the role of vision in business success.

2. Describe the major benefits of planning.

3. Distinguish among strategic planning, tactical planning, and operational planning.

4. Explain the six steps in the strategic planning process.

5. Identify the components of SWOT analysis and explain its role in assessing a firm's competitive position.

6. Describe the importance of relationships with customers, suppliers, employees, and others in achieving a company's objectives.

7. Explain the core elements of buyer-seller relationships.

8. Identify strategies and tactics for building and sustaining relationships with other organizations.

Time Warner Builds a Web of Customer Relationships

Time Warner seems to possess the ingredients needed to become much more than just another Web retailer. After all, this media giant includes divisions as diverse as motion-picture production, Columbia House music clubs, the Book-of-the-Month Club, a collection of cable channels, the Atlanta Braves, and magazines like *Time, Fortune,* and *People*. With inventory like this, Time Warner should be able to build a superstore in cyberspace.

A few short years ago, the Internet was seen as a novelty with little practical application. Too many barriers existed—from concerns about credit-card purchasing to amateurish Web sites—for all but the bravest consumers to purchase anything online. Today, a whole new self-service economy is growing and what was previously unthinkable to companies like Time Warner became not only doable but lucrative.

Catalog giant Spiegel is one example of a company that has boarded the Internet train. While its Internet sales currently account for less than 5 percent of total revenues, they have grown fivefold over the past three years. Spiegel's traditional mail-order and telephone sales from its catalog have plunged over this same period. Dell Computer shoppers spend $3 million a day buying computers from its Web site. Even more important to the Austin, Texas-based company is the fact that direct sales allow Dell to avoid payments to retailers, giving it a 6 percent advantage over its competitors. Although many well-known Internet-based firms are awash in red ink, Eddie Bauer has been generating profits from Web sales of its outdoor clothing since 1997. Of the 2,000 commerce-related sites recently surveyed, nearly half are profitable and an additional 30 percent expect to be within two years. Even though online sales currently account for a tiny share of total U.S. sales, they are impressive in dollar amounts. Internet consumer sales in 2000 reached $20 billion, and online commerce between companies was $175 billion.

Time Warner is not without Web experience. Back in 1994, the company invested heavily to develop Pathfinder, which offered online versions of *Time, Fortune,* and other magazines. The original strategy was to generate revenues from advertisers eager to purchase space and from consumers seeking access to the site. But the venture proved disappointing, as consumers flocked to the site but balked at paying for the privilege. Other cybercompanies (including CDnow and Amazon.com) share Time Warner's experience of spending heavily for years in an effort to draw traffic to their sites but have yet to turn a profit.

www.

www.studiostores.warnerbros.com

Nevertheless, Time Warner is promising to take online retailing to a new level, capitalizing on its vast mail-order experience to quickly turn its cyber superstore into a profitable business. Indeed, the company has an enviable mail-order reputation. Using television ads and toll-free numbers, Time Warner is adept at getting viewers to the phone to buy products "they didn't know they wanted or needed," says Time Inc. CEO Don Logan. The firm is one of the largest U.S. Postal Service customers, already selling more than $2 billion worth of books, videos, and CDs through its Book-of-the-Month Club, Time-Life operations, and Columbia House record club. Its huge mail-order infrastructure should be invaluable for its online superstore, especially since it can tap an existing database of 60 million customers and existing workforce of thousands of employees in huge warehouses located in Indiana, Pennsylvania, and Virginia.

But can all of this be translated to the Internet? Do the typical appeals used in mail-order marketing sustain the relationship that cybershoppers are looking for on the Web? Bauer executive Judy Neuman says the Net "makes you think very differently about your customers." Cybercommerce is about more than building business; it's about more than building a new environment of convenience and speed. It's about relationships. As CDnow's Rod Parker puts it, "You can't reach and grab people." On the Net, soft sell rules. "You want to invite customers in and be of service to them."

Time Warner is starting its retail site off by restricting product offerings to its own items, such as Madonna CDs, Batman videos, Time-Life history books, and Tweety Bird boxers. But the firm has supersize plans—eventually even to sell entertainment merchandise of rival companies. As part of its overall effort, it is promoting the Web sites of other Time Warner units such as Warner Bros. Studio Stores and Atlantic Records. And it already has another advantage: Pathfinder. Consisting of dozens of other sites, Pathfinder attracts 1 billion page-views a month, giving Time Warner considerable power to direct traffic to its cybersuperstore. Other Internet retailers must pay millions to be promoted on popular Web sites (one of the major reasons these cybersellers have such difficulty showing a profit).

The new Net economy offers us the products we want when we want them. More and more cybershoppers are becoming accustomed to online price comparisons, automatic grocery shopping, and 24-hour service. The shopping malls of the 1980s and 1990s redefined how we shopped and even how we spent our time. If Time Warner can offer the types of relationships and shopping experiences that cybershoppers are looking for, its Internet superstore will play a key role in reshaping our shopping habits and expectations yet again.[1]

CHAPTER OVERVIEW

Success in today's business world doesn't just happen. Many factors play a role in a firm's ability to survive, grow, and achieve profitability. Chief among these factors is the ability to envision how a business can satisfy marketplace needs. Effective planning helps managers to meet the challenges of a rapidly changing business environment and to develop strategies to guide a company's future. This management activity involves setting goals and then preparing and implementing plans to reach those goals.

Like Time-Warner, many businesses now include building and managing relationships as core elements in their overall visions and plans. Instead of looking for ways to merely increase transactions with customers, they now focus their management efforts on the broader aim of forging strong, ongoing bonds with customers, employees, and other businesses.

This chapter begins by examining how successful organizations use strategic planning to turn visions into reality. It then explores some of the tools that companies are using to strengthen their links with customers, vendors, employees, and other important stakeholder groups.

THE NEED FOR VISION

As Chapter 1 discussed, business success almost always begins with a **vision,** a perception of marketplace needs and the methods by which an organization can satisfy them. Vision serves as the building block of a firm's actions, helping to direct the company toward opportunity and competitive differentiation. Michael Dell's idea of selling custom-built computers directly to consumers, for example, helped to distinguish Dell from hundreds of other computer industry startups.

Although it is critical to entrepreneurial success, vision isn't just for startup companies. Vision helps established companies to unify the actions of far-flung divisions, keep customers satisfied, and sustain growth.

St. Louis–based Monsanto Co. had long operated as a textile and chemical manufacturer similar to its larger competitor DuPont until Robert Shapiro, the firm's chief executive officer, conceived a different vision for his company. He viewed Monsanto as a biotech firm dedicated to improving human health and protecting the environment by developing what he termed "planet friendly" products. This refocused vision has led the multinational firm to sell off some divisions, acquire successful products such as Equal sugar substitute, and change the direction of others. New products are being developed to fulfill the vision, such as genetically altered vegetable seeds that allow farmers to reduce their use of pesticides. This vision of the future is already paying off in expanded sales and profits and the prices investors are willing to pay for shares of Monsanto stock.[2]

Vision must be focused and yet flexible enough to adapt to changes in the business environment. Retail giant Sears strayed from its department store origins through a series of misguided acquisitions and diversification moves into financial services, real estate, and insurance. Soon, billion-dollar annual profits had turned into losses, and customers began staying away in droves. The Sears board of directors hired a new CEO, Arthur Martinez, to return the firm to its original vision as a reliable retailer offering strong consumer brands. Martinez sold off such subsidiaries as Allstate Insurance, the Discover credit card, and the Coldwell Banker real estate operation. Even though his firm's hardware and appliance brands had maintained strong customer loyalty, particularly among male shoppers, Sears needed to do more to win back female customers turned off by the firm's stodgy retail image. Martinez and his executive team revitalized the Sears image through improved merchandise selection, store redesign, and an advertising campaign inviting consumers to "come see the softer side of Sears." Figure 7.1 illustrates this new image aimed at enhancing growth in sales and profits at Sears.[3]

As these examples demonstrate, however, vision is only the first step along an organization's path to success. While a clear picture of a firm's purpose is vitally important, it takes careful planning and action to turn a business idea into reality. As Nolan Bushnell, founder of Atari, once said, "Everyone who's ever taken a shower has an idea. It's the person who gets out of the shower, dries off and does something about it who makes the difference."[4] The next section takes a closer look at the planning and implementation process.

THE IMPORTANCE OF PLANNING

Managers at the Todo Loco Mexican restaurant were convinced that their new food package was a winner. The product, dubbed "Wraps," was a series of gourmet food entrees, each one wrapped up in a flavored tortilla. Consumer response was so favorable that Todo Loco's owners raised enough money to open 16 stores in their Seattle home market and several more in other West Coast locations, including California.

Business Directory

vision a perception of marketplace needs and methods by which an organization can satisfy them.

Figure 7.1   **Fashionable Clothing as Well as Building Supplies: The New "Softer Side" of Sears**

"I went in for insulation."

"And left with a warm fuzzy feeling."

Come see the softer side of *SEARS*

©1997 Sears, Roebuck and Co. Prices may vary in Alaska, Hawaii and Puerto Rico.

seize opportunities. As Todo Loco management discovered, effective planning requires an evaluation of the business environment and a well-designed road map of the actions needed to lead a firm forward.

A typical outcome of the planning process is the creation of a formal written document called a **business plan.** The business plan states the firm's objectives and specifies the activities and resources required to achieve them. It also includes details about the markets in which the firm plans to compete, its financial resources, and the competitive situation facing each of its products. Both new and existing companies create business plans, but these documents are particularly important for entrepreneurial ventures.

But Wraps did not prove to be a success, at least not for Todo Loco. Competitors found the idea easy to copy, and the new restaurant chain quickly encountered stiff competition from imitators. In addition to regional competitors, international fast-food franchises such as Taco Bell and Wendy's introduced their own versions of the product, and Todo Loco found itself losing money. Expensive marketing efforts didn't work, and layoffs and store closings soon followed. Finally, the company sold several of its remaining restaurants to competitors and closed the rest. Just 3 years after inventing the Wraps concept, Todo Loco was out of business.[5]

Todo Loco's experience underscores the importance of planning based on a realistic assessment of opportunities combined with a clear-sighted evaluation of company strengths and competitive threats.

Planning is the process of anticipating future events and conditions and determining courses of action for achieving organizational objectives. Effective planning can help a business to crystallize its vision, avoid costly mistakes, and

Types of Planning

Planning can be categorized by scope or breadth. Some plans are very broad and typically long-range, focusing on key organizational objectives. Other types of plans specify how the organization will mobilize to achieve these objectives. Table 7.1 explains these basic types: strategic, tactical, operational, adaptive, and contingency planning.

Strategic Planning **Strategic planning**—the most far-reaching level of planning—is the process of determining the primary objectives of an organization and then adopting courses of action and allocating resources to achieve those objectives. Strategic planning evaluates conditions through a wide-angle lens to determine the long-range goals of the organization. British Airways' strategic plan, for example, calls for transforming the air carrier from a British company into a global operator serving increased international routes and distinguishing itself from competitors by offering superior service.

Business Directory

planning the process of anticipating future events and conditions and determining courses of action for achieving organizational objectives.

Table 7.1	**Types of Plans**	
Type	**Description**	**Example**
Strategic	Establish overall objectives; position the organization within its environment for time periods ranging from short-term to long-term	Chase Manhattan's plans to become the largest U.S.-based financial institution by merging with Chemical Bank
Tactical	Implement activities and resource allocations, typically for short-term periods	McDonald's efforts to slow Burger King's growth by introducing a clone of the Whopper, BK's flagship brand
Operational	Set quotas, standards, or schedules to implement tactical plans	Requirement to handle grievances within 48 hours of receipt
Adaptive	Ensure flexibility for responding to changes in the business environment by developing scenarios to take advantage of potential opportunities or respond to foreseeable problems	Nike's investigation of moving its athletic shoe production from Asia to Mexico following the passage of NAFTA
Contingency	Prepare for emergencies	Burger King's ban of beef purchases from Hudson Foods after discovery of *E. coli* contamination at a Nebraska packing plant

Tactical Planning **Tactical planning** involves implementing the activities specified by strategic plans. Tactical plans guide the current and near-term activities required to implement overall strategies. Although strategic and tactical plans apply to different time frames, both contribute to the achievement of organizational objectives. Four key activities are outlined in British Airways' tactical plan:

▼ Develop an international marketing plan

▼ Help employees understand the firm's global vision

▼ Learn from the experiences of other airlines to improve service

▼ Form partnerships with other airlines to expand the route network

Operational Planning **Operational planning** creates the detailed standards that guide implementation of tactical plans. This activity involves choosing specific work targets and assigning employees and teams to carry out plans. Unlike strategic planning, which focuses on the organization as a whole, operational planning often centers on developing and implementing tactics in specific functional areas such as production, human resources, or marketing. Operational plans may state quotas, standards, or schedules. At British Airways, the operational planning process led the firm to develop a new identity program. All planes received new paint jobs displaying logos designed by artists around the world. Onboard its aircraft, British Airlines set new standards for service that included sensitivity to the cultural differences of passengers from diverse societies around the world.

> **They said it**
>
> "No plan can prevent a stupid person from doing the wrong thing in the wrong place at the wrong time—but a good plan should keep a concentration from forming."
>
> **Charles E. Wilson (1890–1961)**
> **U.S. Secretary of Defense during the Eisenhower Administration**

Adaptive Planning All planning, whether at the strategic, tactical, or operational level, needs to develop courses of action fluid and forward-looking enough to adapt to changes in the business environment. To succeed in the volatile business world, companies must emphasize focus and flexibility in their plans. They must practice **adaptive planning.**

In emphasizing focus for planning, managers identify and then build on the company's strongest capabilities. British Airways, for example, already had established a superior reputation for ensuring passenger comfort, and that strength became a key point in differentiating the airline as a global carrier.

To emphasize flexibility in planning, managers must develop scenarios of potential future activities to prepare the firm to take full advantage of opportunities as they occur. British Airways bought large shares in several European airlines specializing in low-cost travel. These investments were intended to allow the airline to take advantage of the growth in consumer demand for low-priced flights.[6]

Contingency Planning As the first news reports confirmed the tragic death of Princess Diana, Weight Watchers President Kent Kreh realized that his company faced a major crisis. Unless he and his management team acted quickly, the problem could permanently damage his company. A few months earlier, Weight Watchers had hired Diana's former sister-in-law, the Duchess of York, as a celebrity endorser. Ads and brochures featuring her likeness had been prepared the same week the Princess of Wales died in a car accident after being chased by photographers. The ad campaign's headline proclaimed that losing weight is "harder than outrunning the paparazzi."

All ads were pulled and Weight Watchers asked its advertising agency to begin work immediately on a new campaign.[7]

Planning cannot always foresee every possibility. Threats such as terrorism, natural disasters, and rapid economic downturns can throw even the best-laid plans into chaos. To handle the possibility of business disruption from negative events like these, many firms are turning to a contemporary innovation in planning, **contingency planning,** which allows a firm to resume operations as quickly and as smoothly as possible after a crisis while openly communicating with the public about what happened. This planning activity involves two components: business continuation and public communication. Many firms have developed management strategies to speed recovery from accidents such as airline crashes, factory fires, chemical leaks, product tampering, and product failure. Contingency planning is more important now than ever; over half of the worst industrial accidents in this century have taken place since 1977.

A contingency plan usually designates a chain of command for crisis management, assigning specific functions for particular managers and employees in an emergency. Contingency planning also involves training workers to respond to emergency events, improving communications systems, and recovering the use of technology such as computer records and telecommunications systems. Additionally, contingency plans look at issues of safety and accident prevention to minimize the risk of crises in the first place.

Another important aspect of contingency planning is setting up a system for communicating with the media and public during and after a crisis. When a crisis occurs, the firm involved must quickly tell the truth. Accepting responsibility, even at the cost of short-term profitability, is a

Contingency planning at Weight Watchers began immediately after the tragic and unexpected death of Princess Diana, former sister-in-law of celebrity endorser the Duchess of York. Out of respect for the Princess of Wales and her family, the company withdrew this ad and initiated a new ad campaign.

critical gesture, since early honesty means so much in the court of public opinion. A crisis management plan must ensure that the firm faces the public and makes amends. These steps may range from simple product replacements to payments of medical or monetary claims. Finally, the underlying cause of the problem must be determined and systems established to make certain that it does not recur. Hiring a highly regarded, independent research group to determine what caused the problem is recommended as a method of ensuring objectivity.

Planning at Different Organizational Levels

Although managers spend some time on planning virtually every day, the total time spent and the type of planning done differ at different levels of management. As Table 7.2 points out, members of top management, including a firm's board of directors and chief executive officer, spend a great deal of time on long-range planning, whereas middle-level managers and supervisors focus on short-term, tactical planning. Employees at all levels can benefit themselves and their company by making plans to meet their own goals.

Planning and the Other Managerial Functions

Each step in planning incorporates more specific information than the last. From the global mission statement to general objectives to specific plans, each phase must fit into a comprehensive planning framework. The framework also must include narrow, functional plans aimed at individual employees and work areas and relevant to individ-

Table 7.2	Planning at Different Management Levels	
Primary Type of Planning	**Managerial Level**	**Examples**
Strategic	Top management	Organizational objectives, fundamental strategies, long-term plans
Tactical	Middle management	Quarterly and semiannual plans, departmental policies and procedures
Operational	Supervisory management	Daily and weekly plans, rules and procedures for each department
Adaptive	All levels	Ongoing, flexible plans; quick response to changes in the environment
Contingency	Primarily top management, but all levels contribute	Ongoing plans for actions and communications in an emergency

ual tasks. These plans fit within the firm's overall planning framework, allowing it to reach objectives and achieve its mission. Planning is a key managerial function and planning activities extend into each of the other functions—organizing, directing, and controlling.

Organizing Once plans have been developed, the next step in the management process typically is *organizing*—the means by which managers blend human and material resources through a formal structure of tasks and authority. This activity involves classifying and dividing work into manageable units by determining specific tasks necessary to accomplish organizational objectives, grouping tasks into a logical pattern or structure, and assigning these elements to specific positions and people.

Included in the organizing function are the important steps of staffing the organization with competent employees capable of performing the necessary tasks and assigning authority and responsibility to these individuals. The organizing process is discussed in detail in the next chapter.

Directing Once plans have been formulated and an organization has been created and staffed, the management task focuses on *directing,* or guiding and motivating employees to accomplish organizational objectives. Directing includes explaining procedures, issuing orders, and seeing that mistakes are corrected.

The directing function is an especially important responsibility of supervisory managers. To fulfill their responsibilities to get things done through people, supervisors must be effective leaders. However, middle and top managers also must be good leaders and motivators, and they must create an environment that fosters such leadership. These topics are discussed in detail in Chapters 8, 9, and 10.

Controlling *Controlling* is the function of evaluating an organization's performance to determine whether it is accomplishing its objectives. The basic purpose of controlling is to assess the success of the planning function. The four basic steps in controlling are to establish performance standards, monitor actual performance, compare actual performance with established standards, and, if performance does not meet standards, determine why and take corrective action. Controlling is discussed in detail in the chapters of Part 3 and Part 5.

THE STRATEGIC PLANNING PROCESS

Strategic planning often makes the difference between an organization's success and failure. Strategic planning has formed the basis of many fundamental management decisions:

▼ PepsiCo's decision to combine its rapidly growing Pepsi-Cola soft drink and Frito-Lay snack foods divisions and reorganize its Taco Bell, KFC Corp., and Pizza Hut operations within a separate restaurant division

▼ Internet provider America Online's decision to acquire rival CompuServe

▼ Motorola's decision to abandon the consumer-goods market and concentrate on industrial products

Successful strategic planners typically follow the six steps shown in Figure 7.2.

To demonstrate how the strategic planning process works, the discussion in this section follows one business through an entire planning cycle. The company is JumboSports, the second largest sporting goods retailer (behind The Sports Authority) in the United States. At the start of the strategic planning process, however, JumboSports had suffered through several years of disappointing performance and management was searching for ways to return to profitability.

Defining the Organization's Mission

Earlier discussion in this chapter pointed out the importance of an underlying vision for an organization. The first step in strategic planning is to translate the firm's vision into a

Figure 7.2 **Steps in the Strategic Planning Process**

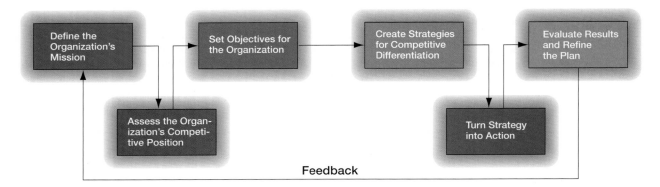

mission statement. A **mission statement** is a written explanation of an organization's business intentions and aims. It is an enduring statement of company purpose, highlighting the scope of operations, the market it seeks to serve, and how it will attempt to set itself apart from competitors. A mission statement guides the actions of people inside the firm and informs customers and other stakeholders of the company's underlying reason for existence. After creating the mission statement, a business should share it with employees, suppliers, partners, shareholders, and customers.

JumboSports's executive team developed a mission statement just 21 words long: "To be the number one sporting goods superstore retailer in each market it serves by focusing on service, selection, and value."

Other companies develop longer mission statements. Coffee retailer Starbucks sums up its mission this way:

To establish Starbucks as the premier purveyor of the finest coffee in the world while maintaining our uncompromising principles as we grow. Starbucks accomplishes this mission with the help of five guiding principles:

1. Provide a great work environment and treat each other with respect and dignity.

2. Apply the highest standards of excellence to the purchasing, roasting, and fresh delivery of our coffee.

3. Develop enthusiastically satisfied customers all of the time.

4. Contribute positively to our communities and our environment.

5. Recognize that profitability is essential to our future success.

The Beckman Instruments mission statement shown in Figure 7.3 illustrates how the manufacturer of scientific laboratory equipment has transformed its corporate vision into a more precise definition of its mission. Beckman's mission statement identifies the broad range of customers it hopes to serve and stresses its aims for meeting the needs of employees and investors.

Although mission statements may seem simple, their development can be one of the most complex and difficult aspects of strategic planning. Completing these statements requires detailed consideration of company values and vision. Effective mission statements state specific, achievable, inspiring principles. They avoid empty promises, ego-stroking, and unrealistic statements.

Assessing Competitive Position

Once a mission statement has been created, the next step in the planning process is to assess the firm's current position in the marketplace. This phase also involves an examination of the factors that may help or hinder the organization in the future. Two frequently used tools in this phase of strategic planning are SWOT analysis and forecasts of future sales performance.

SWOT Analysis A **SWOT analysis** is an organized method of assessing a company's internal *s*trengths and *w*eaknesses and its external *o*pportunities and *t*hreats. The basic premise of this review assumes that a critical internal

Business Directory

mission statement a written explanation of an organization's business intentions and aims.

SWOT analysis an organized method of assessing a company's internal strengths and weaknesses and its external opportunities and threats.

Starting a Business? Have a Plan!

Poor planning has been the downfall of many a would-be entrepreneur. The truth is, every business no matter how new or how small needs a business plan.

Business plans are essential tools for raising money. Most banks and venture capitalists won't lend money to a new business until they become convinced that their investments will likely generate favorable returns.

A good business plan also saves time, stress, and wasted action by spelling out the exact actions to turn a business dream into reality. It helps to minimize mistakes and set priorities for using resources. Finally, the process of business planning helps entrepreneurs to gain realistic insights into the challenges that lie ahead.

What should an entrepreneur's business plan contain? Here's a short list of questions it should answer.

1. **How feasible is your business?**

   Take a realistic look at the challenges and opportunities that lie ahead and compare them to your firm's strengths and weaknesses.

   What business are you in? _____

   What good or service will you offer buyers? _____

   Who are your potential customers? _____

   What is the size of your market? _____

   Who are your competitors? _____

   What are their strengths and weaknesses? _____

   What other factors will affect your potential for success? _____

2. **What's your competitive advantage?**

   Specify your vision for your company.

   What is your firm's mission? _____

   How will you position your good or service to differentiate it from competitors? _____

   What benefits will your good or service provide to customers? _____

   What tactics will you use for marketing, human resources, operations, technology? _____

   _____

3. **What's your financial potential?**

   Determine your income and profit potential based on your sales forecasts.

   Want more information? For a downloadable template of a business plan, you can visit the Money Hunter Web site. The Small Business Administration (SBA) also offers a detailed tutorial on writing a business plan and shareware files outlining business plan elements.

   www.moneyhunter.com   www.sbaonline.sba.gov

and external study of reality will lead managers to select the appropriate strategy for accomplishing their organization's objectives. SWOT analysis encourages a practical approach to planning based on a realistic view of a firm's situation and scenarios of likely future events and conditions. The framework for a SWOT analysis is shown in Figure 7.4.

To evaluate the firm's strengths and weaknesses, the planning team may examine each functional area such as human resources, finance, marketing, and information technology. Entrepreneurs may focus analysis on the individual skills and experience they bring to a new business.

Large firms may also examine strengths and weaknesses of individual divisions and geographic operations. Usually, planners attempt to look at strengths and weaknesses in relation to those of other firms in the industry.

JumboSports management identified several strengths and weaknesses during its strategic planning process. Among its major strengths was a strong network of 85 U.S. outlets, each offering a broad selection of competitively priced sports apparel and equipment. Sales were second only to those of the market leader, The Sports Authority. However, these strengths were countered by significant

| Figure 7.3 | **Vision, Values, and Mission of Beckman Instruments** |

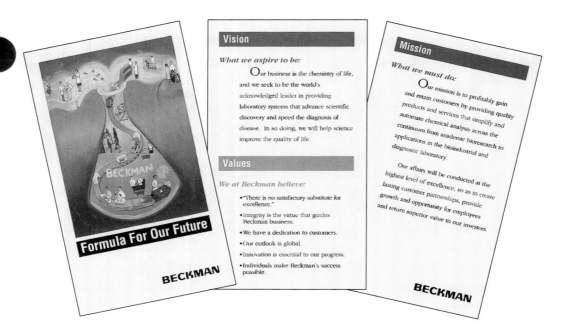

mountable difficulties. A SWOT analysis is a useful tool in the strategic planning process, because it forces management to look at factors both inside and outside the organization. SWOT analysis examines not only the current picture but also necessary current actions to prepare for likely future developments.

Forecasting A second tool used to assess the firm's competitive position and a complement to SWOT analysis is **forecasting,** the process of estimating or predicting a company's future sales or income. Forecasts can focus on the short term (under 1 year), intermediate term (1 to 5 years) or long term (over 5 years).

areas of weakness. Since stores carried different names—Sports Unlimited and JumboSports—in different markets, the chain had developed no national image. The company had no automated inventory control system, which meant that store managers had problems receiving merchandise quickly. Employee training tended to be lackluster and hampered store managers' efforts to provide attentive customer service. These weaknesses combined to produce an overall financial weakness, as the firm posted several years of back-to-back financial losses.[8]

SWOT analysis continues with an attempt to define the major opportunities and threats the firm is likely to face within the time frame of the plan. Environmental factors such as market growth, regulatory changes, or increased competition are all considered. For example, JumboSports saw moderate growth in the sales of sporting goods as an opportunity to improve its revenues. However, consolidation and increased competition in the sporting goods industry posed a very real threat.[9]

If a firm's strengths and opportunities mesh successfully, it gains competitive leverage in the marketplace. On the other hand, if internal weaknesses prevent a firm from overcoming external threats, it may find itself facing insur-

Qualitative forecasting methods are subjective techniques. The company might ask salespeople, managers, executives, or outside consultants to suggest likely levels of short-term sales. Some businesses also survey their customers about purchasing plans and develop forecasts based on the data collected. Because they rely on subjective assessments, qualitative forecasts are limited in their usefulness, and most firms use them only for very short time periods.

Product designers at Wrangler began forecasting by surveying women about what they wanted—and didn't want—in their jeans. A large percentage of respondents suggested that they would be more likely to buy jeans if the back pockets were eliminated. The result was Wrangler's new line of bareback jeans shown in Figure 7.5.

Quantitative forecasting uses historical data and mathematical models to predict how the firm will perform. For example, a business may track sales performance over a period of time, look for ongoing trends, and forecast future growth or declines based on the identified trends. This method is called *trend analysis.*

Forecasts are important because they guide the planning process and support decision making. They can help managers to pinpoint potential opportunities and threats

Business Directory

objectives specific performance targets that an organization hopes to accomplish.

that may interfere with the company's plans. On the other hand, they can become outdated and may require revisions due to environmental changes.

Setting Objectives for the Organization

After defining the company's mission and examining factors that may affect its ability to fulfill that mission, the next step in planning is to develop objectives for the organization.

Objectives set guideposts by which managers define the organi-

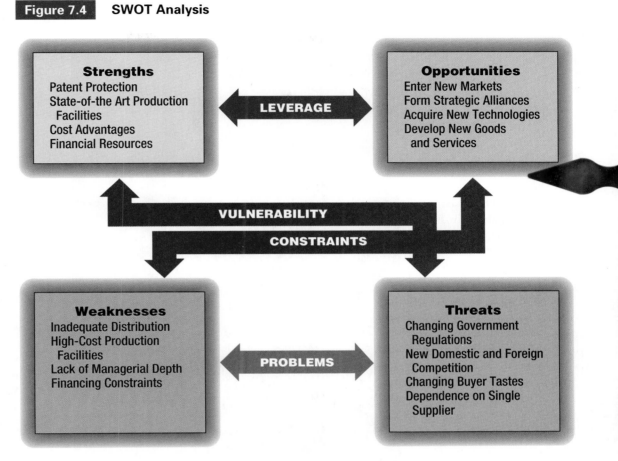

Figure 7.4 **SWOT Analysis**

zation's desired performance in such areas as profitability, customer service, and employee satisfaction. While the mission statement delineates the company's goals in general terms, objectives are more concrete statements. More and more businesses are setting explicit objectives for performance standards other than profitability. As public concern about environmental issues mounts, many firms find that operating in an environmentally responsible manner pays off in good relations with customers. Others channel some of their profits into socially responsible causes, such as funding educational programs and scholarships. Today's businesses offer many additional examples:

▼ In addition to profitability and growth objectives, sports apparel manufacturer Russell Corp. has elaborated a variety of social objectives, including operating a "Stay in School" program aimed at high school students.

▼ An important Procter & Gamble objective is the development of disposable diapers that break down in industrial solid-waste programs.

▼ Rubbermaid has achieved growth objectives by acquiring Little Tikes, a toy company;

Con-Tact, a well-known maker of adhesive coverings; Gott Corp., with its line of insulated containers; Seco Industries, a floor-care products company; and MicroComputer Accessories, a supplier of accessories for personal computers.

JumboSports CEO Stephen Bebis and his management team knew that their firm would fulfill its mission only if they set some tough objectives. The primary objective was to return the company to profitability within 18 months by increasing sales and reducing expenses. Another objective was to build consumer awareness of the company's stores. The team also set standards for service, employee training, and merchandise control.[10]

Creating Strategies for Competitive Differentiation

Developing a mission statement and setting objectives point a business toward a specific destination. To get there, however, the firm needs to map the strategies it will follow to compete with other companies pursuing similar missions and objectives. The underlying goal of strategy development is **competitive differentiation,** the unique combination of a company's abilities and approaches that place it ahead of competitors. Common sources of competitive differentiation include human resources, product innovation, technology, and financial management. Figure 7.6 shows how some firms have leveraged these sources of differentiation to their advantage. The "Solving an Ethical Controversy" box in this chapter discusses some of the challenges faced in gaining a competitive edge. A later section of the chapter examines how firms achieve competitive differentiation through relationship management strategies.

Strategists at JumboSports made some difficult choices in deciding how to differentiate their firm. First, the executive team realized the need to scrap the previous strategy of increasing sales by adding stores, at least temporarily, because of its high cost. Second, the company could no longer avoid strategic applications of technology. Improvements in merchandising and inventory costs required investments in updated computer systems. Most importantly, however, management decided that to reach previously set objectives for increased sales and customer awareness, they would have to build a unified brand image and reputation for the entire company.[11]

Figure 7.5 **Using Customer Surveys to Forecast New-Product Sales**

must begin to put strategy into action by identifying the specific methods and deploying the resources needed to implement the intended plans.

To implement its strategy of building a unified, companywide image, management replaced the jumble of names that had been used on the firm's 85 retail outlets with the JumboSports name. Accompanying the name change, interior redesigns added color changes for signage and employee attire. A series of television, radio, and print ads also helped to build awareness of the new JumboSports image. In addition, a new JumboSports Web page was launched.

Next on the strategic agenda was a project to replace the company's poor inventory-management system. A new computerized system enabled Jumbo Sports buyers to track inventory at each store and minimize out-of-stock situations by quickly resupplying needed products. It also cut the costs involved in ordering and shipping merchandise.

To improve customer service, JumboSports launched an employee training program dubbed *JumboSports College.* Special programs conducted at headquarters and in individual stores communicated product information to managers and employees and focused on customer-service skills. JumboSports addressed the profitability problem by designing a management compensation program that rewarded executives and store managers who met predetermined objectives for improving store profitability.[12]

Implementation: Turning Strategy into Action

Once the first four phases of the strategic planning process are complete, managers face even bigger challenges. They

 www.jumbosports.com

Monitoring and Adapting Strategic Plans

The final stage in the strategic planning process, closely

Business Directory

competitive differentiation the unique combination of a company's abilities and approaches that will place it ahead of competitors.

linked to implementation, consists of monitoring and adapting plans when actual performance fails to match expectations. Monitoring involves establishing methods of securing feedback about actual performance. Common methods include comparisons of actual sales and market share data to forecasts, information received from supplier and customer surveys, complaints received on the firm's customer hot line, and reports prepared by staff members within production, finance, marketing, and other company departments.

Figure 7.6	Sources of Competitive Advantage

Source	Example
Human Resources	Central Parking Corp. only hires college graduates to manage the company's public parking lots. The managers help institute formal management systems, sell new customers, and improve customer satisfaction.
Product Innovation	Cosmetic manufacturer Hard Candy developed a line of nail polishes in unusual shades. The company relies on a continual stream of new, innovative product shades to compete with large manufacturers like Revlon.
Technology	Federal Express has used technology to set itself apart from competitive delivery firms. Each shipment is bar-coded so FedEx customers can receive up-to-the minute status reports over the phone or through the Internet. Investments in technology also lead to higher productivity in FedEx's Louisville, Kentucky, distribution center.
Financial Management	Ross Stores Inc. purchases and sells end-of-season merchandise. Company buyers actively negotiate with manufacturers to get the lowest cost of goods. Tight controls on operating expenses also keep prices low. The savings translate into low prices for customers, a key advantage in the highly competitive retail market.

Ongoing use of such tools as SWOT analysis and forecasting can help management to adapt objectives and functional plans as changes occur. An increase in the price of a key product component, for instance, could dramatically affect the firm's ability to maintain planned prices and still earn acceptable profits. An unexpected strike by UPS may disrupt shipments of products to retail and industrial customers. In each instance, the original plan may require modification to continue to guide the firm toward achievement of its objectives.

The JumboSports turnaround plan produced mixed initial results. Some major strides were made in building a companywide brand image, correcting operating problems, and improving customer service. However, profits remained elusive as the company continued to pile up months of operating losses. CEO Bebis and his executive team continued to monitor feedback received from different sources, but they remained convinced that their strategic plan would ultimately return the firm to profitability. The continuing increase in the number of rivals in an already competitive sporting goods industry worried management, but they were confident that fine-tuning their planning and implementation efforts would result in profitable operations by 2000.[13]

The JumboSports World Wide Web home page reflects its new corporate image that was created when the company changed the names of all of its 85 stores to JumboSports.

SOLVING AN ETHICAL CONTROVERSY

Corporate Espionage or Pure Competition?

Nearly every business keeps tabs in some way on competitors' products, prices, and advertising. Strategic planning would be almost impossible without this kind of information. At what point, however, does gathering competitive intelligence cross an ethical line?

Kodak's research and development team was working on a design for disposable cameras when they uncovered some important competitive information. They learned that arch-rival Fuji was planning to launch its own version of a disposable camera in the near future. Kodak rushed development in order to launch its camera just one day before Fuji. The move gave Kodak the lion's share of media coverage and left Fuji as an also-ran in the minds of consumers and retailers.

Competitive information took on a different slant for General Motors when a high-ranking executive resigned and took a position in Volkswagen's headquarters in Germany. According to a lawsuit filed by General Motors against VW, the executive shared GM's product plans and strategies with his new employer, resulting in unfair competitive advantage for VW. The German firm ended up paying $100 million in damages and firing the former GM ex-

ecutive. The GM case is only the tip of the iceberg in the automotive industry. Over 25 industrial espionage lawsuits are currently active in Michigan courts alone. Other recent suits involving well-known companies include *Campbell* v. *Heinz, Informix* v. *Oracle, Dow* v. *GE,* and *Cadence* v. *Avant.*

 Is gathering competitive intelligence an ethical practice?

PRO

1. Most intelligence-gathering activities don't break the law. When a company prints a brochure, sets up a Web page, or runs a commercial on TV, it willingly shares information with the world. If businesses analyze publicly available information for insights about a competitor's plans and strategies, they are within their rights.

2. Gathering competitive intelligence is just good business sense. Managers can't make decisions about their own strategies in a vacuum. They need information about what other companies in the industry are planning and what methods they're using.

CON

1. Many of the tactics used to collect competitive information lie in ethical and legal gray areas. For ex-

ample, representatives of some companies have rummaged through the trash bins of rivals, cracked computer codes, and even placed electronic bugging devices in order to collect competitive intelligence.

2. Some studies estimate that industrial espionage costs U.S. firms as much as $2 billion a month in lost sales and wasted research and development.

3. Passage of the Economic Espionage Act of 1996 makes stealing trade secrets a federal crime with penalties of up to 15 years in prison and up to $500,000 in fines for each person convicted. Although the law has not yet been tested in the courts, some believe that the collection and use of certain types of competitive intelligence fall within the bill's jurisdiction.

Sources: Daniel Eisenberg, "Eyeing the Competition," *Time,* March 22, 1999, accessed at www.pathfinder.com; "CI Success Stories," downloaded from Fuld & Company Web site, www.fuld.com, August 16, 1997; Stan Crock and Jonathan Moore, "Corporate Spies Feel a Sting," *Business Week,* July 14, 1997, p. 76; and Stephen H. Miller, "Economic Espionage: Now It's a Federal Case," *Competitive Intelligence Review,* Spring 1997.

RELATIONSHIP MANAGEMENT STRATEGIES

As explained in the earlier discussion, a big part of the strategic planning process revolves around deciding how to best use the organization's capabilities in light of market opportunities and threats. The past decade has brought rapid change to most industries, as customers have become better-informed and more demanding purchasers through closely comparing competing goods and services. They expect, even demand, new benefits from the companies that supply them, making it harder for firms to gain competitive advantage based on product features alone.

Meanwhile, most businesses have traditionally focused on **transaction management,** characterized by buyer and seller exchanges with limited communications and little or no ongoing relationship between the parties. In transaction management, the goal is simple: Negotiate hard with suppliers to secure the least expensive raw materials and components, then build products and find customers to buy them at prices high enough to cover costs and still earn a profit.

In today's hyper-competitive era, however, businesses need to find new ways of relating to customers if they hope to maintain long-term growth. Instead of keeping customers at arm's length, businesses are developing strate-

BUSINESS HALL OF FAME

Just For Feet Makes Fun with "Shoppertainment"

In an industry plagued by too many retail stores and lagging sales of high-priced licensed merchandise, Just For Feet is a big exception. The Birmingham, Alabama–based firm operates superstores that specialize in brand-name athletic and outdoor footwear and apparel. But they are far more than just stores. Each Just For Feet outlet is a giant indoor playground for adults and kids, creating a new and exciting shopping experience. As company founder and CEO Harold Ruttenberg puts it, "We take our cue from Walt Disney, a master at making people smile."

Today's sports shoppers are bored—by the hassle of shopping and by the sameness of merchandise. They can turn to giant box stores like Sports Authority and Academy Sports, place orders from mail-order catalogs, or buy on the Internet. How can an independent retailer compete? Just For Feet stands out by offering something called *shoppertainment*, mixing merchandising techniques with entertainment. By making shopping more fun, more educational, and more interactive, Ruttenberg's firm is establishing a new kind of customer relationship.

The typical Just For Feet store features an indoor basketball court, a wall

of video screens, laser light shows, a hot dog stand, and athletic events. "During Wimbledon, we invited the public to watch the matches on the big screen, and we served them doughnuts and coffee," says Ruttenberg. "That was ten years ago. Now we have our own restaurants." The smile campaign is working wonders. Despite increasing competition in the athletic shoe industry, Just For Feet is posting record sales. Its 84 U.S. superstores recently posted annual sales of $600 million—a healthy jump from its 1993 sales of $23 million.

The possibilities for shoppertainment are limited only by the entrepreneur's imagination. Whether it's hands-on product testing, expert advice, in-store food, or special events like slide shows, book signings, lectures, and free classes, most customers like to participate. Experts caution that whatever retailers choose to do, they make sure the entertainment is compatible with their products and their store image. And they must always remember that no entertainment events can make up for poor-quality or inappropriate merchandise, uncompetitive prices, or poor customer service. Top-quality products offered at a fair price with stellar service are essential for success.

Just For Feet succeeds by meeting customers with smiling faces and offering them a sensory roller coaster ride. But the company also offers a huge se-

lection of top merchandise. It claims the world's largest shoe wall, with 3,000 to 4,000 styles of athletic and outdoor shoes. Plus, Just For Feet offers superior customer service. For example, the company invests time and money training its staff. The people at Just For Feet know that entertainment will get customers to come in. They also know that, to succeed, Just For Feet must offer great value.

QUESTIONS FOR CRITICAL THINKING

1. **Suppose you went into business to sell used textbooks. Your store is in a small but charming building close to campus. What shoppertainment ideas could build an exciting relationship with customers?**

2. **What potential drawbacks exist in the use of shoppertainment to attract customers? Can you envision problems with a hobby shop encouraging customers to test their skills with display models? Explain.**

Sources: "Just For Feet, Inc., Announces Record Sales and Comp Stores Sales for the Fourth Quarter," Just For Feet press release, February 2, 1999, accessed at www.feet.com; and Carla Goodman, "That's Entertainment," *Entrepreneur*, December 1998, pp. 124–131.

gies and tactics that draw them into a tighter connection with their customers. Such webs may expand to include stronger bonds with suppliers, employees, and even, in some cases, competitors. Many firms, therefore, are turning their attention away from managing transactions to the broader issues of **relationship management**. Relationship management can be defined as a firm's activities dedicated to building and maintaining ongoing, mutu-

ally beneficial ties with customers, suppliers, employees, and other partners. Unlike transaction management, relationship management targets a more complex goal than just producing goods and services and finding buyers for

Business Directory

relationship management a firm's activities that build and maintain ongoing, mutually beneficial ties with customers, suppliers, employees, and other partners.

them. As Figure 7.7 shows, relationship management seeks to find suppliers and buyers, build relationships with them, and continually fill their needs by creating customer-tailored goods and services.

The emphasis on managing relationships instead of completing transactions often leads to some unique partnerships. The following list reviews a few of the ways businesses are using relationships to reach corporate goals.

▼ *Partnering with customers* Homeowners thinking about putting tile down in their bathrooms or hanging new wallpaper in the living room can get more than supplies for their jobs at Home Depot. The chain's 500-plus stores run weekend how-to seminars that teach customers the skills they need to do home repair and remodeling jobs themselves. Store sales associates prowl the aisles offering advice and tips to do-it-yourself shoppers. Many stores even offer to send interior design consultants out to customers' homes. Working with customers helps Home Depot to ring up $24 billion in sales each year.[14]

▼ *Partnering with suppliers* Ruth Owades says she wouldn't be in business without her suppliers. Owades's firm Calyx & Corolla is a catalog company that sells fresh flowers to customers across the country. To make sure that the highly

perishable products reach customers in peak condition, she formed partnerships with wholesale growers and Federal Express. These partners helped her to devise packaging and shipping methods for efficient delivery of her flowers. When a customer places an order, Calyx & Corolla's growers are alerted and send the order out via Federal Express for next-day arrival.[15]

▼ *Partnering with other businesses* Cardinal Laboratories' new Crazy Dog pet shampoos and sprays were instant hits with customers. In fact, customers clamored for additional products. Since Cardinal's factory wasn't geared to produce them, management invited five small manufacturers to partner with the firm. Each business developed and manufactured new products—from dog toys to pet food—which were marketed jointly under the Crazy Dog label. All six of the partners then split the profits.[16]

▼ *Partnering globally* When General Electric decides to sell appliances in a new country, one of its first moves is to team up with a local company that understands the market. In Japan, its partnership with a large retailer helped to cut the cost of distribution, allowing GE to sell its products at far lower prices than it could have achieved alone. In the first month, GE sold 20,000 appliances.[17]

By presenting weekend "how-to" seminars that teach customers to do home repairs and remodeling jobs themselves, Home Depot uses relationships to increase customer satisfaction.

Relationship Strategy Benefits

Relationship strategies help all parties involved. In addition to mutual protection against competitors, businesses that forge solid links with suppliers and customers are often rewarded with lower costs and higher profits than they would generate on their own. Long-term agreements with a few high-quality suppliers frequently reduce a firm's production costs. Unlike one-time sales, these ongoing relationships encourage suppliers to offer preferential treatment to their customers, quickly adjusting shipments to accommodate changes in orders and correcting any quality problems that might arise.

Any manager will also agree that a firm must spend much more to continually find new customers than it would spend to keep loyal customers. In fact, attracting a new customer can cost as much as five times more than keeping an existing one. Not only do marketing costs go down, but long-term customers usually buy more, require less service, refer other customers, and provide valuable feedback.

Because of these factors, one of the most important measures in relationship management is the **lifetime value of a customer**: the revenues and intangible benefits (referrals, customer feedback, etc.) that a customer brings to the seller over the average lifetime of the relationship, less the amount the company must spend to acquire, market to, and service that customer. Taco Bell, for example, estimates that the lifetime value to the company of a loyal customer is $11,000. To retain as many of these valuable relationships as possible, Taco Bell managers take steps to listen to their customers. In a typical year, the fast-food restaurant chain surveys 800,000 of them.[18]

Customers also benefit from strong relationships with their suppliers. Purchasers who repeatedly buy from one business may find that they save time and gain service quality as the business learns their specific needs. Some relationship-oriented companies also customize goods and services based on customer preferences. Because many businesses now choose to reward loyal customers with discounts or bonuses, some customers may even find that they save money by developing long-term relationships.

Businesses like General Electric that choose to form alliances with other firms also reap rewards. The alliance partners combine their capabilities and resources to accomplish goals that they could not reach on their own. Additionally, alliances with other firms may help businesses to develop the skills and experience they need to successfully enter new markets or improve service to current customers.

The discussion that follows concentrates on the specific strategies, tools, and tactics through which businesses can develop and manage partnerships for competitive advantage. First, the section examines the techniques organizations use to build long-lasting relationships with their customers. Then it discusses how choosing the right partners for business alliances can help firms to reach their objectives.

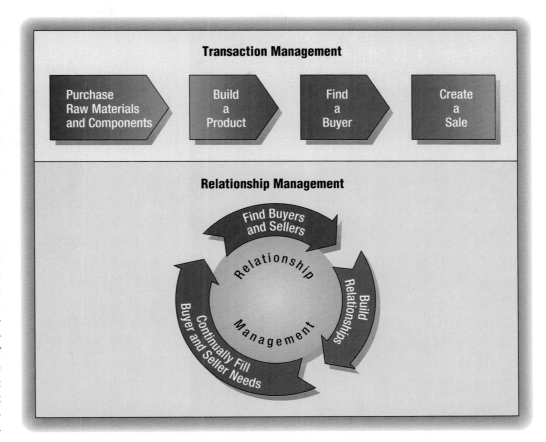

Figure 7.7 **Transaction Management versus Relationship Management**

Business Directory

lifetime value of a customer the revenues and intangible benefits that a customer brings to a seller over the average lifetime of the relationship, less the amount the company must spend to acquire, market to, and service the customer.

| Figure 7.8 | The Contax Camera: Making—and Keeping—Promises |

Kyocera elaborated ten promises to combine the best elements of German and Japanese technology to produce a camera with unparalleled optical characteristics for discerning photographers. Refined viewfinder, focus, and film handling mechanisms ensure exemplary performance for a user who is unwilling to compromise for the sake of reducing cost.

FOUNDATIONS OF BUYER-SELLER RELATIONSHIPS

At the heart of any successful relationship management strategy is the buyer-seller relationship. In order to build that relationship, a business must nurture its links with customers. This section focuses on the core elements of the buyer-seller relationship: the three promises that form the basis of buyer-seller relationships and the four dimensions involved in building that relationship.

Promises in Relationship Management

Promises are the building blocks of successful buyer-seller relationships, whether the buyers are individuals or other companies. Businesses make promises to parties outside their organizations, within their organizations, and in their interactions with customers. This network of promises defines the buyer-seller relationship. Therefore, managing those promises is a central element of efforts to nurture loyalty and trust.

Making Promises Businesses make a variety of promises to their customers, including lower prices, better quality, and more exceptional service than competitors offer. A company must carefully ensure that the promises it communicates to customers are both realistic and consistent with one another.

To satisfy professional photographers, Japanese camera manufacturer Kyocera made ten promises outlined in Figure 7.8. These principles underlie the design of the firm's Contax model, a blend of German artisan culture and Japanese high-tech performance. Camera purists seeking unparalleled quality rank this camera as the Stradivarius of photography tools.

Enabling Promises A relationship management strategy will succeed only if a firm has set up the procedures, systems, and internal capabilities that enable it to fully meet its promises. This condition requires recruiting talented employees and providing them with the tools, training, and motivation they need to achieve effective performance. When businesses do not sell directly to customers, they must make sure that the intermediaries between their own organizations and customers do not hinder their relationships.

For example, although Toyota automobiles have built a favorable reputation for quality and reasonable prices, company research showed that customers were turned off by their experiences at Toyota dealerships. Toyota studied the customer service practices of leaders in other industries, including L. L. Bean and Citibank, to develop new standards for dealer-customer interactions. New customer-service training programs were also implemented at dealerships. The new initiatives were designed to keep customers coming back to Toyota for subsequent car purchases.[19]

Keeping Promises Every time a customer interacts with a business, the transaction reaches a moment of truth, when the seller must meet or surpass customer expectations. The moment of truth typically occurs when the business provides a good or service and the customer receives it. A company that fails to keep its promises at this point in the exchange process destroys any hope of forging a continuing buyer-seller relationship.

Four Dimensions of Buyer-Seller Relationships

Although making, enabling, and keeping promises are crucial elements in creating a relationship with a buyer, other factors also influence the attachment between buyer and seller. The firm needs to develop emotional links with its customers, as well. Figure 7.9 highlights four key dimensions of building these linkages: bonding, empathy, reciprocity, and trust.

| **Figure 7.9** | **Dimensions of Buyer-Seller Relationships** |

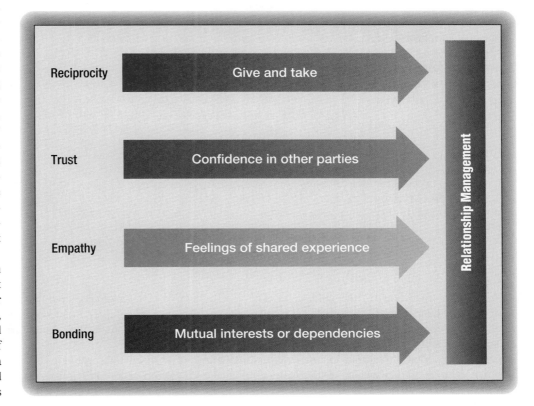

Bonding A long-term relationship between buyer and seller requires a *bond* that joins the two. Mutual interests or dependencies must be identified and satisfied in order to cement the relationship. Customers with strong bonds to a business are more likely to remain committed to continuing their relationships with the firm.

DaimlerChrysler uses bonding strategies to reinforce the attachment many Jeep owners feel toward their vehicles and the company. Throughout the year, it sponsors events designed to foster a feeling of belonging. During these Jeep Jamborees, customers travel together on exciting off-road adventures in destinations like Utah and Colorado. Jeep's World Wide Web site gives full coverage to the twists and turns encountered during each jamboree.

www. **www.jeepunpaved.com**

Each year, more than 6,000 people also travel to Camp Jeep in Colorado's Camp Hale. During the 3-day camp, Jeep owners, accompanied by their families and friends, learn the basics of off-highway driving and participate in activities like white-water rafting and rock-climbing.[20] Jeep 101 is the newest of DaimlerChrysler's programs. Owners and prospective owners drive through a course that

BUSINESS HALL OF SHAME

Steering Car-Rental Companies toward Improved Customer Service

Many travelers encounter the worst experiences of their trips after they reach their destinations. Trudging over to the counters of car-rental agencies, they begin the long and frustrating process of renting cars.

Short-term auto rentals are up 25 percent since 1992, but many customers complain that car-rental companies like Avis, Hertz, and National still lag far behind other industries in their emphasis on nurturing customer relationships. In fact, consumer ratings of the service, convenience, and availability benefits they receive from auto-rental firms have slipped steadily since 1995. Big gripes include long waits, hassles at the counter over insurance and gas, and bills that are all but impossible to decipher. "They're like, 'You booked with me. Now drop dead,'" grumbles one business traveler.

The problems stem from years of struggling to increase sales transaction by transaction. Promotional tools like discount coupons, bargain rates, and tie-ins with airline frequent flyer programs have done little to encourage long-term bonds with customers. Employees have found weak incentives to improve service, because most auto-rental firms tie compensation to sales levels instead of service objectives.

---

simulates trail conditions in the wilderness. They're accompanied by experienced Jeep guides who explain the capabilities of Jeep vehicles. This year, Jeep 101 programs are scheduled in five major cities. "All three programs provide a peak experience that links the owner emotionally to both the activity and their vehicle," says General Manager Martin R. Levine.[21]

Empathy Empathy is the ability to see a situation from the perspective of another party. Understanding customer needs and motivations helps businesses to improve the effectiveness of their goods, services, and programs. Empathy also encourages customer loyalty by reassuring them that the company cares about their concerns.

Patients of health maintenance organizations (HMOs), for example, often complain of feeling dehumanized when they contact their health-care providers for help or information. Connecticut-based Oxford Health Plans recognized this problem and restructured its customer service operation. Previously, different customer service representatives handled different types of inquiries. Now, however, every Oxford Health Plan customer is assigned to a dedicated service manager who handles all of her or his problems and responds to all questions. Because each dedicated service manager serves the same patients on an ongoing basis, Oxford staff members personalize the service they provide and establish stronger relationships with individual patients.[22]

Reciprocity Give-and-take, or *reciprocity*, is a part of every relationship. One party makes allowances and grants favors to the other in exchange for the same treatment when a need arises. In business relationships, this give-and-take process weaves a web of commitment between buyer and seller, binding them ever closer together.

Kingsway Paper is not the lowest-cost supplier of paper shopping bags, but the specialized services it renders to its retail customers more than justify the difference in price. The firm tracks each customer's usage patterns and shipments and then creates a

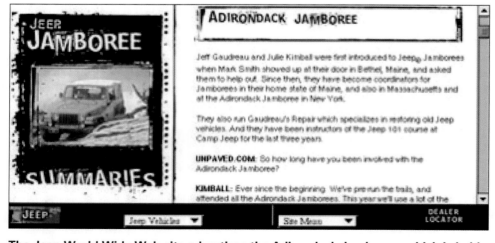

The Jeep World Wide Web site advertises the Adirondack Jamboree, which is held in New York. Jeep owners attending this Jamboree or others in locations such as Utah, or Colorado experience a bonding, which helps to form the attachment they feel toward their vehicles.

The low-price battles between auto-rental companies have also slashed industry profits. As a result, few companies can invest in the new computer systems and employee training programs needed to boost the efficiency of their service. Rental companies have also tried to keep expenses under control by purchasing inexpensive, relatively unpopular car models from automobile manufacturers.

Some companies are trying to stem the tide. National recently launched an employee training program to improve customer care. Alamo is adding airport kiosks that let customers handle transactions over electronic links. Budget has started offering Harley-Davidson motorcycles and convertibles in order to attract customers. A number of mergers have also consolidated the industry. Whether these measures will convince travelers that the firms have changed remains to be seen.

QUESTIONS FOR CRITICAL THINKING

1. **How has the auto-rental industry violated the principles of relationship management?**

2. **What specific strategies and tactics would you recommend to ex-** ecutives in the car-rental industry to help improve customer satisfaction and service?

3. **How could the auto-rental industry use business-to-business partnerships to improve performance?**

Sources: "Thrifty Named Top Car Rental Company by *Entrepreneur* Magazine for Sixth Straight Year," PR Newswire, April 19, 1999; Lisa Miller, "Car Rental Industry Promises that Things Will Improve. Really," *The Wall Street Journal*, July 17, 1997, p. A1; and "Limited Mileage," *The Economist*, January 18, 1997, p. 63.

---

customized report showing the order placement times and quantities that would minimize the company's funds tied up in inventory as well as its shipping and handling costs. Even though Kingsway's products cost up to 7 percent more than those of competitors, customers are willing to pay the difference in exchange for the special services Kingsway offers.[23]

Trust The glue that holds a relationship together is *trust*. Trust is one party's confidence that it can rely on the other's integrity to deliver what it promises. When a business follows through on its commitments to customers, trust grows and allegiance is fortified.

Seattle-based Costco is a master at nurturing customer trust. A recent survey found that 75 percent of the warehouse club's members say they trust Costco implicitly to sell quality products. In fact, they trust Costco enough to pay a $35 a year membership fee for the right to shop there. Costco protects this trust by forging ties with the manufacturers of the products it sells. The retailer even gets involved in its suppliers' production and distribution methods in an effort to enhance customer value. Over the past few years, Costco has pressed its suppliers to improve its fresh salmon fillets by trimming fat, removing bones, and removing skin. It also began buying directly from suppliers in Canada and Chile, shaving prices to $4.79 a pound, about half what local supermarkets charge. Not surprisingly, Costco now sells about 9 million pounds of salmon fillets a year.[24]

MANAGING RELATIONSHIPS WITH BUYERS

Every business establishes relationships of some kind with its customers. The intensity of these relationships varies depending on the type of good or service the company provides and the manner in which it is delivered. Purchases that involve greater risk for the buyer tend to increase the intensity of the relationships.[25]

Relationship intensity can be represented as a continuum of customer commitment to the firm. As shown in Figure 7.10, the strength of commitment between the parties grows as an individual or firm progresses from the lowest level to the highest level in this continuum. At the same time, the likelihood of a business continuing a long-term relationship with its customers also increases. Relationship management seeks to move customers along this continuum whenever it can.

The First Level of Buyer Commitment

At the lowest level of customer commitment, buyer and seller share only a short-term and superficial relationship. Consumers may see little or no distinctions among the offerings provided by different firms. Although they expect quality goods and services at this level, they have little incentive or desire to remain committed to a particular firm. At this level of commitment, customers make choices based on fundamental considerations like price or product features rather than feelings of bonds to a particular firm. Manufacturers of products like toothpaste, soup, laundry detergent, and gasoline generally operate at this level of customer commitment.

Firms seeking to improve this weak customer commitment usually focus their efforts on pricing and other financial considerations to motivate customers to enter into buying relationships. Examples include United Airlines' Mileage Plus frequent-flyer program, the Discovery Card's offer of cash back for every purchase made with the credit card, and value meal promotions at fast-food outlets.

Programs like these offer only a low probability of creating long-term buyer commitment. Although frequent-flyer programs like that offered by United Airlines do offer added value to consumers, they are easily duplicated by competitors, so they do very little to convince buyers to remain loyal to the sponsoring firms over time. A seller must offer more than a low price or other financial incentive to create a long-term relationship with a buyer.

The Second Level of Buyer Commitment

Relationship intensity increases at the second level of buyer commitment to a business. Interactions between buyers and sellers often involve *social* exchanges based on deeper links than the financial motivations of the first level. Consumers begin to believe that they receive unique benefits by continuing their relationships with a particular firm. They are motivated by their perceptions of attentive service, some product customization by the seller to meet their needs, or intangible benefits like a sense of belonging derived from doing business with the firm.

Like Jeep, Harley-Davidson uses social relationships to strengthen customer bonds. Local dealers sponsor

Harley Owners' Groups (HOGs), and the company includes a 1-year free membership with each motorcycle it sells. Harley-Davidson also makes a complete line of accessories and apparel to encourage customers to live the Harley lifestyle.[26] Similarly, Mitre, a well-known soccer equipment manufacturer, invites customers to join Club Mitre. Members receive newsletters that highlight soccer tournaments and offer game tips from soccer professionals.

In other cases, the bonds that customers feel for a particular company can be strengthened by creating an emotional link with a cause or charity important to them. For example, New Jersey–based Catholic Telecom offers long-distance and Internet service to Roman Catholics worldwide. The firm offers added value to its customers by contributing 3 cents of every dollar it receives to the Catholic church and not-for-profit charities related to it.[27]

The Third Level of Buyer Commitment

At the highest level of buyer commitment, the buyer-seller social relationship is transformed into structural changes that forge true partnerships. The buyer and seller find themselves working closely together, developing a dependence on one another that continues to grow over time. Sellers become intimately aware of buyer needs at this level. Buyers hesitate to switch to another company, because they would then have to educate the new seller about their requirements. They see themselves as receiving value-added benefits and specialized services that cannot be found elsewhere.

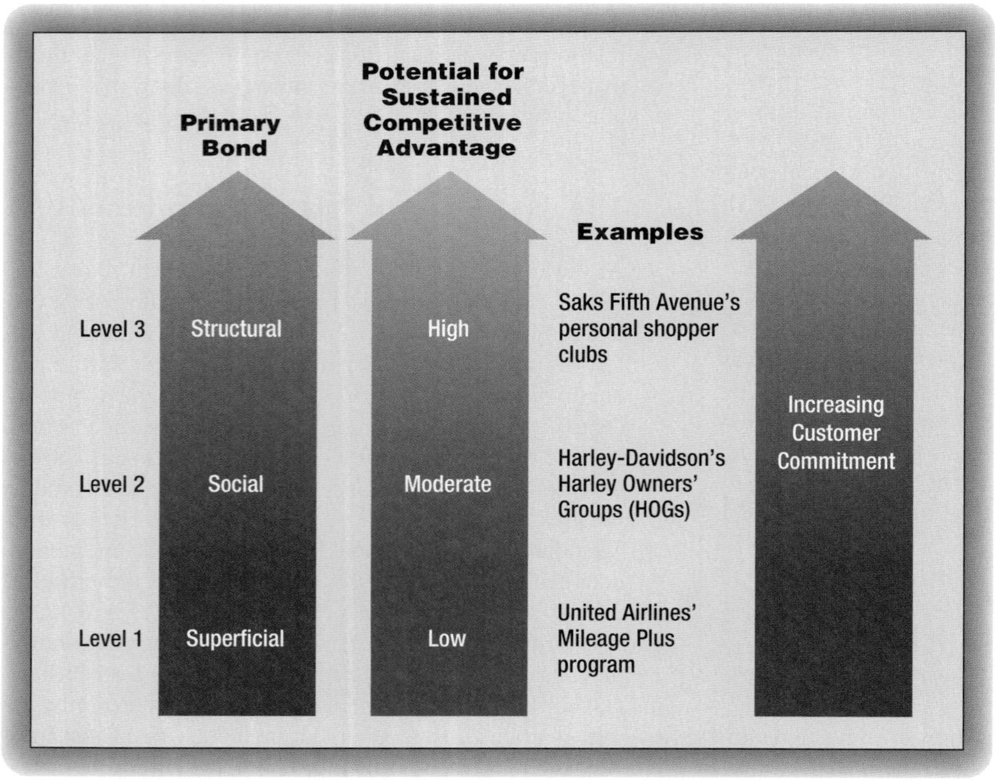

Fashion retailer Saks Fifth Avenue nurtures customer commitment with its Fifth Avenue Clubs. Customers are invited to special personal shopping areas set up away from the stores' main sales floors. While they enjoy refreshments and other amenities, specially trained store associates work with them to identify their wardrobe needs. The associates then put together selections for the customers to approve. When a personal shopper notes the arrival of new merchandise that matches a customer's preferences, the staff member contacts the customer. "We're there only to

Figure 7.10 Three Levels of Buyer Commitment

spoil you," explains Saks's personal shopper supervisor Susan Olden. "We know your figure flaws, what you'd like for lunch, your favorite fitter, and the length of your sleeve." In one case, Saks's personal shoppers put together an entire business wardrobe in 2½ hours for an executive whose suitcase had been stolen en route to London.[28]

Businesses that sell to other businesses also reach high levels of customer commitment by forging partnerships with customers. Process Products Ltd., a maker of nuts, bolts, and other small parts used in manufacturing, places its own employees at the factories of major customers. These representatives help to specify and order the parts that the customers require, a service that adds value for customers by eliminating the cost of assigning this task to their own staff. The service also binds them closer to Process Products.[29]

Table 7.3	Tools for Developing Customer Relationships
Area	**Specific Tactics**
Marketing	Frequency marketing programs
	Affinity programs
	Co-marketing
	Co-branding
Human resources	Employee selection, training, and retention programs
Production	Customization
	Mass-customization
Technology	Internet and extranets
	Electronic data interchange
	Customer databases

Tools for Nurturing Customer Relationships

Although relationship management has important benefits for both customers and business, most relationship-oriented businesses quickly discover that not all customers justify equally vigorous treatment. Some customers generate more profitable business than others. An often-quoted standard asserts that 20 percent of most firms' customers account for 80 percent of their sales and profits. A customer in this category undoubtedly has a higher lifetime value than a customer who buys only sporadically or makes only small purchases.

While businesses shouldn't ignore any customer, of course, their objectives and tactics for managing relationships with individual customers often reflect the overall value to the firm of the resulting business. A firm may choose to custom-manufacture goods or services for high-value customers while working to increase repeat sales of stock products to less valuable customers. An important task in developing relationship strategies, therefore, is to differentiate between customer groups when seeking ways to pull each one closer to an intense

commitment to the firm. The firm can then choose the particular tactics that suit each customer group.[30]

Table 7.3 illustrates some of the tools businesses can use to accomplish their relationship goals. Some of these tactics are suitable for developing relationships with individual consumers, others for developing relationships in business-to-business makets, and some are suitable for both.

The Fifth Avenue Clubs at Saks Fifth Avenue department stores provide their busy male and female clients with efficiency, speed, and personal service, which builds a structural relationship between the seller and the buyer.

Marketing Popular techniques through which firms try to build and protect customer relationships include frequent-buyer and frequent-user programs. Such a marketing initiative, commonly known as a **frequency marketing** program, rewards purchases with cash, rebates, merchandise, or other premiums. Catalog retailer Eddie Bauer enrolls customers in its Rewards program. Members earn 10 points for every dollar they spend on store or catalog purchases. When they collect 5,000 points, they receive a $10 discount on future purchases. Rewards members also receive Eddie Bauer fashion newsletters and opportunities to earn other special bonuses.[31] Hallmark Cards has launched a similar frequency marketing program that awards points to customers for every purchase and then distributes certificates to those who reach purchase goals. Company research shows that customers in the program spend an average of 70 percent more than others each time they visit Hallmark stores.[32]

Affinity programs are another tool for building emotional links with customers. An **affinity program** is a marketing effort sponsored by an organization that solicits involvement by individuals who share common interests and activities. Affinity programs are common in the credit card industry. For example, SunTrust Bank offers a Professional Golf Association (PGA) Tour MasterCard. American Express competes directly by offering its own American Express Golf Card.[33] General Motors' Concept Cure line of vehicles is another example of an affinity program. GM promises to donate a percentage of the proceeds from new-car sales to breast-cancer research.[34]

Many businesses have also used co-marketing and co-branding for some time. In a **co-marketing** deal, two businesses jointly market each other's products. Many personal computer manufacturers use co-marketing to promote the Intel Pentium processors in their machines. The PC makers gain credibility through their association with the high-quality, cutting-edge reputation of Intel Corp., and Intel benefits by having its name appear in more places and more often than it could achieve on its own.

When two or more businesses team up to closely link their names for a single product, **co-branding** occurs. Several restaurant companies have joined forces to house more than one restaurant choice under one roof. Inside many Subway or Blimpies restaurants, you can also order a frozen yogurt from a stand run by the TCBY frozen yogurt chain.[35] Nestlé USA and Frito-Lay teamed to develop Pretzel Flips, a co-branded candy snack combining Nestlé's chocolate and Frito-Lay's Rold Gold Pretzels.[36] Toymaker Hasbro and sunscreen maker Nantucket Gold developed a line of kid-targeted sunblock products that feature the Playskool logo.[37] The chapters on marketing management in Part IV will focus on additional marketing tools that can help firms

| Figure 7.11 | **Building Successful Relationships through Human Resources** |

The right relationship begins with the right people.

The way we see it, everything that makes us unique, makes our work force that much stronger in a diverse world. Our commitment is to create an environment in which the best people do their best work, and that means building a global organization in which differences are respected and valued. We recognize that this goal is a challenging one, and we know we're not there yet. But our candor is matched only by our determination in reaching this goal — to cultivate a broader base of people whose differences can help to create successful relationships for ourselves and with our clients.

CHASE. The right relationship is everything.

© 1997 The Chase Manhattan Corporation.

to build more solid customer relationships.

Human Resources As mentioned earlier, a firm can fulfill the promises it makes to its customers only through properly trained and equipped employees. Most relationship-oriented organizations try to develop human resource tactics to support their relationship management initiatives. Financial institutions, like Chase Manhattan Bank and Boston-based Fleet Capital Corp. build long-term relationships with customers on a foundation of long-term relationships with employees. The banks' training programs help employees to understand the firms' missions and empathize with customer needs. The banks have also redesigned their employee compensation and rewards systems to encourage employee loyalty.[38] This commitment to serve customers with highly-trained, motivated employees is illustrated in Figure 7.11.

Entrepreneur Steve Lauer owns and operates 31 Subway franchises. "Everything is based on getting and keeping good employees," he says. "You have to focus on your employees before you can serve customers." When Lauer hires managers for his restaurants, he looks for people with positive personalities and attitudes. He knows the managers will have a big impact on how employees feel about their jobs—and how they treat customers. "I look for managers who can make coming to work fun. Employees who are happy at their jobs are more likely to make customers happy."[39]

The next four chapters take a closer look at the tactics for human resource management that promote development of a solid workforce that effectively serves customers.

Production Adapting production processes to meet customer needs is an important component of relationship management. In some industries, the ability to customize a good or service to suit the individual requirements of customers offers competitive advantage. Salespeople for Nordstrom Valves carry laptop computers that run specially

BUSINESS TOOL KIT

How Good Are Your Networking Skills?

The old saying, "It's not what you know but who you know" is more accurate today than it ever was. Networking, or parlaying your social, business, and educational connections into helpful relationships, can often provide invaluable assistance in business. How good are your networking skills? To find out, check the appropriate line to the left of each of the following ten questions.

Yes No

❏ ❏ 1. I treat everyone I meet with respect and honesty.

❏ ❏ 2. I believe I have skills and experience that are worth sharing with others.

❏ ❏ 3. I take an active role in learning about other people's interests.

❏ ❏ 4. I'm able to remember other people's interests when I meet them for a second or third time.

❏ ❏ 5. I enjoy introducing people to one another.

❏ ❏ 6. When I join a club or organization, I don't mind taking on responsibility.

❏ ❏ 7. I am a good team player.

❏ ❏ 8. When someone does something especially nice or helpful for me, I make it a point to thank them with a personal note or follow-up phone call.

❏ ❏ 9. I keep in touch with friends, teachers, employers, and co-workers from my past.

❏ ❏ 10. I'm a good listener.

Interpreting Your Answers

If you answered Yes three times or less, your networking skills need work. To build solid networking relationships you have to be willing to give before you expect to receive. Answering Yes four to seven times means that you recognize the importance of developing bonds with others, but you're still uncertain about how to develop them. If you answered Yes eight to ten times, congratulations! You understand some of the key factors involved in creating a network of contacts who will be willing to help you in the future.

For more information on networking, read *The Secrets of Savvy Networking* by Susan Roane, Warner Books, 1993.

---

designed software. When salespeople meet with customers the computer program allows them to customize the design of the tire products on the spot. Customers can instantly see a product simulation and receive data on the cost of buying and using the finished product. Nordstrom customers are willing to pay prices 15 to 20 percent higher than those of competing products in order to buy customized products.[40]

Some businesses plan the locations of their factories to strengthen customer relationships. Nypro Inc. is a Massachusetts firm that produces plastic products through injection molding. In order to reinforce bonds with its major customers, Nypro has built dedicated factories close to their sites. Nypro's Oregon plant is only 3 miles from one of its largest customers, Hewlett-Packard. The facility was even designed with space for a development center to be used by Hewlett-Packard engineers.[41]

Some businesses strive for **mass-customization,** a production method that allows for mass production of goods and services in lot sizes of one or just a few at a time. Want a new pair of jeans guaranteed to fit? Levi Strauss' Personal Pair jeans can be personalized according to your actual body measurements. Salespeople enter the measurements into a computer, which selects from 500 design choices to find the best match. The order is then sent via modem to Levi's factory where the jeans are made by altering standard Levi's patterns. For about $65, the firm will deliver a pair of personalized jeans in about 3 weeks.[42]

Technology Rapid technological advances have enabled businesses to develop new capabilities for managing customer relationships. The ability to customize and rapidly deliver goods and services has become increasingly dependent on investments in technology like computer-aided design and manufacturing.

The Internet offers a way for businesses to connect with customers in a much more intimate manner than was previously available. Beneficial National Bank's mortgage division lets potential customers learn the details of mortgages by combining the Internet and telephone contact. Mortgage seekers dial into Beneficial's Web page and access a special area that automatically establishes a phone connection with a live customer service representative in the bank's mortgage department. The representative answers questions over the phone while simultaneously directing additional information to the customer's computer screen.[43]

Another communications tool helps businesses to communicate with their business customers. **Electronic data interchange (EDI)** is a quick and highly cost-efficient computer-to-computer exchange of invoices, orders, and other business documents. Later chapters on communications and technology revisit EDI.

Customer databases use information from company computers to identify and target specific groups of potential customers. This refinement allows a business to focus on marketing and management efforts that target its best customers. British Airways uses a customer database to enhance the traveling experiences of its most valued customers, members of the airline's Executive Club frequent-flier program. The database records details about the specific preferences of each club member. When a member makes a flight reservation, the information is available on the system so that ticketing representatives and flight attendants can make sure the member's preferences are met.[44]

Data warehouses are sophisticated customer databases that allow managers to combine data from several different organizational functions. Managers can then use the information to create a centralized, accurate profile of each customer's relationship with the firm as an aid to decision making. Kentucky Fried Chicken's data warehouse lets planners access up-to-the-minute data on exactly what food items customers are ordering in each of the company's 9,000 restaurants. KFC uses this information to improve menu selection and make adjustments to purchasing and staffing levels.[45]

Many supermarkets also track the purchases of their customers, storing the information in data warehouses. Using such a customer database, a supermarket can then send tar-geted promotions to customers based on their past preferences. For example, Food Lion supermarkets may send previous buyers of Dove brand soap a discount coupon for the product. This encourages customers to deepen their relationships with the store, because they believe that it recognizes and caters to their needs and preferences.[46]

Giant retailer Wal-Mart teamed with NCR to build a data warehouse capable of serving the needs of 3,000 Wal-Mart outlets worldwide. As Figure 7.12 explains, the system supplies buyers and vendors with information they need to make informed decisions on stock replenishment, buying trends, and pricing. Chapters 17 and 18 will look closer at these and other technological advances.

BUILDING AND MANAGING BUSINESS PARTNERSHIPS

Customer relationships aren't the only relationships that organizations form. To compete effectively in today's global marketplace, businesses must also manage their relationships with other businesses. Some business-to-business relationships revolve around buyer-seller connections. One firm provides materials or services that the other firm uses in serving its customers. Other business-to-business relationships link two or more firms to work together toward common goals. For example, two firms may use co-branding to boost the sales and market exposure of their individual products, or several firms may form a cooperative venture to jointly develop new technology. Increasingly, businesses are viewing their relationships with other businesses as partnerships.

A **partnership** is an affiliation between two or more companies that assist each other in achieving common goals. Partnerships can involve a single function or activity, such as product distribution, or all functions, such as the research and development, manufacturing, and marketing for a new product. Business partnerships help a firm to control its uncertainty and reduce its risk, in the process increasing profits. Organizations are motivated to form partnerships for

| Figure 7.12 | **The Wal-Mart Data Warehouse** |

a variety of reasons. They may seek to protect or improve their positions in existing markets or gain access to new domestic or international markets. Other motives include sharing resources, reducing costs, warding off competitive threats, raising or creating barriers to entry, and learning new skills.

Types of Business Partnerships

Each business-to-business partnership can be classified as one of three types: buyer-seller, internal, or lateral partnerships.

Buyer-Seller Partnerships In a buyer-seller partnership, a firm purchases goods and services from one or more intimately related providers. For example, one firm may contract with an advertising agency to develop and place advertisements. Another company may depend on a partner to supply important components used in its manufacturing process. In a buyer-seller business partnership, however, the relationship may go much deeper than just supplying goods or services. Both parties may begin to rely on each other to provide additional value beyond exchanges of goods.

The mutually beneficial partnership between Levi Strauss and JCPenney is illustrated by their jointly sponsored promotion shown in Figure 7.13. Levi depends on retailers like JCPenney as the final link in its distribution channel to reach jeans buyers. To strengthen the bonds between partners, Levi ads feature JCPenney as a local source for the company's jeans. The firm also works closely with the retailer to provide specialized training for store employees, quick shipments of out-of-stock products, and special promotions. Both manufacturer and retailer benefit from this successful relationship.

Buyers, for example, may begin to expect special benefits such as price reductions, quick delivery, and high quality in return for directing their business to the seller. Department stores often demand that manufacturers guarantee specific profit margins as a condition of carrying their product lines. Retailers may also insist that sellers meet stringent requirements for packing and shipping or pay fines for failing to do so. Some retailers even specify that apparel manufacturers must ship merchandise on comparatively expensive hangers.[47]

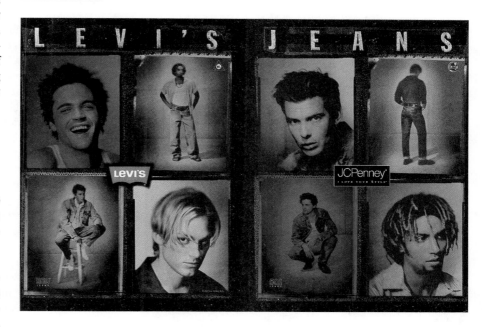

Figure 7.13 **The Levi-JCPenney Business Partnership**

Why would a manufacturer agree to demands like these? The answer is a simple concept: Sellers have needs, too. Sellers depend on steady streams of cash to stabilize their finances, and they recognize potential opportunities to control marketing and even manufacturing costs by developing long-term relationships with buyers. The pressure to build and maintain buyer-seller partnerships is especially intense for small businesses. As a result, many sellers see the job of meeting buyer demands simply as part of their work of protecting their partnerships. "If your life is tied to these people, then you have to do business this way," explains the chief executive officer of one apparel company.[48]

A growing form of buyer-seller partnership is outsourcing. **Outsourcing** occurs when one business decides to hire another to perform tasks or functions previously handled by internal staff and systems. The benefits of outsourcing include reduced operating expenses, improved company focus on core strengths, and access to capabilities the firm lacks on its own. Businesses currently outsource a wide variety of functions such as data processing, telemarketing, accounting, manufacturing, and even human resource management. Altogether, U.S. businesses spend about $108 billion on outsourcing.[49]

Business Directory

outsourcing an arrangement in which one business hires another to perform tasks or functions previously handled by internal staff and systems.

Help future astronauts **take pictures**

First Mark asked his buddy Joel to take his picture with the school's new Kodak digital camera and downloaded the image on to a computer.

Then he hopped on the World Wide Web and found a great interplanetary image of Saturn on the NASA Web site.

Mark drew a few aliens, scanned them into the computer using a Kodak photo scanner, and created his own take on space exploration.

He sent it out into cyberspace, where he met a few future colleagues at, of all places, an astronomy class in Australia.

To learn more about how Kodak products and solutions are bringing the classroom into the 21st century, visit our Web site: http://www.kodak.com/edu/. Or give us a call at 1-800-939-1630.
Kodak is a trademark. ©Eastman Kodak Company 1997.

Kodak partnered with four of its main competitors—Canon, Fuji, Minolta, and Nikon—to develop the digital camera, which Mark (inside spacesuit) used to have his photo taken. Mark downloaded the image to a computer, added a Saturn image from the NASA World Wide Web site, drew some aliens and scanned them into the computer, and created the space exploration photo that was used in this ad.

The Southland Corp. operates 5,000 7Eleven stores in the United States, Canada, and Japan, all of them with heating and air conditioning requirements. Previously, each store handled maintenance of these systems. This arrangement proved costly and inefficient, however, so Southland decided to centralize maintenance by outsourc-

ing it to a tight network of contractors. As a result, Southland has gained greater control over the cost of repairs and reduced downtime because preventive maintenance is scheduled from one central source.[50]

Even the U.S. Postal Service relies on outsourcing. When the USPS had trouble delivering packages through its 2-day priority mail service, the agency turned to Emery Worldwide Airlines for help. To meet USPS needs, Emery will set up, staff, and manage ten priority mail processing plants on the eastern seaboard.[51] Outsourcing is discussed in more detail in Chapter 9.

Internal Partnerships As outsourcing has increased in popularity, many businesses are also recognizing the importance of internal partnerships. The classic definition of the word *customer* as the buyer of a good or service is now more carefully applied to *external customers*. This change recognizes that customers within an organization also have their own needs. For example, in a company that manufactures cellular phones, the team that assembles the phones is a customer of the firm's purchasing department. In essence, the manufacturing plant buys cellular phone parts from the purchasing department, and the purchasing department acts as a supplier. In this partnership, the purchasing department must continue to fulfill the needs of manufacturing by selecting vendors that provide the parts needed within price, quality, and time frame specifications from manufacturing. Without recognizing, building, and maintaining internal partnerships, an organization will experience difficulties meeting the needs of its external partnerships.

Lateral Partnerships Lateral partnerships result from strategic relationships between separate businesses or organizations. Lateral partnerships involve no buyer or seller interactions; rather, the partners join to promote progress toward common aims by sharing resources, knowledge, or capabilities. Co-branding and co-marketing, discussed in the previous section, are two forms of lateral partnership. Another important form of lateral partnership is the strategic alliance.

Business Directory

strategic alliance a partnership between two or more businesses designed to create competitive advantage for all participants.

Strategic Alliances

A **strategic alliance** is a partnership formed to create competitive advantage. Companies form strategic alliances when each believes that the other can offer an important benefit. Businesses of all sizes, all kinds, and in many locations have formed strategic alliances. One study found that American companies are entering strategic alliances 48 percent more often than they did just 3 years ago. Companies engaging in strategic alliances report greater growth in revenues and productivity than firms without alliances.[52]

Companies serving the same or different industries form many types of strategic alliances. Although alliances occur in all types of industries, they are particularly common among industrial manufacturers, electronics companies, and computer hardware and software firms. One study of leading U.S. and Canadian oil companies found that 84 percent expected future improvements in their performance to come mainly from alliances with other firms rather than from internal actions of their own.[53]

Strategic alliances can involve competition between a market leader and a follower or even between rivals. Most partnerships between competitors involve cooperative efforts to introduce new, industrywide standards or systems. Industrywide partnerships can help to build consumer confidence in such new products, which improves their chances of succeeding. Arch-rivals Eastman Kodak, Canon, Fuji, Minolta, and Nikon teamed up to develop and introduce the Advanced Photography System, which combines digital and conventional photography technologies. The four companies shared their research and development capabilities and patented technology to create a unique system that they hope will become a new standard in photography.[54]

The global marketplace offers additional opportunities for success through strategic alliances. By partnering with a firm already established in another country, a firm hoping to expand into that market can reduce its risk. In either arrangement, the partners agree in advance on the skills and resources that each will contribute to the alliance to achieve their mutual objectives and gain a competitive advantage. When Starbucks decided to expand into Japan, for example, the company joined forces with Japanese retailer Sazaby, Inc., to open five coffee shops. Sazaby helped Starbucks to identify retail sites and to understand Japanese consumer preferences.[55]

Ingredients of Successful Partnerships

Just as organizations must manage their relationships with customers, they must manage their relationships with other businesses, as well. Central to this process is a careful process for selecting appropriate partners. The first priority is to locate firms that can add value to the partnership, perhaps by supplying funding, extra manufacturing capacity, technical know-how, contacts, or distribution capabilities. The desirability of forming a partnership increases along with the value that partners can add. In many cases, the attributes of each partner complement each other.

The same elements that tie customers to a particular business—bonding, empathy, reciprocity, and trust—also play roles in the success of business partnerships. Long-term partnerships require bonds based on common values and goals. A highly ethical firm, for example, probably would not maintain a long-term relationship with a partner who suggested compromising product safety to boost short-term profits.

Both firms must feel that they receive adequate benefits from the partnership if it is to continue for the long term. Giant computer maker Digital Equipment Corp. has formed a strategic alliance with tiny Dragon Systems, a leading specialist in voice recognition systems for computers. Digital relies on Dragon to provide technological breakthroughs and enhancements that put Digital's products at the forefront of the market. Dragon, with only 200 employees, needs Digital to reach international markets and to gain credibility with other potential customers.[56]

Finally, trust is critical in business partnerships. Each party must trust that the other works to promote the interests of the partnership and not only its own concerns. Without trust, business partnerships crumble and relationships wither. Both parties must believe that each is fully committed to the other and that they share a desire to continue the relationship until mutual goals are satisfied.

SUMMARY OF LEARNING GOALS

1. Explain the role of vision in business success.

Vision is the ability to perceive the needs of the marketplace and develop methods for satisfying those needs. Vision helps new businesses to pinpoint the actions needed to take advantage of opportunities. In an existing firm, a clear vision of company purpose helps to unify the actions of far-flung divisions, keep customers satisfied, and sustain growth.

2. Describe the major benefits of planning.

The planning process identifies organizational goals and develops a road map of the actions necessary to reach them. Through realistic assessments of current and future conditions, planning helps a company to turn vision into action, take advantage of opportunities, and avoid costly mistakes.

3. Distinguish among strategic planning, tactical planning, and operational planning.

Strategic planning is a far-reaching process. It views the world through a wide-angle lens to determine the long-range focus and activities of the organization. Tactical planning focuses on the current and short-range activities required to implement the organization's strategies. Operational planning sets standards and work targets for functional areas such as production, human resources, and marketing.

4. Explain the six steps in the strategic planning process.

The first step of strategic planning is to translate the firm's vision into a mission statement that explains its overall intentions and aims. Next, planners must assess the firm's current competitive position by examining its strengths and weaknesses as well as probable future opportunities and threats. Based on this information, managers set specific objectives that elaborate what the organization hopes to accomplish. The next step is to develop strategies for reaching objectives that will differentiate the firm from its competitors. Managers then develop an action plan that specifies the specific methods for implementing the strategy. Finally, the results achieved by the plan are evaluated and the plan is refined as needed.

5. Identify the components of SWOT analysis. Explain its role in assessing a firm's competitive position.

SWOT analysis focuses on a firm's *s*trengths, *w*eaknesses, *o*pportunities, and *t*hreats. This organized procedure assesses a company's internal capabilities in order to avoid threats and take advantage of future market opportunities. SWOT analysis helps the firm to see its current situation in the competitive environment and the steps it must take to compete effectively in the future.

6. Describe the importance of relationships with customers, suppliers, employees, and others in achieving a company's objectives.

Effective management of relationships with customers helps a firm to protect itself against competitors and perhaps to increase profits. Forging relationships with employees helps to reduce turnover and, ultimately, to serve customer needs. Relationships with other businesses, such as partnerships and strategic alliances with suppliers, pay off by increasing the firm's capabilities and resources.

7. Explain the core elements of buyer-seller relationships.

A buyer-seller relationship is built around a network of promises that specify essential conditions for nurturing customer loyalty and trust. Emotional links with customers, such as bonding, empathy, reciprocity, and trust, knit together the interests and needs of both buyer and seller. Not all customers are equally committed to a relationship with a firm. Whenever possible, businesses should move customers toward greater commitment through mutually beneficial activities. Businesses can use methods based on marketing, production capabilities, human resources, and technology to develop strong links with customers.

8. Identify strategies and tactics for building and sustaining relationships with other organizations.

Businesses often seek to form partnerships with their suppliers and other organizations. This activity helps to control a firm's uncertainty and reduce its risk while increasing its profits. Partnerships with suppliers can be strengthened by working closely together to solve mutual problems and anticipate demand. Two or more businesses form strategic alliances when they believe they can achieve better results by joining forces than they can by competing as separate entities. Firms must manage their business-to-business relationships so that empathy, reciprocity, and trust bond the parties.

TEN BUSINESS TERMS YOU NEED TO KNOW

vision	competitive differentiation
planning	relationship management
mission statement	lifetime value of a customer
SWOT analysis	outsourcing
objectives	strategic alliance

Other Important Business Terms

business plan	affinity program
strategic planning	co-marketing
tactical planning	co-branding
operational planning	mass-customization
adaptive planning	electronic data interchange (EDI)
contingency planning	
forecasting	customer database
transaction management	data warehouse
frequency marketing	partnership

REVIEW QUESTIONS

1. Choose a well-known company and explain how vision has been important to its success or failure.
2. Distinguish between strategic, tactical, and operational planning. Review several magazine and newspaper business sections, and find examples of business planning at all three levels.
3. Why is contingency planning important? How large should a company grow before it begins to develop such plans?
4. What is a mission statement? How do objectives differ from mission statements? Write a mission statement for your school, church, team, or other organization.
5. Explain how the four elements of SWOT analysis help a business to focus on the future.